BEYOND THE LAND ETHIC

SUNY Series in Philosophy and Biology

David Edward Shaner, editor

BEYOND THE LAND ETHIC

*More Essays in
Environmental Philosophy*

J. Baird Callicott

STATE UNIVERSITY OF NEW YORK PRESS

Published by
State University of New York Press

Printed in the United States of America

For information, address the State University of New York Press,
State University Plaza, Albany, N.Y. 12246

Marketing by Patrick Durocher
Production by Bernadine Dawes

Library of Congress Cataloging-in-Publication Data

Callicott, J. Baird.
    Beyond the land ethic : more essays in environmental philosophy /
J. Baird Callicott.
        p.   cm. — (SUNY series in philosophy and biology)
    Includes bibliographical references and index.
    ISBN 0-7914-4083-4 (hc : alk. paper). — ISBN 0-7914-4084-2 (pbk.
: alk. paper)
    1. Environmental sciences—Philosophy. 2. Environmental ethics.
    I. Title. II. Series.
    GE40.C35   1999
    179'.1.—dc21   98-53504
                                                                   CIP

10 9 8 7 6 5 4 3 2 1

For Evelyne Baird Callicott, my mother,

who taught me the meaning of unconditional love

CONTENTS

ACKNOWLEDGMENTS

More people than I can name have read and criticized these essays in various stages of their composition. I thank them all. More broadly, I am indebted to my colleagues at the University of Wisconsin-Stevens Point and at the University of North Texas for their support and indulgence. Over the last decade, my work has benefited from a change of scenery and from the intellectual stimulation of associates at institutions—the University of Hawaii; the University of California, Santa Barbara; the University of Kansas; James Cook University of North Queensland; and Presbyterian College—where I have been privileged to be a visiting professor. I am also indebted to all the members of the international community of environmental philosophers for the ongoing, dialectical conversation to which these essays contribute. My voice could not be heard were it not for theirs.

"Environmental Philosophy *Is* Environmental Activism: The Most Radical and Effective Kind" first appeared in *Environmental Philosophy and Environmental Activism,* ed. Don E. Marietta and Lester Embree (Lanham, Md.: Rowman and Littlefield, 1995), 19–35. "How Environmental Ethical Theory May Be Put into Practice" first appeared in *Ethics and the Environment* 1 (1996): 3–14. "Just the Facts, Ma'am" first appeared in the *Environmental Professional* 9 (1987): 279–88. "Can a Theory of Moral Sentiments Support a Genuinely Normative Environmental

Ethic?" first appeared in *Inquiry* 35 (1992): 183–98. "The Case against Moral Pluralism," "Rolston on Intrinsic Value: A Deconstruction," and "Do Deconstructive Ecology and Sociobiology Undermine the Leopold Land Ethic?" first appeared, respectively, in *Environmental Ethics* 12 (1990): 99–124; 14 (1992): 129–43; and 18 (1996): 353–72. "Moral Monism in Environmental Ethics Defended" first appeared in the *Journal of Philosophical Research* 19 (1994): 51–60, and is used with permission of the Philosophy Documentation Center (Bowling Green, Ohio). "Genesis and John Muir" first appeared in *Covenant for a New Creation,* ed. Carol Robb and Carl Casebolt (Maryknoll, N.Y.: Orbis Books, 1991), 106–38. "Intrinsic Value in Nature: A Metaethical Analysis" first appeared in a special issue—*Justifying Value in Nature*—of the *Electronic Journal of Analytic Philosophy* 3 (1995), located at http://www.phil.indiana.edu/ejap/1995.spring/callicott.abs.html. "The Metaphysical Transition in Farming: From the Newtonian-Mechanical to the Eltonian-Ecological" first appeared in the *Journal of Agricultural Ethics* 3 (1990): 36–49, and is republished here with kind permission from Kluwer Academic Publishers. "Environmental Wellness" first appeared in *Literature and Medicine* 15 (1996): 148–62, and is republished here with the permission of Johns Hopkins University Press. "After the Industrial Paradigm, What?" first appeared in French translation under the title "Après le Paradigm Industriel" in *La Crise Environnementale,* ed. Catherine Larrère and Raphaël Larrère (Nancy: INRA Editions, 1997). "Whither Conservation Ethics?" and "Ecological Sustainability as a Conservation Concept" first appeared in *Conservation Biology* 4 (1990): 15–20, and 11 (1996): 32–40, respectively; they are reprinted by permission of Blackwell Science, Inc. "Aldo Leopold's Concept of Ecosystem Health" first appeared under the title "Aldo Leopold's Metaphor," in *Ecosystem Health: New Goals for Environmental Management,* ed. Robert Costanza, Bryan G. Norton, and Benjamin D. Haskell (Washington, D.C.: Island Press, 1992), 42–56. "The Value of Ecosystem Health" first appeared in *Environmental Values* 5 (1995): 345–61.

Introduction:
Compass Points in Environmental Philosophy

ENVIRONMENTAL PHILOSOPHY AND
MAINSTREAM ACADEMIC PHILOSOPHY

During the decade that has elapsed since the publication of *In Defense of the Land Ethic*, environmental philosophy has developed explosively. I have no hard data to prove it, but the anecdotal evidence I collect, as President of the International Society for Environmental Ethics, suggests that a majority of colleges and universities in the United States, Canada, and Australia offer a course in environmental ethics (though in some cases it may not be taught in the philosophy department). So does the market evidence. An instructor has more than a dozen textbooks in environmental philosophy from which to select. And I can say from personal experience that the scholarly literature in the field has become so voluminous that it is impossible for even a full-time devotee, such as I, to read it all.

Nevertheless, environmental philosophy remains something of a pariah in the mainstream academic philosophical community. The environmental turn taken in other traditional disciplines, such as history and literature, is not so reviled. Consider the difference in professional status between the leading environmental philosophers and the leading environmental historians. Donald Worster, dean of environmental historians, is Hall Distinguished Professor of History at the University of Kansas and oversees a number of doctoral students. Holmes Rolston III, dean of environmental philosophers, fills no endowed chair and toils at Colorado's second-tier university, Colorado State, which offers only a master's degree in philosophy. William Cronon, the heir apparent for the deanship in the field of environmental history, is Frederick Jackson Turner Professor of History, Geography, and Environmental Studies at the University of Wisconsin-Madison, a world-renowned research institution; and, like Worster, Cronon supervises more than his share of doctoral candidates. And J. Donald Hughes, President of the American Society for Environmental History, is John Evans Professor of History at the University of Denver. Until recently, I was a plain, no-name philosophy professor at the University of Wisconsin-Stevens Point, a self-styled "undergraduate teaching institution" offering no advanced degrees, and I am now employed in another brand-X position by the University of North Texas—which can plausibly claim, while offering only a master's degree, to have the best graduate program in environmental philosophy in the United States. Eugene C. Hargrove, now chair of the UNT Department of Philosophy and Religion Studies, first received tenure at another university, but only after an international letter-writing campaign resulted in an appeals committee override of the philosophy department's decision to let him go. The letters, written by indignant and outraged scholars from a wide variety of disciplines all over the world, pointed out that Hargrove was the most distinguished member of his department, having virtually established the field of environmental philosophy by founding and editing *Environmental Ethics*, the journal. Of course, his mainstream colleagues attempted to deny him tenure, not despite that fact, but because of it. The outcast estate of environmental philosophy used to be something of a mystery to me, but I think I now understand the reasons for it.

For one thing, environmental philosophy has been relegated to the "applied ethics" barrio. Hence, it is snubbed by the mandarins of academic philosophy who regard themselves to be advancing the "pure" stuff. There is an irony in this ghettoization. Environmental philosophy has, for the most part, been pressing the envelope of theory, especially ethical theory. Applied ethics, on the other hand, as the name suggests, applies the standard ethical theories—that hail ultimately from the Olympians of the Western tradition, such as Aristotle, Hobbes, Locke, Kant, and

Bentham, and that have been refined by their twentieth-century custodians, such as MacIntyre, Rawls, Nozick, Harman, and Hare—to novel moral problems created by Modern technology. But, because the whole of the Western tradition of moral philosophy has been resolutely (and often militantly) anthropocentric, environmental philosophers have been largely preoccupied with the more fundamental intellectual business of devising new, more nature-oriented and environment-friendly ethical theories than with the pedestrian work of applying off-the-rack ethical theories to moral problems in the environmental arena.

However, looked at from another angle, environmental philosophy is properly regarded as a species of applied philosophy. For contemporary environmental philosophers are attempting to apply the traditional *methods* of philosophy, conceptual criticism and invention, if not the traditional ethical theories, to a well-defined spectrum of actual problems— biological impoverishment, ecological and environmental degradation, and so on—that we human beings collectively face. Mainstream academic philosophers who do realize what is actually going on in environmental philosophy—theoretical reflection provoked by the twentieth century's environmental crisis—seem to become, nevertheless, even more antagonistic; for two reasons, I think. First, twentieth-century philosophers, fearing the hegemony of the sciences, attempted to transform philosophy into one compartmentalized academic discipline among others, with its own unique set of special problems, its own private turf. And theoretical environmental philosophy steps beyond the self-imposed disciplinary bounds of mainstream academic philosophy. Second, staunchly to maintain the ideological status quo in service of the imperium is a central role of the academic powers that be. In part, this is effected in mainstream academic philosophy by a diversionary tactic: focusing the considerable critical faculties of philosophy on specialized arcane intellectual puzzles, such as the referential relationship between words and objects, and away from common and pressing real-world problems—the solving of which might necessitate profound social, economic, and political change. (The highest compliment that a mainstream academic philosopher can win today from his or her peers is to be called "clever"—not wise, not profound, not insightful, not far-seeing, but, merely, clever. That's quite revealing, I think.) And theoretical environmental philosophy is revolutionary; it challenges the most cherished assumptions of the venerable Modern Western philosophical tradition, upon which rest, in turn, the prevailing social, economic, and political institutions.

The intellectual revolutionaries of earlier periods in philosophy have, of course, now become pillars of the tradition. But in their own day, they too were the outcasts, the upstarts, the dangerous boat-rockers, shunned by the scholastic establishment, denied professorships at the better places, marginalized, sometimes even martyred. So, I feel very encouraged, though often personally aggrieved, by the indifference on the part of most, and the outright hostility on the part of some, mainstream academic philosophers shown to us environmental philosophers and to our work.

The history of Western philosophy is conventionally ordered by centuries. In the ancient period, the sixth, fifth, and fourth centuries B.C.E., for example, each had its own distinctive philosophical concerns and style, as had the seventeenth, eighteenth, and nineteenth centuries, respectively, in the Modern period. Twentieth-century philosophy was marked by an effort, on the part of its practitioners, to make philosophy over into a rigorous, narrow, science-like discipline. In the Anglo-American philosophical community, the result was analytic philosophy; in the Continental philosophical community, the result was phenomenology. With the advent of the twenty-first century, not only a new century, but a new millennium will have arrived. And, in the twenty-first century, analytic philosophy and phenomenology will have become curiosities of intellectual history discarded by future philosophers with the same bemused contempt as was nineteenth-century absolute idealism by early twentieth-century philosophers, such as Moore and Russell, or as was Medieval scholasticism by early Modern philosophers, such as Descartes and Hobbes. Husserl and Davidson will be about as influential in the twenty-first century as Fichte and Bradley were in the twentieth. Future historians of philosophy will doubtless regard analytic philosophy and phenomenology as aberrations, born of physics envy, in a tradition of expansive, transdisciplinary speculative and critical thought going back more than 2,500 years.

What will succeed analytic philosophy and phenomenology as the twenty-first century ripens? I've bet my life on the belief that environmental philosophy will be regarded by future historians as the bellwether of a twenty-first-century intellectual effort to think through the philosophical implications of the profound paradigm shifts that occurred in the sciences during the twentieth century. Hasn't philosophy of science, a twentieth-century innovation, been doing just that all along, you may be thinking? Not really. Philosophy of science has been a mainstay of twentieth-century academic philosophy to be sure, but, for the most part, twentieth-century philosophy of science was devoted to an analysis of the scientific method and the formal logico-mathematical relationships between scientific hypotheses and their experimental verification or falsification. When profound paradigm shifts were noted and studied by philosophers of science, attention was focused on the etiology of the shift, not its broader metaphysical and moral implications. Speculative ontological questions, for example, about the nature of physical reality in the light of the special and general theories of relativity and quantum theory did not head the research agenda of twentieth-century philosophy of science. But speculative ontological questions about the nature of terrestrial nature in the light of ecology have been at the forefront of inquiry in environmental philosophy, as have moral questions about the relationship of human beings to nature in the light of the theory of evolution.

In this regard, note that, in the 2,500-year-old Western philosophical tradition, changes in moral philosophy follow upon and adjust to changes in natural philosophy. The first philosophers in the tradition, the pre-Socratics, raised questions about the composition of the physical world and its principles of order and movement. Their success in persuasively answering such questions contributed to an ethical and political crisis in ancient Greek society—which crisis stimulated a shift in intellectual attention from natural to moral philosophy. And the first ancient Greek attempt to understand the origin and nature of justice, the social contract theory of ethics, was modelled on the atomic paradigm in natural philosophy. (Solitary, egoistic individual human beings in the "state of nature" are, in effect, social atoms, chaotically colliding with one another. And social contracts are supposed to order and coordinate their movements, reducing collisions to some tolerable minimum.) Socrates (who seems not to have been a social contract theorist) and his contemporary moral philosophers, the sophists (who were), lived and worked a century or so after Anaximenes and Heraclitus. Moral philosophy did not mature until the mid-fourth century in the work of Plato, Aristotle, and their contemporaries, a century or so after the zenith of Greek natural philosophy in the mid-fifth century. After the recovery of Greek natural philosophy in the European Renaissance and its further development in the course of the scientific revolution of the sixteenth century, a similar response of moral philosophy was led in the seventeenth century by Descartes, in epistemology, and by Hobbes and Locke, in ethics. Thus it appears that the lag time between fundamental changes in natural philosophy—that is, in what today we call the scientific worldview—and subsequent changes of equal profundity in moral philosophy is about a century. The twentieth-century revolution in natural philosophy—led by Planck, Einstein, Heisenberg, Bohr, and others in physics, and by Clements, Elton, Tansley, Haldane, and others in biology—if history is a reliable guide, will be followed by a parallel revolution in moral philosophy. The environmental philosophy of the last quarter of the twentieth century is, I submit, the harbinger of things to come.

PRACTICING ENVIRONMENTAL PHILOSOPHY

The essays in the first section of this volume provide a more sustained discussion of the relationship of environmental philosophy to the larger discipline of which it still remains a small, professionally despised, and peripheral part, and to the contemporary environmental crisis that provoked it. The first, "Environmental Philosophy *Is* Environmental Activism: The Most Radical and Effective Kind," attempts to defend environmental philosophy as I have pursued it, not against attacks by my reactionary mainstream colleagues, who would like to nip it in the bud, but against attacks by environmental "antiphilosophers," as I call them, who seem to think that theoretical environmental philosophy is not radical enough. It was written for a small conference of scholars, organized by Don E. Marietta and Lester Embree, on environmental philosophy and environmental activism, held in the spring of 1993 at a pleasant oceanside resort in South Florida. The second, "How Environmental Ethical Theory Can Be Put into Practice," argues that unlike other ethics, environmental ethics requires more social and political than personal commitment to be effective. I speculate on how new worldviews seep into the collective consciousness of a culture such as ours and begin to shape its values and eventually to inform its changing policies and laws. It was written for an international interdisciplinary conference, open to the public, organized by Frederick Ferré and others, held at the University of Georgia in the spring of 1992. The third, "Holistic Environmental Ethics and the Problem of Ecofascism," takes up a perennial problem for "ecocentric" environmental ethics. I try to locate the Leopold land ethic, the leading example of a holistic environmental ethic, in the history of Western moral philosophy, and indicate why it has not been better understood and given a more sympathetic hearing by Modern moral philosophers. In brief and in sum, I trace the philosophical pedigree of the Leopold land ethic first to Darwin's evolutionary account of the origin and development of the "social instincts" and "the moral sense" in *The Descent of Man*, which evidently directly informed Leopold's thinking, and then to the sentimental communitarianism of Adam Smith and David Hume, which evidently directly informed Darwin's thinking. And I dispel the pseudoproblem of ecofascism that has bedevilled holistic environmental ethics for more than fifteen years—at last, hopefully, once and for all. This chapter has not been presented or published elsewhere.

REVISITING THE LAND ETHIC

Aldo Leopold is routinely called a prophet—for two reasons. First, he studied the Bible, not as an act of faith, but for a model of literary style. As a result, his writing has a sort of biblical compulsion to it. Second, he thought far ahead of his time; he anticipated intellectual things to come. He was an environmental philosopher, before environmental philosophy came on the scene. He was an amateur twenty-first century philosopher, exploring the moral implications of the biological sciences, living in the twentieth century—and only during the first half of it, at that. Many of the essays on environmental philosophy in *In Defense of the Land Ethic* attempt to explore the submerged part of an intellectual iceberg, only the tip of which is visible in Aldo Leopold's *A Sand County Almanac*. There I also deal with obvious theoretical problems confronting the land ethic, such as why we human beings may have moral obligations to nature while to suppose that nature might have moral obligations to us is patently absurd. As it seems to me, the most obvious theoretical problem facing the land ethic is how, in view of the divorce between facts and values decreed in twentieth-century academic philosophy, science can inform ethics, more especially how the theory of evolution and ecology can inform the land ethic.

I touched on that problem in *In Defense of the Land Ethic;* here I return to it in "Just the Facts, Ma'am," an essay written for a theme issue of the *Environmental Professional* on environmental ethics, published in 1987. In addition to a more thorough theoretical treatment, I illustrate the interplay between our human rational faculties and moral sentiments with a case study: Leopold's well-known reversal of attitude toward predators—such as the gray wolf, the brown bear, and the mountain lion—from one of fear and loathing to one of affection and concern.

My essays in the earlier SUNY Press collection did not, however, anticipate and obviate all the theoretical problems to which the land ethic is heir. Kristin Shrader-Frechette and Warwick Fox both argue that the land ethic, as I have interpreted it, lacks "normative force." I may be able satisfactorily to explain, that is, how someone like Leopold, who acquires an evolutionary and ecological worldview, might come to love and respect predators after contemning and persecuting them, but I cannot, with the conceptual resources of the land ethic alone, demonstrate that anyone (Leopold included) ought, morally ought, to love and respect predators. Or so argue Shrader-Frechette and Fox, quite independently of one another. Here, in "Can a Theory of Moral Sentiments Support a Genuinely Normative Environmental Ethic?" I wrestle with this problem. The essay was written as the Invited Address to the sixty-fifth annual meeting of the Pacific Division of the American Philosophical Association in the spring of 1991. (The Pacific has long been the most progressive of the three divisions of the APA. Further evidence that environmental philosophy is garnering at least a little bit of professional respect is that an environmental philosopher was asked to give, not an, but *the* invited address to the division meetings that year. I should also add, in the same vein, that between the writing of this introduction and its publication Kristin Shrader-Frechette, my successor as president of the International Society for Environmental Ethics, has become Alfred C. DeCrane Professor of Philosophy and Concurrent Professor of Biology at Notre Dame University.)

In my opinion, the biggest problems for the land ethic arise not from its philosophical, but from its scientific foundations. *Sand County's* "The Land Ethic" was put together at almost the midpoint of the twentieth century. Then the ecosystem concept was in ascendancy in ecology. It represented living nature to be an integrated set of structures in dynamic equilibrium, maintained in such an equilibrium by negative feedback processes, such as predator-prey relationships, similar to that of a thermostat. But virtually all the models and metaphors in ecology up until then assumed, in one way or another, that to be in a state of equilibrium was nature's normal condition. In F. E. Clements's superorganism model in early twentieth-century ecology, for example, one "association" of organisms succeeded another until a mature climax association was attained. Then the climax reproduced itself in perpetuity until the successional series leading up to the climax was restarted by some external (often anthropogenic) disturbance. In Charles Elton's community model, widely current in ecology by the 1920s, the magnitude of potentially explosive species populations composing biotic communities remained constant or fluctuated around some mean, each species population held in "balance," in respect to the others, by various invisible hands, such as competition and predation. Sometime around 1975, the equilibrium or balance-of-nature worldview in ecology gave way to one in which nature is constantly changing, often chaotically, and in which violent disturbance is a normal and healthy, not an abnormal and pathological, occurrence. Further, after Leopold composed "The Land Ethic," evolutionary accounts of the origin and development of ethics more sophisticated than Darwin's own have also been advanced. In "Do Deconstructive Ecology and Sociobiology Undermine the Leopold Land Ethic?," I document and confront these and similar challenges to the scientific foundations of the land ethic. I answer "No" to the title's question, but argue that late twentieth-century developments in the ecological and evolutionary sciences may necessitate revising the precepts of the land ethic.

HOW MANY EARTH AND OTHER ETHICS DO WE WANT?

In 1989, I was drawn into a debate about moral pluralism by another invitation to present a paper at the annual meeting of the APA-Pacific—this time as one of the critics in an increasingly popular "author-meets-critics" session celebrating the publication of *Earth and Other Ethics* by Christopher D. Stone. Stone advanced a position that he styled "moral pluralism," a position that I found to be philosophically untenable. My critique, "The Case Against Moral Pluralism," was eventually published in *Environmental Ethics*, the journal. It provoked a firestorm of protest.

Pluralism is politically correct. How could I or any other well-meaning, magnanimous, progressive person be against it? I endorse personnel pluralism in the academy and in the bureaucracy, and pluralism in sexual orientation, why do I not endorse pluralism in ethics? My case against moral pluralism is directed toward the very specific form of it recommended by Stone, not moral pluralism under any and every possible interpretation of the term. I do not think that we should adopt one *theory* of ethics to guide action in *this* type of moral quandary, another to guide action in *that* very different sort of moral quandary, a third moral *theory* to guide action in still *another* equally different kind of moral quandary, and so on, as Stone suggests. Why? In short, because moral theories are embedded in moral philosophies, most of which are mutually inconsistent. Hence, moral pluralism, as Stone advocates it, implies intrapersonal inconsistency and self-contradiction.

If by "moral pluralism" you mean the right of different moral agents to select the moral theory and associated moral philosophy most persuasive to each, severally, certainly I have nothing against that. On the other hand, I think that the very nature of moral philosophy requires that we assume a commitment on the part of all moral agents to *reasoned* persuasion. To adopt a moral theory arbitrarily or because it is self-serving is contrary to a commitment to reasoned persuasion. Hence, if I am persuaded by the land ethic—and as modified along the lines I just sketched, I am—I assume that, after sufficient discussion between us, you will be too. Or, after sufficient discussion, you will convince me to adopt the theory that you find most persuasive. This, of course, is an ideal. No discussion is ever sufficient. New and unexpected considerations are always emerging. So the adoption of any moral theory, as of any scientific theory, is always provisional and open to modification or wholesale replacement. And, because universal agreement is an ideal, at any given time there are going to be a number of viable candidates in mutual contention for best moral theory. That's what I call "interpersonal moral pluralism," and it is a very good and healthy thing. In this good and healthy climate of interpersonal moral pluralism, each moral philosopher has not only a right but a duty to argue that his or her preferred moral theory is superior to all the others—that is, that it uniquely takes account of all the relevant considerations and does so self-consistently. By the same token, if each moral philosopher expects everyone else to be persuaded by reasoned argument that his or her preferred moral theory is superior to all the others, then he or she also has a duty to be genuinely open to persuasion by the reasoned arguments of others. I have been criticized for changing my mind. I consider changing my mind not to be a philosophical weakness or vice—as if philosophy consisted in staking out a position, digging in one's heels, refusing to budge, and shamelessly concocting any and every sophistry to fend off criticism—but evidence of my commitment to reasoned persuasion. How can I expect everyone else to be open to persuasion by my arguments, if I am unwilling to be open to persuasion by theirs? And what better way to prove that one is open to persuasion by someone else's arguments than occasionally to be persuaded by them?

In academic ethics, "moral pluralism" often refers to the view that an agent might appropriately employ a multiplicity of moral *principles* to guide action in various, different moral quandaries. I do object to such a pluralism of principles *if* one's principles are grounded in inconsistent moral philosophies, as I just explained. Again, for example, if one adopted the utilitarian "greatest happiness" principle to guide one's actions in one quandary and then adopted the Kantian "universalization" principle to guide one's actions in another moral quandary, one would be committing oneself to the mutually inconsistent and contradictory ethical theories and moral philosophies that ground and justify these principles. But one might, quite properly, in my opinion, adopt a single moral philosophy, say Plato's, and subscribe, within that moral philosophy, to a plurality of principles: say, Be just; Be temperate; Be courageous; Be wise; Be pious; and Be generous. Having a single moral philosophy in which these several principles are grounded and by means of which they are justified, unifies them theoretically. And if they should come into conflict in practice or application, one can compare each with the others in the commensurable terms of the common and self-consistent moral philosophy in which they are located. One can thus adjudicate between them, or "prioritize," as we now sometimes say, among them. Suppose, to continue with the Platonic-virtue-ethics example, that I am a college student and that my moral quandary is, Should I or should I not attempt to drink a quart of whisky at one gulp on the dare of my fraternity brothers? We are all enrolled in a course in classical Greek philosophy, being campus "Greeks" ourselves, in the expectation of learning something about how the ancient inventors of Greek-letter organizations initiated their pledges and what and how much they drank when they partied down with their "little sisters." Not to try to chug it, my frat brothers argue, would be cowardly, and thus contrary to the Platonic principle Be courageous. To try, I reply, would be intemperate, and unwise as well, given the toxicity of alcohol, and its potential, in such quantity, to kill me. Moreover, it might involve impiety, if not toward the gods (Dionysus might approve, while Apollo might not—we were just assigned the *Euthyphro*, and I read it) then "filial" impiety, as my professor called it, toward my parents, who certainly would not want me to try to do such a foolish thing. If they should explore Plato's moral philosophy more deeply, I go on to point out, my frat brothers might discover that he views courage as a species of wisdom, the knowledge of what to fear and what not to fear. And the taunts of one's peers, I argue triumphantly, is not something to fear—or at least such taunting should be feared less than abject drunkenness and possible suicide. All things considered, the virtuous thing to do is to demur.

At first, I understood the Leopold land ethic to posit a single moral principle, comparable in this regard, not to the Platonic ethic, but to the more familiar Christian, utilitarian, and Kantian ethics, each of which endorse one and only one master moral principle. The Golden Rule is the monistic principle of the Christian ethic; the greatest happiness principle is the monistic principle of the utilitarian ethic; and the categorical imperative is the monistic principle of the Kantian ethic. The golden rule of the land ethic is, "A thing is right when it tends to preserve the integrity, stability, and beauty of the biotic community; it is wrong when it tends otherwise." Raised in a predominantly Christian culture and schooled in Modern consequentialist and deontological ethics, I naively just assumed moral monism at the level of principle. And so at first I argued that the land ethic required us to assess the rightness or wrongness of *all* our actions to the extent that they conform to this principle, just as the Christian, utilitarian, and Kantian ethics assess the rightness or wrongness of all our actions to the extent that they conform to the Golden Rule proper, the greatest happiness principle, or the categorical imperative, respectively. My critics gleefully pointed out that actually guiding all our actions by the summary moral maxim of the land ethic would entail monstrous, homicidal consequences. Here, by the way, my commitment to interpersonal pluralism and openness to persuasion may be demonstrated. I was persuaded that my critics were right: Guiding *all* our actions by the golden rule of the land ethic would indeed entail monstrous, homicidal consequences. And, then and there, I would have abandoned the land ethic, had it not occurred to me that I had been wrong to interpret it as positing a single moral principle as do the Christian, utilitarian, and Kantian ethics. Leopold characterizes the land ethic, I noted, as an "accretion," that is, an addition to our familiar human-to-human ethics; it is not intended to replace or eclipse our familiar human-to-human ethics. But if the summary moral maxim of the land ethic is a new principle to be added to others, we can only do so consistently, that is, without self-contradiction, if we can locate it within an ethical theory and moral philosophy that accommodates a plurality of principles, human, humane, and environmental. As noted, the Christian, utilitarian, and Kantian moral philosophies each accommodate only a single master principle—the Golden Rule, the greatest happiness principle, and the categorical imperative, respectively. But the Platonic moral philosophy coherently accommodates a plurality or multiplicity of principles—the justice principle, the temperance principle, and so on—or, more precisely put, a plurality or multiplicity of cardinal virtues. I find a moral philosophy that will accommodate a plurality or multiplicity of ethical principles—or, more precisely, a multiplicity of duties and obligations—including the summary moral maxim of the Leopold land ethic (as modified to take into account recent developments in ecology), in the sentimental communitarianism first advocated by David Hume and Adam Smith and later biologicized by Charles Darwin. And, in the final analysis, I claim that the golden rule of the Leopold land ethic (as modified to take into account recent developments in ecology) is but one of a multiplicity of community-generated duties and obligations, unified by sentimental communitarianism. It is generated by our membership in the biotic community. But our many other community memberships—in families, municipalities, nation-states, the global human village—generate many other duties and obligations than the land ethical duty to disturb the biotic community only at normal spatial and temporal scales (which is how I suggest that the summary moral maxim of the land ethic might be modified to take into account recent developments in ecology).

My defense of the land ethic against the charge that it entails a hideous "environmental fascism" opens it to the charge that it is a "paper tiger." It has no bite. Just how do we prioritize when our land ethical duties and obligations conflict with our familial, municipal, national, and humanitarian duties and obligations? I suggested that the duties and obligations associated with our more venerable and intimate community memberships are the more primitive and urgent. Thus, if one has severely limited resources, one should share them with family members, not distribute them indiscriminately to total strangers. By the same token, I have stronger obligations to my fellow human beings and to the human community than to my fellow creatures and to the biotic community. But in that case, it would seem that our environmental ethics would always be eclipsed by our human ethics. And they would be, rightly so I think, if all our duties and obligations were of equal strength. But they are not. Many of our environmental problems could be ameliorated if we sacrificed not the necessities of human life, which we have a strong duty to provide ourselves and others, but some of the more excessive and extravagant luxuries of human lifestyles. We have a much stronger obligation to save endangered species from extinction, for instance, than we have to raise the Dow Jones Industrial Average by a percentage point or two. In "Moral Monism in Environmental Ethics Defended" (written in 1993 for presentation at the ninety-first annual meeting of the APA-Central Division, and originally published in the *Journal of Philosophical Research*), I clarify just what sort of moral pluralism I find philosophically untenable. And I take up the paper-tiger problem alleged to bedevil the land ethic and indicate how the land ethic might help guide us in resolving the notorious timber-industry-versus-spotted-owls conflict in the Pacific Northwest.

ANOTHER CONTROVERSIAL TOPIC

Though environmental philosopher Bryan Norton wishes it were not so, the intrinsic-value-in-nature question has been, and remains, the central and most persistent cluster of problems in theoretical environmental philosophy. Two special issues of general philosophy journals—the *Monist*, volume 75, number 2 (1992) and the *Electronic Journal of Analytic Philosophy*, volume 3, number 3 (1995)—were devoted to that topic; I guest-edited the former and contributed to the latter. Anthropocentrists, such as Norton and Hargrove, refuse to attribute intrinsic value to nature, and reserve it only for human beings, both those presently living and future generations. That is why, indeed, they are called anthropocentrists. Non-anthropocentrists, such as practically everyone else of note in the field, all agree that nature has intrinsic value, but we disagree profoundly on the extent to which it can be found (or ought to be distributed) in nature and on its ontological status. As to its distribution in nature, some claim that only individual organisms can be properly said to possess intrinsic value (or inherent worth, as it is sometimes called). Others, I among them, argue that superorganismic wholes—species, biotic communities, ecosystems, the whole biosphere—are intrinsically valuable. As to ontological status, some nonanthropocentrists claim that intrinsic value exists objectively—no less objectively than, say, backbones or wings—as a fact of nature. Others, I among them, claim that intrinsic value is subjectively conferred—that is, that if there existed no valuing subjects, nothing would be of value, intrinsic or otherwise.

The first of the three papers in this volume on intrinsic value in nature was presented at the 1989 meeting of the American Society for Environmental History at Evergreen State College in Olympia, Washington, on the shores of Puget Sound. In retrospect, that meeting represents an intellectual watershed. At it, Donald Worster debuted his essay, "The Ecology of Order and Chaos," in which he summarized and documented, for the community of environmental humanists, the ethically untoward and disturbing shift in ecology from the mid-century "balance of nature paradigm" to the fin-de-siècle "flux of nature paradigm" (as the principal proponent of the latter, Stewart Pickett, styles them)—the ecology of order and the ecology of chaos, respectively, of Worster's title. It was Worster's paper that first convinced me that, to remain viable, the Leopold land ethic must be revised in light of this recent paradigm shift in ecology.

For some time, at any rate, I had been playfully thinking about a third interpretation of the environmental implications of Genesis, to which Lynn White Jr. had called attention in his notorious "Historical Roots of Our Ecologic Crisis," published in *Science* in 1967. (Scrutinizing that paper a quarter-century later, it appears to have, more generally, set out an agenda for a future environmental philosophy and inspired us, the founders of the field, to get moving on it.) White had sketched the mastery interpretation which Judeo-Christian apologists had immediately countered with the stewardship interpretation. The more I thought about it, the more convinced I became that an environmental ethic far more radical than the Judeo-Christian stewardship environmental ethic, or even than the Leopold land ethic, could be teased out of the biblical worldview. Then I noticed that in *A Thousand Mile Walk to the Gulf,* John Muir had adumbrated just such a radical Judeo-Christian citizenship environmental ethic as I had been mulling over. "Genesis and John Muir" amalgamates my ruminations on Genesis with Muir's. It is included in this section on intrinsic value because, as it seems to me, Genesis clearly imputes intrinsic value to nature, and does so in the clearest and most direct way imaginable—by divine fiat.

The second of the three papers in this volume on intrinsic value in nature, "Rolston on Intrinsic Value: A Deconstruction," was also occasioned by an invitation to serve as a critic at another APA-Pacific author-meets-critics session. For this one, the author was Holmes Rolston III; the book was *Environmental Ethics*; and the year was also 1989. Rolston is a staunch advocate of objective intrinsic value in nature. I hold a less doctrinaire, more relative opinion. I think that intrinsic value in nature cannot exist objectively *within the constraints of the Modern worldview*, the general parameters of which were set out by Descartes in the seventeenth century. A cornerstone of the Modern worldview is the divorce, decreed by Descartes himself, between the *res extensa* and the *res cogitans*, between the objective physical and the subjective psychological domains. Corollary to this divorce is the one decreed between objective primary and subjective secondary qualities, first by Galileo Galilei and later affirmed (and so named) by John Locke, and the one decreed by David Hume between objective facts and subjective values. In the Modern worldview, values are, as it were, subjectively conferred tertiary qualities of objects. In *Environmental Ethics*, the book (and elsewhere), Rolston challenges the Humean distinction, arguing that intrinsic value actually exists in nature, while expressly affirming the Galilean-Lockean distinction between primary and secondary qualities and nowhere challenging the more fundamental distinction from which the other two are derived, the Cartesian distinction between purely psychological subjects and purely physical objects. Hence, his case for objective intrinsic value in nature fails to convince.

To mount a convincing case for objective intrinsic value in nature, one must go beyond the Modern worldview. In *In Defense of the Land Ethic,* I suggested that a postModern worldview useful for solving environmental philosophy's intrinsic-value-in-nature problems might be constructed from the conceptual resources provided by quantum theory in the New Physics. For in the worldview of the New Physics, the Cartesian distinction between the *res extensa* and *res cogitans* is blurred. Corollary to this postModern remarriage of subjects and objects, I also there argued that all properties of objects—their primary quantitative properties, their secondary sensory properties, and their tertiary valuative properties—had the same ontological status. All were "virtual" (or potential) properties of objects that are actualized only by interaction with physical subjects. Short of some such foundational project as this, hard as we try to conjure it, intrinsic value cannot be shown to exist objectively in nature.

But short of some such foundational project as constructing a post-Cartesian worldview from the conceptual resources of the New Physics, we can get by just fine, in environmental ethics, with a normatively equivalent theory of subjectively conferred intrinsic value in nature. Normatively, intrinsic value serves as a foil for instrumental value. When something is valued instrumentally, it is valued by some valuing subject as a means only. On the other hand, if something has intrinsic value, it is also an end-in-itself. The normative function of finding objective intrinsic value in nature is to transform nature (or some elements or aspects of it) from the status of a mere means to the status of an end-in-itself. We can, however, preserve the distinction between means and ends without challenging the Cartesian cleft between the *res extensa* and the *res cogitans*. For we psychological Cartesian subjects (assuming that that's what we are) are perfectly capable of valuing entities other than ourselves intrinsically—that is, for their own sakes, as ends in themselves—as well as instrumentally.

In "Intrinsic Value in Nature: A Metaethical Analysis" (originally published in the *Electronic Journal of Analytic Philosophy*) I try to prove, against Norton, that intrinsic value "exists," in the sense that most everyone values him- or herself intrinsically, and that the concept of intrinsic value has a powerful function in ethics. An intrinsically valuable end cannot be appropriated as a mere means, without overwhelming justification for doing so. As things stand, only the instrumental value of nature is widely recognized. To prevent the destructive exploitation of nature, environmentalists are, thus, compelled to show that the instrumental value of nature left alone and whole (its ecological services, its potential for recreation and for aesthetic gratification) outweighs its instrumental value as fodder for the industrial maw. Now suppose that the intrinsic value of nature (or some elements or aspects of it) were to become as widely recognized as is the intrinsic value of human beings. Then the burden of proof would shift from those who would protect nature to those who would exploit it as only a means. Intrinsically valued people are often called "human resources" and millions of us human resources are exploited every day by our employers. Though we employees are acknowledged to be ends-in-ourselves, we are also means to our employers' ends. Hence in those societies that intrinsically value human life, ethical constraints—hour maximums, wage minimums, workplace safety standards—are institutionalized to mitigate the exploitation of human beings. If nature were intrinsically valued, it could, ethically, still be exploited, but similar constraints would apply.

Wide recognition of the intrinsic value of nature, as we see, would work in the environmental arena similar to the way in which wide recognition of human rights works in the political arena. Few philosophers who study human rights ascribe to a metaethical theory of natural rights—a theory that asserts that human rights are something objective which human beings may coherently be said to possess in the same straightforward sense in which we may coherently be said to possess shoes or teeth or even thoughts. A metaethical theory of the ontological status of human rights which denies that they are anything objective, however, does not undermine—nor is such a theory intended to undermine—the considerable normative efficacy of human rights. Similarly, a Modern metaethical theory of the ontological status of the intrinsic value of nature, such as mine, which denies that the intrinsic value of nature is objective, and asserts instead that it is subjectively conferred by valuing subjects, would in no way compromise—nor is it intended to compromise—the considerable impact on environmental policy and law that a wide recognition of the intrinsic value of nature would make.

Conflating, I suppose, metaethical and normative discourse, moral philosophers going all the way back to Kant have, nevertheless, tried, within the constraints of the Modern worldview, to convincingly claim that some limited set of entities—rational human beings and interested organisms, are the two candidate sets that I examine in "Intrinsic Value in Nature: A Metaethical Analysis"—possess objective intrinsic value. None, including Kant, succeed, in my opinion. However, in the course of his most recent attempt, *Conserving Natural Value*, Rolston, I suggest, gradually and inadvertently transcends the Modern worldview by first systematically democratizing, then deconstructing and decentering the Cartesian psychological subject. Rolston thus hints at a postModern theory of intrinsic value that is very different from the reconstructive one, distilled from the New Physics, that I offer. He, rather, points toward a poststructuralist approach, the viability of which can only be judged if and when it is more fully and deliberately developed.

BAROMETERS OF CHANGE

Signs are everywhere that the Modern worldview is decaying and that its hold on the Western mind and institutions is weakening. In my opinion, the most irresistible force undermining the very foundations of Modernism is the shift from print to electronic information media. The shift from orally transmitting and mnemonically storing information to storing and transmitting information by means of writing was accompanied by a profound transformation of human consciousness—from the mythopoeic mind to the rational mind and from the communal self to the individual self. Print completed and perfected the changes initiated by writing. Modernity is the legacy of a more or less universal literacy, made possible by print. But now, we educators lament, no one reads anymore. People watch TV instead or, more recently, surf the net. And information is stored and retrieved electronically. What equally profound transformation of human consciousness will that create?

A deconstructed and decentered self? Maybe the fragmented, rapidly shifting images on MTV are, it is feared, an objective correlative of the postModern mind—a shattered, post-rational self that is nowhere and everywhere at once, a far cry from the focused, rational, synoptic Modern ego, so ably characterized by Descartes. There is a more hopeful possibility than this, however. The political balkanization of the planet, the bickering domestic politics of difference ("identity politics," as it is sometimes called) in pluralistic societies such as the United States of America, the empty consumerism of this *fin de millennium* may not be the end point of the sea changes in progress, but the transitional phase. To what? Perhaps to an ecological or, more generally, a systems worldview and to a gradual reification of such a worldview in the material of social, political, and economic organization.

Two universals in human experience are eating and getting sick. Irrespective of one's cultural identity, everyone must eat and everyone is liable to get sick. Though the necessity of getting food and the possibility of getting sick are human universals transcending the myriad cultural differences between us, the means of obtaining something to eat and of warding off and curing illness are deeply embedded in and understood in terms of the many and various cultural worldviews. In *In Defense of the Land Ethic*, I characterize some aspects of the traditional woodland American Indian representation of their means of getting food (and getting sick) by hunting and gathering. Game animals and forage plants were believed to be persons who would voluntarily give themselves up to needy and worthy hunters and gatherers. Success in obtaining food was, therefore, believed to depend less on developing capture skills with such technologies as the bow and arrow and more on developing a proper relationship with the other-than-human persons in the hunters' and gatherers' greater-than-human community. Illness, similarly, was explained as retaliation for some social offense against a mystically empowered human or other-than-human person. If, for instance, a hunter were to take more game than needed or fail respectfully to dispose of an animal's inedible remains, either the animal's spirit or it's spiritual warden could and would cause the errant hunter to fall ill. Curing illness involved restoring the afflicted person's good relationship with his or her neighbors—human or other-than-human, as the case may be—often diagnosed and mediated by a shaman.

Eating and getting sick are not only universal in human experience, they are vital and fundamental. How we go about getting food and warding off and curing sickness reveal, therefore, perhaps more reliably than any profession of faith or statement of philosophy, our foundational beliefs, our worldview. In "The Metaphysical Transition in Farming: From the Newtonian-Mechanical to the Eltonian-Ecological" (originally published in the *Journal of Agricultural Ethics*) and in "Environmental Wellness" (originally published in *Literature and Medicine*), I argue that Modern agriculture and medicine are clear manifestations, indeed manneristic manifestations, of the mechanical worldview. But mechanical (or "industrial") agriculture and "conventional" (or mechanico-chemical) medicine are, increasingly, much criticized, and alternative farming and medical methods, informed by alternative philosophies of agriculture and medicine, are currently being tried. A sea change in our conception and practice of such universal, vital, and fundamental human activities as getting food and warding off and curing sickness is indicative of a sea change in our cultural worldview. And an examination of the direction of change now underway in both agriculture and medicine—from a reductive and mechanical to a holistic and systemic paradigm—confirms my contention that the scientific revolutions of the twentieth century are informing a new, more "ecological" twenty-first-century *Weltanschauung.*

During January 1994, I was invited to participate in a symposium in Paris entitled La Crise Environnemental et ses Enjeux: Ethique, Science, et Politique. There I presented a paper, "Après le Paradigm Industriel," which was published three years hence in the symposium proceedings, *La Crise Environnemental.* Included here is "After the Industrial Paradigm, What?," the English translation of that paper, in which I try to crystallize my understanding of Modernism and postModernism. More particularly, I try to indicate the shape of a reconstructive postModern epistemology, ontology, and, upon this basis, a reconstructive postModern paradigm for self, society, and technology.

THE PHILOSOPHY OF CONSERVATION

The blinkered gaze of mainstream academic philosophy in the twentieth century, falling on a vary narrow range of specialized problems, has, until recently, left discussion of the philosophical dimensions of many emergent concerns to amateurs, such as Aldo Leopold. One such concern is conservation, and it has a rich history of philosophical dispute, going back about a hundred years. Over the last decade I have tried, more systematically, to apply the tools and methods of philosophical exposition, criticism, and reconstruction to developments in contemporary conservation. The most dramatic development in contemporary conservation is the emergence of conservation biology. Conservation biology is characterized as a "transdiscipline," that is, an architectonic discipline that embraces and incorporates a number of traditional disciplines. In addition to genetics, population biology, island biogeography, and ecology, environmental philosophy and ethics are routinely listed in conservation biology manifestos and textbooks as being among the disciplines that this new transdiscipline embraces and incorporates. More recently, another conservation transdiscipline has emerged called "ecosystem health" or, sometimes, "clinical ecology." The final section of this collection include some of my philosophical contributions to the transdisciplines of clinical ecology and conservation biology.

The first of the four essays in this section, "Whither Conservation Ethics?," was originally published in *Conservation Biology*, the journal, in 1990. It sketches the century-old history of American conservation philosophy. Two conservation ethics dominated the twentieth century—the Resource Conservation Ethic and the Nature Preservation Ethic, the former institutionalized primarily in government agencies, such as the United States Department of Agriculture Forest Service and the several state departments of natural resources. Aldo Leopold, I argue, quietly formulated a third conservation ethic envisioning the ideal of a human harmony with nature that fosters both economic and ecosystemic health—which is better suited to inform conservation policy in the twenty-first century, than is either Resourcism or Preservationism.

The very idea of ecosystem health is problematic and controversial. Do ecosystems as such exist? Are they enough like organisms that we can intelligibly speak of them as in a condition of health or ill-health? If so, to what extent should human interests be incorporated into the concept of ecosystem health? Or is ecosystem health a condition of ecosystems that is independent of human interests? These are just a few of the distinctly philosophical questions raised by the emergence of clinical ecology in conservation. "Aldo Leopold's Concept of Ecosystem Health" was written for a symposium on ecosystem health at the 1991 American Association for the Advancement of Science meeting in Washington, D.C. It was originally published as "Aldo Leopold's Metaphor" in *Ecosystem Health: New Goals for Environmental Management*, edited by Robert Costanza, Bryan G. Norton, and Benjamin D. Haskell. In "Aldo Leopold's Concept of Ecosystem Health," I point out that because health is a concept that at once has both objective and normative dimensions, its metaphorical use is particularly potent in moral discourse. The health metaphor was, for that reason, exploited by Plato in the *Republic*. There Plato argues that virtue is the health of the soul. Leopold seems to have been the first thinker in the philosophy of conservation to exploit the health metaphor—with his concept of "land health." Such a potent idea as ecosystem health is bound to draw criticism from those who, for one reason or another, wish to frustrate the political ambitions of environmentalists. In "The Value of Ecosystem Health," first published in the journal *Environmental Values*, I try to defend the concept from attacks by reactionary ecologists and philosophers who variously doubt its viability.

The final essay in this volume is entitled "Ecological Sustainability as a Conservation Concept." It was written with a coauthor, Karen Mumford, who from 1995 to 1998 was a Ph.D. candidate in conservation biology at the University of Minnesota and served as my research assistant under the auspices of a grant from the Great Lakes Fishery Commission to explore new Great Lakes management policies for the twentieth-first century. Sustainability has a long history in conservation philosophy, appearing first in the form of the concept of maximum sustainable yield. After several United Nations conferences on environment and development and after the famous *Brundtland Report*, a great deal of interest in the conservation community has focused on the concept of sustainable development. In this essay, Mumford and I explore the concept of ecological sustainability, which we link intimately to the concept of ecosystem health. More generally, we envision a twenty-first-century conservation philosophy of "complementarity." We note that there are two basic approaches to the science of ecology, evolutionary-community ecology and ecosystem ecology. In the former, the natural environment is understood to consist of organisms composing species populations that interact in biotic communities; in the latter, solar energy drives a congeries of interlinked hierarchically ordered processes, such as photosynthesis, nutrient cycling, and disturbance regimes. From the former perspective, the preservation of biological diversity and ecological integrity are the paramount goals of conservation; from the latter perspective, the paramount goals of conservation are the preservation of ecosystem health and ecological sustainability. Both these approaches to ecology are valid and complementary. A similar complementarity should govern conservation policy. The preservation of biological diversity and ecological integrity is best facilitated by large, thoughtfully sited and interconnected reserves; ecosystem health and ecological sustainability are the appropriate conservation norms for the humanly inhabited and economically exploited regions of the world.

As the discerning reader may already have observed, this book moves from more abstract philosophical concerns to the practical application of environmental philosophy and ethics in agriculture, medicine, and the transdisciplinary contexts of ecosystem health and conservation biology. Most of the essays included here first appeared elsewhere. I collect them into a single volume primarily because they were originally published in such diverse places—from the *Journal of Philosophical Research* and the *Electronic Journal of Analytic Philosophy* to *Ecosystem Health* and *Conservation Biology*—that only the most dedicated scholar would have been able, otherwise, to find them, or even to be aware of them all. Together they track developments in my thinking on themes familiar to readers of *In Defense of the Land Ethic* and introduce new themes emerging in my work over the last decade. Because each of these essays was written for a particular audience and most of them for a particular occasion, they vary widely in style and tone. I believe, however, that they are mutually consistent and complementary. And also, because each of these essays once stood alone, some may go over ground gone over by another. Such repetition is unavoidable if each essay is to remain largely unchanged. And I think it is important to correct only incidental errors in order to ensure that an essay cited here is nearly identical to an essay of mine under the same title cited elsewhere.

PART I

PRACTICING
ENVIRONMENTAL ETHICS

Environmental Philosophy *Is* Environmental Activism: The Most Radical and Effective Kind

THE SOCIAL EFFICACY OF PHILOSOPHY: TWO VIGNETTES

Here is one picture of philosophy. It goes on in an ivory tower pursued by cloistered academics who endlessly dispute the contemporary equivalents of questions like "how many angels can dance on the head of a pin?" It is far removed from the "real world," even when philosophers spin theories about what is "real." (In the real world, everyone knows what's real, without having to have philosophers to inform or misinform them.) Here is another picture of philosophy. Socrates is hauled into court, tried, and sentenced to death—not for anything he might have done, such as sell state secrets to the Lacedaimonians or conspire to assassinate Kleon, but for questioning religious ideas and moral ideals, thus bringing about the precipitous transformation of Athenian society. In the first picture, philosophy seems socially irrelevant. In the second, it seems to be the most potent force of social change imaginable.

ENVIRONMENTAL ANTIPHILOSOPHY

There does seem to be a lot of ivory-tower philosophy—a kind of new scholasticism—going on today in academe. Only future historians will be in a position to judge whether or not it will prove to have actually been socially transformative. But let's grant, for the sake of argument, that the test of time will prove that what seems to be irrelevant ivory-tower philosophy is indeed just that. The postsixties "applied" movement in late-twentieth-century philosophy has been an attempt, on the part of many academic philosophers, to descend from the ivory tower and directly engage real-world issues. The advent of business ethics, biomedical ethics, animal welfare ethics, engineering ethics, and environmental ethics illustrates two points: first, that many young academic philosophers then believed that business-as-usual analytic philosophy, phenomenology, philosophy of science, and the like is, as many non-philosophers suspect, socially irrelevant; and second, that an attempt was deliberately made to reorient philosophy so as to apply its rich heritage of theory and powerful methods of argument to illuminate and help solve real-world problems.

The "pure" philosophers, as if to confirm the suspicion that their preoccupations are ivory-tower irrelevancies, have responded with contempt. Applied philosophy is scorned as not "real" (that is genuine) philosophy and as merely yeoman's (and yeowoman's) work, appropriating the creative ideas of the true, the pure, the real philosophers and mechanically applying them to current social "issues." Applied work is perhaps suitable for academic philosophers toiling in bush league undergraduate departments, but not for those holding prestigious chairs in major league research departments.

Since environmental philosophy came into being in such circumstances—in deliberate reaction to what was perceived as the reigning neo-scholasticism and in a deliberate attempt to help society deal with real-world problems—it is surprising to find some people now suggesting that environmental philosophy is itself an ivory-tower preoccupation of little practical moment. Though the people I have in mind occupy positions in philosophy departments and publish papers in philosophy journals, I hesitate to call them philosophers, since they seem to think that philosophy, even environmental philosophy, is worse than an irrelevancy, it's a subterfuge.

Kenneth Sayre

One such environmental antiphilosopher is Kenneth Sayre. He writes,

> In no case does the reasoning of an ethical theorist actually cause a norm to be socially instituted or cause a norm once in force to lose that status. Whether a moral norm is actually in effect within a given community depends not at all on ethical theorizing. . . . If norms encouraging conservation and proscribing pollution were actually in force in industrial society, it would not be the result of ethical theory; and the fact that currently they are not in force is not alleviated by any amount of adroit ethical reasoning. (Sayre 1991, 200)

Sayre's understanding of ethical theory is very narrow and formal. No doubt there is a kernel of truth in his claim, if by "ethical theory" we refer to some arid inferential exercise in which a philosopher deduces that (4) action X should be proscribed, since (3) X is wrong, because (2) X has the property A and (1) all actions that have A are wrong. The alternatives to ethical theorizing, so conceived, that Sayre suggests would seem to dissolve environmental ethics into various social sciences, much as sociobiology would absorb the social sciences into biology. "Environmental ethics," he writes, "should join forces with anthropology, economics, and other areas of social science in hopes of generating a basis for empirical information about how moral norms actually operate" (Sayre 1991, p. 195).

For Sayre "moral norms" seem just to exist in splendid isolation from the larger cognitive culture. Sayre's example of a norm that is socially "in place" is honesty. An example of an environmental ethical norm that is not in place is recycling. Sayre seems to think that eventually, people may just up and adopt the recycling norm; and a new breed of environmental ethicists transformed into sociologists, social psychologists, and economists can empirically describe the mysterious process by which such a norm shift will have occurred, if it does. Or empirically examining how new norms, such as antislavery, came to be adopted in the recent past, environmental ethicists can help socially engineer new environmental norms, such as recycling, in the near future. One thing Sayre is sure of is that no amount of theorizing is going to induce most people to believe that recycling is simply the right thing to do in the same way that most people believe that honesty is simply the best policy.

Doubtless he is right if environmental ethical theory conforms to Sayre's caricature. But such formal reasoning is not what actually goes on in theoretical environmental philosophy. Environmental philosophers, rather, are attempting to articulate a new worldview and a new conception of what it means to be a human being, distilled from the theory of evolution, the New Physics, ecology, and other natural sciences. On this basis, we might suggest how people ought to relate to the natural environment, but there is rather little deducing of specific rules of conduct. People come to believe that old norms (such as "stone adulterers" and "burn witches") should be abandoned, and new ones adopted (such as "abolish slavery" and "feed the starving") only when their most fundamental ideas about themselves and their world undergo radical change. Much of the theoretical work in environmental ethics is devoted to articulating and thus helping to effect such a radical change in outlook. The specific ethical norms of environmental conduct remain for the most part only implicit—a project postponed to the future or something left for ecologically informed people to work out for themselves.

Bryan Norton

Bryan Norton, another environmental antiphilosopher, thinks that theoretical environmental ethics is not only an irrelevant subterfuge, but that it is also downright pernicious. Environmental ethicists arguing with one another about whether nature has intrinsic as well as instrumental value and about whether intrinsic value is objective or subjective divide environmentalists into deep and shallow camps. While these two camps spend precious time and energy criticizing one another, their common enemy, the hydra-headed forces of environmental destruction, remains unopposed by a united and resolute counterforce. But according to Norton (1991), a long and wide anthropocentrism "converges" on the same environmental policies—the preservation of biological diversity, for example—as nonanthropocentrism. Hence, the intellectual differences between anthropocentrists and nonanthropocentrists, deep ecologists and reform environmentalists are, practically speaking, otiose. Environmental philosophers, in Norton's view, should therefore cease spinning non-anthropocentric theories of the intrinsic value of nature and, as Norton himself does, concentrate instead on refining environmental policy. Norton (1991) opts for anthropocentrism because it is the more conservative alternative. Most people are anthropocentrists to begin with, and when the instrumental value of a whole and healthy environment to both present and future generations of humans is fully accounted, anthropocentrism, he believes, is sufficient to support the environmental policy agenda.

Norton's "convergence hypothesis," however, is dead wrong. If all environmental values are anthropocentric and instrumental, then they have to compete head to head with the economic values derived from converting rain forests to lumber and pulp, savannas to cattle pasture, and so on. Environmentalists, in other words, must show that preserving biological diversity is of greater instrumental value to present and future generations than is lucrative timber extraction, agricultural conversion, hydroelectric impoundment, mining, and so on. For this simple reason, a persuasive philosophical case for the intrinsic value of nonhuman natural entities and nature as a whole would make a huge practical difference. Warwick Fox (1993) explains why. Granting an entity intrinsic value would not imply "that it cannot be interfered with *under any circumstances*." Believing, as we do, that human beings are intrinsically valuable does not imply that human beings ought *never* be uprooted, imprisoned, put at grave risk, or even deliberately killed. Intrinsically valuable human beings may—ethically may—be made to suffer these and other insults *with sufficient justification*. Therefore, Fox points out,

[T]he mere fact that moral agents must be able to justify their actions in regard to their treatment of entities that are intrinsically valuable means that recognizing the intrinsic value of the nonhuman world has a dramatic effect upon the framework of environmental debate and decision-making. If the nonhuman world is only considered to be instrumentally valuable then people are permitted to use and otherwise interfere with any aspect of it for whatever reasons they wish (i.e., no justification is required). If anyone objects to such interference then, within this framework of reference, the onus is clearly on the person who objects to justify why it is *more useful* to humans to leave that aspect of the nonhuman world alone. If, however, the nonhuman world is considered to be *intrinsically valuable* then the onus shifts to the person who wants to interfere with it to justify why they should be allowed to do so: anyone who wants to interfere with any entity that is intrinsically valuable is morally obliged to be able to offer a *sufficient justification* for their actions. Thus recognizing the intrinsic value of the nonhuman world shifts the *onus of justification* from the person who wants to protect the nonhuman world to the person who wants to interfere with it—and that, in itself, represents a fundamental shift in the terms of environmental debate and decision-making. (Fox 1993, 101)

Just as Sayre seems to think of moral norms as hanging alone in an intellectual void, so Norton seems to think of environmental policies in the same way. We environmentalists just happen to have a policy agenda—saving endangered species, preserving biodiversity in all its forms, lowering CO_2 emissions, and so forth. To rationalize these policies—to sell them to the electorate and their representatives—is the intellectual task, if there is any. (Much of Norton's research for his book, *Unity Among Environmentalists*, consisted of interviewing the Washington-based lobbyists for "big ten" environmental groups. Such cynicism may be characteristic of revolving-door lobbyists who are hired to pitch one policy today and its opposite tomorrow, but starting with a policy and looking for persuasive reasons to support it is not how sincere environmentalists outside the Beltway actually think.) People don't just adopt a policy the way they decide which color is their favorite. They adopt it for what seem to them to be good reasons. Reasons come first, policies second, not the other way around.

Most people, of course, do not turn to philosophers for something to believe—as if they didn't at all know what to think and philosophers could and should tell them. Rather philosophers such as Thoreau, Muir, Leopold, and Rolston give voice to the otherwise inchoate and inarticulate thoughts and feelings in our changing cultural *Zeitgeist*. A maximally stretched anthropocentrism may, as Norton argues, rationalize the environmental policy agenda, but anthropocentrism may no longer ring true. That is, the claim that all and only human beings have intrinsic value may not be consistent with a more general evolutionary and ecological worldview. I should think that contemporary environmental philosophers would want to give voice and form to the still small but growing movement that supports environmental policies for the right reasons—which, as Fox points out, also happen to be the strongest reasons.

Granted, we may not have the leisure to wait for a majority to come over to a new worldview and a new nonanthropocentric, holistic environmental ethic. We environmentalists have to reach people where they are, intellectually speaking, right now. So we might persuade Jews, Christians, and Muslims to support the environmental policy agenda by appeal to such concepts as God, creation, and stewardship; we might persuade humanists by appeal to collective enlightened human self-interest; and so on. But that is no argument for insisting, as Norton seems to do, that environmental philosophers should stop exploring the real reasons, the best reasons, why we ought to value other forms of life, ecosystems, and the biosphere as a whole.

The eventual institutionalization of a new holistic, nonanthropocentric environmental ethic will make as much practical difference in the environmental arena as the institutionalization of the intrinsic value of all human beings has made in the social arena. As recently as a century and a half ago, it was permissible to own human beings. With the eventual institutionalization of Enlightenment ethics—persuasively articulated by Hobbes, Locke, Bentham, and Kant, among others—slavery was abolished in Western civilization. Of course, a case could have been made to slave owners and an indifferent public that slavery was economically backward and more trouble than it was worth. But that would not have gotten at the powerful moral truth that for one human being to own another is wrong. With the eventual institutionalization of a holistic, nonanthropocentric environmental ethic—today persuasively articulated by Aldo Leopold, Arne Naess, Holmes Rolston, and Val Plumwood, among others—the wanton destruction of the nonhuman world will, hopefully, come to be regarded as equally unconscionable.

Anthony Weston

Anthony Weston seems to believe that systematic environmental philosophy is premature. In an article entitled "Before Environmental Ethics," he suggests that it is much too early in the sea change of values that is presently taking place to try to articulate and systematize a new environmental ethic. We should let these new environmental values ferment and bubble up organically. Instead of theorizing, philosophers should help to create "quiet zones," or "ecosteries" (on analogy with Medieval monasteries) where people can "reinhabit" the land; and, through "enabling practice," unpredictable but ultimately appropriate environmental values will "emerge" (Weston 1992).

Specifically criticizing my case against moral pluralism, Weston (1991, 284) writes,

The flaw in this argument, I believe, is that it greatly overrates the role of metaphysical views in shaping and justifying values. . . . Values and their larger explanatory contexts evolve together . . . . At least sometimes we may even rearrange our metaphysics to suit our values. Inconsistent metaphysics, anyway, are just the price we sometimes pay for keeping all our essential values in play. . . .

Weston apparently agrees with Ralph Waldo Emerson that "consistency is the hobgoblin of little minds." It is, I rather suppose, the very foundation of critical judgment. Certainly the intellectual virtue of self-consistency or noncontradiction has enjoyed a long tenure of solid support in the Western tradition. Is Socrates the little mind and Euthyphro the great one when Socrates rejects Euthyphro's account of piety because it is self-contradictory? I'm sure that Euthyphro would also have gladly agreed with Emerson. To abandon consistency as a criterion of what one permits oneself to believe is to abandon the examined life, personally, and Western civilization, culturally.

THE INESCAPABILITY OF METAPHYSICS

For Sayre, norms seem independent from a supporting matrix of ideas; for Norton, policies seem to be equally free-floating, and for Weston, values are much less embedded in and dependent upon a worldview than I suggest they are.

To think as I do that ideas shape our values, that moral norms depend upon a cognitive context, and that policies reflect a worldview may seem like a typical intellectual, and more especially philosophical, myopia. Only intellectuals, and more especially philosophers, live in a world of ideas, concern themselves with self-consistency, and ask questions like, Given that this is the kind of world we live in and this is the kind of being we are, how should we relate to the world and to one another? As Sayre (1991, 205) ingenuously remarks, most people

treat the relevant actions as [prescribed or] proscribed simply because they have been taught to do so by their parents or teachers, but for no reason amounting to a rationally perceived cause. Although various members of contemporary American society, for instance, may be aware that lying often causes distress, the reason lying is actually proscribed (to the extent that it is) has more to do with the fact that responsible persons have learned to abide by that norm as they take their place in mature society.

Of course Sayre is right. Most people acquire their moral norms through a process of socialization. When children are chastised for, say, telling a lie, most parents probably answer, "because I told you so," when their children ask why lying is proscribed. Most people acquire their most basic values—"family values" as they were called in the 1992 presidential campaign—in the same way. I guess that's why we call them family values, they're instilled by the process of primary socialization, without the benefit of ethical theory or moral philosophy. And for most people, new values, such as an acute concern for the pain and suffering of animals or for endangered species, just seem spontaneously to bubble up in consciousness.

Still, I think, though most people may not be at all aware of it, that every day of our lives—from our tenderest years to our old age—we live, move, and have our being in an ambient intellectual ether. That ordinary people interpret their experience by means of a conceptual framework, quite unbeknownst to them, may not be evident to us when we are reflecting on our own culture, because we too may take the prevailing worldview for granted. We routinely mistake for reality itself an elaborate cognitive superstructure imposed upon phenomenal consciousness. But students of another and very different culture are keenly aware that ordinary people in that culture unconsciously filter sensory and affective experience through a conceptual framework. Because that framework—and thus that culture's "reality"—is often so strikingly different from his or her own, the inquiring outsider cannot help but notice it.

For example, anthropologist A. Irving Hallowell, a student of woodland American Indian peoples writes,

Human beings in whatever culture are provided with cognitive orientation in a cosmos; there is "order" and "reason" rather than chaos. There are basic premises and principles implied, *even if these do not happen to be consciously formulated and articulated by the people themselves.* We are confronted with the philosophical implications of their thought, the nature of the world of being as they conceive it. If we pursue the problem deeply enough we come face to face with a relatively unexplored territory—ethnometaphysics. (Hallowell 1960, 20, emphasis added)

We live today in a culture undergoing a profound paradigm shift. Like the anthropologist confronting the strange cognitive orientation of people in another, very foreign culture, we are also keenly aware that our compatriots have a worldview—whether they know it or not—because the waxing new set of ideas uncomfortably coexists with the waning old set. Students of another culture are also keenly aware how intimately linked to a more general conceptual framework are its norms, values, ethics, and morality. For example, anthropologist Clifford Geertz writes,

In recent anthropological discussion the moral and aesthetic aspects of a given culture, the evaluative elements, have been summed up in the term "ethos," while the cognitive, existential aspects have been designated by the term "worldview." A people's ethos is the tone, character, and quality of their life, its moral and aesthetic style and mode; it is the underlying attitude toward themselves and their world that life reflects. Their worldview is the picture of the way things in sheer actuality are, their concept of nature, of self, of society. It contains their most comprehensive ideas of order. (Geertz 1973, 126–27)

But Geertz goes on to draw attention to the fact that although ethos and worldview may be distinguished for purposes of analysis, in the living context of culture they are thoroughly blended together. "The powerfully coercive 'ought' is felt to grow out of the comprehensive, factual 'is,'" he says, and by his choice of language indicates sensitivity to the academic philosophical controversy dating from Hume, often mislabelled, "the Naturalistic Fallacy." "The tendency to synthesize worldview and ethos at some level, if not logically necessary, is at least empirically coercive; if it is not philosophically justified, it is at least pragmatically universal" (Geertz 1973, 127).

PHILOSOPHY AND THE WESTERN WORLDVIEW

Although anthropologist Paul Radin wrote an influential work entitled *Primitive Man as Philosopher*, the consensus of anthropological opinion seems to be that the prevailing worldview in most nonliterate cultures, like Topsy, just grew, just evolved, without significant input from native philosophers. Nonliterate cultural worldviews, in other words, seem not to have been self-consciously created by an intellectual elite, by a cadre of speculative shamans, who think them up and disseminate them to everyone else. And indeed, if we imagine the process of worldview and ethos genesis like that, it is just as implausible to suppose that the prevailing literate Western worldview is a product of philosophical excogitation.

Anthony Weston correctly points out that the prevailing Modern "ethic of persons" and the intimately associated concept of "rights" gradually evolved in Western civilization. Material cultural forces, such as the printing press and the availability of the Bible in vernacular languages, helped to create persons and their rights. Weston asks us to "Imagine the extraordinary self-preoccupation created by having to choose for the first time between rival versions of the same revelation, with not only one's *eternal soul* in the balance, but often one's *earthly life* as well. Only against such a background of practice did it become possible to begin to experience oneself as an individual, separate from others, beholden to inner voices and 'one's own values,' 'giving direction to one's life' oneself . . . and bearing the responsibility for one's choices" (Weston 1992, 331, emphasis added).

On the other hand, there can be little doubt that past philosophers have left an indelible stamp on the prevailing Western worldview. Notice how Weston assumes that the early Modern protoperson is a dualist, concerned with his or her "eternal soul" as well as with his or her "earthly life." Right down to the present, most Moderns take it for granted that their "physical" bodies are inhabited by an independently existing psychic substance. Keeping up with my general reading in the field, for example, I came across the following sentence in the *Journal of Philosophy*: "Friends, of course, inhabit separate bodies" (Meyer 1992, 476). Friends usually inhabit separate houses and often inhabit separate bioregions, but do they inhabit separate bodies? "Of course" they do, the author avers. He can be so sure only because he uncritically accepts the popular view that persons are psychic substances; and while sojourning in "this world" they *inhabit* bodies. Aren't nearly all contemporary Christian children taught to recite the following prayer at bedtime?: "Now I lay me down to sleep, I pray the Lord my soul to keep; if I should die before I wake, I pray the Lord my soul to take."

Such a prayer would make no sense to Buddhists who hold the doctrine of *anatman* or no-self and hope not for eternal spiritual life, but extinction—liberation from samsara—if they should die before they wake. The Hebrew Bible has practically nothing to say about the soul or about what doubtless to Moses would have seemed the paradoxical, indeed, the apparently self-contradictory idea of life after death. Could Moses, by the way, even comprehend the verbally simple proposition that "Friends inhabit separate bodies"? "Tents, do you mean?," Moses might quizzically reply, "I thought I heard you say 'bodies.'"

The concept of the soul was introduced into Western thought by Pythagoras. It was developed and enriched by Plato. This essentially Greek philosophical notion—that one's true self is an independently existing immortal soul temporarily residing in an alien earthy body—became a cornerstone of the Hellenistic hybrid religion, Christianity. And with the eventual triumph of that religion in the West, the concept of the soul became a key element of the prevailing Western worldview.

Another characteristic feature of the prevailing Western worldview is mechanism, the view that the physical world is ultimately composed of externally related inert material particles which are assembled into various macroscopic aggregates, that all events in the physical world are causally determined, and that all causal relations are ultimately mechanical, the direct transfer of kinetic energy from one material mass to another.

Proof that mechanism is a fundamental feature of the prevailing Western worldview is the fervent faith placed by most people in Modern medicine, the great prestige of medical doctors, and the proportion of the gross national product of the United States and other industrialized nations spent on health care. When peoples' health or in some cases their very lives are on the line, their actions betray their beliefs. And in such circumstances most people turn unquestioningly to the medical establishment. But Modern medicine is almost a caricature of mechanism. The whole human being is reduced to a body which is objectified and discussed—by the doctor with the body's resident soul—in impersonal terms. Diagnosis consists of identifying the broken part and a cure is effected either by means of surgery, a mechanical procedure par excellence, or by prescribing chemical medicines, which work mechanically at the molecular level of organization.

But who could say that this fundamental element of the prevailing

Western worldview was not the creation of philosophers? Leucippus and Democritus invented the concept of the atomic particle and, I would argue, the complementary concept of homogeneous, isotropic physical space. Geometry, the analysis of space so conceived, was begun by Pythagoras, advanced in the Academy of Plato, and systematized by Euclid. In the seventeenth century, Galileo, Descartes, and Newton synthesized the Democritean ontology and Euclidian geometry to create the mechanical natural philosophy. Engineers applied the concepts that Newton so powerfully and persuasively articulated to create an array of machines—weaving machines, sewing machines, steam engines, automobiles, airplanes, rockets, etc., etc. Recall Weston's cogent argument that the advent of the printing press helped to create the ethics of persons. But the printing press itself was an early embodiment of the mechanical intellectual motif. (In this connection it is revealing to remember that when Aristotle discusses atomism he uses the letters of the alphabet to illustrate how the atoms differ from one another.) Look around you at this thoroughly mechanized environment. It didn't just happen. It isn't just the result of an inevitable process of blind technical evolution. It is, rather, the direct legacy of Western natural philosophy going all the way back to the pre-Socratics. As Ludwig von Bertalanffy perceptively comments,

The *weltanschauung*, the view of life and the world, of the man in the street—the chap who repairs your car or sells you an insurance policy—is a product of Lucretius Carus, Newton, Locke, Darwin, Adam Smith, Ricardo, Freud, and Watt—even though you may safely bet that the high school or even the university graduate has never heard of most of them or knows of Freud only through the *Dear Abby* column of his newspaper. (Bertalanffy 1967, 124)

If Western philosophy played a major role in the creation of the prevailing dualistic-mechanistic Western worldview, then Western philosophy would seem to have a major role to play in deconstructing it and reconstructing a new ecological-organic worldview. (By "philosophy" I mean "philosophy" in the old-fashioned sense of the word inclusive of theory in the natural and social sciences, as well as in history and the humanities, generally, not just philosophy as practiced by today's narrowly specialized professional philosophers. In this sense, Albert Einstein, Niels Bohr, and Werner Heisenberg are philosophers as are Aldo Leopold, Rachel Carson, and Eugene Odum.)

THE IMPORTANCE OF RETHINKING THE WESTERN WORLDVIEW:
THE POWER OF IDEAS

In my opinion, the seminal paper in environmental ethics is "The Historical Roots of Our Ecologic Crisis," by Lynn White Jr. (1967). White's brassy and cavalier critique of Christianity as the ultimate cause of our contemporary environmental malaise overshadows a more general (and more credible) subtext in that essay. Four or five times he reiterates the claim that what we do depends upon what we think and thus that if we are to effect any lasting changes in behavior, we must first effect fundamental changes in our worldview: "What shall we do?," he asks, about our environmental crisis. "No one yet knows. Unless we *think about fundamentals*, our specific measures may produce new backlashes more serious than those they are designed to remedy" (White 1967, 1204). Is White right about this? Sure. For example, the Green Revolution and eucalyptus afforestation programs, couched in the Modern industrial paradigm, have proved to be socially and environmentally disastrous in recipient countries (Guha 1990; Shiva 1991). Certainly they created "new backlashes more serious than those they were designed to remedy." In the next paragraph, White (1967, 1204) adds, "The issue is whether a democratized world can survive its own implications. Presumably we cannot unless we *rethink our axioms*." Toward the middle of his infamous essay, White returns to this subtext:

What people do about their ecology [that is, how people treat their natural environments] depends on what they *think* about themselves in relation to things around them. Human ecology is deeply conditioned by *beliefs about our nature and destiny*—that is, by religion. To Western eyes this is very evident in, say, India or Ceylon [that is, Sri Lanka]. It is equally true of ourselves and of our Medieval ancestors. (White 1967, 1205)

And in his peroration White (1967, 1206) writes,

What we do about ecology [that is, what we do about environmental problems] depends on our *ideas of the man-nature relationship*. More science and more technology are not going to get us out of the present ecologic crisis until we find a new religion or *rethink* our old one.

White, of course, rejects the first alternative, finding a new religion, and opts for the second, rethinking our old ones, Judaism, Christianity, and Islam. Finally, in his penultimate sentence, White (1967, 1207) writes, "We must *rethink* and refeel our nature and destiny."

The agenda for a future environmental philosophy thus was set. First, we identify and criticize our inherited beliefs about the nature of nature, human nature, and the relationship between the two. White himself initiated this stage with a critique of those most evident biblical ideas of nature, "man," and the man-nature relationship. Other environmental philosophers, I among them, went on to identify and criticize the more insidious intellectual legacy of Western natural and moral philosophy going back to the Greeks. Second, we try to articulate a new natural philosophy and moral philosophy distilled from contemporary science. We try, in other words, to articulate an evolutionary-ecological worldview and an associated environmental ethic.

This two-phase program of environmental philosophy has been gaining momentum for the past two decades. In that amount of time—which is really not very much time to bring off a cultural revolution comparable to the shift from the Medieval to the Modern world—how effective has environmental philosophy been? In so short a time, the rethinking of our old religion that White called for is virtually a fait accompli. The stewardship interpretation of the God-"man"-nature relationship set out in Genesis is now semiofficial religious doctrine among "people of the Book"—Jews, Catholics, Protestants, even Muslims (anonymous 1980; anonymous 1982; Bakr et al. 1983; Ehrenfeld and Bently 1985). Such an interpretation and its dissemination would not have come about, or at least it would not have come about so soon, had White's despotic interpretation not provoked it. The currently institutionalized Judeo-Christiar-Muslim stewardship environmental ethic was a dialectical reaction to White's critique. It has now trickled down into the synagogues and churches, and may be on its way into the mosques. Sunday school children learning about God's creation and our responsibility to care for it and pass it on intact to future generations may never hear Lynn White Jr.'s name, or the names of John Black, James Barr, Robert Gordis, Jonathan Helfand, Francis Schaeffer, Albert Fritsch, Thomas Berry, Wendell Berry, Matthew Fox, Iqtidar Zaidi, and the other Jewish, Christian, and Muslim theologians whom White provoked, but what they are being taught—and as a result of that teaching how in future they may try to be good stewards of God's creation—

owes a lot to Lynn White Jr. and those whom he challenged to reconceive Judeo-Christian-Muslim attitudes and values toward nature.

But if you think I'm impossibly biased—a philosopher affirming the power of ideas and defending the practical efficacy of philosophy—then perhaps you can trust Dave Foreman, environmental activist par excellence, to provide a candid assessment of the role that environmental philosophy has played in shaping the contemporary environmental movement. Remember that it was Foreman who wrote, "Let our actions set the finer points of our philosophy" (1983, 95) in a debate with Eugene C. Hargrove about the wisdom of monkey-wrenching; and it was Foreman (1983, 95) who dismissed environmental philosophers in the following terms: "Too often, philosophers are rendered impotent by their inability to act without analyzing everything to absurd detail. To act, to trust your instincts, to go with the flow of natural forces, *is* an underlying philosophy. Talk is cheap. Action is dear."

Eight years later, Dave Foreman changed his tune. In "The New Conservation Movement," Foreman identified four forces that are shaping the conservation movement of the 1990s. They are, and I quote, first, "academic philosophy," second, "conservation biology," third, "independent local groups," and fourth, "Earth First!." That's right, "academic philosophy" heads the list. This is some of what Foreman has to say about it:

> During the 1970s, philosophy professors in Europe, North America, and Australia started looking at environmental ethics as a worthy focus for discussion and exploration. . . . By 1980, enough interest had coalesced for an academic journal called *Environmental Ethics* to appear. . . . An international network of specialists in environmental ethics developed, leading to one of the more vigorous debates in modern philosophy. At first, little of this big blow in the ivory towers drew the notice of working conservationists, but by the end of the '80s, few conservation group staff members or volunteer activists were unaware of the Deep Ecology–Shallow Environmentalism distinction or of the general discussion about ethics and ecology. At the heart of the discussion was the question of whether other species possessed intrinsic value or had value solely because of their use to humans. Ginger Rogers to this Fred Astaire was the question what, if any, ethical obligations humans had to nature or other species. (Foreman 1991, 8)

And part of the way that Earth First!, last but not least on Foreman's list, helped to shape the new conservation movement was by bringing "the discussion of biocentric philosophy—Deep Ecology—out of dusty academic journals" (Foreman 1991, 10).

Clearly Dave Foreman understands the power of ideas. Of course, we philosophers do not simply create new environmental ideas and ideals ex nihilo. Rather, we try to articulate and refine those that the intellectual dialectic of the culture has ripened. To employ a Socratic metaphor, we philosophers are the midwives assisting the birth of new cultural notions and associated norms. In so doing we help to change our culture's worldview and ethos. Therefore, since all human actions are carried out and find their meaning and significance in a cultural ambience of ideas, we speculative environmental philosophers are inescapably environmental activists.

All environmentalists should be activists, but activism can take a variety of forms. The way that environmental philosophers can be the most effective environmental activists is by doing environmental philosophy. Of course, not everyone can be or wants or needs to be an environmental philosopher. Those who are not can undertake direct environmental action in other ways. My point is that environmental philosophers should not feel compelled to stop thinking, talking, and writing about environmental ethics, and go *do* something about it instead—because talk is cheap and action is dear. In thinking, talking, and writing about environmental ethics, environmental philosophers already have their shoulders to the wheel, helping to reconfigure the prevailing cultural worldview and thus helping to push general practice in the direction of environmental responsibility.

3

How Environmental Ethical Theory
May Be Put into Practice

WHY WE ENVIRONMENTAL ETHICISTS HARDLY
PRACTICE WHAT WE PREACH

At a meeting of minds pondering the nature of nature and the human-nature relationship at the Hastings Center think tank, someone pointed out that environmental values seem somehow softer, less compelling than many other moral beliefs. Those of us who profess to hold them don't seem to be putting them into practice, at least not as thoroughly and as consistently as other values seem to be put into practice.

Just consider. Most women who believe that abortion is murder will refuse to undergo an abortion except under the most extraordinary circumstances. Most people who believe that animals have rights will refuse to patronize zoos and circuses or to wear fur and eat meat. Pacifists who believe that war is categorically immoral will refuse to serve in the military. But most of us environmental ethicists own and operate a personal automobile; and most travel long distances by airplane, knowing full well that both automobiles and airplanes are major sources of greenhouse gases. Speaking only for myself, I dutifully recycle cans, bottles, and papers, but I live in a house with a chlorofluorocarbon refrigerator, a flush toilet, and a fossil-fuel furnace. I occasionally eat seafood, though I am fully cognizant that the planet's oceans are seriously overfished. I'm not suggesting that backsliding and hypocrisy in the other domains of ethics just mentioned do not exist, but there does seem to be a greater commitment to practicing what one preaches among pacifists, animal liberationists, and antiabortionists than among us environmentalists.

Why? Are we environmentalists morally weaker than people with other preoccupying convictions? Maybe. But I don't think that simple *akrasia* is the explanation for the greater disparity between theory and practice in environmental ethics than in other morally charged fields of conduct. Let me relate my own personal odyssey in the realm of environmental ethical praxis as, perhaps, a typical and, hopefully, a revealing case study.

Soon after I began teaching environmental ethics in the early 1970s, I tried to set a practical example for my students and neighbors as well as explore eco-philosophical theory. I kept my old Volkswagen bug in the garage most of the time and instead walked or biked around town and out to the surrounding countryside. For one whole year, I swear I didn't leave Portage County, Wisconsin. If we all stayed put and reduced our personal gasoline consumption by 75 percent that would significantly cut down on CO_2 and other air pollutants. I converted my back yard into a big garden and grew most of my own food—organically, without using polluting chemicals. If we all grew 60 percent of our food on small plots, soil erosion and the pollution attendant upon industrial agriculture could be greatly reduced. Believing that we ought to leave petroleum where nature deposited it and rely instead on recently stored solar energy, I heated with wood—wood that I myself laboriously collected and sawed and split by hand. I spent a considerable portion of my discretionary income putting in state-of-the-art storm windows and insulating my old house, to save even more energy. I wore out-of-style clothes and patched them up instead of throwing them away. I stopped having children after only one. To put it succinctly, I was Joe Bioregionalist.

Meanwhile, the U.S. economy kept growing and most everyone else went on consuming fossil fuels—limited, if at all, only by the formation of OPEC, not conscience. Industrial agriculture expanded. More consumer items than ever came on the market. Shopping malls sprang up in erstwhile hayfields and wetlands around Milwaukee, Madison, and even Stevens Point just as they did all over North America from coast to coast and from Canada to Mexico. And adding insult to injury, while I was trying to live, to practice an environmental ethic at a considerable cost of time and effort, to say nothing of money, my colleagues in the field at other universities were publishing papers, attending conferences, and getting ahead professionally. When the man who believed that trees caused pollution was elected president of the United States in 1980, I decided that it was high time to reassess my strategy for infusing an environmental ethic at the practical level.

THE FUTILITY OF ASSUMING INDIVIDUAL RESPONSIBILITY FOR PRACTICING HOLISTIC ETHICS

What was that strategy? It was simple. I recently heard it articulated by an Earth Hippie still hanging in there in these reactionary 1990s at a little benefit concert for the local alternative energy fair in the village of Amherst, Wisconsin. If only each one of us will do his or her bit, she said, to conserve, to recycle, to shun polluting chemicals, and so on, then the environment can be saved. Surely she was right about that, but the problem is that each one of us isn't doing his or her bit. Only a few of us are or were and our efforts have been swamped by the indifference shown to environmental ethics by the overwhelming majority. I was pissing in the wind (if you'll excuse the masculinist metaphor). So, I gave up making a lifestyle out of environmental ethics more than a decade ago because my bit (slightly to shift metaphors) was but an insignificant drop in a very leaky bucket. My personal practice of environmental ethics had absolutely zero positive effect on soil erosion, on air and water quality, and on biodiversity. I finally grasped, at the visceral level, the operational meaning of Garrett Hardin's insight that in a commons only mutual coercion mutually agreed upon will avert tragedy.

The other ethical domains just mentioned are different because they are not holistic, they do not involve a commons. Each ethically motivated decision to eschew abortion and carry to term an unplanned and unwelcome pregnancy saves the precious life of a human fetus. Each ethically motivated decision to eschew the purchase of a fur coat saves the skins of a score or more individually precious minks. Each person who refuses to engage in lethal combat may save the life of another precious person. Human rights, fetus rights, and animal rights are all *individualistic* ethics.

If a single human life is saved, or a single fetus is allowed to be born, or a single animal is spared suffering and a premature death, then one's self-imposed, morally motivated limitation on freedom of action will not have been in vain. But environmental ethics concerns populations of animals and plants, species, ecosystems, and the biosphere as a whole. No purely personal practice of environmental ethics that I undertook or any that I could have undertaken would have prevented global warming or soil erosion or species extinction. For any significant environmental benefits to occur our whole society and culture will have to undertake fundamental structural changes. We will have to: totally eliminate the manufacture of chlorofluorocarbons, and meticulously recover and destroy those still in use; abandon a fossil fuel economy; undertake a wholesale shift to commercial organic agriculture; assiduously implement a rigorous policy of population stabilization and decrease; preserve all the remaining old growth forests; allow second and third growth forests to mature undisturbed; preserve and restore wetlands and prairies; help, financially as well as technologically, the nations of the South to implement bottom-up sustainable development consistent with rain forest preservation; and so on and so forth.

So, I decided to try another strategy. How do we achieve mutual coercion mutually agreed upon in a democratic society—the worst form of government there is, as Winston Churchill quipped, except for all the others? Through persuasion. If people could be brought up to speed about the ecological facts, if the dire straits that the environment is really in could be impressed upon the public, then the environmental values would follow. And when, in a democratic society, a majority comes to share a set of values, they enact them into law through their elected representatives. Then those who are too lazy or too stupid to become enlightened or are or too warped by greed to care may be forced, coerced to comply. If everyone had to limit his or her number of children, give up his or her personal automobile, rigorously recycle, make a downward shift on the food chain, consume fewer forest products, etc., etc., etc., then, I dare say, significant improvement of environmental quality would follow.

So I bought some decent clothes and a new car, quit wasting my time gardening and making firewood, and joined the cadre of ecologists, conservation biologists, ecophilosophers, and environmental activists writing articles and books and travelling around the country and the world lecturing on the desirability of making the fundamental structural changes that are necessary to avert the environmental disaster looming on the horizon. This idea is pretty simple too. And we don't seem to be making much more real progress by way of this approach than by the doing-one's-own-personal-bit approach. We preach to the choir while the congregation politely ignores us.

This painfully real problem of environmental ethical praxis has set me to thinking very hard about how changes in environmental behavior can be effected. The incremental approach—you change, I change, the next person changes, and after a while we all will have changed our environmental behavior—seems futile. So does the educational-political approach—first we spread the gospel and enlighten people and soon they will pack their representatives off to local, state, federal, and global institutions of government to enact laws and negotiate treaties that will fairly compel everyone to change their environmental behavior.

THE NEED FOR UNIVERSAL ECOLOGICAL LITERACY

So far, I have tried to diagnose why the first simple idea hasn't worked. Environmental problems are problems of the commons and environmental ethics is commensurately holistic. Hence there is little practical payoff for isolated individual environmentally ethical acts. Maybe the second simple idea hasn't worked because all values, including environmental values, are, as many philosophers believe, surds, and thus lie beyond the reach of rational persuasion. If this were so, then debates between us environmentalists and antienvironmentalists like Ronald Reagan, George Bush, Phil Gramm, Newt Gingrich, and their academic minions like Milton Friedman and Julian Simon, would be like arguments between children about which color is the prettiest. One child likes red best, the other blue; and there is no rational way for either child to persuade the other that his or her preference is objectively correct. If values are divorced from facts, then it seems that we environmentalists just happen to prefer biodiversity and a healthy biosphere, while the antienvironmentalists just happen to prefer shopping malls, parking lots, dog tracks, golf courses, conditioned air, and oodles of money, hot and now.

But, as I have argued extensively elsewhere (chapter 5), our environmental values are *not* independent moral surds. They are informed by "facts."

Anthropologist Clifford Geertz sagely points out that "The powerfully coercive 'ought' is felt to grow out of a comprehensive, factual 'is.' . . . The tendency to synthesize worldview and ethos at some level, if not logically necessary, is at least empirically coercive; if it is not philosophically justified it is at least pragmatically universal."

How so?

The natural world is, for one thing, the theater of human action. How we picture the world, what we conceive it to be, will at the very least set limits on and suggest possibilities for action. Only if we think that the world is round will we attempt to get to the Far East by sailing West. And only if we picture the natural world as an aggregate of independent objects—animals, plants, minerals of various kinds distributed over an inert landscape like so much furniture in a room—will we entertain the possibility of rearranging it to suit our tastes. When, on the other hand, we come to picture the natural world as an internally related whole, as more like a very complex organism than like a vast auto parts warehouse full of inventory, then we shall probably be more solicitous of its structural integrity and functional health.

What we imagine to be the rightful, natural, or intended "place" of people in the world, furthermore, serves as an ideal or model of human nature that most people, consciously or not, strive to realize or fulfill. Believing that human beings are set apart from the rest of nature—either that we are created in the image of God and given dominion over the earth or that we are uniquely endowed with self-consciousness and reason—inspired us to seek mastery over nature and to bend it to our will. When, on the other hand, we come to believe that we human beings are only fellow voyagers with other living beings in the odyssey of evolution, then we might well, as Aldo Leopold suggested, acquire "a sense of kinship with other creatures; a wish to live and let live; [and] a sense of wonder over the magnitude and duration of the biotic enterprise."

I think that we all share certain basic human values, moreover, rooted in our common human nature. In addition to being robustly self-interested, we all altruistically value, as ends-in-themselves, our spouses, children, parents, siblings, friends, neighbors, colleagues, fellow citizens, humanity in the abstract, and our social institutions as such—our families, churches, schools and universities, civic communities, countries, and the like. I don't think that the leading antienvironmentalists just named are evil people who are indifferent to the natural legacy that they will leave their children, their grandchildren, and more remotely related future generations. Rather, I think that though clever, they are, like most of us, simply ill-informed—not necessarily ill-informed about this fact or that, but ill-informed in the sense that they see the world through false and outmoded cognitive lenses. Put positively, I think that the political implementation of environmental ethics—the only implementation that can make a significant practical difference—will follow upon the transition of the prevailing worldview from a Baconian-Cartesian-Newtonian model to a Darwinian-Einsteinian-Leopoldian model. When we—we the people, not just we environmentalists—come to see nature as a systemic whole and ourselves as thoroughly embedded in it, a part of nature, not set apart from it, then what is called the "political will" necessary for mutual coercion mutually agreed upon may materialize.

MEDIA AND MESSAGES

In the previous section I have in so many words reaffirmed the educational-political approach to the practical implementation of environmental moral theory. But I think that that approach will only succeed through more subliminal methods of mass communication than the overt, direct, and self-conscious methods that we believe to be at our disposal. The Rachel Carsons, Barry Commoners, and Paul Ehrlichs, and more recently the Edward O. Wilsons, Michael Soulés, and Holmes Rolston the Thirds have tried to impress the new integrative and systemic worldview on the public via classroom teaching, books, and public lectures; the Jacques Cousteaus, Tom Lovejoys, and David Suzukis have tried to impress the new integrative and systemic worldview on the public via didactic television documentaries. Such efforts are entirely praiseworthy; and they are indeed a necessary first step. But unfortunately the vast majority of people who don't read serious books and had rather watch *Wheel of Fortune* and *Night Court* than *The Planet Earth* and *The Flooded Forest* just don't get the message that way.

Nevertheless, I think that the message may soon get through to the public. Nature is not static. Culture is even more demonstrably dynamic. I recall witnessing environmental historian Donald Worster during a colloquium at Berkeley being wearied by graduate students who insisted that American agriculture was doomed to eventual collapse because capitalistic forces relentlessly pressure farmers to adopt unsustainable practices. Finally, Worster waved his hand and said, "Look, capitalism came from somewhere and it's going to go somewhere." Indeed, the whole conceptual complex of which capitalism is an integral element, the modern Baconian-Cartesian-Newtonian worldview, so ill-adapted to the ecological exigencies of nature, came from somewhere and it's going to go somewhere. The one thing we can be sure of is that the prevailing worldview of the future and its associated prevailing values will be different from those that prevail now. We are, further, living in a period of revolutionary intellectual change, a time, in this respect, very like post-Renaissance Europe. And the pace of cultural change today is enormously accelerated in comparison with any past era.

The obsolescing Baconian-Cartesian-Newtonian worldview that currently dominates public policy is no less abstract than the emerging Darwinian-Einsteinian-Leopoldian worldview and was also at first limited to a small circle of literate intellectuals. How then has *it* become so widespread?

Just think. People in the Middle Ages lived in a world in which a flat earth was firmly at rest in the center of the universe; the sun, moon, stars, and planets literally circled over head once a day; kings ruled by divine right; ordinary people were bound to the soil and lived by subsistence agriculture; benign miracles and malign witchcraft were commonplace; and heaven and hell had actual physical locations. The vast majority of Bacon's, Descartes's, and Newton's European contemporaries still experienced the world in much the same terms. Indeed, Newton himself secretly indulged in alchemy. But during the two centuries after the publication of *Philosophiae Naturalis Principia Mathematica*, a massive and, relatively speaking, rapid change of consciousness occurred.

Maybe if we understood how the Baconian-Cartesian-Newtonian worldview became so pervasive, we can get a grip on how the new Darwinian-Einsteinian-Leopoldian worldview may soon itself pervade popular consciousness. Galileo, Newton, and Descartes wrote books and gave lectures in which they portrayed the universe as a vast machine. Descartes, especially, portrayed rational human consciousness as independent from the inert physical world. And Bacon, especially, argued that scientific knowledge of nature was the key to exercising power over it. Steeped in and inspired by Newtonian science, Cartesian psychology, and the Baconian creed, intellectuals with a practical bent went on to make actual machines that were images in miniature of the idealized world machine. The longer ordinary people lived in an increasingly mechanized world, a world of steam engines, cotton gins, factories, and later tractors, automobiles, airplanes, etc., the more widespread and deeply ingrained, I suggest, the Modern mechanical worldview and associated psychology and value system became. Technologies, I submit, are not only conveniences, they are also communicators. We live in a machine-saturated environment, so naturally the machine became the pervasive metaphor for all reality in the collective Modern mind—and only a few generations after the mechanical philosophy was conceived in the minds of a few seventeenth-century thinkers.

The history lesson seems to be this. The original scientific revolution was followed by a technological application of the Baconian-Cartesian-Newtonian paradigm, which was followed in turn by a revolution in the popular worldview. The mystical, religious worldview of the Middle Ages was thus gradually replaced by Modernism as the then new science with its associated attitudes and values was translated into hardware during the Industrial Revolution. By now, practically every last person in the street has become, quite unwittingly, a Baconian-Cartesian-Newtonian: a Modern, in short. They're buying the Modern classical worldview like its going out of style.

POSTMODERN TECHNOLOGY AND
THE POSTMODERN WORLDVIEW

Theoretically speaking, mechanism and dualism *are* going out of style and have been for most of the twentieth century. Modern classical science is defunct. A second scientific revolution has already occurred—effected by Albert Einstein, Max Planck, Niels Bohr, Werner Heisenberg, and Ilya Prigogine in physics; and by Charles Darwin, Gregor Mendel, Frederick Clements, Charles Elton, Aldo Leopold, Raymond Lindeman, Eugene Odum, T. F. H. Allen, Robert O'Neill, and S. T. A. Pickett in biology. Relativity and quantum theory portray a universe that is systemically integrated and internally related. The objective world of nature cannot be completely isolated from subjects. Even in the apparently innocent act of knowing nature we change it. Theoretical ecology posits a similar, conceptually resonant holistic, interactive, interdependent, and organically unified portrait of terrestrial nature. And evolution analogously embeds us in nature. Gradually, this new scientific paradigm is being technologically applied.

Ah, but isn't technology at the root of our contemporary environmental problems? The answer to that question is both "yes" and "no."

The *Modern* technology of the nineteenth and twentieth centuries is certainly part of the problem, not the solution. Go back to the litany of ills that I recited at the beginning of these remarks. Virtually every one of them is an untoward effect of some Modern mechanical or chemical technology. No chain saws and bulldozers, no massive rain forest destruction. No coal and oil burning, no greenhouse effect. No chlorofluorocarbons, no hole in the ozone.

But is Modern technology the only technology conceivable? It may be true that, as Gertrude Stein said, "a rose is a rose is a rose." But I don't think it would be equally true to say that "technology is technology is technology." Some technologies are "appropriate." They do not compromise the structural integrity and ecological functioning of the ecosystems to which they are adapted. However, in order to envision a genuine symbiotic reintegration of humanity with nature we shall require not merely a piecemeal substitution of destructive technologies by more appropriate ones, but a wholesale shift of technological *esprit* or *motif*. What I have in mind is a shift to a postModern technology that is inspired and informed by the New Physics and biology. The much discussed shift from a fossil fuel to a solar energy base would represent such a profound conceptual change. So would a shift from industrial to organic agriculture.

I think that we can observe right under our noses the gradual emergence of technologies based on the new science. Hopefully, we shall soon see the disappearance of technologies based on the old.

Television, for example, is a direct application of quantum theory. So are compact disc players. We all sense what a profound force television technology has already become in transforming the collective consciousness of Western civilization. To us academics, it appears to be a mostly evil force responsible for rendering a whole generation nearly illiterate. But it has also helped to create the global village, factious and quarrelsome though it may be. And TV may have played a major role in the recent spectacular collapse of soviet statism. Try as they might, "communist" dictators could not keep the seductive (and one might add, largely illusory) image of the Western consumer society from beaming through the iron curtain via TV.

I would like to distance these comments as much as possible from the speculations of Marshall McLuhan in the 1960s about media and messages. His distinction between "hot" and "cool" communications technology was entirely impressionistic and totally vague. Today, similar— though more definite—speculations abound about how television has served to shorten the attention span of children to the length of a thirty-second commercial spot or music video and, further, about how within such abbreviated program units, the rapidly changing, fragmentary, and disconnected images have served to deconstruct the Modern sense of a synoptic, spatially and temporally continuous reality. Obviously, rigorous research into the effects of television on normal human consciousness (here please understand "normal" as in "normal science") is needed before any specific conclusions can be drawn. But surely history amply indicates that information technologies do profoundly affect normal human consciousness and that a major shift in a culture's primary medium of information transforms its erstwhile normal human consciousness into another mode. As Walter Ong and Eric Havelock have persuasively argued, literacy revolutionized the human mind. Doubtless electronic communications technology will too, though certainly I would hesitate to say just how.

In a single decade, the personal computer technology has become ubiquitous. Computers do not as directly apply the New Physics as do television and laser technology. But they beautifully translate systems theory into hardware . . . and software. Think about your old Underwood typewriter. One keystroke, one mark on the paper. The typewriter with its linked rods transferring the motion of the finger to the motion of the rods to the motion of the metal letter is a mechanism par excellence. With a PC, one keystroke can dramatically and instantaneously change the whole configuration of a paragraph or a spreadsheet or a graphic. Here we have a technological analog of an ecosystem in which the extirpation of a single keystone species can precipitate cascading reverberations throughout a biotic community. People who use PCs have grown accustomed to systems experience. The present generation of kids, who grow up with computers in their bedrooms, will think systemically—including, I hope, *eco-*systemically.

These are just a few obvious examples of how new technologies insidiously change our concept of nature as they saturate our living space. While we still love our cars and other mechanical transportation technologies, in some aspects of life there seems to be emerging a contempt for the old mechanical appliances. For example, a vinyl long-playing record album is so inferior—not just in sound, but in technical elegance—to a CD that people are literally throwing out their turntables and LPs. In the first decade of the twenty-first century, will solar voltaic lighting, space heating, and transportation technologies make oil furnaces and gasoline automobiles equally uncool? Will people be taking to solar energy devices as they now take to TV, PCs, CDs, and microwave ovens?

Suppose there does develop an intuitive, wholesale appetite for the now-emerging postModern solar-electronic genre of technologies. Obviously, that would be a plus for ecosystem health. A global transition to appropriate technology is the only way we can maintain a mass consumer culture and a functioning, healthy biosphere, the only way we can achieve a sustainable society. Just as important, however, in my opinion, is the bootstrapping effect of such technologies. I believe that they will communicate the postModern holistic, systemic, dynamic, concept of nature with us smart monkeys as creative, interactive components of it. Hopefully, that will set the stage for a positive feedback cultural process: more holistic-systemic-interactive thinking leading to more technological innovation in the same motif and esprit leading to more thinking in the same vein and on and on. Ultimately, we should hope to see corresponding changes in politics, economics, agriculture, medicine, and other primary aspects of civilization.

Ecology and the New Physics are cognitively resonant and complementary. The emerging solid-state solar-electronic generation of technologies embodies the systemic and holistic foundations of the New Physics. Extrapolating from what seems to be the way the concepts of the previous scientific revolution trickled down into the consciousness of the masses, my thesis is that living in an environment in which solid-state solar-electronic technologies are omnipresent will insidiously inoculate the minds of the present and future generations with the systemic and holistic conceptual modalities of the New Physics, even if the majority of the population is more computer literate than literally literate and even if Pac Man enjoys more celebrity than Albert Einstein. As the analogous and complementary concepts of ecology are increasingly applied in agriculture, the systemic and holistic revolution in consciousness currently taking place may be further reinforced and accelerated.

Agriculture is a major sector of the human economy leading the transition from a mechanical to an ecological paradigm. The so-called Green Revolution—essentially Baconian-Cartesian-Newtonian in spirit—has been a mixed blessing at best and a debacle at worst in lesser developed countries. The shift to water- and chemical-dependent hybrid strains of grains has led to the collapse of local social and economic institutions. Costs of the Green Revolution may also be measured in the currency of pollution, soil erosion and compaction, and the loss of agricultural information, genetic as well as cultural, accumulated over thousands of years. In the wake of such bitter experience, the current philosophy of agricultural development is increasingly shifting back to traditional—essentially organic and ecological—forms and methods of farming, augmented by scientific information and technical imagination. To be sustainable, agroecosystems must both fit into the specific conditions of their regional biomes and imitate the tiered structure and nutrient cycles of natural ecosystems. For about half a century industrial agriculture enjoyed limited, ephemeral success in the United States. But in 1989, the National Academy of Sciences Board on Agriculture recommended a massive shift away from increased scale, mechanization, and the use of chemical fertilizers, pesticides, and herbicides toward "alternative" organic forms, methods, and techniques of farming. My point here is that a global transition to organic-ecological farming would represent not only relief from the burden imposed by industrial agriculture on both society and the environment, it may also hasten the global transition from the prevailing Baconian-Cartesian-Newtonian mind set to its Darwinian-Einsteinian-Leopoldian successor.

SUMMARY AND CONCLUSION

How to translate theoretical environmental ethics into public policy and ultimately into practice? That is the question. Here in sum and in short is my answer. Because environmental ethics concerns natural wholes not individuals, putting one's environmental ethics into practice personally, in the absence of public policy implementation, is, for the most part, futile. In a democracy we can hope to translate environmental ethics into public policy only if the public acquires ecological attitudes and values. The new systemic understanding of nature, human nature, and the human-nature relationship along with its associated values may trickle down into the popular mind less through its direct and didactic representation in books and TV documentaries than through its embodiment in post-Modern solar-electronic technology and organic-ecological agriculture. The new solar-electronic technologies have already shown themselves to be seductive. People want them. These new technologies may thus inspire further application of the same systemic ideas which they embody and our present unsustainable mechanistic civilization may rapidly evolve into a new more sustainable systemic configuration, not only technically, but socially, politically, and economically as well.

4

Holistic Environmental Ethics
and the Problem of Ecofascism

THE DARWINIAN ROOTS OF THE LAND ETHIC

Of all the environmental ethics so far devised, the land ethic, first sketched by Aldo Leopold, is most popular among professional conservationists and least popular among professional philosophers. Conservationists are preoccupied with such things as the anthropogenic pollution of air and water by industrial and municipal wastes, the anthropogenic reduction in numbers of species populations, the outright anthropogenic extinction of species, and the invasive anthropogenic introduction of other species into places not their places of evolutionary origin. Conservationists as such are not concerned about the injury, pain, or death of nonhuman specimens—that is, of individual animals and plants—except in those rare cases in which a species' populations are so reduced in number that the conservation of every specimen is vital to the conservation of the species. On the other hand, professional philosophers, most of them schooled in and intellectually committed to the Modern classical theories of ethics, are ill-prepared to comprehend morally such "holistic" concerns. Professional philosophers are inclined to dismiss holistic concerns as nonmoral or to reduce them to concerns about either human welfare or the welfare of nonhuman organisms severally. And they are mystified by the land ethic, unable to grasp its philosophical foundations and pedigree.

Without a grasp of its philosophical foundations and pedigree, however, it is difficult to know how the land ethic might be related to the more familiar moral concerns that loom large in the Modern era (roughly the seventeenth through the twentieth centuries)—such as human happiness, human dignity, and human rights—and how it might be applied to and illuminate cases other than those Leopold himself considers in his brief sketch of it in *A Sand County Almanac*. In this essay, I outline the philosophical foundations and pedigree of the land ethic and indicate how it might be related to more familiar Modern moral concerns and how it might be applied to those contemporary environmental concerns that Leopold himself could not have considered. In particular, I address the most serious and disturbing theoretical and practical challenge to the land ethic raised by professional philosophers—the problem of ecofascism.

To discover its philosophical foundations and pedigree, we may begin by looking for clues in the text of "The Land Ethic." Leopold provides the most important clue in the second section of the essay, entitled 'The Ethical Sequence.' Having observed that ethics have grown considerably in scope and complexity during the three thousand years of recorded history in Western civilization, Leopold (1949, 202) writes,

This extension of ethics, so far studied only by philosophers [and, Leopold's insinuation is clear, therefore not very revealingly studied] is actually a process in ecological evolution. An ethic, ecologically, is a limitation on freedom of action in the struggle for existence. An ethic, philosophically, is a differentiation of social from anti-social conduct. These are two definitions of one thing. The thing has its origin in the tendency of interdependent individuals or groups to evolve modes of cooperation.

Leopold, I should hasten to point out, was no better a student of philosophy, than most professional philosophers are of conservation and its concerns. Hence his characterization of an ethic, "philosophically," is, put most charitably, incomplete. In any case, what he hints at, rather insistently and unmistakably, is some sort of evolutionary interpretation of ethics. Leopold's use here of such words and phrases as "evolution," "struggle for existence," "origin," "evolve," "social and anti-social conduct" evokes not only a general evolutionary context in which to locate an understanding ethics, it alludes, more particularly, to the classical evolutionary account of ethics in Charles Darwin's *The Descent of Man*, the third chapter of which is devoted to "the moral sense." Doubtless, therefore, Darwin's account of the origin and development of "the thing" is what mainly informed Leopold's thinking about ethics.

THE EVOLUTIONARY ORIGIN OF ETHICS

The existence of ethics presents a problem for Darwin's attempt to show how all things human can be understood as gradually evolved by natural (and sexual) selection, from traits possessed by closely related species, his project in *The Descent of Man*. Ethics demands that moral agents selflessly consider other interests in addition to their own. The theory of evolution would seem to predict, however, that the selfish would outcompete the selfless in the "struggle for existence," and thus survive and reproduce in greater numbers. Therefore greater and greater selfishness, not selflessness, would seem to be selected for in any population of organisms, including those ancestral to Homo sapiens. But history indicates the opposite: that our remote human ancestors were more callous, brutal, and ruthless than are we. At least so it seemed to a refined English gentleman who, while serving as naturalist on the round-the-world voyage of the *H. M. S. Beagle*, had observed first hand what he and his contemporaries regarded as states of savagery and barbarism similar to those from which European and Asian civilizations were believed to have emerged. Absent a convincing evolutionary explanation of its existence and progressive development, Darwin's pious opponents might point to ethics among human beings as a clear signature by the hand of Providence on the human soul.

To the conundrum presented him by the existence and putatively progressive development of ethics, Darwin's resolution is straightforward and elegant. For many kinds of animals, and especially for Homo sapiens, life's struggle is more efficiently prosecuted collectively and cooperatively than singly and competitively. Poorly armed by nature, as solitaries hominids would fall easy prey to their natural enemies or starve for lack of the wherewithal to obtain food. Together our primate ancestors might stand some chance of fending off predators and attacking prey larger than themselves. Like many other similarly situated species, evolving human beings thus formed primitive societies; or, stated more precisely, those hominids that formed primitive societies evolved. But without some rudimentary ethics, human societies cannot stay integrated. As Darwin (1871, 93) puts it, "No tribe could hold together if murder, robbery, treachery, &c., were common; consequently such crimes within the limits of the same tribe 'are branded with everlasting infamy'; but excite no such sentiment beyond these limits."

Darwin's speculative reconstruction of the evolutionary pathway to ethics begins with altruistic "parental and filial affections" which motivate parents (perhaps only the female parent in many species) to care for their offspring and their offspring to desire the company of their parents. Such affectionally bonded nuclear families are small and often ephemeral societies, lasting, as in the case of bears, only until the next reproductive cycle. But the survival advantage to the young of being reared in such social units is obvious. Should the parental and filial affections chance to spill beyond the parental-filial relationship to that between siblings, cousins, and other close kin, such plurally bonded animals might stick together in more stable and permanent groups and defend themselves and forage communally and cooperatively. In which case there might also accrue additional advantages to the members of such groups in the struggle for life. Thus do mammalian societies originate in Darwin's account.

By themselves, the social impulses and sentiments are not ethics. An ethic is a set of behavioral rules, or a set of principles or precepts for governing behavior. The moral sentiments are, rather, the foundations of ethics, as David Hume and Adam Smith argued a century or so before Darwin considered the matter. In addition to the social sentiments and instincts, Homo sapiens evolved a high degree of intelligence and imagination and uniquely possesses a symbolic language. Hence, we human beings are capable of generally representing those kinds of behavior that are destructive of society ("murder, robbery, treachery, &c.") and articulating prohibitions of them in emotionally colored formulae—commandments—which today we call moral rules.

THE ALTERNATIVE MODERNIST ACCOUNT
OF THE ORIGIN OF ETHICS

Darwin's account of the origin of ethics is quite different from the account of the origin of ethics inherited by most professional philosophers.

That account was originally advanced by thinkers contemporary with Socrates in the fifth century B.C.E., and was reasserted in the early Modern period by Thomas Hobbes in the seventeenth century. The social contract theory, as it is called, treats human society as discontinuous with animal societies—or, rather, animal societies are not acknowledged to exist at all—and to be something that was deliberately created by its members. In the "state of nature," with which the social contract theory begins, fully human human beings are imagined to roam the world as solitary individuals engaged in a war of each against all. In this circumstance of universal war, the life of each person is, in the famous characterization of Hobbes, not only "solitary, [but] poor, nasty, brutish, and short." Further, in such a circumstance neither agriculture nor industry is possible, because no enforceable property rights exist; no one would bother to sow, tend, and harvest crops or laboriously produce anything else that others might appropriate at will. Observing that such a rude condition of human life is untoward, at some point in time people are imagined, by social contract theorists, to decide to declare a truce, hold a convention, and hammer out some rules of behavior (moral codes and laws), and settle on some means to enforce them (a sovereign), thus hoping to make their lives more pleasant and predictable, less hazardous and capricious. Ethics thus are founded upon selfish rationality, not selfless sentimentality. Society, moreover, is an artifice, a deliberate *human* contrivance, not something rather common in nature that naturally evolved.

Because the social contract theory reduces morality to enlightened self-interest, one might argue that it is not a theory of *ethics* at all. A proper ethic, one might insist, requires moral agents to respect others or give due regard to the interests of others. In the utilitarian school, founded by Jeremy Bentham in the eighteenth century, happiness, defined in terms of pleasure and pain, is the summum bonum and a moral agent is required to act in such a way as to maximize happiness (pleasure) and minimize misery (pain), no matter whose happiness or misery is at stake, the agent's own or someone else's. In the deontological school, founded by Immanuel Kant also in the eighteenth century, a moral agent should never use another moral agent as a means only, but should treat other moral agents as intrinsically valuable ends in themselves. But to the hard question, Why should a moral agent give due regard to others or their interests?, both schools end by generalizing egoism. I demand that others consider my happiness (if I am inclined to be a utilitarian) or my intrinsic value as a morally autonomous being (if I am inclined to be a deontologist) in choosing a course of action that might affect me; therefore, to be logically self-consistent, I must consider either the happiness or intrinsic value of others in choosing courses of action that might affect them. Though both utilitarianism and deontology, by far the two most pervasive and influential Modern schools of ethics, are putatively other-oriented, at the end of the day, they prove to be no less founded on rational self-regard than the nakedly egoistical social contract theory of ethics.

The social contract theory and its subtler and more palatable descendants, utilitarianism and deontology, were not useful to Darwin because they ground ethics in reason, the most advanced and delicate of animal capacities. From an evolutionary point of view, however, reason could only have emerged in an intensely social environment, complete with a fully articulate language. But the emergence, persistence, and development of such a social environment depends, in turn, on the existence of ethics—"no tribe could hold together . . . &c."—as already noted. Therefore, from an evolutionary point of view, the social contract theory and its variants put the cart before the horse. Indeed, from an evolutionary point of view, the hypothesized state of nature—the supposition that rational human beings ever actually lived as solitaries in a condition of universal war—is absurd and preposterous. Darwin, therefore, turned to the now nearly forgotten sentiment-based moral philosophies of the Scottish Enlightenment, citing Hume's *Enquiry Concerning the Principles of Morals* and Smith's *Theory of Moral Sentiments* in *The Descent of Man*.

THE DEVELOPMENT OF ETHICS CORRELATIVE TO THE DEVELOPMENT OF SOCIETY

So much, then, for the origin of ethics; Darwin goes on to account for the development of ethics. As human social groups competed with one another for resources, the larger and better organized outcompeted the smaller and less well organized. Hence, clans, firstly, merged into tribes; tribes, next, into nations; and nations, eventually, into republics. The emergence of each of these levels of social organization was attended by a corresponding extension of ethics. Darwin (1871, 100–101) sums up this parallel growth of ethics and society as follows: "As man advances in civilisation, and small tribes are united into larger communities, the simplest reason would tell each individual that he ought to extend his social instincts and sympathies to all the members of the same nation, though personally unknown to him. This point being once reached there is only an artificial barrier to prevent his sympathies extending to the men of all nations and races."

Quite remarkably, the influence of Hume, who lived long before evolutionary thinking was habitual, can be found even in Darwin's speculations about the development of ethics correlative to that of society. Compare the passage quoted from Darwin in the previous paragraph with this one from Hume ([1751] 1957, 23):

> But suppose the conjunction of the sexes to be established in nature, a family immediately arises; and particular rules being found requisite for its subsistence, these are immediately embraced; though without comprehending the rest of mankind within their prescriptions. Suppose that several families unite together into one society, which is totally disjoined from all others, the rules which preserve peace and order, enlarge themselves to the utmost extent of that society. . . . But again suppose that several distinct societies maintain a kind of intercourse for mutual convenience and advantage, the boundaries of justice still grow larger in proportion to the largeness of men's views and the force of their mutual connexions. History, experience, reason sufficiently instruct us in this natural progress of human sentiments, and in the gradual enlargement of [them].

Further, with the emergence of each new level in the social hierarchy—the clan, the tribe, the nation, the republic, the global village—the content of the moral code changed or was supplemented to reflect and facilitate the novel structure of each newly emerged level. At the tribal level of society, "when the question is put . . . , is it worse to kill a girl of a foreign tribe, or to marry a girl of one's own, an answer just opposite to ours would be given," Darwin (1871, 91) observes. Since Darwin's day, matrimonial ethics have developed further still. In contemporary post-patriarchal society, we would still answer that it is certainly wrong to *kill* a girl of any ethnic group, but we would add that neither is it right to marry a *girl* of one's own ethnic group or, for that matter, any other. Among ourselves, mature men are allowed to marry only women some four to six years beyond menarche—otherwise they would be guilty of "statutory rape"—and it is, though lawful, "inappropriate" for men to marry or sexually consort with women much younger than themselves.

THE LAND ETHIC AS THE NEXT STEP IN THE DARWINIAN SOCIETY–ETHICS PAS DE DEUX

During Darwin's lifetime, as during Hume's, a universal ethic of human rights was only dimly visible on the horizon. By the mid-twentieth century, when Leopold was gestating the land ethic, a universal human rights ethic may have seemed more nearly attainable. In any case, Leopold, often called a prophet, looked farther ahead than did Darwin himself, indeed farther ahead than Darwin could have looked in the absence of a well-developed ecological worldview. Leopold (1949, 203) summarizes Darwin's natural history of ethics with characteristic compression: "All ethics so far evolved rest upon a single premise: that the individual is a member of a community of interdependent parts." Then he adds an ecological element, the community model of the biota espoused most notably by Charles Elton (1927): Ecology "simply enlarges the boundaries of the community to include soils, waters, plants, and animals, or collectively: the land" (Leopold 1949, 204). When we all learn to "see land as a community to which we belong," not as "a commodity belonging to us" (Leopold 1949, viii), that same "simplest reason," of which Darwin speaks, might kick in. And, when it does, what results will be a land ethic that "changes the role of *Homo sapiens* from conqueror of the land community to plain member and citizen of it" (Leopold 1949, 204).

So, now the philosophical foundations and pedigree of the land ethic should be manifest. Basically, what Leopold did to cook up the land ethic was to take over Darwin's recipe for the origin and development of ethics, and add an ecological ingredient, the Eltonian "community concept." Darwin in turn had taken over a sentiment-based theory of ethics from Hume and Smith. Leopold may never have studied Hume's or Smith's moral philosophies; certainly he never cites them; indeed he may have known of Hume only as a historian and Smith only as an economist. But because he surely did read Darwin and allude in "The Land Ethic" to Darwin's account of the origin and development of ethics, the philosophical foundations and pedigree of his land ethic are traceable through Darwin to the sentiment-based ethical theories of Hume and Smith.

THE HOLISM OF THE LAND ETHIC AND ITS ANTECEDENTS

According to Leopold (1949, 204, emphasis added), "a land ethic implies respect for . . . fellow-members *and also for the community as such.*" The land ethic, in other words, has a holistic dimension to it that is completely foreign to the mainstream Modern moral theories going back to Hobbes. The holistic dimension of the land ethic—respect for the community as such, in addition to respect for its members severally—is, however, not in the least foreign to the Darwinian and Humean theories of ethics upon which it is built. Darwin (1871, 96–97) could hardly be more specific or emphatic on this point: "Actions are regarded by savages and were probably so regarded by primeval man, as good or bad, solely as they obviously affect the welfare of the tribe,—not that of the species, nor that of an individual member of the tribe. This conclusion agrees well with the belief that the so-called moral sense is aboriginally derived from the social instincts, for both relate at first exclusively to the community." Gary Varner (1991, 179) states flatly that "concern for communities as such has no historical antecedent in David Hume." But it does. Demonstrably. Hume ([1751] 1957, 47) insists, evidently against Hobbes and other social contract theorists, that "we must renounce the theory which accounts for every moral sentiment by the principle of self-love. We must adopt a more publick affection, and allow that the interests of society are not, even on their own account, entirely indifferent to us." Nor is this an isolated remark. Over and over we read in Hume's ethical works such statements as this: "It appears that a tendency to publick good, and to the promoting of peace, harmony, and order in society, does always by affecting the benevolent principles of our frame engage us on the side of the social virtues" (Hume [1751] 1957, 56). And this: "Everything that promotes the interests of society must communicate pleasure, and what is pernicious, give uneasiness" (Hume [1751] 1957, 58).

That is not to say that in Hume, certainly, and even in Darwin there is no theoretical provision for a lively concern for the individual members of society, as well as for society per se. The sentiment of sympathy being so central to it, I should expressly acknowledge that in the moral philosophy of Adam Smith, one finds little ethical holism. *Sympathy* means "with-feeling." And that "all-important emotion of sympathy," as Darwin (1871, 81) styles it, can hardly extend to a transorganismic entity, such as society per se, which has no feelings per se. Hume and Darwin, however, recognized other moral sentiments than sympathy, some of which—patriotism, for example—relate as exclusively and specifically to society as sympathy does to sentient individuals.

In the Leopold land ethic, at any rate, the holistic aspect eventually eclipses the individualistic aspect. Toward the beginning of "The Land Ethic," Leopold, as noted, declares that a land ethic "implies respect for fellow-members" of the biotic community, as well as "for the community as such." Toward the middle of "The Land Ethic," Leopold (1949, 210) speaks of a "biotic right" to "continue" but such a right accrues, as the context indicates, to species, not to specimens. Toward the end of the essay, Leopold (1949, 224–25) writes a summary moral maxim, a golden rule, for the land ethic: "A thing is right when it tends to preserve the integrity, stability, and beauty of the biotic community. It is wrong when it tends otherwise." In it there is no reference at all to "fellow members." They have gradually dropped out of account as the "The Land Ethic" proceeds to its climax.

Why? One reason has already been noted. Conservationists, among whom Leopold counted himself, are professionally concerned about biological and ecological wholes—populations, species, communities, ecosystems—not their individual constituents. And the land ethic is tailored to suit conservation concerns, which are often confounded by concerns for individual specimens. For example, the conservation of endangered plant species is often most directly and efficiently effected by the deliberate eradication of the feral animals that threaten them. Preserving the integrity of a biotic community often requires reducing the populations of some component species, be they native or non-native, wild or feral. Certainly animal liberation and animal rights—advocated by Peter Singer and Tom Regan, respectively—would prohibit such convenient but draconian solutions to conservation problems. So would a more inclusive individualistic environmental ethic, such as that proffered by Paul Taylor (1896). Another reason is that ecology is about metaorganismic entities—biotic communities and ecosystems—not individuals, and the land ethic is expressly informed by ecology and reflects an ecological worldview. Its holism is precisely what makes the land ethic the environmental ethic of choice among conservationists and ecologists. In short, its holism is the land ethic's principal asset.

Whether by the end of the essay he forgets it or not, Leopold does say in "The Land Ethic" that "fellow-members" of the "land community" deserve "respect." How can we pretend to respect them if, in the interest of the integrity, stability, and beauty of the biotic community, we chop some down, gun others down, set fire to still others, and so on. Such brutalities are often involved in what conservationists call "wildlife management." Here again, to resolve this conundrum, we may consult Darwin, who indicates that ethics originated among Homo sapiens in the first place to serve the welfare of the community. Certainly, among the things that threaten to dissolve a human community are "murder, robbery, treachery, &c." However, as ethics evolve correlatively to social evolution, not only do they widen their scope, they change in content, such that what is wrong correlative to one stage of social development, may not be wrong correlative to the next. In a tribal society, as Darwin observes, exogamy is a cardinal precept. It is not in a republic. Nevertheless, in all human communities—from the savage clan to the family of man—the "infamy" of murder, robbery, treachery, &c. remains "everlasting." But the multispecies *biotic* community is so different from all our human communities that we cannot assume that what is wrong for one human being to do to another, even at every level of *social* organization, is wrong for one fellow member of the *biotic* community to do to another.

The currency of the economy of nature, we must remember, is energy. And it passes from one member to another, not from hand to hand like money in the human economy, but from stomach to stomach. As Leopold (1949, 107) observes of the biotic community, "The only truth is that its members must suck hard, live fast, and die often." In the biotic community there are producers and consumers; predators and prey. One might say that the integrity and stability of the biotic community depends upon death as well as life; indeed, one might say further, that the life of one member is premised squarely on the death of another. So one could hardly argue that our killing of fellow members of the biotic community is, prima facie, land ethically wrong. It depends on who is killed, for what reasons, under what circumstances, and how. The filling in of these blanks would provide, in each case, an answer to the question about respect. Models of respectful, but often violent and lethal, use of fellow members of the biotic community are provided by traditional American Indian peoples (Callicott and Overholt 1993).

THE PROBLEM OF ECOFASCISM

Its holism is the land ethic's principal strength, but also its principal liability. Remember that according to Leopold, evolutionary and ecological biology reveal that "land [is] a community to which we belong" not "a commodity belonging to us" and that from the point of view of a land ethic, we are but "plain members and citizens of the biotic community." Then it would seem that the summary moral maxim of the land ethic applies to Homo sapiens no less than to the other members and citizens of the biotic community, plain or otherwise. A human population of more than six billion individuals is a dire threat to the integrity, stability, and beauty of the biotic community. Thus the existence of such a large human population is land ethically wrong. To right that wrong should we not do what we do when a population of white-tailed deer or some other species irrupts and threatens the integrity, stability, and beauty of the biotic community? We immediately and summarily reduce it, by whatever means necessary, usually by randomly and indiscriminately shooting the members of such a population to death—respectfully, of course—until its numbers are optimized. It did not take the land ethic's critics long to draw out the vitiating—but, as I shall go on to argue directly, only apparent— implication of the land ethic. According to William Aiken (1984, 269), from the point of view of the land ethic, "massive human diebacks would be good. It is our duty to cause them. It is our species' duty, relative to the whole, to eliminate 90 per cent of our numbers." Its requirement that individual organisms, apparently also including individual *human* organisms, be sacrificed for the good of the whole, makes the land ethic, according to Tom Regan (1983, 262), a kind of "environmental fascism." Frederick Ferré (1996a, 18) echoes and amplifies Aiken's and Regan's indictment of the land ethic: "Anything we could do to exterminate excess people . . . would be morally 'right'! To refrain from such extermination would be 'wrong'! . . . Taken as a guide for human culture, the land ethic—

despite the best intentions of its supporters—would lead toward classical fascism, the submergence of the individual person in the glorification of the collectivity, race, tribe, or nation." Finally, Kristin Shrader-Frechette adds her voice to those expressing moral outrage at the land "ethic": "In subordinating the welfare of all creatures to the integrity, stability, and beauty of the biotic community, then one subordinates individual human welfare, in all cases, to the welfare of the biotic community" (Shrader-Frechette 1996, 63).

Michael Zimmerman (1995) has defended the land ethic against the charge of ecofascism, pointing out that in addition to subordinating the welfare of the individual to that of the community, fascism involves other characterizing features, salient among them nationalism and militarism. And there is no hint of nationalism and militarism in the land ethic. But however one labels it, if the land ethic implies what Aiken, Regan, Ferré, and Shrader-Frechette allege that it does, it must be rejected as monstrous. Happily, it does not. To think that it does, one must assume that Leopold proffered the land ethic as a substitute for, not an addition to, our venerable and familiar human ethics. But he did not. Leopold refers to the various stages of ethical development—from tribal mores to universal human rights and, finally, to the land ethic—as "accretions." Accretion means an "increase by external addition or accumulation." The land ethic is an accretion—that is, an addition—to our several accumulated social ethics, not something that is supposed to replace them. If, as I here explain, Leopold is building the land ethic on theoretical foundations that he finds in Darwin, then it is obvious that with the advent of each new stage in the accreting development of ethics, the old stages are not erased or replaced, but added to. I, for example, am a citizen of a republic, but I also remain a member of an extended family, and a resident of a municipality. And it is quite evident to us all, from our own moral experience, that the duties attendant on citizenship in a republic (to pay taxes, to serve in the armed forces or in the Peace Corps, for example) do not cancel or replace the duties attendant on membership in a family (to honor parents, to love and educate children, for example) or residence in a municipality (to support public schools, to attend town meetings). Similarly, it is equally evident—at least to Leopold and his exponents, if not to his critics—that the duties attendant upon citizenship in the biotic community (to preserve its integrity, stability, and beauty) do not cancel or replace the duties attendant on membership in the human global village (to respect human rights).

PRIORITIZING THE DUTIES GENERATED BY MEMBERSHIP IN MULTIPLE COMMUNITIES

This consideration has led Varner (1991) to argue that any proponent of the land ethic, Leopold presumably included, must be a moral pluralist. True enough, if by moral pluralist one means only that one tries simultaneously to adhere to multiple moral maxims (Honor thy Father and thy Mother; Love thy Country; Respect the Rights of All Human Beings Irrespective of Race, Creed, Color, or National Origin; Preserve the Integrity, Stability, and Beauty of the Biotic Community, for example). But if being a moral pluralist means espousing multiple moral philosophies and associated ethical theories, as it does in Christopher Stone's celebrated and influential *The Case for Moral Pluralism* (1987), then proponents of the land ethic are not necessarily committed to pluralism. On the contrary, the univocal theoretical foundations of the land ethic naturally generate multiple sets of moral duties—and correlative maxims, principles, and precepts—each related to a particular social scale (family, republic, global village, biotic community, for parallel example) all within a single moral philosophy. That moral philosophy is the one sketched here, beginning with the Humean social instincts and affections that evolve into ethics proper and grow more expansive and complicated apace with the Darwinian scenario of social evolution.

The land ethic involves a limited pluralism (multiple moral maxims, multiple sets of duties, or multiple principles and precepts) not a thoroughgoing pluralism of moral philosophies *sensu* Stone (1987)—Aristotelian ethics for this quandary, Kantian ethics for that, utilitarianism here, social-contract theory there (chapters 8 and 9). Thus, as Shrader-Frechette (1996, 63) points out, the land ethic must provide "second-order ethical principles and a priority ranking system that specifies the respective conditions under which [first-order] holistic and individualistic ethical principles ought to be recognized." Leopold provides no such second-order principles for prioritizing among first-order principles, but they can be easily derived from the communitarian foundations of the land ethic. By combining two second-order principles we can achieve a priority ranking among first-order principles, when, in a given quandary, they conflict. The first second-order principle (SOP-1) is that obligations generated by membership in more venerable and intimate communities take precedence over those generated in more recently emerged and impersonal communities. I think that most of us, for example, feel that our family duties (to care for aged parents, say, to educate minor children) take precedence over our civic duties (to contribute to United Way charities, say, to vote for higher municipal taxes to better support more indigent persons on the dole), when, because of limited means, we are unable to perform both family and civic duties. The second second-order principle (SOP-2) is that stronger interests (for lack of a better word) generate duties that take precedence over duties generated by weaker interests. For example, while duties to one's own children, all things being equal, properly take precedence over duties toward unrelated children in one's municipality, one would be ethically remiss to shower one's own children with luxuries while unrelated children in one's municipality lacked the bare necessities (food, shelter, clothing, education) for a decent life. Having the bare necessities for a decent life is a stronger interest than is the enjoyment of luxuries, and our duties to help supply proximate unrelated children with the former take precedence over our duties to supply our own children with the latter.

These second-order principles apply as well in quandaries in which duties to individuals conflict with duties to communities per se. In a case made famous by Jean-Paul Sartre in *L'existentialisme est un Humanisme*, a young man is caught in the dilemma of going off to join the French Free Forces in England during the Nazi occupation of France in World War II or staying home with his mother. Sartre, of course, is interested in the existential choice that this forces on the young man and in pursuing the thesis that his decision in some way makes a moral principle, not that it should be algorithmically determined by the application of various moral principles. But the second-order principles here set out apply to the young man's dilemma quite directly and, one might argue, decisively—existential freedom notwithstanding. SOP-1 requires the young man to give priority to the first-order principle, Honor Thy Father and Thy Mother, over the other first-order principle at play, Serve Thy Country. But SOP-2 reverses the priority dictated by SOP-1. The very existence of France as a transorganismic entity is threatened. The young man's mother has a weaker interest at stake, for, as Sartre reports, his going off—and maybe getting killed—would plunge her into "despair." His mother being plunged into despair would be terrible, but not nearly as terrible as the destruction of France would be if not enough young men fought on her behalf. So the resolution of this young man's dilemma is clear; he should give priority to the first-order principle, Serve Thy Country. Had the young man been an American and had the time been the early 1970s and had the dilemma been stay home with his mother or join the Peace Corps and go to Africa, then he should give priority to the first-order principle Honor Thy Father and Thy Mother and stay home. Had the young man been the same person as Sartre constructs, but had his mother been a Jew whom the Nazis would have sent to a horrible death in a concentration camp if her son did not stay home and help her hide, then again, he should give priority to the first-order principle, Honor Thy Father and Thy Mother, and stay home.

THE PRIORITY PRINCIPLES APPLIED TO
THE OLD-GROWTH FOREST QUANDARY

Let me consider now those kinds of quandaries in which our duties to human beings conflict with our duties to *biotic* communities as such. Varner (1996, 176) supplies a case in point:

Suppose that an environmentalist enamored with the Leopold land ethic is considering how to vote on a national referendum to preserve the spotted owl by restricting logging in Northwest forests. . . . He or she would be required to vote, not according to the land ethic, but according to whatever ethic governs closer ties to a human family and/or larger human community. Therefore, if a relative is one of 10,000 loggers who will lose jobs if the referendum passes, the environmentalist is obligated to vote against it. Even if none of the loggers is a family member, the voter is still obligated to vote against the referendum.

The flaw in Varner's reasoning is that he applies only SOP-1—that obligations generated by membership in more venerable and intimate communities take precedence over those generated in more recently emerged and impersonal communities. If that were the only second-order communitarian principle then he would be right. But SOP-2—that stronger interests generate duties that take precedence over duties generated by weaker interests—reverses the priority determined by applying SOP-1 in this case. The spotted owl is threatened with preventable anthropogenic extinction—threatened with biocide, in a word—and the old-growth forest biotic communities of the Pacific Northwest are threatened with destruction. These threats are the environmental-ethical equivalent of genocide and holocaust. The loggers, on the other hand, are threatened with economic losses, for which they can be compensated dollar for dollar. More important to the loggers, I am told, their lifestyle is threatened. But livelihood and lifestyle, for both of which adequate substitutes can be found, is a lesser interest than life itself. If we faced the choice of cutting down millions of four-hundred-year-old trees or cutting down thousands of forty-year-old loggers, our duties to the loggers would take precedence by SOP-1, nor would SOP-1 be countermanded by SOP-2. But that is not the choice we face. The choice is between cutting down four-hundred-year-old trees, rendering the spotted owl extinct, and destroying the old-growth forest biotic community, on the one hand, and displacing forest workers in an economy that is already displacing them through automation and raw-log exports to Japan and other foreign markets. And the old-growth logging lifestyle is doomed, in any case, to self-destruct, for it will come to an end with the "final solution" to the old-growth forest question, if the jack-booted timber barons (who disingenuously blame the spotted owl for the economic insecurity of loggers and other workers in the timber industry) continue to have their way. With SOP-2 supplementing SOP-1, the indication of the land ethic is crystal clear in the exemplary quandary posed by Varner, and it is opposite to the one Varner, applying only SOP-1, claims it indicates.

CONCLUSION

The holistic Leopold land ethic is not a case of ecofascism. The land ethic is intended to supplement, not replace, the more venerable community-based social ethics, in relation to which it is an accretion or addition. Neither is the land ethic a "paper tiger," an environmental ethic with no teeth (Nelson 1996). Choice among which community-related principle should govern a moral agent's conduct in a given moral quandary may be determined by the application of two second-order principles. The first, SOP-1, requires an agent to give priority to the first-order principles generated by the more venerable and more intimate community memberships. Thus, when holistic environment-oriented duties are in direct conflict with individualistic human-oriented duties, the human-oriented duties take priority. The land ethic is, therefore, not a case of ecofascism. However, the second second-order principle, SOP-2, requires an agent to give priority to the stronger interests at issue. When the indication determined by the application of SOP-1 is reinforced by the application of SOP-2, an agent's choice is clear. When the indication determined by the application of SOP-1 is contradicted by the application of SOP-2, an agent's choice is equally clear: SOP-2 countermands SOP-1. Thus, when holistic environment-oriented duties are in conflict with individualistic human-oriented duties, and the holistic environmental interests at issue are significantly stronger than the individualistic human interests at issue, the former take priority.

PART II

THE CONCEPTUAL FOUNDATIONS
OF THE LAND ETHIC REVISITED

Just the Facts, Ma'am

THE CLASSIC FACT/VALUE DICHOTOMY

Since the eighteenth century, it has been generally held by those partici-
pating in the Enlightenment and its philosophical and scientific legacy
that facts are objective and concrete—out there for everybody to see and
for everybody to see the same way—while values are subjective, vague,
elusive, and vary according to persons, places, and times. Facts are the
subject of exact science—of physics, chemistry, and quantitative biology;
values the subject of sociology, psychology, anthropology, and philosophy—the soft sciences and the humanities. Facts are garnered by disinterested, reasoned observation; values are felt, emotional responses. Facts
and values are, above all, cleanly, neatly separable.

For example, it is a fact that today human activities are destroying
species at a rate and number rivalling the demise of the dinosaurs. But
that this episode of abrupt, massive, anthropogenic extinction is regrettable, unconscionable, bad, is a "value judgment." Many people are morally indifferent to this fact.

It is also a fact that thousands of people die every day from malnutrition
and outright starvation in a world in which enormous food surpluses exist. That mass human starvation is regrettable, unconscionable, and bad is
also a subjective value judgment, although we are less likely to acknowledge

that it is in part because it expresses a widely shared and deeply held value—the value "we place" (as, revealingly, we sometimes say) on human life.

And it is also true, and a fact, that whole groups of people (gens) have been and are being systematically, methodically, and brutally slaughtered (genocide). That genocide is outrageous, intolerable, and evil too is only a subjective value judgment, although in such cases of willful mass murder the value of human life is so thoroughly flouted that many people would insist that genocide must be, somehow, objectively wrong.

But, strictly speaking, from the point of view of both Modern science and mainstream Modern moral philosophy, all values, no matter how deeply held and widely shared, are merely subjective. If all consciousness were obliterated at a stroke, if the subjective realm suddenly disappeared, there would remain only impassive facts. All beauty and ugliness, goodness and badness, right and wrong would disappear with the beholder.

THE RECEIVED VIEW QUALIFIED

This orthodox "enlightened" view of course is easily overstated—but not, in my opinion, on the side of the thorough subjectivity of values. Rather, the complementary conventional assumption that "facts" are thoroughly objective is much more open to question.

Primary and Secondary Qualities

The fact/value dichotomy characteristic of Modern moral theory was first clearly drawn by David Hume (1739). Hume articulated the ethical implications latent in the more general subject/object (or "thought/extension") dichotomy which had earlier been drawn by René Descartes (1641). Descartes's distinction had provided the metaphysical foundations for the distinction first drawn still earlier by Galileo Galilei (1623) between the real or actual properties of an object and those properties that are dependent upon subjects for their existence.

An object's solidity or mass, shape, size, and state of motion are all, according to Galileo, real objective properties, while its color, flavor, odor, and so on, are, so to speak, subjective readouts of its objective characteristics. Hotness, for example, doesn't really inhere in a skillet sitting on the fire. Rather, the fire causes the atoms of iron, which make up the skillet, to move more rapidly than those in a subject's finger. When he or she touches the skillet, the skillet's state of molecular motion relative to the subject's finger is perceived to be not what it actually is—faster motion—but heat. Similarly, grass is not *in fact* green, nor honey *in fact* sweet, and so on. These commonly acknowledged "facts" are no less subjective, from a strict Modern scientific point of view, than the "fact" that murder is evil.

There is, however, an important difference between the subjectivity of values and the subjectivity of color and the other so-called—first by John Locke (1690)—"secondary qualities." The secondary qualities, from this modern orthodox epistemological point of view, are the terminal *effects* upon consciousness of the "primary" or genuinely objective qualities of objects. A certain definite wavelength of light is perceived as green, another as red. And so, in general, for each peculiar secondary quality there actually exists a definite and distinct corresponding primary quality (or combination of primary qualities) really inhering in objects.

In the case of values, however, there appear to be no such corresponding primary or combination of primary qualities. In other words, there seem to be no definite wavelengths of light or molecular motions or chemical conditions that exactly correspond to and normally produce in the beholder sensations of goodness and badness, beauty and ugliness. These value qualities that we associate with facts, sometimes called "tertiary qualities," seem to originate spontaneously in subjects as emotional responses and then to be projected onto objects, actions, or events. If all consciousness were obliterated at a stroke, if the subjective realm suddenly disappeared, there would be no more color, flavor, or odor either, but there would remain their primary analogs in the objective world—in the realm of facts. There would remain in other words, radiation frequencies, molecular motions, and so on. Hence, to say roses are red, vinegar is sour, ice is cold, and the like is just a harmless, colloquial way of stating certain facts—certain real, objective, quantitative conditions—which scientists understand as a kind of imprecise shorthand for what is really denoted.

Facts Theory-laden

From a more sophisticated postModern epistemological point of view, all so-called facts—especially the primary, quantifiable properties of the "realities" recognized by Modern classical science—are theory-laden, and theories are mental constructs (Suppe 1977). What is and what is not a fact and especially what is and what is not a scientifically interesting and/or significant fact is often determined by theories—and perhaps just as often by values (Bohm 1977). For example, Aristotle cites the following "facts": that fire goes "up," i.e., as he explains, away from the center of the cosmos, and earth "down," i.e., toward the same center, and the stars and other heavenly bodies execute a diurnal rotation around the center; all as evidence for his assertion that the simple natural bodies or "elements"—earth, water, air, and fire—manifest natural motions toward their respective natural places where they come naturally to rest (as explained in Nichomachou's *De caelo*, c. 330 B.C.). These "facts" clearly depend, as facts, on Aristotle's theory that the universe, as a whole, has a unique center point. In Galilean space, there is no center and therefore no up nor down, and the local behavior of fire and earth are much less crucial (as redescribed facts) to Newtonian mechanics than to Aristotelian mechanics.

Facts Value-laden

Facts are value-laden to the extent that in the overwhelming "blooming, buzzing, confusion," which is the world, we select for attention among an infinity of potential facts those that interest us for any of potentially an infinity of reasons. Our interests—what we value—in a sense create actual facts. Hence, if we cannot share others' subjective values, we will not acknowledge their alleged facts to be important or even actual or genuinely objective. Commonly, in cases of conflict of interest, especially over environmental issues, the facts asserted by one party to support its side are regarded as irrelevant and unimportant by the other. For example, those opposed to nuclear power because, in their view, it represents an incalculable hazard to human life and to the environment, will treat all the engineering and economic data presented by proponents as otiose. The factuality of risk-benefit analyses, especially, will be contested, not only because they are necessarily based upon assumptions and speculations about the future, but also because the "benefits" projected—kilowatt hours for a growing, increasingly consumptive society—will not appear to opponents to be *benefits* at all.

Objectivity Called into Question

The so-called New Physics, relativity and quantum theory, have posed a more profound and, so to speak, metaphysical challenge to the very concept of objectivity. The ultimate *objects* of classical physics, the hard particles moving through time along straight lines in empty three-dimensional space, have been dissolved into ephemeral configurations of multidimensional space-time *fields*. The concept of discrete objects in space, in other words, has given way to the notion of a universal space-time continuum with various local patterned perturbations (Jones 1982; Bohm 1983).

Descartes's radical distinction between the subjective and objective domains (or, in his own terminology, the *res cogitans* and the *res extensa*) has, furthermore, proved untenable in contemporary physics with extremely profound and portentous consequences. Because energy is, among other things, information and information is energy, to observe—to get information about—an object, energy must be exchanged between the observer and the system under observation. At the macroscopic level the implacably physical nature of information can be ignored, for the most part, but at the subatomic level—since the energies of subatomic structures are so slight—the energetic interaction between "object" and observer necessarily disturbs the system under observation. To observe, to know, the ultimate "realities"—the most basic structures of the physical universe— therefore, necessarily, changes those realities. In the subatomic realm the physical act of knowing, thus, in a sense, partially constitutes the object of knowledge. At this level, the objective world becomes inseparably entangled with the subjective (Heisenberg 1962).

THE MORAL IMPLICATIONS OF THE FACT/VALUE DICHOTOMY

These cautionary reservations about facts, objects, and objectivity notwithstanding, the fact/value distinction remains useful for practical purposes in the ordinary middle-sized world—the world between the astronomical and infinitesimal—in which, day in and day out, we live. However epistemologically fastidious we wish to be, it remains true in some ordinary sense that here on Earth rain falls and plants grow, that animals of all sorts abound, that rivers run to the sea, that the tensile strength of steel is greater than that of stone, that dioxin, PCBs, and other synthetic compounds are highly toxic, that there exist some six billion human beings (and counting), that marsh hawks feed on mice and voles, that aspen springs up in clear-cut northern forests and is succeeded in turn by maple, and so on, and so on. It is also true, in some ordinary sense, that these environmental facts are without value except the value we confer upon them.

But the subjectivity of value has been supposed to involve several implications that are ethically untoward—and, therefore, *a fortiori,* untoward for any *environmental* ethic: First, It has been assumed that since values are subjective they are therefore necessarily subject-centered. In other words, it has been assumed that since there is no value without valuers, valuers only value themselves. An important corollary to this assumption is that only self-serving actions are *rational:* A *rational* agent is one who consistently acts in such a way as to further his or her own interests. Second, because values are subjective and hence cannot be true or false—as statements of fact are true or false depending upon whether or not they correspond with the objective reality—it has been assumed that values must be radically relative: If I like, say, blue whales and pristine wilderness, and you like, say, fast-food hamburgers and dune buggying, my values are no more right, no more correct, than yours. Third, because values and facts are separate and distinct, it has been assumed that facts and values are completely independent: Values are emotional, arbitrary, and irrational; facts do not inform them, nor do values change when new facts come to light.

Egoism Revisited

Certainly, valuing subjects can and do value themselves, but they value a myriad of other things as well. Nevertheless, it has often been supposed that the value of other things is ultimately reducible to the premium value that valuing subjects place upon themselves (or upon certain of their experiences, like pleasure or satisfaction). Other things are valuable "instrumentally." They are means to an end—the end in the final analysis being the subject making the valuation. For example, I value my house, my car, and my job. But I do not value them for the sake of themselves; rather, I value them—and any number of other things, from foodstuffs to elec-

tronic gadgets—for their "utility." Things other than actual tools and commodities are also, in an only slightly extended sense, valued instrumentally—i.e., for what they do for the valuing subject. I value my job not
only because it affords me income, but because it affords me a certain
degree of creative satisfaction and sense of worth—*my experiences,* which
I value for the sake of themselves. I value *Gone with the Wind* because it
entertains me and paintings by Picasso because they move me aesthetically, and so on. Indeed, I value other valuers—other people—instrumentally: my secretary for office services, my colleagues for collegiality,
my friends for companionship, and thousands of other people—editors,
farmers, postal clerks, policemen, etc.—for the anonymous services they
provide me, large and small, in the complex world as today it is economically and socially structured.

Some moral philosophers—the social contract theorists—have made
virtue out of necessity and argued that morality itself is, in the final analysis, reducible to "enlightened self-interest" (Gough 1957; Macpherson
1962). One must refrain from murder, theft, deceit, injustice, and the
like, not only to avoid stigma and punishment, but to support the stability and integrity of society—apart from which one's own interests cannot
be served. Immanuel Kant (1785) took a slightly different tack and urged
a cold and bloodless disinterested "respect" for "others" because they bear
within themselves the same self-conscious self-regard that one has for oneself. Others too are, from their point of view, "ends-in-themselves." And
morality consists in acting as though one belongs to a "Kingdom of Ends,"
according to Kant.

Hume ([1739] 1960), on the other hand, who so clearly and forcefully articulated the fact/value dichotomy, insisted that things other than
oneself (or one's own experiences) may be valued for their own sakes.
Consider, as perhaps the most obvious instance, one's own offspring. Parents can put children to economic use—mowing the lawn, baby sitting,
and doing other chores—for little or no wages. Children also often occasion amusement, delight, pride, and joy. They can be regarded, in other
words, as both an economic and psychospiritual *resource* for their parents.
But would anyone really say that such an analysis exhausts the value that
a child has in the eyes of its parents? Do not parents, at least most parents,
value their children for the sake of the children themselves, as ends-in-
themselves, as well as instrumentally? And isn't it also true that we value

other relatives and friends in the same unselfish way—though perhaps less palpably, less viscerally, than our own offspring? Other things being equal, Hume believed that most people less passionately, but nevertheless very genuinely, value, selflessly, anyone and everyone. In modern parlance our selfless affections are called "altruism." Adam Smith (1759), a younger contemporary of Hume, called them the "moral sentiments" and argued that they, not either an enlightened or generalized egoism, lay at the foundations of ethics.

According to Hume ([1739] 1960), empirical knowledge of the facts and sound reasoning from premises to conclusions by themselves can never motivate action. We are moved to act exclusively by "passions," that is, by feelings, our values among them. Our actions may properly be called "rational" if the *means* we devise to serve our ends are actually causally connected to those ends. For example, if I wish to relieve world hunger and devote the major portion of my modest income at considerable personal sacrifice to a charitable organization like Oxfam, my behavior may be called "irrational" only if the efforts of Oxfam and similar charities are ineffectual or counterproductive. One does not behave irrationally simply because one acts upon altruistic values. Values—whether selfish or unselfish—determine our ends, empirically informed reason our means.

Relativism Revisited

Charles Darwin (1871) in his own estimation was the first person to offer an account of "the moral sense or conscience . . . exclusively from the side of natural history." Darwin himself, in other words, attempted to construct a biological account of the origin and evolution of ethics. The existence of altruism is an evolutionary paradox: In a world red in fang and claw, a keen and narrow selfishness would seem to be a sine qua non for survival and reproductive success, while a disposition to act altruistically would appear to be a lethal mutation.

For many species, however, Homo sapiens preeminent among them, life's struggle is more efficiently pursued collectively and cooperatively than singly and competitively. Hence, animal *societies* evolved. The prehuman ancestors of Homo sapiens could not have been intelligent enough to figure out for themselves the long-term personal advantages of cooperative behavior. Their egoism could not have been so "enlightened." So

Darwin (1871) argued that for social organization to be possible, members must be genetically endowed with "social instincts"—genuine caring for fellow members of the same social group and for the group per se—which in our own species evolved into the moral sentiments upon which we have erected the noble notion of duty and systems of ethics and law.

Darwin's biosocial account of the origin of moral values explains how values in general, and moral values in particular, have become more or less fixed, standardized by natural selection. Having the right values is every bit as necessary to our survival and reproductive success as having keen eyesight, sharp hearing, good health, strength, and so on. We must have a robust sense of what Hume and Smith called "self-love"; that is, we must each value as an end-in-itself our own life and *instrumentally* value those things that really are means to our own well-being—for us twentieth-century editions, our jobs, houses, vehicles, and so on. And in order that our familial and social institutions might flourish, we must value, as *ends-in-themselves,* our parents, siblings, spouses, friends, neighbors, colleagues, fellow citizens *and* these social institutions as such—our families, communities, countries, etc.

Having the "right" values is not exactly the same as having the "right" opinions, but it is similar. If you believe that the Mississippi River is east of the Rocky Mountains, you have the right opinion because your belief *corresponds to* the geographical facts. If you care about yourself, wish others well, and delight in social prosperity, you have the "right" values, but not because your values correspond to any moral facts. Rather, one may be said to have the right values in the same sense that one may be said to have the right number of fingers if one has five on each hand. Values, like physical features, have been normalized, standardized by natural selection. And, just as many human physical characteristics (normal height and weight, normal rest heart rate and blood pressure, for example) sometimes exhibit a wide range of normalcy, so likewise do many human psychological characteristics, human values among them. The normal human psychological profile like the normal human physical profile, in other words, exhibits considerable individual variability. Hence, some people are more cautious than others, some more generous and loving, some more spiteful and quarrelsome, and so on.

Thus, while a given value is neither true nor false, something pragmatically equivalent and functionally analogous to truth and falsity serves

to make some values correct and others incorrect. Values are not, therefore, radically relative. To be sure, what is valued by one person may not
be valued by another, but just as in disputes about matters of fact, so in
disputes about value one person may be right and another wrong. A person who delights in torture, for example, is wrong, depraved, and perverse.
Such a person's values clearly fall outside the range of normalcy for the
human species. While it might not be just to punish a person for having a
psychological birth defect or for having been morally maimed by trau-
matic social circumstances, we are certainly justified in calling torture wrong
and abominable and in forcibly preventing a person who thinks otherwise
from acting upon their perverse proclivities.

The Irrelevancy of Facts to Values Revisited

Garden variety disputes about values are never so ridiculously cut and
dried as these examples suggest, however. No one openly commends torture or condemns mother love. Rather, some people value nuclear power
plants, agricultural and industrial development of the moist tropics, stamp-
ing out the spread of communism at all costs. . . . Others value wilderness
preservation, clean air and water, organically grown foods, cultural and
political pluralism. . . . How can these value differences be adjusted and
reconciled? We may say what is wrong or incorrect about valuing torture—to do so is inhuman—but what's *wrong* with valuing dune buggying
and the "golden arches"?

I have, in effect, argued, following David Hume, Adam Smith, and
Charles Darwin, that certain basic values (allowing for a wide range of
normalcy and thus for considerable individual variability) are universal
characteristics of human nature. Let us call those values about which there
is little or no disagreement or debate "ultimate" human values; and those
values (or things valued) about which there is very often a great deal of
disagreement and debate (among parties whose humanity is not in doubt)
let us call "proximate" human values.

Which are and are not the correct proximate values depends upon
being right about the facts. The reason we value certain things in the
proximate class is that we believe that they will serve our ultimate, shared
human ends. Whether they do or do not is, as Hume pointed out, a matter of fact, a matter of "cause and effect," and is thus amenable to *rational*

discussion and resolution. Our debates about proximate values are debates about means, not ends, and thus fall to the office of empirically
informed reason, not emotion.

Here is a simple example: Everyone values his or her health. Health is
an ultimate human value. A person with normal values does not, except
in very unusual or special circumstances, say that he or she would rather
be sick than well. Now, it was once widely believed that people suffering
from arthritis could be cured by bathing in certain mineral springs to
which sufferers travelled long distances at considerable expense and in-
convenience. Mineral springs were thus proximately valued because they
were believed to have a therapeutic effect for victims of arthritis. With the
empirical advance of medicine and a shift of belief in the medical community about the etiology of arthritis, mineral springs have lost their value,
at least their therapeutic value. Victims of arthritis who proximately valued mineral springs (for their curative powers) might thus be rationally
persuaded that they were wrong to value them (as a cure for arthritis) by
the facts. Facts thus inform our values. And a change in our beliefs about
matters of fact can change what we do and do not value.

Consider another, somewhat more complicated, example—cigarette
smoking. I took up smoking in the late fifties, before overwhelming evidence that it was bad for your health had been accumulated and widely
publicized. I smoked for the usual reasons: I thought it made me look
more grown up and sophisticated; it "gave me something to do with my
hands"; the people I wanted to be friends with smoked; I enjoyed the
mild narcotic effect of the nicotine; it "relaxed" me. Upon becoming aware
of the facts, I, along with a lot of other people, quit. A great many people,
however, still smoke, most of them knowing full well that it could cause
them to suffer from heart disease and lung cancer. Does this mean that
they do not value their health, that they had rather be sick than well? No,
it just means that health is only one among our ultimate values and that
we discount probable future debits in weighing them against actual present
assets. Normal people in ordinary circumstances would no more voluntarily smoke than voluntarily drink sulfuric acid if smoking made them
certainly and immediately terminally ill. Some people proximately value
smoking because apparently they believe that smoking serves other ultimate values—self-indulgence, peer group acceptance, identification with
a certain cultural mystique (the Marlboro man or Virginia Slims woman),

and present gratification of desire. And they can pay the piper later, if they have to pay at all.

We can approach differences of opinion about some environmental issues by means of this simple model drawn from cigarette smoking. We can, I think, begin to understand most environmental pollution-type issues by means of the smoking example. Many people are simply unaware—unacquainted with the fairly recently discovered facts—that certain of their (by now) culturally institutionalized, habitual activities contribute to pollution. When they discover, for example, that fluorocarbon propellants harm the upper ozone layer of the Earth's atmosphere and what effect that has on life at the surface, some people will switch to spray products with manual pumps or forgo the use of such products altogether. Those who do not cannot be said to positively value an increased incidence of skin cancer and the destructive effects of increased ultraviolet radiation on other forms of life. Rather, more likely, the facts may not have been impressed upon them, or they may not have believed or understood them. And, as in the case of those who are fully aware of the facts and still continue to smoke, other immediate values may be preemptive—the comfort of habit, convenience, supposed personal and/or general economic welfare, and so on.

Although they are real-world examples about the relevancy of facts to values, the two analogies drawn from medical etiology do not quite capture the problematic and puzzling relationship of environmental facts to environmental values. For one thing, the primary untoward effects of our environmental activities, unlike our cigarette smoking example, are often suffered by other people and/or other forms of life (acid polluted rain, for example, by Canadians and fish) and may not be fully felt for several generations—atmospheric CO_2 pollution, for example, will have significantly warmed the planet only by the middle of the twenty-first century.

More disturbing and still more puzzling, however, is the fact that a great many people just do not seem to care about environmental quality and ecological integrity, *period*—while others are passionately concerned about them. In my opinion, as I have just explained, this difference reflects not just an arbitrary and irremediable difference of taste; it reflects a difference in the assessment of relevant facts. The environmental facts relevant to environmental values are vast, complex, and heavily theory-laden—the relationship between fluorocarbons, the atmospheric ozone zone, ultraviolet radiation, melanin, and organic life on the Earth's surface is an excellent case in point. Furthermore, differing larger theoretical models—differing paradigms, worldviews, Big Pictures, the different ways we conceptually organize and interpret environmental facts—are as deeply implicated in differences of environmental values as being informed or not, as the case may be, of the facts themselves.

A CASE STUDY: THE VALUE OF A VARMINT

Aldo Leopold has been touted as the twentieth century's most distinguished professional conservationist (Fox 1981). His *A Sand County Almanac* has become the bible of the contemporary environmental movement and Aldo Leopold its principal "prophet" (Stegner 1987). In "Thinking Like a Mountain," one of *Sand County's* most memorable essays, Leopold apologetically describes killing a wolf. The essay really sugarcoats his actual attitude at the time of the killing—since it focuses on an isolated incident and Leopold represents himself to have undergone, then and there, a conversion experience, like Paul on the road to Damascus. Actually, while a forest ranger and president of the New Mexico Game Protective Association, Leopold relentlessly campaigned for the complete eradication of large carnivores—bobcats, mountain lions, and grizzly bears, as well as wolves—from the "southwestern game fields" (Flader 1974; Meine 1988). Leopold was, in fact, slow to come around on the matter of the value of predators, but come around he did—180 degrees. Toward the end of his life, ironically, predator protection and even predator restoration were among the highest of his conservation priorities (Leopold 1949).

How can we understand this shift—as an arbitrary and irrational change of *heart* or as a change of *mind* ? If the foregoing abstract analysis is correct, given what we know about Leopold's basic values, it was a change of mind. Leopold did not just soften toward predators. It was not as if he did not like them at first and then he did. Rather, he came to better understand the facts about predators—about how predators were related to things of ultimate value. But beyond that and more significantly, he came to espouse a new worldview, a new synthesis and integration of environmental facts, which reversed the proximate disvalue he had formerly placed upon predators.

Leopold's Basic Values

Leopold was born in 1887 to a commercially and professionally successful civic-minded aristocratic family of German descent living in Burlington,
Iowa (Flader 1974; Meine 1988). From his father he acquired a love of
nature and of hunting. Probably in the spirit of noblesse oblige Leopold's
father, before the advent of legal restrictions, voluntarily imposed upon
himself and his sons a hunting ethic—including bag limits and a cessation of spring shooting of waterfowl (Meine 1988). Leopold's romance
with the natural world grew as he grew, and he decided to professionalize
his interests with a career in forestry—the first environmental profession
in the nation. Upon graduation from the Yale Forest School, he was assigned to District 3 of the United States Forest Service in the Arizona and
New Mexico territories. He naturally gravitated to "secondary" forest utilities—hunting, especially, and other forms of recreation—as his professional specialty. Leopold's professional background as well as his family
background was morally charged. The Forest Service was established during the Progressive Era in response to the wanton destruction of America's
vast natural resources by, among others, lumber barons and cattle and
sheep emperors. The Forest Service was the front line of defense in the
hinterlands against their greed and waste.

Leopold's Early neo-Darwinian Worldview

Leopold understandably translated this good-guys-versus-bad-guys mentality into the natural world. "Game" animals—deer especially, and other
wild ungulates; turkey, grouse, and quail; waterfowl of every variety—
were the good animals. "Varmints"—wolves especially, the brown bear,
wild felines, and birds of prey—were the bad animals. Self-disciplined
sportsmen shot and killed, but—in an emotionally complex relationship—
loved, cherished, and, above all, conserved their game. Song birds, ground
squirrels, and all the other animals too small to shoot were morally neutral
creatures that rounded out the landscape and were valued by the cultivated
observer for their aesthetic or scientific interest. Venal market hunters,
"game hogs" and "slobs," even subsistence-hunting American Indian
"poachers" *and* varmints were the enemy of game and sportsmen alike.

They threatened mindlessly to destroy the faunal recreational resource, as the lumber-, cattle-, and sheepmen once threatened to destroy the floral material resource. In this case, as in that, the Forest Service to the rescue. Legislation and strict enforcement would control the human menace; the Biological Survey's bounty hunters, public spirited cowboys and sportsmen would help the forest ranger control the varmint (Leopold 1918).

During the first two decades of the twentieth century "ecology" was definitely not a household word. Plant ecology had by then become a vigorous new science, but it remained, if it were a part at all, a peripheral part of the curriculum of the aspiring professional forester. A biologically informed professional conservationist was more likely to view the world through a neo-Darwinian cognitive lens: The natural world was the scene of an incessant and ubiquitous struggle for existence—grass against trees, owls against mice, fox against rabbits, etc., etc. Competition, not cooperation and symbiosis, was the only law of the jungle. Each species had its "natural enemies." It was only logical, therefore, to believe, as Leopold seems to have, that if one wanted to conserve certain valued species, one must wage war on their natural enemies, their competitors in life's struggle.

Leopold's Dawning Ecological Awareness

While still with the Forest Service, Leopold self-consciously and deliberately sketched the outlines of a new environmental profession—game management—analogous to timber management (Leopold 1918). Above all, he argued, to be successful, game management, like timber management, must have a scientific foundation. After moving to Wisconsin and resigning from the Forest Service, Leopold was given a chance to lay the foundations for scientific game management—by the Sporting Arms and Ammunitions Manufacturers Institute, which hired him to make an unprecedented survey of game in seven Midwestern states. Leopold thus began meticulously to collect and assemble the facts, the empirical data for the scientific foundations of his new environmental profession. Not long thereafter he wrote his classic *Game Management* and was appointed to a professorship in the field he pioneered at the University of Wisconsin.

Leopold's most innovative idea and the key concept of *scientific* game management was to augment the beneficial effect of predator control and bag-limit and closed-season laws with habitat manipulation (Leopold 1933a). To conceive of game-*in-situ*, the animal in its habitat, is to begin to think ecologically. It is to think of animals not just as haphazardly arrayed upon the range or moving among the trees of the forest, but as an intimate part of or indeed as an expression of the floral community.

The Community Concept

The concept of a "biotic community," elegantly articulated by British zoologist Charles Elton (1927), replaced Frederick Clements's controversial superorganism model as the principal paradigm of the rapidly developing science of ecology (McIntosh 1985). Leopold's research began to show that in fact, contrary to his earlier assumptions, predation was for most game species a negligible element in their precipitous decline (Leopold 1931). Intensive, "fencerow-to-fencerow" farming was the primary culprit. For some, predation was actually beneficial and necessary for their population equations. More importantly, however, predators and prey alike—upon the new working model of ecology, the community model— filled niches, or more colorfully, performed roles, or more colorfully still, occupied professions in the "economy of nature." All were functioning members of the biotic community. His deepening conception of the living natural world as one whole and integrated biota, as one humming community of cooperations and competitions—the latter no less essential than the former—gradually transformed Leopold's understanding of predators. From the point of view of ecology, predators were not villainous marauders, but members in good standing and upright citizens of the biotic community. They had a "biotic right" to continuation. And as "plain members and citizens" of the biotic community *we* had no right to deny them their place in community life.

Leopold's *ultimate* values remained unchanged. As a normal human being he selflessly valued the fellow members of his society and the commonweal itself. Perhaps in Leopold these values were unusually strongly held. In any case, they were reinforced by his family and profession. And during the course of his life they simply became newly informed and expanded by his growing ecological awareness. Ecology represented plants and animals (including predators), soils and waters as fellow members of a single community of which we human beings are also members.

The Ecosystem Concept

To free it from the potentially misleading and distracting analogies with organisms and societies of its earlier models, British ecologist Arthur Tansley (1935) proposed the nonmetaphorical concept of an "ecosystem" as a governing scientific model for ecology. Indeed, the ecosystem model was inspired less by earlier thought in biology than by earlier thought in physics (Worster 1979). And it had the distinct scientific advantage of quantifiability. Solar energy falling on the surface of the planet, converted to biomass by plants, captured by herbivorous animals, and in turn by secondary (omnivorous) and tertiary (carnivorous) consumers, could be represented in essentially thermodynamic terms. Elton's metaphorical "biotic community" with its descriptive, qualitative food chains and food webs became a pyramidal array of flow paths of energy, measurable at each point of capture.

Over the course of geologic time, evolution had gradually lengthened the flow paths of incident energy—adding layer upon layer to the pyramid of life—and elaborated alternate pathways from one layer to the next: from plant producers through animal consumers to bacterial and fungal decomposers. Predators, in Leopold's (1949) ripe expression of his ecological worldview, are the end points of the complex circuitry of this "fountain of energy." To deliberately eradicate, extirpate, and finally to render predators extinct, from this point of view, is to "lop off the apex of the pyramid"; it is tantamount to undoing evolution's crowning achievement.

This comprehensive, expansive, and holistic conception of nature brought Leopold full circle back to his father's incipient conservation ideals—but at a higher level of understanding. Mankind has a responsibility to conserve nature—not only waterfowl and other game, nor more generally only "natural resources," but the biosphere in its entirety and as a whole. All of Earth's species in all their diversity make up the richness and splendor of the whole. Game animals would not be the animals they are apart from their coevolution with their predators. Earth's ecosystem may not continue to function if its full complement of species is significantly eroded. Predators are instrumentally valuable. But like our family, friends, neighbors, and coworkers, upon all of whom we depend for the necessities of life, their value transcends their utility. Predators especially are to

be valued as both the sign—the indicator species—and symbol of a healthy
and complete biota.

CONCLUSION

Today the world in which we live is marked by virulent divisiveness, not
only in the environmental arena, but in virtually every domain of public
policy. One might, therefore, fairly conclude that fundamental and irreconcilable value differences lie at the roots of these conflicts. It is my contention that they do not. Shared ultimate human values define in part our
common humanity. For all our cultural and genetic diversity, we are one
species, standardized by natural selection in our psychological faculties—
including our regard for self, fellows, and society—no less than in our
physical characteristics. The apparent conflicts of value that confront us
at every turn are differences of opinion about "matters of fact," "cause and
effect," i.e., about the best *proximate means* to achieve our *ultimate ends.*

But if I am right that differences in proximate environmental values
are factual, not temperamental, why are they not quickly and amicably
resolved? Partly because, although we share the same ultimate values, these
values are not always mutually consistent—as the examples earlier discussed
indicate. Some people temperamentally give greater weight to (collective
human) self-interest than to (biotic) community welfare and vice versa.
But such idiosyncratic differences should average out in the process of
policy formation so that a balance may be struck; for finally (collective
human) self-interest and the integrity of the (biotic) community coverage
in the long run. The current state of seemingly hopeless confusion about
what to do—how best to get on with our shared human project—reflects
in greater measure the torrential proliferation and maddening complexity
of the facts themselves. The rate and volume of new information accumulation is more than most people seem to be able to handle.

Or want to handle. As we race headlong into an unknown and fright-
ening future, we drag along with us a global legacy of obsolete worldviews
(some of which go back two thousand or more years) to which many
people obstinately cling and by means of which they organize and interpret
the contemporary flood of environmental facts—or, more often, distort
and suppress them. Indeed, the deeper obstacle to a scientifically informed

environmental policy consensus seems to be an active, often even militant resistance to information and especially to a broad paradigm change. There is a widespread "fear of facts"—perhaps because vested interests stand to lose by the profound changes in proximate values that new environmental facts and the attendant new ecological worldview imply.

Nevertheless, despair and cynicism, pursuant to these reflections, is, I think, premature. The spectacular evolutionary success of our species so far rests precisely upon the flexibility of culture and the rapidity of cultural adaptation. The environmental facts, overwhelming and complex though they may be, and state-of-the-art ecological theory that renders them whole and meaningful, in all its subtlety and transformative power, can be, with effort and dedication, more or less generally disseminated and assimilated. Today's complacency, fundamentalism, and dreamy nostalgia for a simpler past may be the darkness before dawn—before the sunrise of a global environmental/ecological awakening now just barely breaking on the horizon.

In any case, however formidable our value conflicts may appear, at least we can take courage in the knowledge that a solution is *in principle* possible. If environmental conflicts turned upon irreconcilable differences of ultimate value, then we would face a hopeless surd. Debates about proximate environmental values—about the value of biodiversity and atmospheric ozone—would be like debates among children over which is the prettiest color. There would be no *rational* end in sight. As it is, if we can envision a future society in which ecological awareness and biological literacy are as commonplace as mechanical facility and fascination with gadgets are today, we can reasonably expect that such a society may obtain a broad consensus regarding proximate environmental values and policy. And we can reasonably expect that such a society, united by a common understanding, will find a way to heal the planet for sake of the common good.

Can a Theory of Moral Sentiments Support a Genuinely Normative Environmental Ethic?

THE PROBLEM OF NORMATIVE FORCE FOR A BIOSOCIAL ETHIC

When I began seriously to explore the theoretical outlines of a nonanthropocentric environmental ethic a quarter century ago, I found an enticing point of departure in the seminal "land ethic," as he styled it, adumbrated by Aldo Leopold in the 1949 conservation classic, *A Sand County Almanac*. Leopold's land ethic embraces not only our "fellow members" of the biotic community—individual animals and plants—it also provides respect for "the community as such" (Leopold 1949, 204). That is, it has a holistic as well as an individualistic aspect.

There would be no need for an environmental ethic if we had no dire environmental concerns. Leading the list is the "biodiversity crisis" (narrowly interpreted), the current episode of abrupt, massive anthropogenic species extinction. Running a close (and of course not unrelated) second is the incremental eradication of *ecosystems*—tropical rain forests, temperate rain forests, long-grass prairies, the Everglades, and so on. An environmental ethic that cannot provide moral considerability for wholes—for species as well as specimens, for ecosystems as well as their components—is therefore of little practical interest. Given its prima facie promise, I made it my business to uncover the historical roots of Leopold's abbreviated environmental ethic and to provide it with a more complete and express theoretical development.

I found the immediate intellectual forebear of the land ethic to be Charles Darwin's account of the origin and evolution of morality in *The Descent of Man*. Darwin (1871, 106, 109) writes freely of "the moral sentiments" and cites both Adam Smith and David Hume in his own account of ethics "exclusively," as he put it, "from the side of natural history" (Darwin 1871, 97). The intellectual pedigree of Leopold's land ethic is thus traceable through Darwin to the Scottish Enlightenment in the eighteenth century. Therefore, however novel and radical it may seem at first blush, the land ethic actually has a legitimate ancestry in the Western philosophical canon. Because no less eminent a biologist than Darwin had concerned himself with the origin and evolution of morality, a body of moral theory in biology has since grown up and diverges considerably from contemporaneous philosophical thought about ethics. Notable contributors to the biological literature are T. H. Huxley, Petr Kropotkin, J. B. S. Haldane, and recently the more notorious (in liberal circles) than notable E. O. Wilson. Sociobiology is just the latest round of biological moral theory in a tradition which we could say, most expansively, was founded by Aristotle and given its modern cast by Darwin. And current biological thought about ethics remains not only essentially Darwinian, but essentially Humean as well. Wilson (1975, 3), for example, revealingly writes, "the emotional control centers in the hypothalamus and limbic system of the brain . . . flood our consciousness with all the emotions—hate, love, guilt, fear, and others—that are consulted by ethical philosophers who wish to intuit the standards of good and evil."

I think that it is fitting and elegant for a non-anthropocentric environmental ethic, which practically by definition has the biological world as its beneficiary, to be grounded in evolutionary and ecological biology. But because biological and philosophical thought about ethics have gone their separate ways for the past century and a half, an environmental ethic largely informed by biological moral theory will, *qua* ethics, appear to philosophers to have fatal flaws.

One such apparent flaw, by no means the only one, is that the land ethic, as I have explicated it, lacks "normative force," or so Warwick Fox (1985) has alleged. Nor should an allegation such as this come as a surprise, since, whatever other divergences characterize biological and philosophical moral theory, certainly the former is primarily intended to be descriptive and explanatory, while the latter is usually intended to be normative. Writes Fox (1985, 21), "Callicott grounds his subjectivist environmental ethic in the work of Hume, Darwin, and Leopold, and claims that the theory . . . derived from this lineage 'provides for' the moral considerability of the non-human world. But what should we understand by this? While some readers might think that Callicott's Hume-Darwin-Leopold axiology has normative and not just explanatory force, Callicott does not actually claim this, nor can he."

Fox is half right, I have not, so far, expressly claimed for the Hume-Darwin-Leopold environmental ethic any "normative force." But I am not so sure that he is right that it cannot validly be done. Kristin Shrader-Frechette has recently joined Fox in dissent. She writes, "Callicott's use of biology to undergird his environmental ethics . . . destroys the normative dimension of his ethics. He avoids relativism by postulating that ethical uniformity/unanimity is achieved by means of natural selection. He says, 'human feelings have been standardized by natural selection.' [But] be-havioral uniformities explained through natural selection are descriptive not normative" (Shrader-Frechette 1990, 189).

NORMATIVE FORCE IN THE PREVAILING MODERN MORAL PARADIGM

First, let me develop more fully the deficiency that Fox and Shrader-Frechette find in my theory of environmental ethics, and then argue that they are mistaken. There is a particularly strong sense of "normative force" with which it is useful to begin. One might argue, though this is not the point of attack developed by either Fox or Shrader-Frechette, that a proper ethic should *rationally coerce* a moral agent into doing something or into leaving something undone, irrespective of her feelings. For example, I may not be inclined to help a lost child find her parents, but an ethic worthy of the name should force me to do so, on pain of self-contradic-tion. If I would have other people aid my child were he lost, then, to be consistent, I should aid the lost children of others. On the other hand, the child's fright may stir pity in me, and as this feeling is complemented by sympathy for her parents when I imagine the anguish they feel, I may experience a strong emotional inclination to help her and promptly drop my pressing personal projects to do so. But, if rational coercion is essential to moral action, such feelings should play no decisive role in my distinctly ethical deliberations about what I should or should not, ought or ought not, do in such a case.

As everyone knows, Immanuel Kant made "normative force," so understood, the very measure of the moral quality of an action. Any action, however beneficent and however accordant with duty, done from mere inclination, Kant asserts, has no ethical significance. He points out that some people, happily, are "so sympathetically constituted that without any motive of vanity or selfishness they find an inner satisfaction in spreading joy, and rejoice in the contentment of others which they have made possible" (Kant 1959, 14). But an action motivated by such constitutional kindness does not pass Kant's test for genuinely *ethical* action. "However dutiful and amiable it may be, that kind of action has no true moral worth," he declares (Kant 1959, 14). Kant stamps his moral seal of approval instead on the outwardly similar action performed by a person who is "by temperament cold and indifferent to the sufferings of others" but who is moved to act in a kind way exclusively by the rational consideration that kindness is capable of universalization and its opposite is not (Kant 1959, 14–15).

Similarly, I suppose, one might think that an environmental ethic worthy of the name should force us, whether we care about them or not, to act in ways that respect our fellow members of the biotic community and the community as such. A truly ethical action toward the environment would be carried out, not by someone like Leopold, for whom life without wild things would be no life at all, but by someone who is insensible to the charms of nature and indifferent to biodiversity, yet who rancorously does her bit to preserve the critical habitat of an endangered species because she thinks that if everyone acquiesced in species extinction the ecosystem would collapse and the maxim of her action would therefore prove self-contradictory.

Upon this interpretation of "normative force," to charge that the Leopold land ethic lacks normative force reduces to the charge that it is not Kantian. And the appropriate reply to that charge is, "So what?" The Leopold land ethic also lacks "non-natural qualities," thus it is not Moorean. It lacks a "veil of ignorance," thus it is not Rawlsian. And so one could go on and on: no "ideal observer," thus it is not Sidgwickian; no "principle of reflection," thus it is not Butlerian; etc. To insist that any ethic, environmental or otherwise, must answer to one moral philosopher's criterion for ethics is surely the most patent sort of question begging. Leopold's land ethic has its roots in Hume, and Hume, unlike Kant, grounded ethics precisely in inclination—in unselfish feelings such as sympathy, beneficence, and humanity, not in dispassionate reason. Leopold thought that "when we see land as a community to which we belong, we may begin to use it with love and respect" (Leopold 1949, viii). And much of *A Sand County Almanac* is crafted to cultivate a love of nature in its readers, from which, Leopold hoped, benevolent and respectful actions toward nature would flow.

But Kant is hardly just "one moral philosopher" on a par with Moore, Sidgwick, or Butler. His is the archetype of the whole venerable deontological school of Modern ethics. Normative force, as here so far understood, moreover, is also a fundamental feature of the other major school of Modern ethics, the protean utilitarian school, for whom Jeremy Bentham's moral philosophy is the prototype if not the archetype. A nice example of the invocation of utilitarian normative force is provided by Peter Singer, perhaps the purest Benthamite among contemporary ethical expositors. In the preface to *Animal Liberation,* Singer (1977, x) pointedly informs his readers that he doesn't "own any pets," is not particularly "fond of dogs, cats, or horses," and, in general, doesn't "'love' animals." He writes,

The portrayal of those who protest against cruelty to animals as sentimental, emotional "animal lovers" has had the effect of excluding the entire issue of our treatment of non-humans from serious . . . moral discussion. . . . This book makes no sentimental appeals for sympathy toward . . . animals. . . . Nowhere in this book do I appeal to the reader's emotions where they cannot be supported by reason. . . . It is an appeal to basic moral principles which we all accept, and the application of these principles . . . is demanded by reason, not emotion. (Singer 1977, xi–xii)

In his book Singer argues that we expect others to consider the deleterious consequences of their actions on us because we are capable of suffering. For the very same reason, we ought to give equal consideration to the deleterious consequences of our actions, not just on other human beings, but on any sentient creature. One may not love animals; one may not feel one jot of sympathy for them; indeed, one may actively loathe them. No matter, those animals who qualify—those capable of suffering—deserve moral enfranchisement.

Kenneth Goodpaster has provided an insightful analysis of the normative force common, for the past two hundred years, to both major schools of moral philosophy. According to Goodpaster (1979, 28), "the two major foundational accounts of morality share, both in their classic formulations and in their contemporary interpretations, a fixation on egoism . . . which in essence generalizes or universalizes that egoism." Baldly stated, the generic Modern moral paradigm comes to this: I insist that others consider my interests or respect my person. If challenged, I may defend my demand for consideration or respect by appeal to a psychological characteristic or capacity that I possess which is arguably relevant to moral considerability or respectability. But then—if I am to be consistent, to be rational—I must accord others, who possess the same morally relevant psychological characteristic or capacity upon which I rest my claim to consideration or respect, exactly the same consideration or respect that I demand from them. I am compelled, in other words, by the logic of my own moral claim upon others to grudgingly grant their similar claims upon me.

But such a general paradigm, though easily and directly adapted to accommodate sentient animals, as Singer (1977) has done, and even all living things, whether conscious or not, as Paul Taylor has done, cannot be adapted to accommodate natural wholes. Like us, other animals can suffer. Like us, other living beings, whether conscious or not, have natural *teloi* that can be frustrated. But we can hardly find a capacity comparable or analogous to reason, sentiency, or conation that we share with a species or with a rain forest. If we are to have a holistic, as well as a nonanthropocentric environmental ethic, we shall have to depart from the prevailing Modern paradigm. A Humean paradigm, which openly and honestly affirms the role of feeling in moral deliberation, motivation, and judgment, may not be the only alternative, but it is the alternative that undergirds the popular land ethic.

Granted, normative force of the kind just explained has been a practically ubiquitous feature of all Modern moral philosophy for two hundred years, so it is understandable that many philosophers have come to expect to find it in any system of ethics and may feel that something is missing if they do not. But the history of Western moral philosophy goes back two-and-a-half-thousand years. To insist that to be worthy of the name, an ethic must logically compel moral behavior, either in defiance of our selfish inclinations or in the abeyance of our generous ones, is to be temporally parochial. Plato argued that the Good was an objective form that could be discovered through reason. But he did not argue that an agent must be coerced by reason to act in accordance with the Good in order for her actions to be considered ethical. Indeed, Plato believed that the Achilles heel of the then prevailing social contract theory of ethics was its assumption that people are naturally solitary and egoistic and therefore that they must be rationally persuaded to be just. He himself held that "virtue is a kind of health and beauty and good condition of the soul," like physical health and beauty and good condition, something integral to one's own well-being and thus something one cultivates for its own sake and the happiness that comes from its possession. Aristotle thought of a good person as like a good horse, a being that exemplifies the particular virtues of her species. As human beings are social animals, Aristotle argued that human happiness is realized only in community. A good human being exemplifies not only personal virtues like temperance and courage, but social virtues like justice and generosity. Again, Aristotle's ethics, like Plato's, is utterly devoid of "normative force," understood as logical compulsion. But surely it would be an intolerable Modernist presumption to say that the ethical theory of the person who bequeathed to ethics its very name was not worthy of that name.

What Plato, Aristotle, Hume, and Smith have in common is a vision of human nature embedded in community. Apparently, between the 1740s and 1750s, when Hume's *Enquiry* and Smith's *Theory of the Moral Sentiments* were published, and the 1780s, when Kant's *Foundations* and Bentham's *Principles of Morals and Legislation* were published, a reductive vision of human society as an aggregate of essentially rational social atoms had taken hold of the Western imagination. The only way to make a reasoning monad moral is to universalize her egoism, to argue that others' claims on her rest on exactly the same basis as her claims on others. Contemporary theorists are, of course, breaking out of the Modernist mold. Alasdair MacIntyre and Bernard Williams, for example, have repaired to the ancients for ethical insights more fitting to a systemic postModern worldview—the former to Aristotle, the latter to Plato. Feminist ethical theory, especially (and perhaps most notably) as represented by Carol Gilligan (1982), has, like Hume's and Smith's, emphasized the moral importance of feelings, such as "caring," that are correlative to relationship and embedded in context.

THE PROBLEM OF RADICAL RELATIVISM FOR A THEORY OF MORAL SENTIMENTS

However, out of the frying pan of Modernism and into the flames of relativism. If one follows Hume and Smith and grounds ethics in feeling, emotion, sentiment, or passion one will invite the charge of radical relativism. Hume explicitly draws an analogy between judging beauty and ugliness, on the one hand, and vice and virtue on the other. In his view, "the distinct boundaries and offices of reason and taste are easily ascertained. The former conveys the knowledge of truth and falsehood, the latter of beauty and deformity, vice and virtue" (Hume [1751] 1957, 112). What is good and what is evil, what is right and what is wrong, like what is beautiful and what is ugly, are, Hume here avers, in the eye of the beholder. But judgments of beauty and ugliness are notoriously personal and variable. I may find Picasso's cubist paintings beautiful, another beholder may find them ugly. Similarly, I may find murder odious, another beholder (Jeffrey Dahmer, for instance) may find it delectable. If ethics, as Hume here expressly says, is ultimately a matter of taste (!), then there can be no objective standards of conduct, no moral norms. The issue now is not normative force, but the very possibility that any uniform norms of conduct at all may be cut from the fickle fabric of feeling. A sentiment-based ethic seems to collapse into the most decadent emotivism and the rankest relativism.

But Hume did not agree. Shortly before the rational universalization of egoism gained a stranglehold on moral philosophy, Hume attempted, theoretically, to achieve universality, if not objectivity, in standards of conduct through a putative common or shared humanity. "While the human heart is compounded of the same elements as at present," he writes,

it will never be wholly indifferent to publick good, nor entirely unaffected by the tendency of characters and manners. And though this affection of humanity may not generally be esteemed so strong as vanity and ambition, yet being common to all men, it can alone be the foundation of morals or of any general system of blame or praise. One man's ambition is not another man's ambition, nor will the same event or object satisfy both; but the humanity of one man is the humanity of everyone; and the same object touches this passion in all human creatures. (Hume [1751] 1957, 93–94)

Objective norms, such as Plato's Good or Moore's non-natural qualities, of course, do not exist in Hume's opinion. His is a subjectivist theory. But because Hume supposed the faculty of moral judgment, of ethical taste, to be no less common and univocal in human nature than Kant supposed the faculty of reason to be, something functionally equivalent to objective norms exist in Hume's moral philosophy. In this respect, aesthetic and moral taste are different. The former may be personal and variable, but the latter is common and universal.

How so? Hume ([1751] 1957, 112) only says in the "Conclusion" of the *Enquiry* that, "the standard [of moral judgment], arising from the internal frame and constitution of animals, is ultimately derived from that Supreme Will which bestowed on each being its peculiar nature and arranged the several classes and orders of existence." Why Hume chose suddenly to speak of the "internal frame and constitution of *animals*," and of "the several classes and orders of existence," rather than of the internal frame and constitution of human beings and of human nature, is a mystery to me. That he did so may have been especially suggestive to Darwin; I don't know. In any case, as Darwin substituted natural selection for the Divine Will in accounting for the external frame and observable constitution of animals and the peculiar natures of the several classes and orders of biological existence in *The Origin of Species,* so he substituted the same principle for the Divine Will in accounting for the uniformity of the moral sentiments in *The Descent of Man.*

Darwin's account begins with the parental-filial affections common to all mammals. Bonds of affection and sympathy between parents and offspring permitted the formation of small, closely kin social groups, he argued. Should the parental-filial affections bonding nuclear family members chance to extend to less closely related individuals, that would permit the formation of extended family groups; and should such expanded communities more successfully defend themselves and more efficiently provision themselves, the inclusive fitness of their members severally would be increased, Darwin reasoned. Thus, the "social sentiments" would be spread throughout the species. Darwin then imagined the "social instincts" and "moral sentiments," thus evolved from the emotional ties binding kinship groups, to have become "more tender and widely diffused" as communities developed in size and complexity in response to the human evolutionary principle that if membership in comparatively large, complex societies is a good thing, then membership in even larger, more complex societies is better.

Now to be sure, inherited social feelings and moral sentiments may vary from person to person. But they vary within a range of normalcy, not unlike physical characteristics. People of normal height may be either short or tall. Then, there are midgets and NBA centers. Analogously, some people are longer on sympathy and similar sentiments than others who are more consumed by vanity, ambition, greed, or spite. Thus, upon Darwin's account, we can explain how ethical dispositions vary, as they obviously do, while insisting that neither are they radically relative. Hence Darwin's descriptive and explanatory theory of the origin and evolution of ethics provides moral norms that are not unlike the norms provided by the descriptive and explanatory science of medicine. If a human being's blood pressure falls within a certain range, it is normal; outside that range, it is aberrant. Similarly, a certain modicum of sympathy, concern, and benevolence is humanly normal, very little or none at all is aberrant.

Therefore, the sentiment-based theory of ethics first expounded by Hume and given a natural grounding in human evolution by Darwin, is certainly not liable to the charge that whatever feels good to an agent is right and good—for that agent—and whatever feels bad is wrong and evil. A sentiment-based theory of ethics may find a "normative dimension" in what might be called a "consensus of feeling." An agent's abnormal moral sensibilities may not be untrue, but by the human consensus of feeling, they may be "wrong," morally, if not epistemically.

THE PROBLEM OF BIOLOGICAL DETERMINISM FOR A DARWINIAN THEORY OF MORAL SENTIMENTS

Out of the flames of relativism and onto the hot coals of biological determinism. As I understand my critics, Fox and Shrader-Frechette, the real problem rears up just here. Neither dogmatically insists on the Modern egoism-*cum*-generalization paradigm, so incisively exposed by Goodpaster, although Fox's choice of the term "force" suggests that he may not have entirely escaped its intellectual hegemony. And both eschew taking a cheap shot at an ethical theory grounded in naturally selected and generally distributed unselfish feelings by conflating it with emotivism and falsely charging that it collapses into a morally intolerable radical relativism. Rather, the problem, both allege, is that the theory provides us with no means of criticizing the medical-like descriptive norms derived from common innate moral sentiments. There may be a consensus of feeling that murder is evil, but there also seems to be a consensus of feeling that only people are worthy of moral considerability.

If the final court of appeal of moral judgments is a consensus of feeling, how can we possibly argue that although something is generally felt to be right or good, say speciesism, it *ought* not to be? If our moral sentiments are "derived from that Supreme Will which bestowed on each being its peculiar nature," they are immutable as well as universal. If they are naturally selected, we are hardly liberated. In that case, any change in prevailing values would appear to have to await a genetic mutation and the slow process of natural selection. And even then, such a shift in values could only be said to be different, not better. Certainly the existing consensus of feeling would seem to be immune to cognitive criticism of any sort. As Hume would say, a passion can be opposed only by another passion, not by reason. This, Fox and Shrader-Frechette think, is the important missing normative dimension of a theory of moral sentiments grounded in human nature. And it would seem to be a problem that is especially vitiating, not to mention ironical, for a biologically tethered, sentiment-based nonanthropocentric and holistic *environmental* ethic—an ethic that would oppose anthropocentrism on cognitive grounds and introduce, at a single stroke, wildly new (or newly wild) values.

This general concern, of course, has been at the eye of the storm of liberal protest against the latest version of Darwinian moral theory. Sociobiology, it has been indignantly alleged, would institutionalize racism and sexism, let alone speciesism. Their defense against charges of racism and sexism has not been aided by the sociobiologists themselves, who regularly commit either the fallacy of composition or the genetic fallacy (no pun intended).

Some argue that altruism among human beings is illusory because our behavior is orchestrated by "selfish" genes (Dawkins 1976). That is the fallacy of composition. To argue that we are necessarily selfish because our genes are selfish makes about as much sense as to argue that we are necessarily microscopic because our genes are microscopic. The sociobiological theory of kin selection plausibly explains how genuinely altruistic organisms may have evolved because their selflessness works to increase the representation in future generations of the genes that they share with close kin. To put the point mythopoeically, our designing genes (pun intended) have deviously created genuinely altruistic carriers in order to vouchsafe their own future representation.

Ah, but wouldn't that imply that genuine altruism is necessarily narrowly limited to close kin? That is the genetic fallacy. Further elaborating his critique of my approach to environmental ethics, Fox (1990, 264) recapitulates this fallacy:

J. B. S. Haldane . . . said that he "would lay down his life for more than two brothers or sisters, eight cousins, thirty two second cousins, etc., these numbers corresponding to the proportions of his own genes shared by these relatives." Thus sociobiology explains—and serves to legitimate—the fact that we generally tend to favor our "nearest and dearest" over and against those to whom we are not genetically related or those who are not useful to us in the business of transmitting our genes.

Altruism evolved in small, aboriginal kinship groups and its expression therefore usually benefited close kin. But evolved behavioral dispositions and the emotions that animate them are often blunt as well as blind instruments. Obviously the parental affections were selected because those who felt them most strongly were most successful at rearing their offspring to sexual maturity. But for all of that, adoptive parents may cherish their adopted child no less ardently than if she were their own flesh and blood and make innumerable selfless sacrifices rearing her. Kin selection, it will be countered, may just as readily explain the emergence of the phenomenon of adoption: it is avuncular nurturing in aboriginal societies. Granted. But adoptive parents in large, pluralistic contemporary societies, who often adopt genetically unrelated children, are, from a biological point of view, wasting their time and energy. How could this be possible and so routine if a naturally selected affection were precisely limited in its range of intention to the actual kin it evolved to benefit? Our feelings are not calculating. Precisely because our primitive ancestors had no idea that they had genes, any conscious interest in their transmission, or the intellectual sophistication to carry out a benefit-cost analysis, in the currency of inclusive fitness, such as that reputedly performed by Haldane, evolution endowed them with broadcast altruistic feelings and impulses, which originally served to enhance their own genotypic reproduction, but which were deflected to broader social ends in changed circumstances.

Not only is it obviously true that the social dispositions and affections, evolved in aboriginal human kinship groups, are neither calculating nor limited in their intentional range to actual kin, it is also obviously true that they may be cognitively massaged. It is an irony of history that Darwin himself was not a Social Darwinist. He did not attempt to legitimate the supremacy of one person over another or of one group over another by means of simplistic analogies between nature and society. In view of the sociobiology row, it is also an irony of history that Darwin himself, the original sociobiologist, was not a biological determinist. Human morality, properly speaking—that is, morality as opposed to a set of mere social instincts—requires, in Darwin's terms, "intellectual powers" sufficient to recall the past and imagine the future, "the power of language" sufficient to codify "common opinion," and habituation to patterns of behavior deemed, by common opinion, to be socially acceptable and beneficial. Ethics is grounded in naturally selected feelings, to be sure, but there is also a large cultural component of morality that gives shape and direction to our selfless sentiments. In general, we may say, culture informs the moral sentiments.

Here is an analogy better to appreciate the interplay that Darwin suggested exists between nature and nurture in ethics. Human beings have an innate disposition to speak, and part of the human brain is specifically devoted to language. But which language, among the thousands of mutually unintelligible human languages, one learns to speak is not determined by one's genes. All normal human beings are linguistic, but which language we learn to speak and to whom it is appropriate to say what is shaped by our cultural environment.

Similarly, all normal human beings are endowed, some more generously than others, with moral sentiments, but to whom they pertain and just how they ought to be behaviorally expressed is shaped by our cultural environment. The moral sentiments are in themselves underdetermined and plastic. To put my point in Aristotelian terms, they are in themselves potentialities that become actual only in a cultural context. So we are not stuck with a set of inflexible moral norms determined by our biology. We are not innately racists, sexists, or speciesists. We may indeed feel a special regard for our relatives and our fellows, but which beings are *believed* to be included in these classes is determined by cultural representation, not biology. Christian preachers regularly declaim, with palpable effect, that we are all brothers and sisters under the skin and address nonrelatives in kinship terms—"Brother Jones," "Sister Smith"—and refer to our universal, "Father in Heaven." A tribal person may even believe herself to be closely kin to members of another species, her totem species, and may actually behave as if she were. (And Aldo Leopold argued that such notions of interspecies kinship are not so farfetched.) What I have characterized as the genetic fallacy in the sociobiology debate might better be characterized as the fallacy of equivocation. "Father," "mother," "brother," "sister," "uncle," "aunt," "grandfather," "grandmother," and "cousin" have a precise biological sense and a vernacular, cultural sense, which sometimes are, but often are not, the same. The mistake made by both parties to the sociobiology debate is to suppose the biological sense to be the effective one, the one that influences how we behave, when of course it is the vernacular, cultural sense that counts when it comes to how we feel about some other being and thus how we relate to him, her, or it.

THE COGNITIVE NORMATIVE DIMENSION OF
A THEORY OF MORAL SENTIMENTS

But this rejoinder may only seem to propel me off the hot coals of biological determinism and back into the flames of relativism. As Fox (1990, 191) puts it, "even though Callicott's sociobiological approach can be used to overcome the extreme case that he refers to as radical relativism, . . . there is still plenty of room for the common, everyday kinds of relativism that have typically been held to render subjectivist approaches impotent."

Let me review the argument to this point. Having dismissed as an obsolete Modernist preoccupation "normative force" (understood as the logical coercion of a consistent-at-all-costs rational egoist into doing the right thing), a postModern return to a theory of moral sentiments may be rescued from reduction to emotivism and radical relativism by appeal to human nature. But that leads to the charge that, if they are built into human nature, we have no way to criticize and argue for changing prevailing values, moral dogmas, and conventions. The charge that a theory of moral sentiments lacks such a normative dimension may be answered by observing that while human beings are naturally ethical, by nature we are only generically ethical, and that the all-important details of ethics are specified by culture. But, in that case, haven't we exchanged a normless radical relativism for a normatively deficient cultural relativism? Speciesism is a "value" specified by almost all literate cultures. Sexism is a "value" specified by Moslem culture. Racism was a "value" specified by German culture in the 1930s and, more recently, in white South African culture. Katherine Ellen Rawles (1990) has recently evoked the specter of (the now erstwhile) policy of *apartheid* in South Africa and argued that the ethical theory that I espouse will not permit me to say that apartheid is categorically wrong and ought to be abolished.

But it certainly does. And quite easily. For now, at last, I have landed on cool cognitive terra firma. Speciesism, sexism, and racism are not free-floating cultural "values." A culture is, among other things, a shared worldview. A culture's values and ethical ideals rest upon and are justified by suppositions of fact and supposed relations among supposed facts. A racist believes that members of other races are all subhuman or are deficient in certain laudable human qualities, such as intelligence or decency. We condemn racism and attempt to purge it from our own culture—or from any other for that matter—principally by debunking the alleged "facts" on which it is based and by which it is justified. Similarly do we condemn sexism and argue that it ought to be purged from our society and from all others. Animal liberationists argue that the supposed "facts" justifying speciesism are spurious. Animals are conscious despite Descartes (1641). Animals have desires and interests despite R. G. Frey (1980). Since animals are so like us in the ways that appropriately stimulate our sense of sympathy—though Singer may pretend to abjure to play on sympathy—then they too, a Humean animal liberationist might argue, ought to be extended moral considerability.

Aldo Leopold tried to persuade us that we ought to feel a sense of kinship with our fellow voyagers in the odyssey of evolution and love and respect for the land because ecology has reorganized our understanding of nature. He did not try to change the human heart or instill a novel affection in us, although it may be of passing historical interest to note that Leopold at first may have believed that we must await a genetic change in the normal human psychological profile in order for a land ethic literally to evolve. In the 1935 paper in which he turned the phrase, "land ethic," for the first time, he wrote, "the breeding of ethics is yet beyond our powers. All science can do is to safeguard the environment in which ethical mutations might take place" (Leopold 1991a). But the mature Leopold realized that while human nature changes very slowly, our *ideas* about who we are, what sort of world we live in, and our relationship to the natural environment change rapidly and not at all arbitrarily or blindly. They change in response to scientific discovery and to intra- and intercultural critical reflection and debate. He thought that the expanded kinship with other organisms implied by the evolutionary epic and the representation of terrestrial nature in ecology as a biotic community might especially appeal to our moral sentiments which are so evidently excited by the prospect of kinship, fellowship, and society. But can Leopold say not only that as a matter of fact we may come to love and respect the environment when we come to see it through the lenses of evolution and ecology, but that we *ought* to as well? Has his land ethic, grounded in the moral sentiments, any normative force, any normative dimension? Its normative force is not of the Modernist rationally coercive kind. But the land ethic certainly has a normative dimension. And that normative dimension lies precisely in the realm of reason or cognition. As Hume ([1739] 1960, 469) put it, "reason in a strict and philosophical sense can have an influence on our conduct only after two ways: either when it excites a passion by informing us of the existence of something which is a proper object of it; or when it discovers the connexion of causes and effects, so as to afford us means of exerting any passion."

Is nature a "*proper* object" of human sympathy, loyalty, benevolence, or respect? If animals are, as Descartes believed, mere automata, then they are no more proper objects of sympathy than is a pencil sharpener. Whether we ought or ought not extend them moral considerability, for psychologically healthy people who have a normal amount and complement of moral sentiments, turns thus on a matter of fact. Just what sort of beings are animals, and what connections have they to us? This is a question capable of cognitive resolution. Are plants, like animals, conscious beings? So it was alleged in *The Secret Life of Plants*. But the claims in that book have been decisively discredited. Paul Taylor (1986) has made a good case, however, that plants at least are conative, if not conscious beings, that they are "teleological centers of life." If plants are not conscious then we have no grounds for sympathizing with them, but if they are conative we may appropriately feel benevolent toward them. Are we, along with plants and animals, coevolved, distantly kin members of a biotic community, as ecology alleges? If so, then indeed we ought to feel sympathy or benevolence toward our fellow members and loyalty and respect toward the community as such.

Of course, to claim, as I have, that the normative dimension of a sentiment-based environmental ethic, depends, surprisingly, on matters of fact and scientific revelation, raises a whole 'nother set of problems— epistemological problems. Are there "facts"? Does science provide us with a "true" representation of "reality"? And so on. These questions are important and critical to an environmental ethic erected on a theory of moral sentiments. And I have addressed them elsewhere (chapter 5). Rather, what I hope to have shown is that what we should and should not care about, that what we ought and ought not value, that how we ought and ought not act in relation to what—that all such questions are cognitive questions and that the remaining normative problems attending a sentiment-based environmental ethic are in essence epistemological. And that I think is a clear advance.

Do Deconstructive Ecology and Sociobiology Undermine the Leopold Land Ethic?

THE ECOLOGICAL SIEGE OF NATURE

In an essay entitled "The Social Siege of Nature," Michael Soulé, one of the architects of conservation biology, directly confronts the insidious challenge to nature conservation posed by poststructuralists. There he defends nature protection from a deconstructive assault by "humanists who feel they must attack and redefine the concept of living nature and its protection as part of the struggle to liberate the less powerful classes of Homo sapiens from oppression by economically and politically stronger subgroups of the species" (Soulé 1995, 138). From the point of view of Critical Theory, *nature* and its *crisis* are but elements of a "socially constructed" (patriarchal) Western worldview that serves to "oppress" various "Others" (including women).

Ironically, however, Soulé is quite complacent about the deconstruction, going blithely on in contemporary ecology, of the popular conception of living nature as a symbiotic, delicately balanced, well-integrated, orderly system. Indeed, he warmly endorses what might be called the new deconstructive ecology:

Certainly the idea that species live in integrated communities is a myth. So-called biotic communities, a misleading term, are constantly changing in membership. The species occurring in any particular place are rarely convivial neighbors; their coexistence in certain places is better explained by individual physiological tolerances. Though in some cases the finer details of spatial distribution may be influenced by positive interspecies interactions, the much more common kinds of interactions are competition, predation, parasitism, and disease. Most interactions between individuals and species are *selfish*, not symbiotic. Current ecological thinking argues that nature at the level of local biotic assemblages has never been homeostatic. The principle of balance has been replaced with the principle of gradation—a continuum of degrees of . . . disturbance. (Soulé 1995, 143)

Nature, so described, is not exactly the appealing beneficiary of conservation portrayed by Jacques Cousteau television programs on the Discovery Channel. With scientific friends like Soulé, nature doesn't need any humanistic enemies. His impassioned call to protect a threatened nature, thus characterized, is about as appealing, morally and politically, as a call to protect endangered street gangs and terrorist organizations. The deconstructive siege of nature that Soulé laments is as much a subversion from within the scientific establishment as an attack from antiscientific liberal humanists without. This disturbing turn in ecology might be called "deconstructive" because the old master narratives of ecology—organicism, community, ecosystem—are currently being reviled, and there is an apparent contentment with either no organizing paradigm or a plurality of mutually inconsistent organizing paradigms in ecology.

Two of the most fundamental organizing concepts of modern ecology, the ecosystem concept and the biotic community concept, are indeed presently being deconstructed (Shrader-Frechette and McCoy 1993). Just what *are* ecosystems as objects of scientific study? They seem ontologically vague and ambiguously bounded. Indeed, in "Ecology of Order and Chaos," Donald Worster (1990, 8) reports that "A survey of recent ecology textbooks shows that the [ecosystem] concept is not even mentioned in one leading work and has a much diminished place in the others." A more sanguine assessment is provided by Frank Golley (1994) in *A History of the Ecosystem Concept in Ecology*, but even Golley's partisan account reveals the ecosystem concept to be problematic. A severe blow to the community concept was struck by Margaret B. Davis (1984). A community was once believed to be a unit of interdependent species populations that come and go as one. But studies of the pollen record suggest that species populations formed very different associations in the past.

A hallowed "law" of ecology, that ecological stability depends on biological diversity, has been all but repealed. Daniel Goodman (1975) provides a summary of research results through the mid-seventies on the diversity-stability hypothesis. His conclusion drips with sarcasm and contempt: "The diversity-stability hypothesis may have caught the lay conservationists' fancy, not for the allure of its scientific embellishments, but for the more basic appeal of its underlying metaphor. It is the sort of thing that people like, and want, to believe. Thus, though better theories supplant it in scientific usage, we may be certain that the 'hypothesis' will persist for awhile as an element of folk science. Eventually that remnant, too, may vanish in light of discordant facts, and the imagery of this once-scientific hypothesis will recede to a revered position in the popular environmental ethic, where it doubtless will do much good" (Goodman 1975, 261).

The very idea that nature is somehow stable—that is, in a static equilibrium of countervailing forces, such as that once believed to exist between a predator and its prey—is passé (Shrader-Frechette and McCoy 1993; Sagoff 1985). Rather, nature is dynamic (Botkin 1990). It is, moreover, chaotic, changing unpredictably (Degan et al. 1987; Gleik 1987; May 1974). And disturbance ("perturbation")—by wind, flood, fire, pestilence—not freedom from such disruption is nature's normal state (Pickett and White 1985).

What implications for environmental ethics have these deconstructive developments in contemporary ecology?

That depends on which environmental ethic you have in mind. The Judeo-Christian stewardship environmental ethic would seem to be little affected. From the prevailing autecological point of view, the planet's complement of species may not be rivets holding Spaceship Earth together, as they were represented to be in *Extinction* by Paul and Anne Ehrlich (1981). Indeed, according to David Ehrenfeld (1988, 215), the species "whose members are the fewest in number, the rarest, the most narrowly distributed—in short, the ones most likely to become extinct—are obviously the ones least likely to be missed by the biosphere. Many of these species were never common or ecologically influential; by no stretch of the imagination can we make them out to be vital cogs in the ecological machine." But they are still God's creatures and He declared each and every one of them to be good—intrinsically valuable—immediately after He created them (Dobel 1994). And the biocentric environmental ethic of Paul W. Taylor (1986), which was never very well informed by ecology, would also seem to be little affected. That we ought to respect each and every *individual* shrub, bug, and grub remains just as true as it ever was, whether such teleological centers of life can be considered members of biotic communities and components of ecosystems or not. The Leopold land ethic, on the other hand, is extremely vulnerable to the current deconstructive turn in ecology (Cahen 1988; Comstock 1995; Steverson 1994). For of all the systems of environmental ethics so far articulated, the Leopold land ethic is the one most thoroughly grounded in evolutionary and ecological biology (Callicott 1987). From the 1970s through the 1990s, its scientific foundations have undergone a series of seismic tremors. In addition to the recent deconstructive turn taken in ecology, sociobiology has also come along and significantly altered the evolutionary account of the origin and development of human morality upon which Leopold builds the land ethic. Will we find that the land ethic has collapsed into a heap of rubble when we turn around to look at it again?

THE EVOLUTIONARY CORNERSTONE OF THE LAND ETHIC

In *The Descent of Man*, Darwin (1871) dealt with what at first glance appears to be an evolutionary anomaly—the existence of ethics. Ethics appears anomalous, from an evolutionary point of view, because the more aggressively, selfishly, and treacherously inclined specimens of Homo sapiens would be expected to out compete, on average, their more cooperatively, altruistically, and deferentially inclined conspecifics. Thus, as time goes on, human beings should become more aggressive, selfish, and treacherous rather than more cooperative, altruistic, and deferential; in short, more unethical rather than more ethical. But, however morally flawed actual human behavior may be, ethics do exist; and moral sensibilities *seemed* (to Darwin and most of his contemporaries) to be more refined and more broadly cast in nineteenth-century European civilization than among the Stone Age ("savage") peoples Darwin encountered while voyaging on the *Beagle*.

Go figure. And Darwin did. Human survival and reproductive success, he argued, is possible only in a social setting. But cooperative societies could not exist if their members did not observe certain limits in the usual course of their interactions with one another. "No tribe," Darwin (1871, 93) writes, "could hold together if murder, robbery, treachery, &c., were common; consequently, such crimes, within the limits of the same tribe, 'are branded with everlasting infamy,' but excite no such sentiment beyond these limits." In short: no ethics, no community; no community, no survival (and, more importantly, no reproduction). Darwin (1871, 100–101) then goes on to imagine the expansion of the moral community as smaller societies merge to form larger, more complex, and more efficient societies:

As man advances in civilisation, and small tribes are united into larger communities, the simplest reason would tell each individual that he ought to extend his social instincts and sympathies to all the members of the same nation, though personally unknown to him. This point being once reached, there is only an artificial barrier to prevent his sympathies extending to the men of all nations and races.

The literary Leopold is not one to impede the flow of his prose by citing sources. But that he is thinking of Darwin's evolutionary scenario of the origin and development of ethics is indicated by allusion in a 1933 essay that foreshadowed "The Land Ethic," entitled "The Conservation Ethic." After having suggested the existence of an advance in moral sensibilities over the three-thousand-year course of Western civilization from the days of Odysseus down to our own, he writes,

This extension of ethics, so far studied only by philosophers, is actually a process in ecological *evolution*. Its sequences may be described in *biological* as well as in philosophical terms. An ethic, *biologically*, is a limitation on freedom of action in the *struggle for existence*. *An ethic*, philosophically, *is a differentiation of social from anti-social conduct*. These are two definitions of one thing. The thing has its origin in the tendency of interdependent individuals or societies to evolve modes of cooperation. (Leopold 1933b, 634, emphasis added)

ECOLOGICAL PARADIGMS AND THE LAND ETHIC

To readers of *A Sand County Almanac*, all this will sound familiar. Leopold worked this very passage from "The Conservation Ethic" into "The Land Ethic" with only slight revision. (One could argue that the revisions—changing "biological" in the second sentence to "ecological" and changing "biologically" in the third sentence to "ecologically"—were ill-advised. Darwin's account of the origin and evolution of ethics was less an exercise in human ecology than in human evolution, thus it was more generally biological than specifically ecological.) But in the "The Land Ethic" he immediately added a new ecological element: the now-problematic "community concept." Basically, Leopold just extends Darwin's reasoning from the correlation of ethics with our various human community memberships—family, clan, tribe, nation, all humanity—to the newly discovered biotic community. Putting Darwin's analysis in a nutshell, Leopold (1949, 203–4) writes, "All ethics so far evolved rest upon a single premise: that the individual is a member of a community of interdependent parts." Ecology, he then goes on to note, "simply enlarges the boundaries of the community to include soils, waters, plants, and animals, or collectively: the land."

In "The Land Ethic," Leopold does not keep his ecological paradigms clearly sorted out. Residual traces of the early twentieth-century Clementsian superorganism paradigm—the ethical implications of which Leopold (1979) had flirted with as early as 1923—turn up in the 'Land Health and the A-B Cleavage' section of "The Land Ethic." And 'The Land Pyramid,' the longest section of "The Land Ethic," is devoted to an exposition of the then state-of-the-art, physics-inspired thermodynamical ecosystem paradigm—introduced by Arthur Tansley (1935), operationalized by Raymond Lindeman (1942), and then institutionalized by Eugene Odum (1953, 1959, 1971)—and to a derivation of the specific land-ethical implications of that paradigm. In the same section of "The Land Ethic"—'The Land Pyramid' section—Leopold (1949, 214) even uses the phrases *biotic mechanism* and *land mechanism*, although in his 1923 paper on environmental ethics, "Some Fundamentals of Conservation in the Southwest," he had sharply contrasted an organismic with a "mechanistic conception of the earth" (Leopold 1979. 139).

Two postModern elements, however, also appear in 'The Land Pyramid' section of "The Land Ethic."

First, Leopold (1949, 214) expressly abjures the balance of nature idea: "The image commonly employed in conservation education is 'the balance of nature,'" he writes. "For reasons too lengthy to detail here, this figure of speech fails to describe accurately what little we know about the land mechanism." In "A Biotic View of Land," Leopold (1939, 728) elaborates his misgivings about the balance of nature metaphor:

To the lay mind, balance of nature probably conveys an actual image of the familiar weighing scale. There may even be danger that the layman imputes to the biota properties which exist only on the grocer's counter. To the ecological mind, balance of nature has merits and also defects. Its merits are that it conceives of a collective total, that it imputes some utility to all species, and that it implies oscillations when balance is disturbed. Its defects are that there is only one point at which balance occurs and that balance is normally static.

Second, Leopold (1949, 216–17) goes on in 'The Land Pyramid' section of "The Land Ethic" to emphasize nature's inherent dynamism: "When a change occurs in one part of the circuit," he writes, "many other parts must adjust themselves to it. Change does not necessarily obstruct or divert the flow of energy [through ecosystems]; evolution is a long series of self-induced changes, the net result of which has been to elaborate the flow mechanism and to lengthen the circuit."

LEOPOLD ON THE RELATIONSHIP BETWEEN
DIVERSITY AND STABILITY

One of the two principal themes of the immediately preceding section, 'Substitutes for a Land Ethic,' is the dependence of stability on diversity. Speaking of economically worthless wildflowers and songbirds (which had not yet been shadow-priced by industrious neoclassical economists), Leopold (1949, 210) avers that "these creatures are members of the biotic community, and if (as I believe) its stability depends on its integrity, they are entitled to continuance." Leopold's scientific scruples are evident in the parenthetical phrase "as I believe." He does not, that is, state the dependence of stability on diversity (or integrity, that is, the presence of the characteristic species of a biotic community in their characteristic numbers) as a well-established fact, but as his own well-educated opinion.

Three or four years before Leopold pieced "The Land Ethic" together, he more fully expressed his views on the relationship between diversity and stability in a paper entitled "Conservation: In Whole or In Part?" which was written in 1944 but remained unpublished until 1991. Stability is a notoriously ambiguous concept in ecology, and has more recently been parsed into several more specific concepts—persistence, resistance, and resilience (Pimm 1991). In "Conservation in Whole or In Part?" Leopold seems to mean by *stability* what more precisely might be called *community persistence*. In the following quote, it is evident that Leopold (1991b, 312) supposes a typological biotic community to be a persistent unit that comes and goes as such:

The Wisconsin land was stable . . . for a long period before 1840 [when settled by Europeans]. The pollens embedded in peat bogs show that the native plants comprising the prairie, the hardwood forest, and the coniferous forest are about the same now as they were at the end of the glacial period, 20,000 years ago. Since that time these major plant communities were pushed alternatively northward and southward several times by long climatic cycles, but their membership and organization remained intact. . . . The bones of animals show that the fauna shifted with the flora, but its composition or membership likewise remained intact.

Leopold then goes on to point out that the biotic communities of the upper Midwest were diverse—that is, they were composed of many different species. And he also points out that while "tooth and claw competition" was the principal mode of interspecies relations, species extinction was rare. From these "facts" Leopold (1991b, 315, emphasis added) reaches a conclusion, and, though it is that stability (persistence) is caused by (species) diversity, his conclusion is remarkable for its caution:

The *circumstantial* evidence is that stability and diversity in the native community were associated for 20,000 years, and *presumably* depended on each other. Both now are partly lost, *presumably* because the original community has been partly lost and greatly altered. *Presumably* the greater the losses and alterations, the greater the risk of impairments and disorganizations.

Better resolution of the pollen record now reveals a very different picture. Linda Brubaker (1988, 41) sketches it:

Because species have responded individualistically to climatic variations, plant communities have been transient assemblages, seldom persisting more than 2,000 to 5,000 years. . . . . Most of the tree species dominating North America today became common 8,000 to 10,000 years ago when they expanded from ice-age refugia. Most species spread at different rates and in different directions, reaching their current range limits and populations only 3,000 to 5,000 years ago. Thus present-day North American forests should not be considered stable over evolutionary time scales.

Where then does that leave the summary moral maxim of the land ethic—"A thing is right when it tends to preserve the integrity, stability, and beauty of the biotic community. It is wrong when it tends otherwise"—? Apparently biotic communities lack integrity. They are mere "transient assemblages" of species that are "individualistically" adapted to the same edaphic and climatic gradients. And apparently they lack stability: apparently, that is, they do not *persist*; nor, apparently, do they *resist* alteration (species mix and match opportunistically); and, apparently, assemblages do not reconstitute themselves when the climate oscillates back to a former state—they are not *resilient* (at least not in response to long-term climate perturbation cycles). All that seems left to preserve is the beauty of the biotic community. That may satisfy Gene Hargrove (1989) and Mark Sagoff (1988), who ground environmental ethics in natural aesthetics. But the individualistic-dynamic paradigm in deconstructive community ecology seems to undercut two out of three of the land ethic's cardinal values.

A WORD OR TWO OF CAUTION ABOUT SUMMARILY DISMISSING THE DIVERSITY-STABILITY HYPOTHESIS

The science that informed Leopold's land ethic may be out of date, but Leopold's scientific epistemology seems to be much more advanced than that of some of the contemporary deconstructive ecologists. Note once more Leopold's caution in asserting a causal relationship between diversity and stability. Surely, an equal degree of caution should accompany the claims of those who assert that there is no such relationship, especially as the environmental risk of their being wrong is very great.

Daniel Goodman (1975) reports that ecologists looking for a correlation between diversity and various kinds of stability did not find it, but found instead that *some* monophytic communities (spartina-dominated salt marshes) are remarkably persistent, resistant, and resilient. He also reports that mathematical models involving a few variables are more stable (persistent, resistant, resilient) than multifactored models, with strongly connected variables. But what does that prove? That in *all* biotic communities there is an inverse correlation between diversity and stability? It may only mean that empirical ecologists have not looked hard enough in the right places for a positive correlation between diversity and stability or that mathematico-theoretical ecologists are not clever enough to model the real world correctly. To positively conclude that something does not exist—the correlation between diversity and stability, in this case—because scientists do not observe it or because they cannot model it is to commit the fallacy of *argumentum ad ignorantum.*

The diversity-stability hypothesis, as a matter of fact, is currently making a comeback. A recent study of grasslands by David Tilman and John Downing (1994, 363) "shows that primary productivity in more diverse plant communities is more resistant to, and recovers more fully from, a major drought." Tilman and Downing explicitly apply their results to the now-classic debate about the diversity-stability hypothesis: "Our results support the diversity-stability hypothesis," they write, "but not the alternative hypothesis that most species are functionally redundant. This study implies that the preservation of biodiversity is essential for the maintenance of stable productivity in ecosystems" (Tilman and Downing 1994, 363).

Further, if nature is chaotic—that is, describable by deterministic, nonlinear equations that are sensitive to initial conditions, and we cannot know all the relevant initial conditions, and therefore cannot predict the outcome of changes that we impose upon it—then surely that too calls for erring on the side of caution. If anything, what Donald Worster calls the new "ecology of chaos" makes Leopold's much-quoted cautionary advice more sound now than ever: "To keep every cog and wheel is the first precaution of intelligent tinkering" (Leopold 1953, 146–47).

EVOLUTIONARY KINSHIP AND THE LAND ETHIC

Though Darwinian evolutionary theory has been refined since mid-century and fundamental challenges to Darwin's gradualism, such as punctuated equilibrium, have been advanced, the idea that all extant species, including Homo sapiens, are descended from one urform or from very few such forms is not in doubt. As Soulé (1995, 142) notes, "There is now no question that all life on earth evolved from a common ancestor. The genetic material and the codes embedded within it reveal that every living kind of plant and animal owes its existence to a single-celled ancestor that evolved some three and a half billion years ago. All species are *kin*." Hence, human beings are a part of nature, and we are kin—literally, though more or less distantly kin—to all other kinds of life. These assumptions are common to all secular nonanthropocentric developments in ethics—animal liberation/rights and biocentrism no less than the land ethic (Rachels 1990; Taylor 1981). Leopold (1949, 109) states the general ethical implication of evolutionary theory with his usual charm and simplicity:

It is a century now since Darwin gave us the first glimpse of the origin of species. We know now what was unknown to all the preceding caravan of generations: that men are only fellow voyagers with other creatures in the odyssey of evolution. This new knowledge should have given us, by this time, a sense of kinship with fellow creatures; a wish to live and let live; a sense of wonder over the magnitude and duration of the biotic enterprise.

SOCIOBIOLOGY AND THE LAND ETHIC

This statement is as credible now as it was in 1949. However, Darwin's more specialized account of the origin and development of ethics—which is foundational to the Leopold land ethic—has been elaborately developed as "sociobiology," which emerged simultaneously with deconstructive ecology in the mid-1970s. Many of its proponents as well as critics believe that sociobiology reduces altruism to egoism and ethics to reproductive prudence (Chandler 1991). These conclusions are fallacious. The first involves the fallacy of composition; the second the genetic fallacy (no pun intended).

First, sociobiology takes altruism at the level of organisms at face value. As a matter of fact, some organisms *do* make sacrifices for the sake of others; no doubt about it. According to Edward O. Wilson (1975, 3), "the central theoretical problem of sociobiology [is] how can altruism, which by definition reduces personal fitness, possibly evolve by natural selection?" The problem for the evolutionary biologist is to account for the existence of genuine altruism in nature consistent with Darwinian principles. Kin selection solves the problem (Hamilton 1964). Since off-spring represent their parents' genes in the next generation, natural selection has selected parents who will behave altruistically toward their own offspring, rather than selfishly at the expense of their offspring. For similar reasons—the same genes are represented in siblings, cousins, and so on—altruism toward other close kin also evolved.

Now, let us grant that *genes* are selfish (though using morally charged language to characterize molecular entities is, to say the least, suspect). The point is that our selfish genes have deviously designed genuinely altruistic organisms to further their reproduction. Thus to conclude that, because our genes are selfish, therefore, *we* are selfish is to commit the fallacy of composition—which is, in general, to argue that because all the parts of a whole have a certain characteristic, therefore, the whole, which the parts compose, also has that characteristic. To argue that we are necessarily selfish because our genes are selfish makes about as much sense, in other words, as to argue that we are necessarily microscopic because our genes are microscopic or that we ourselves necessarily have a nucleus because we are composed of cells and our cells have a nucleus.

Doesn't this, however, imply that genuine altruism—and palpable ethical concern by implication—is necessarily limited to *close* kin? As Warwick Fox (1990, 264) reports, "J. B. S. Haldane . . . said that he would lay down his life for more than two brothers or sisters, eight cousins, thirty-two second cousins, etc., these numbers corresponding to the proportion of his own genes shared by these relatives." Thus, Fox (1990, 264) goes on, "sociobiology explains—and serves to legitimate—the fact that we generally tend to favour our 'nearest and dearest' over against those to whom we are not genetically related."

It may—and rightly—do so. The practical absurdity of the universalism characteristic of Modern ethical theory is unwittingly captured by Peter Singer (1982), who argues that he has failed in his duty because he does not donate the greatest portion of his modest income to help allevi-ate the suffering of hungry people living halfway around the world, even though doing so would sorely impoverish not only himself but his own children. If he actually did what his theory leads him to think he ought to do, Singer would be badly judged—not only by his nearest and dearest, but by practically everyone else as well. While sociobiology may explain and legitimate moral partiality, however, it does not preclude a gradated expansion in the embrace of our moral sensibilities, short of indiscrimi-nate universalism (Hardin 1982). The limited duties, felt by many people, to help alleviate world hunger or save imperiled species are not inconsis-tent with a sociobiological construction of ethics. On the other hand, such things as imposing hunger on one's nearest and dearest to relieve it elsewhere, or inflicting genocide on a human population to preserve spe-cies, are indeed inconsistent with a sociobiological construction of ethics, as well as with commonly accepted morality.

Evolved behavioral dispositions and the emotions that animate them are often blunt as well as blind instruments of inclusive fitness. Altruism evolved in small kinship groups and its expression therefore usually ben-efited close kin. But adoptive parents may cherish their adopted child no less ardently than if she were their own flesh and blood and make innu-merable sacrifices rearing her. How could this be possible and so routine if naturally selected altruism were limited in its range of application to the actual kin which it evolved to benefit? Precisely because our primitive ancestors had no idea that they had genes, any conscious interest in their transmission, or the intellectual sophistication to carry out a benefit-cost analysis in the currency of inclusive fitness (such as that reputedly per-formed by Haldane), evolution endowed them with broadcast altruistic feelings and impulses—which originally served to enhance their own ge-notypic reproduction, but which were deflected to broader social ends in changed circumstances.

Human ethics are complex expressions of naturally selected altruism, but there is a very large cultural component of morality which gives shape and direction to our sympathetic impulses. To argue that a sociobiologi-cal analysis of ethics limits the purview of ethical regard to our close kin commits the genetic fallacy (again, no pun intended)—the fallacy of attrib-uting the properties of a cause to its effects. Altruism and eventually ethics may have evolved to serve selfish genes, but that fact does not necessarily limit them to the purpose for which they evolved. Christian preachers regularly declaim, with palpable effect, that we are all brothers and sisters under the skin and address non-relatives in kinship terms—"Brother Jones," "Sister Smith"—and refer to our common Father in Heaven. And contemporary environmental ethicists, including Leopold, point out—with similar moral-rhetorical intentions—that we are kin to other species and that, with them, we are fellow members of a common community: the biotic community.

Science has expanded our worldview. The Earth is a "small planet" in an immense, inhospitable universe. We and its other denizens *are*, from a cosmic point of view, *close* kin. And, from the same cosmic point of view, we do in fact depend for our existence—with every breath we take, with every morsel of food we eat—on our fellow voyagers in the odyssey of evolution.

THE COMMUNITY CONCEPT

As noted, our evolutionary kinship with other extant species is not in doubt, in scientific circles, but, in light of contemporary deconstructive ecology, one may well wonder if we and they are really fellow members of a common biotic community.

No poststructuralist ecological theory of which I am aware asserts that organisms are entirely independent of one another. However individualistic and self-seeking each organism may be, consumers cannot exist without producers and producers cannot exist without decomposers. In trying to repair some of the damage done to environmentalism by deconstructive ecology, Worster, in the second edition of *Nature's Economy* (1994, 429), evokes "the principle of interdependency": "No organism or species of organism has any chance of surviving without the aid of others." Though the two-species "daisy world" envisioned by James Lovelock (1988) may be of heuristic value in illustrating how the Earth might have evolved an organic thermostat, a world consisting of only two species of the same genus is not ecologically feasible.

The community concept in ecology is a metaphor. The metaphor assimilates the way proximate organisms are mutually dependent to the way proximate human beings are mutually dependent. Now let's consider human communities, the paradigms to which biotic communities are assimilated. Human communities—at least recent human communities—are neither stable nor typological. They change over time and in the process of change they do not come and go as units.

Take my (now erstwhile) community, Stevens Point, Wisconsin, as an example. It began as a logging community in the 1840s. After the old-growth Wisconsin pinery was levelled, the Scandinavian loggers who cut it down moved on to virgin forests farther west, and the land was settled by Polish dairy farmers. But second growth woods sprang up here and there and some lumber mills hung on, so that while the pestilential Scandinavian arboreal parasites diminished in number, some remained and adapted to the new colonizers, supplying lumber for houses and barns. Loggers and farmers like to drink beer. So an empty niche opened up and German *Braumeisters* invaded the nascent Stevens Point community and established a brewery. Pretty soon, tavern keepers, butchers, bakers, candlestick makers, grocers, farm implement dealers, hardware merchants, Protestant ministers, Catholic priests, doctors, journalists, lawyers, and eventually, college professors, all drifted in. Journalists, lawyers, and college professors use lots of paper. The old pinery was spontaneously growing back to scrubby aspen and jack pine, and the Wisconsin River runs through it. In addition to nearby woody fiber, there was a handy supply of water power and waste transport, so dams went up and paper mills and mill workers came to town.

Notice, none of these invasive species—with the problematic exception of ministers on a mission, priests following a vocation, and doctors being faithful to their Hippocratic Oath—were primarily motivated by altruism. Nor did they all move in at once, as a unit. In the formative period each person came because an economic opportunity to which he or she was individually adapted presented itself. Community succession in Stevens Point proceeded from timber mill town to paper mill town. Now Stevens Point has become quite diverse with its social analog of species populations organized into many economic guilds—paper making, hazard insurance, higher education, retailing, manufacturing, and family farming, being most salient. After the community was established, some people who were born there stayed there. Others left. And many people who now immigrate to Stevens Point will leave (as did I) when greater opportunity presents itself elsewhere. Further, the boundaries of the town

expanded with the passage of time. The posted "city limits" are not help-
ful in demarcating the actual community, which comprises several smaller
adjacent municipalities and includes, more or less, hundreds of people
living on nearby ten-to-forty-acre rural estates and eighty-to-one-thousand-
acre farms. But does all this mean that there is no such thing, no community *as such*, that we can call Stevens Point, Wisconsin, that all that exists
is just a standing crop of various types of transient, selfish individuals who
happen to be adapted to similar socioeconomic gradients in an ill-defined
place?

Try to tell that to Stevens Pointers, a very community-minded lot.
Sure, most people in Stevens Point, like most people everywhere, devote
most of their time to private gain and leisure pursuits. Economic competition is vigorous. But the people of Stevens Point nevertheless respect the
fellow members of their municipal community: no one is homeless or
hungry; every kid who wants to can join the YMCA, whether his or her
parents can pay the dues or not (I supported one or two such memberships myself); and the "developmentally challenged" are well integrated
into the social mainstream. Stevens Pointers also have respect for the community as such: people root for the home sports teams; a local ordinance
prohibiting fringe shopping malls was passed to preserve Main Street
(though, I'm sorry to say, Stevens Point still has tacky strip development);
and people impose relatively high property taxes on themselves to support good schools and well-maintained roads, public buildings, and municipal parks.

My point is that paradigmatic human communities are no more integrated, nor less dynamic, nor any easier to demarcate than biotic communities as represented in deconstructive ecology. Yet human communities
such as Stevens Point are still recognizable entities and engender moral
duties and obligations both to fellow members and to the community as
such. On this crucial point my conclusions, therefore, are these. First,
that though biotic communities are not now conceived to be so unified
and persistent as they once were, they do exist: Proximate plants and animals, however competitive, predatory, and parasitic, are no more independent of one another than are proximate persons. And second, if paradigmatic human communities are sufficiently robust to engender civic
duties and obligations both to fellow members and to such communities
per se, then biotic communities, which are not less robust than paradig-

matic human communities, are, by parity of reasoning, also sufficiently robust to engender analogous environmental duties and obligations.

They would be, at any rate, if we were members of them. I am aware of two environmental philosophers who deny that we are members of biotic as well as of human communities—John Passmore and Brian K. Steverson.

Passmore intends expressly to criticize the Leopold land ethic with a bacteria counterexample to ethics-generating interspecies community membership. His example of "bacteria and men" (sic) having no "common interests" is a spectacularly poor choice, given the mutualistic symbiosis between Homo sapiens and the bacteria in our intestines, which are essential for our capacity to digest food (Passmore 1974, 116). But free-living bacteria in the soil are also essential to human agriculture, to say nothing of the myriad ecological services performed by bacteria, beautifully documented by Lynn Margulis and her son, Dorion Sagan (1986). Bacteria, those little buggers! We Homo sapiens just couldn't live without them.

Steverson seems to think that we are inhabiting Biosphere Two, hermetically sealed off from Biosphere One. "Human-engineered biotic communities," he writes, meaning agricultural systems, "are, at least structurally, significantly detached from nonengineered ones. Except for some common dependencies on sunshine, soils, and sources of water, human-engineered biotic communities and those resulting from nonhuman processes have essentially distinct structures" (Steverson 1994, 81). Wow! This is a good object lesson in the need for environmental philosophers to acquire at least a rudimentary ecological literacy before attacking an ecologically grounded environmental ethic like Leopold's. Ignorance of the degree to which human-engineered environments—from industrial forests and farms to urban factories and tenements—are integrated into and dependent upon the nonengineered ecosystems that they are imposed on and that they are nestled into is the principal source of concern that they may not be sustainable (Ehrlich 1989). Tilled soil is alive with nonengineered microorganisms without whose services plantation forests and food crops would fail. Crops are pollinated by bees and other nonengineered insects, birds, and bats. Steverson (1994, 81) wants us to know that he does not think that "humans are totally disconnected from the functioning of nonengineered biotic communities." However, besides the aforementioned "common dependencies on sunshine, soils, and sources of water," the only interface between "human-engineered" and "nonengineered" communities that he acknowledges is "the harvesting of seafood and exotic [as opposed to indigenous?] wild plants" (Steverson 1994, 82). I don't think further comment from me is needed. Steverson's breathtaking ecological naiveté is self-refuting.

THE LAND ETHIC DYNAMIZED

But *what* environmental duties and obligations does human membership in biotic communities generate? To preserve the integrity, stability, and beauty of the biotic community? These cardinal values of the Leopold land ethic may have to be revised—dynamized, to coin a word—if they are to be ecologically credible. As noted, Leopold was aware of and sensitive to environmental change. He knew that conservation must aim at a moving target. How can we conserve a biota that is dynamic, ever changing, when the very words *conserve* and *preserve*—especially when linked to *integrity* and *stability*—connote arresting change? The key to solving that conundrum is the concept of scale. Scale is a general ecological concept that includes rate as well as scope; that is, the concept of scale is both temporal and spatial. And a review of Leopold's "The Land Ethic" reveals that he had the key, though he may not have been aware of just how multiscalar change in nature actually is.

In 'The Land Pyramid' section of the "The Land Ethic," Leopold (1949, 217) writes, "Evolutionary changes . . . are usually slow and local. Man's invention of tools has enabled him to make changes of unprecedented violence, rapidity, and scope." As noted, Leopold was keenly aware that nature is dynamic, but, under the sway of mid-century equilibrium ecology, he conceived of natural change primarily in evolutionary, not in ecological terms. Nevertheless, scale is equally normative when ecological change is added to evolutionary change, that is, when normal climatic oscillations and patch dynamics are added to normal rates of extinction, hybridization, and speciation.

The scale notion is currently being employed to refine the ecosystem concept in ecology. As also noted, a major problem with the ecosystem concept in ecology is the problem of bounding ecosystems. The field-defining paper by Lindeman (1942) focused on Cedar Bog Lake in Minnesota. The influential work of Herbert Bormann and Gene Likens (1976) focused on Hubbard Brook. Thus, one way that ecosystems came to be defined was to regard them as coextensive with watersheds (Golley 1994). But such a method of defining ecosystems is crude at best and inapplicable at worst to marine ecosystems and to other study areas that are not easily divisible into watersheds. The watershed method of defining ecosystems is also inapplicable to transwatershed problems such as demarcating the Greater Yellowstone Ecosystem or determining the ecosystemic needs and functions of wide-ranging species like bears and wolves.

However, with the development of hierarchy theory in ecology, ecosystems may be defined quite precisely—albeit both abstractly and relativistically—in reference to temporally scaled processes. According to Tim Allen and Tom Hoekstra (1992, 94, 98–100),

Ecosystems are not readily defined by spatial criteria. Ecosystems are more easily conceived as a set of interlinked, differently scaled processes that may be diffuse in space, but easily defined in turnover time. . . . Thus a single ecosystem is itself a hierarchy of differently scaled processes. . . . There are differently scaled processes inside a single ecosystem, as well as sets of differently scaled, more inclusive and less inclusive ecosystems. . . . The degree to which processes of different types express themselves and the length of time they do so, are both ways of describing the uniqueness of particular ecosystems. Much of what we observe in ecosystems is better set in time rather than space. . . . The ecosystem is a much richer concept than just some meteorology, soil, and animals, tacked onto patches of vegetation. . . . Ecosystems can be seen more powerfully as sequences of events rather than things in a place. These events are transformations of matter and energy that occur as the ecosystem does its work. Ecosystems are process-oriented and more easily seen as temporally rather than spatially ordered.

Homo sapiens is a part of nature, "a plain member and citizen" of the "land-community"—*pace* Passmore and Steverson—as Leopold (1949, 204) puts this evolutionary-ecological point. Hence, anthropogenic changes imposed on nature are no less natural than any other. But, since Homo sapiens is a moral species, capable of ethical deliberation and conscientious choice, and evolutionary kinship and biotic community membership add a land ethic to our familiar social ethics, anthropogenic changes may be land-ethically evaluated. But by what norm? The norm of appropriate scale.

Let me first elaborate Leopold's use of the temporal scale of evolutionary change as a norm for evaluating anthropogenic change. Consider the current episode of abrupt, anthropogenic, mass species extinction, which many people, I included, intuitively regard as the most morally reprehensible environmental thing going on today. Episodes of mass extinction have occurred in the past, though none of those has been attributed to a biological agent (Raup 1991; Raup and Sepkoski 1984). Such events are, however, abnormal. Normally, speciation out paces extinction—which is the reason why biodiversity has increased over time. So, what is land-ethically wrong with current anthropogenic species extinction? Species extinction is not unnatural. On the contrary, species extinction—anthropogenic or otherwise—is perfectly natural. But the current *rate* of extinction is wildly abnormal. Does being the first biological agent of a geologically significant mass extinction event in the 3.5-billion-year tenure of life on Planet Earth morally become us Homo sapiens? Doesn't that make a mockery of the self-congratulatory species epithet: the sapient, the wise species of the genus *Homo?*

Earth's climate has warmed up and cooled off in the past. So what's land-ethically wrong with the present episode of anthropogenic global warming? We are a part of nature, so our recent habit of recycling sequestered carbon may be biologically unique, but it is not unnatural. A land-ethical evaluation of the current episode of anthropogenic climate change can, however, be made on the basis of temporal scale and magnitude. We may be causing a big increase of temperature at an unprecedented rate (Schneider 1989). That's what's land-ethically wrong with anthropogenic global warming.

Temporal and spatial scale in combination are key to the evaluation of direct human ecological impact. Violent nonanthropogenic perturbations regularly occur (Pickett and White 1985). Volcanoes bury the biota of whole mountains with lava and ash. Tornadoes rip through forests, levelling trees. Hurricanes erode beaches. Wild fires sweep through forests as well as savannas. Rivers drown floodplains. Droughts dry up lakes and streams. Why therefore are anthropogenic clear cuts, beach developments, hydroelectric impoundments, and the like environmentally unethical? As such, they are not. Once again, it's a question of scale. In general, frequent, intense disturbances, such as tornadoes, occur at small, widely distributed spatial scales. And spatially broadcast disturbances, such as droughts, occur less frequently. And most disturbances at whatever level of intensity and scale are stochastic (random) and chaotic (unpredictable). The problem with anthropogenic perturbations—such as industrial forestry and agriculture, exurban development, drift net fishing, and such— is that they are far more frequent, widespread, and regularly occurring than are nonanthropogenic perturbations.

Stewart Pickett and Richard Ostfeld—exponents of the new natural disturbance/patch dynamics paradigm in ecology, which they dub "the flux of nature" (in contrast to the old "balance of nature")—agree that appropriate scale is the operative norm for ethically appraising anthropogenic ecological perturbation. They note that

the flux of nature is a dangerous metaphor. The metaphor and the underlying ecological paradigm may suggest to the thoughtless and greedy that since flux is a fundamental part of the natural world, any human-caused flux is justifiable. Such an inference is wrong because the flux in the natural world has severe limits. . . . Two characteristics of human-induced flux would suggest that it would be excessive: fast rate and large spatial extent. (Pickett and Ostfeld 1995, 273–74)

Among the abnormally frequent and widespread anthropogenic perturbations that Leopold (1949, 217) himself censures in "The Land Ethic" are the continent-wide elimination of large predators from biotic communities; the ubiquitous substitution of domestic species for wild ones; the ecological homogenization of the planet resulting from the anthropogenic "world-wide pooling of faunas and floras"; the ubiquitous "polluting of waters or obstructing them with dams."

SUMMARY AND CONCLUSION

So . . . let me return, by way of summary and conclusion, to the question that is the title of this essay, Do deconstructive ecology and sociobiology undermine the Leopold land ethic? Or, more generally, do changes in the biological sciences—evolutionary as well as ecological—on which it is erected undermine the Leopold land ethic?

The answer is No.

We remain a part of nature, kin to other species. The Darwinian evolutionary ethical theory on which the land ethic is based has become sociobiology, but, when correctly interpreted, sociobiology does not explain morality away or gainsay the Darwinian correlation, fundamental to the land ethic, between morality and multiple community membership.

Biotic communities may be ever-changing assemblages of organisms of various species that happen to be adapted to the same edaphic and climatic gradients. But that makes them even more analogous to human communities than the old static-holistic representation. Ever-changing, imprecisely bounded communities of human individualists are robust enough to be identifiable entities and to generate special obligations to fellow members and to such communities per se. Why should a communitarian environmental ethic such as Leopold's have to meet any higher standard of community robustness?

The summary moral maxim of the land ethic, however, must be dynamized in light of developments in ecology since the mid-twentieth century. Leopold acknowledged the existence and land-ethical significance of natural environmental change, but seems to have thought of it primarily on a very slow evolutionary temporal scale. But even so, he thereby incorporates the concept of inherent environmental change and the crucial norm of scale into the land ethic. In light of more recent developments in ecology, we can add norms of scale to the land ethic for both climatic and ecological dynamics in land-ethically evaluating anthropogenic changes in nature. One hesitates to edit Leopold's elegant prose, but as a stab at formulating a dynamized summary moral maxim for the land ethic, I will hazard the following: *A thing is right when it tends to disturb the biotic community only at normal spatial and temporal scales. It is wrong when it tends otherwise.*

Tom Birch (personal communication) and Holmes Rolston (personal communication) both point out that this reformulation of the summary moral maxim of the land ethic is incomplete (at best): Must we disturb ecosystems to be doing the right thing? Is it wrong to just leave nature alone? Further, ecological restoration and rehabilitation are good things *and* the more rapidly they are effected the better. I agree with these reservations. Faster is better where ecological restoration and rehabilitation are concerned. And ofttimes—though not always as, for example, in the case of prescribed burns—refraining from any disturbance is the right thing to do to ecosystems. Being incomplete is, however, an endemic problem with summary moral maxims: utilitarianism's summary moral maxim—the greatest happiness for the greatest number—infamously fails to take account of the way individual rights trump aggregate utility; Kant's categorical imperative fails to take account of mitigating circumstances; in the land ethic's original summary moral maxim, "fellow members" of the biotic community are not mentioned. A summary moral maxim has to be general and pithy to be a summary moral maxim. But general and pithy statements are necessarily incomplete.

PART III

MORAL MONISM
VERSUS
MORAL PLURALISM

The Case against Moral Pluralism

WHY MORAL PLURALISM SHOULD ARISE ESPECIALLY IN CONNECTION WITH ENVIRONMENTAL ETHICS

It is not at all accidental—or, now that it is here, surprising—that moral pluralism would pop up in close association with *environmental* ethics. Twenty years ago a few academic philosophers went looking for a moral theory that would ethically enfranchise nonhuman natural entities and/ or nature as a whole. We wanted to articulate, as Tom Regan (1982, 20) so forcefully put it in the third volume of *Environmental Ethics*, the journal, not an ethic for the *use* of the environment, a "management ethic," but "an ethic *of* the environment." Or, put another way, we wanted to develop what I had called a "direct," not an "indirect," "environmental ethic," or what Holmes Rolston III, had still earlier called a "primary," not a "secondary," "ecological ethic"—an ethic, in any case, that situates the environment as the object, not merely the arena, of human moral concern (Callicott 1979; Rolston 1975).

We wanted to bring the natural environment within the purview of ethics, to be sure, but we also wanted to keep human well-being and the human social fabric in sharp moral focus. Between lie a spectrum of concerns—the welfare of future people, of domestic animals, and so on—

neglected in traditional Western moral theories that many other philosophers also felt compelled, either by novel circumstances (modern technology) or by the dialectic of rapidly evolving moral sensibility (civil rights, followed by women's liberation, followed by universal human rights), to try to bring within the reach of ethical theory. By working with *one* ethical theory, chosen to accommodate our special concern for the environment, how can we also account for our traditional interpersonal responsibilities and social duties, accommodate all these intermediate new moral concerns to boot, and then order and mutually reconcile the whole spectrum of traditional and novel ethical domains?

Christopher Stone, one of the founders of environmental ethics and an early architect of the extensionist enterprise, now claims, in *Earth and Other Ethics: The Case for Moral Pluralism*, that we cannot. Earth and other ethical requirements simply stretch any given moral theory to the breaking point. One thus seems confronted with two choices: moral cynicism or moral pluralism. We can either give in to moral overload and theoretical burn out, or pick up the pieces, one by one, and work theoretically with each separately. I am not attracted to either alternative and propose a third in the last section of this discussion.

In a précis of his book, published in *Environmental Ethics*, the journal, Stone (1988, 139) laments that environmental ethics has "reached a plateau. The signs include a tendency to reiterate the well-worn 'need' for an environmental ethics 'whose time has come' and then work over the increasingly familiar themes about the restricted reach of mainstream theories, et cetera." Stone (1988, 140) claims to draw this conclusion from a survey of the first ten volumes of *Environmental Ethics*, the journal (which he modestly declines to "presume to summarize"), and allied monographs that appeared during the same decade—1979–89. But both his book and spin-off article give the lie to that claim. The "need" for an environmental ethic was in fact the burden of the 1970s generation of philosophical environmental literature (Goodpaster 1978; Rolston 1975; Routley 1973). Over the 1980s and 1990s, thanks in large measure to the forum for exploration and critical discussion—*Environmental Ethics*, the journal—provided by Eugene C. Hargrove, environmental philosophers have actually developed an impressive array of fairly well worked out theories of environmental ethics (Attfield 1983; Callicott 1989; Rolston 1988; Sagoff 1988; Taylor 1986). State-of-the-art environmental ethics also exhibits lateral theoretical diversity, in other words, as each theoretician attempts his or her own vertical integration of multiple moral spheres. It is partly our success in creating a wide variety of compelling, but distinct and mutually inconsistent, environmental ethical systems—however great their tendency may be to weaken when asked to cover all our moral concerns— that has resulted in an embarrassment of riches, ripe for pluralist plucking.

In any case, there now exists a fairly wide selection of nonanthropocentric ethical theories, each of which, proclaim its proponents, is superior to all the others. Though many distinct voices may be heard in the environmental ethics choir, most are improvising on one or another familiar melody.

A neo-Kantian family of environmental ethics (united by conation as a criterion for moral considerability) seems to be attracting more converts as time goes on. The biocentrism of Paul Taylor (1981, 1986) is the purest neoclassical exemplar of this type. But more baroque variations on the conation theme have been set out by Robin Attfield (1981, 1983) and Holmes Rolston (1988). Contemporary conativism in environmental ethics is traceable to a loose remark made by Joel Feinberg (1974, 49–50): "A mere thing . . . has no good of its own. The explanation of that fact, I suspect, consists in the fact that mere things have no conative life: no conscious wishes, desires, and hopes; or urges and impulses; or unconscious drives, aims, and goals; or latent tendencies, direction of growth, and natural fulfillments. Interests must be compounded somehow out of conations; hence mere things have no interests." The implication, clearly, is that a minimally conative life—absent conscious wishes, desires, hopes, urges, and impulses, but possessing latent tendencies, directions of growth, and natural fulfillments—has a good of its own. Tom Regan (1976) toyed with the theoretical possibilities for environmental ethics inadvertently provided by Feinberg, but eventually gave up on its having conations as a sufficient condition for something to have a good of its own in favor of conscious wishes, desires, hopes, urges, and impulses, summed up in his concept of "subject-of-a-life" (Regan 1983). Kenneth Goodpaster (1978), next picked up on the idea, but Paul W. Taylor (1981, 1986) brought Feinberg's offhand remark to its full fruition—inventing, parallel to Regan's notion of a subject-of-a-life, the notion of a teleological-center-of-a-life. The earlier work of Rolston (1975) was theoretically promiscuous, in my opinion, but has, in *Environmental Ethics*, the book, settled into a stable relationship with conativism. Although Rolston (1988) frequently quotes Aldo Leopold and shares certain temperamental affinities with the great American conservationist, the immediate intellectual ancestor of contemporary conativism is the reverence-for-life ethic of Albert Schweitzer (1923). I discuss more fully the intellectual affinities between Schweitzer and the conativists in contemporary environmental ethics elsewhere (Callicott 1984, and here in chapter 12).

A second family of environmental ethics (united by "a more tender and widely diffused" altruism, to quote Darwin, with intellectual roots in Hume) has sprung, in fact, from the Aldo Leopold land ethic. I have been the most vocal champion of this theoretical approach, but fellow travellers include Edward O. Wilson (1984), William Godfrey-Smith (1980), and Richard Sylvan and Val Plumwood (Routley and Routley 1980).

A third family—centered upon Self- (with a capital *S*) realization, based upon the unity between self and world suggested by ecology—has been advocated by the more philosophical exponents of Deep Ecology (Fox 1990; Mathews 1988; Naess 1987).

Now that we have a good feel for the lay of the theoretical land, I assumed—before Stone came along with his powerful and seductive case for moral pluralism—that we could begin to work toward the creation of an intellectual federation and try to put an end to the balkanization of nonanthropocentric moral philosophy. I already took a step in that direction. In "Animal Liberation: A Triangular Affair," I contemptuously dismissed the moral enfranchisement of *individual* animals qua individuals, because the ecocentric ethic adumbrated by Leopold—that had at first inspired me, and that I was attempting rigorously to ground—posited the integrity, stability, and beauty of the biotic *community* as the ultimate measure of the rightness and wrongness of human actions (Callicott 1980). Although I now wince at its stridency when I reread "Triangular Affair" and wish that I were not so closely identified with this particular piece of work, that essay did serve to delineate sharply the theoretical differences between animal welfare ethics and one approach—ecocentrism, as it has come to be called—to a primary or direct environmental ethic (Callicott 1980). Personally, however, I am not unmoved by the pain and suffering of individual sentient animals and believe that we ought to extend them moral considerability, if not rights. So I tried to effect a reconciliation between animal welfare ethics and environmental ethics with a little palinode entitled "Animal Liberation and Environmental Ethics: Back Together Again," which I held out as an olive branch to our colleagues interested primarily in the study of ethics and individual animals (Callicott 1988). But in that paper I didn't simply say, "well, what the heck, where animals are concerned, I'll go with Singer (or Regan), but you guys meet me half way and agree to go with me (or Rolston) on species and ecosystems." Rather, I tried to find a coherent theory that would provide at once for the moral considerability of individual animals—differently "textured," incidentally, for domestic animals, on the one hand, and for wild animals on the other—*and* for species and ecosystems. ("Texture" is one of the many quasi-technical terms in Stone's wonderfully rich and creative book. I hope that I have used it correctly here.)

In "Triangular Affair" I even argued that the worth of individual *human* beings must, *if* one acceded to a demand for ruthless consistency, be measured against Leopold's holistic summum bonum, and suggested that its degree of misanthropy might be the litmus test of whether a stance or policy was in agreement with the land ethic. I never actually endorsed such a position. It is obnoxious and untenable. And I now no longer think that misanthropic prescriptions can be deduced from the Leopold land ethic, as I have subsequently explained (Callicott 1986, 1987; and here in chapter 4). I certainly feel that we have duties and obligations to fellow humans (and to humanity as a whole) that supersede the land ethic, although I have by no means abandoned the land ethic (chapter 4). Before Stone, I just *assumed* that a complete environmental ethic would begin with a carefully chosen theory of interpersonal and human social ethics, and unite animal welfare and environmental ethics under the same theoretical umbrella. I still think that this is the appropriate way to proceed, but Stone has offered an easy and appealing alternative that demands a thoughtful reply.

Moral pluralism, crudely characterized—I hope not crudely caricatured—invites us, instead, to adopt one theory to steer a course in our relations with friends and neighbors, another to define our obligations to fellow citizens, a third to clarify our duties to more distantly related people, a fourth to express the concern we feel for future generations, a fifth to govern our relationship with nonhuman animals, a sixth to bring plants within the purview of morals, a seventh to tell us how to treat the elemental environment, an eighth to cover species, ecosystems, and other environmental collectives, and perhaps a ninth to explain our obligations to the planet,

Gaia, as a whole and organically unified living thing. Stone (1987, 118) himself provides an illustration of a pluralist posture in the following image:

The Moral Pluralist holds that a public representative, a senator, for example,
might rightly embrace utilitarianism when it comes to legislating a rule for social
conduct (say, in deciding what sort of toxic waste program to establish). Yet, this
same representative need not be principally utilitarian, nor even a consequentialist
of any style, in arranging his personal affairs among kin or friends, or deciding
whether it is right to poke out the eyes of pigeons. And surely being committed
to utilitarianism as a basis for choosing legislation does not entail judging a person's
character solely by reference to whether, on balance, he advances the greatest
good for the greatest number of persons.

THOSE WHO ADVOCATE PLURALISM IN ENVIRONMENTAL ETHICS AND THOSE WHO DON'T

Since environmental ethics so invites pluralist parsing, and since Christopher Stone has now put together such a frank, strong, and eminently
reasonable case for moral pluralism, one wonders if a pluralistic turn can
be detected in the earlier unconventional ethics literature.

In "Back Together Again" I gave critical attention to the plea of Mary
Anne Warren (1983) for moral pluralism published in the early 1980s
(Callicott 1988). Warren argues that animals, like human beings, have
rights. But she also argues that animals do not enjoy the same rights as
human beings and, *pace* Regan, that the rights of animals do not equal
human rights. Animal rights and human rights are grounded in different
metaphysics of morals. Human beings have "strong" rights because we are
autonomous, à la Kant (1785). Animals have "weaker rights" because they
are sentient, à la Bentham (1823) and Singer (1977). Plant liberation, à la
Paul Taylor (1986), had not been vociferously championed or well formulated when Warren was writing, and so she has nothing specifically to
say about the moral entitlements of individual living, but merely conative,
beings. A holistic environmental ethic, Warren (1983) suggests, rests upon
still other foundations—the instrumental value of "natural resources" to
us and to future generations, à la Gifford Pinchot (1947), and the "intrinsic value" we may intuitively find in species, "mountains, oceans, and the
like," à la Aldo Leopold (1949).

Mary Anne Warren doesn't come right out and say that she is advocating moral pluralism, but that's what her eclectic program amounts to. In "Back Together Again" I thought that it was enough simply to point out that Warren's approach was eclectic and pluralistic, in order to set it aside and get on with the serious business of searching for the Holy Grail of environmental ethics—the coherent, inclusive supertheory (Callicott 1988).

Although neither does he actually so label his posture, pluralism, nevertheless, is also detectable in Eugene C. Hargrove's metaethical discussion of the role of rules in ethical decision making. In light of recently emerged "moral perceptions" respecting animals and the environment, writes Hargrove, "moral philosophers will have to abandon for the most part the search for a rational set of universal principles which moral agents can mechanically follow" (1985, 30). (Here Hargrove, incidentally, anticipates Stone's comparison of moral theorizing to map making.) Hargrove, in another conceit (that Stone seems not to have thought of but might find useful), suggests that we understand moral rules to be somewhat like nonconstitutive chess rules—not the rules of the game that inflexibly govern the movement of the pieces, but the ad hoc rules for effective play in various situations. According to Hargrove (1985, 32), in ethics as in chess,

the body of rules has no ultimate unifying principle, the principles themselves are not logically related to one another (the omission of one or the addition of another in no way affects the group as whole), they are not organized in any meaningful hierarchy, . . . and there are innumerable cases which can be brought forward with regard to each of them in which following the proper rule leads to disaster in a board [or, analogously, in a real-life] situation.

Almost simultaneously with Stone's extensive case for moral pluralism, Andrew Brennan (1988) and Peter Wenz (1988) have expressly advocated "ethical polymorphism" and a "pluralistic theory" of environmental ethics, respectively. Brennan (1988, 186) remarks that "an ethic by which to live is not to be found by adopting one fundamental, substantive principle relative to which all our deliberations are to be resolved. Instead we are prey to numerous different kinds of consideration originating from different directions, many of them with a good claim to be ethical ones."

In *Thinking About Nature*, Brennan (1988) goes on to rummage through a few of these different kinds of consideration, showering most of his attention on the competing claims of environmental individualism and environmental holism to which our ethical intuitions are prey. In the introduction to *Environmental Justice*, Wenz (1988) tells how as a boy he and his friend Billy used to divide a pizza. One cut it in half and the other chose first. Wenz often returns to this childhood image of distributive justice throughout his discussion. For Wenz, the environment, it seems, is a big pizza. The ethical question is how to divide it equitably among human consumers. In any case, Wenz, after glossing the same (by now familiar) biocentric (Taylorian) and ecocentric (Callicottian) theories, as something of an afterthought at the end of an elaborate review of conventional theories of justice and an evaluation of the direction they each give for equitably dividing the environmental pie, feels less inclined to settle on one best approach than to float them all at once:

We found . . . that none of the above theories of justice was flexible enough to accommodate all of our considered views about how particular matters of environmental justice should be decided. . . . But because each theory and many of the principles contained in each theory seem reasonable when applied to certain kinds of cases, they should not be abandoned entirely. They should be modified and blended to form an all embracing pluralistic theory. A theory is pluralistic when it contains a variety of principles that cannot be reduced to or derived from a single master principle. (Wenz 1988, 310)

Wenz is aware that the phrase "pluralistic theory" may seem to be an oxymoron to some philosophers. Nor does he do more than name it; no actual pluralistic *theory* is developed in *Environmental Justice*. In his review of *Earth and Other Ethics*, Gary Varner (1988, 264) underscores, correctly I think, "the fundamental metaethical challenge" to environmental ethics posed by Stone. In casting about for harbingers of pluralism, Varner (1988), quite understandably, completely overlooks Warren's essay—one small, dated item in a literature that is growing exponentially—and Hargrove's, which is about ethics in general, not environmental and animal welfare ethics specifically. Wenz's and Brennan's books, on the other hand, could not have come to his attention before his review of Stone was all but set in stone. Varner does find, incorrectly I think, intimations of pluralism in the work (respectively) of one well-known environmental philosopher and in that of one minor luminary. "There are hints," Varner (1988, 264) writes,

—but still only hints—of pluralism emerging in recent work by Paul Taylor and Baird Callicott. In *Respect for Nature*, Taylor stresses that environmental ethics rests on very different foundations than human ethics, and that it accordingly embodies very different principles. In his recent "Search for an Environmental Ethic," Callicott similarly abandons the vitriolic rhetoric of his "Triangular Affair" article and stresses that Leopold characterizes the land ethic as an accretion that supplements, rather than replaces, previous ethics.

How accurately my work may be characterized as pluralistic may be gathered from this essay. As to Paul Taylor, his theory strikes me as about as clear a case of what Stone calls moral monism as any theory of environmental ethics could possibly be. While Taylor (1986) grants moral rights to human teleological-centers-of-life and withholds them from nonhuman teleological-centers-of-life, he insists that, their rights notwithstanding, the former are in no way morally superior to the latter and that *all* teleological-centers-of-life are of *equal* inherent worth.

Basically, Taylor, as Bryan Norton (1987) notes, slips conation into the slot reason fills in Kant's moral philosophy. To be sure, Taylor, a neo-Kantian, cannot bring himself to completely renounce the classical Kantian emphasis on special respect for persons and sometimes speaks of "both systems of ethics"—respect for persons and respect for nature—as if he were juggling two independent principles. But Taylor's moral theory is monistic, as Wenz (1988) clearly recognizes. When he considers conflicts of interest, Taylor does not treat respect for persons and respect for nature as two mutually incommensurable systems of ethics. For Taylor (1986, 259), "the good of other species and the good of humans make claims that must equally be taken into consideration." It's just that human beings, as self-conscious and morally autonomous beings, have certain goods that other teleological-centers-of-life lack. Thus, while it may be contrary to a tree's good to cut it down, it is not contrary to a tree's good, as it is to a human being's, to be lied to or to be fenced in. Respect for persons (and associated human rights) takes into account the peculiar, but not better-making, endowment of human beings in comparison with other forms of life.

Taylor does not, in other words, resort to other theories than his basic biocentrism in order to guarantee that we human beings (at least we genteel, culturally rich, but materially modest human beings) can go on living the lives to which we have grown accustomed. He tries to make things come out right—so that we can eat vegetables, and build wooden houses, and generally get on with our human projects (at least our more refined, low-impact human projects)—by means of an elaborate set of hedges enabling us consumptively to use our fellow entelechies within the limits of his extremely broad egalitarian theory. To show that Taylor's attempt to deal, under the auspices of a single theory, with all our considered moral sensibilities—from respect for human rights to the moral enfranchisement of individual plants—collapses under the load, Wenz (1988) employs, very effectively in my opinion, a technique of philosophical refutation delightfully satirized by Stone (1987, 117): He "volleys hypothetical quandaries onto" Taylor that his "principles cannot handle."

Varner might more profitably have looked into Holmes Rolston's theory of environmental ethics for "hints" of pluralism. In *Environmental Ethics,* the book, Rolston devotes a chapter each to the intrinsic value of, and corresponding duties owed, "higher animals," "organisms," "species," and "ecosystems." Along the way he finds intrinsic value in evolutionary *processes*—going all the way back to the Big Bang. Rolston does not strive for unambiguous clarity and clean, crisp definitions, as Taylor does. So, it may seem that in each of these chapters he develops independent arguments—not all of which, even within each chapter, are univocal—for the value of each of these natural things. But I think that most of his arguments for intrinsic value in nature cluster around a central, pivotal notion—conation, once again. Organisms have, each of them, a telos, Rolston reminds us—unconscious drives and aims, or (at least) latent tendencies, directions of growth, and natural fulfillments. His defense of their intrinsic value seems to settle upon the fact that organisms, even unconscious organisms, compete for nutrients and a place in the sun, and defend their own lives—in an astonishing variety of ingenious ways. They have, thus, a good of their own. Sentient organisms are aware of their strivings, and feel urges and impulses, some more keenly than others; and we human organisms are *self*-aware, conscious of ourselves as beings with wishes, desires, hopes, and goals. Though Taylor does not, Rolston assigns a value bonus to consciousness and a double bonus to self-consciousness which he adds on to the value base constituted by conation.

From this value epicenter, conation, Rolston hoes the row the other way. Each organism, Rolston (1988, 143) says, in a characteristic argument by verbal trope, represents—i.e., "re-presents"—its species. Each struggles, not only to survive and flourish, but also to reproduce. Each is a token of its type. Its type is indeed its telos, just as Aristotle would have it. Each strives to be "good-of-its-kind" and to "defend its own kind of good" (Rolston 1988, 101). Hence, each kind—each species—is intrinsically valuable, even though species are holistic entities which are not conative per se. Ecosystems, similarly, are the matrix which give birth to the myriad intrinsically valuable kinds. Rolston says that ecosystems and evolutionary processes are "projective." They do not themselves possess *teloi* (Rolston observes with strict consistency the ateleological conventions of evolutionary biology) but they have, as we see, "projected," thrown up, a good many ordered systems and organized entities. The quasi-conative character of ecosystems and evolutionary processes earns them a value dividend in Rolston's theory of environmental ethics.

So Rolston, as it turns out, is not really a pluralist after all. One begins to wonder, then, why our best, most systematic and thoroughgoing environmental philosophers cling so desperately to moral monism? One can find scattered outbreaks of pluralism in the literature, but so far pluralism has not become epidemic. Stone, a lawyer, makes moral pluralism seem so reasonable, and its opposite a silly and parochial preoccupation. Yet Taylor and Rolston have mounted veritably epic efforts to save the philosophical integrities of their respective systems. Taylor will save his biocentrism at the cost of patent sophistries (which Wenz revels in exposing) and Rolston can save his only by resorting to ambiguity and courting equivocation. Why? Why don't we all just become merry moral pluralists? I take that to be the metaethical challenge that Varner says that Stone has thrown down.

MORAL PLURALISM'S ACHILLES HEEL: THE HARD CHOICE BETWEEN CONTRADICTORY INDICATIONS

Wenz (1988, 313), pluralist convert though he may have become, clearly articulates one reason to beware its siren lure: "Without a single master principle in the background, what is to be done . . . when one of the independent principles in the pluralistic theory requires a course of action different from and incompatible with the course of action required by one of the other independent principles . . . ? In this kind of situation, the theory yields either no recommended course of action or contradictory recommendations."

Consistency is not just a shrine before which philosophers worship. There is a reason for wanting consistency, ensured by organization around or derivation from a "master principle," among one's practical precepts. Attempting to *act* upon inconsistent or mutually contradictory ethical principles results in frustration of action altogether or in actions that are either incoherent or mutually cancelling.

Stone, of course, has thought of this. It is worth noting, he points out, that a multiplicity of independent principles might just as well all converge on a single course of action. The practical necessity of such a plurally mandated course of action would be reinforced, rather than frustrated or negated. *Earth and Other Ethics* is wonderfully creative, not only in its advocacy of the idea of pluralistic ethics, but in working out methods for solving ethical conundrums drawing upon the resources of a variety of moral systems. Stone asks us to think of various maps of a single territory. One map might show human population distribution, another land use patterns, a third the vegetation types, a fourth contours, and so on. If we regard a situation in which we must do something as the "territory" and various theories as the "maps" (or "planes," as Stone later calls them), we may overlay, as it were, the "planes"/"maps" and see if they indicate a clear path of action. Why should we expect several overlays to yield interference patterns more usually than sympathetic vibrations?

Still, what do we do when we put all our systems down, each "plane" (theory) layered over the "territory" (the actual or hypothetical moral quandary in which we find ourselves), and the indications are inconsistent or contradictory? The actual case of a bison trapped in the frozen Yellowstone River, a case that Stone fully develops in his book, serves as a good example. Animal welfare ethics indicate that we ought to try to save individual animals from unnecessary pain, suffering, and eventual death, while ecocentric environmental ethics indicates that we ought to let bison (and all the other nonhuman members of the biotic community) alone to struggle for their lives and live and pass their tested genes on to the next generation or die and become food for the carrion eaters. Stone tells us what happened to this particular bison on this particular occasion, and how the moral theories that various people held affected their actions and inactions, but he never tells us what these people ought to have done or not done for the animal.

One problem with moral pluralism, noticed by Hargrove—but that neither Wenz nor Stone directly address—is that it invites a kind of moral promiscuity. Hargrove (1985, 26) notes a potential "fear that the open form in which decisions naturally and normally take place will allow un-scrupulous or weak moral agents to waiver and [choose] principles to their own immoral advantage." With a variety of theories at our disposal, each indicating different, inconsistent, or contradictory courses of action, we may be tempted to espouse the one that seems most convenient or self-serving in the circumstances.

If Stone can, in a charming and friendly way, tweak us philosophers about our foibles, then turnabout is fair play. Lawyers are notoriously adversarial. They are trained to use scholarship and logic, not to seek the truth, or implement justice, but to represent a client or win a case—re-gardless of where the truth and the right lies. The overall structure of *Earth and Other Ethics* does not give one much comfort about the worry that moral pluralism might provide a sophisticated scoundrel with a bag of tricks to rationalize her convenience or self-interest—rather than a box of tools to work her way through the moral complexities of life in the late twentieth and early twenty-first centuries.

In the 1970s, Stone began with a desideratum—how *legally* to en-franchise "non-persons," as he calls everything from ships and corporations to wild rivers and endangered species. Extend them (limited) legal rights, operationally defined, was his answer in *Should Trees Have Standing?* (Stone 1974). Since then the courts have considerably liberalized standing, but "standing . . . does nothing but get you through the courthouse door" (Stone 1987, 10). The law can provide all sorts of legal fictions and de-vices for the legal considerateness of nonpersons. That's no problem. But once environmentalists or animal liberationists get a hearing for their "wards," Stone asks, then how do they go about "justifying" legal accom-modation and how can they prevail against competing interests? (Stone 1987, 42). That leads Stone from the realm of law to the realm of ethics. In other words, like a lawyer, he begins with a spectrum of practical ends in view—leaving some resources and wilderness for the use and enjoy-ment of future generations, protecting animals from pointless or needless suffering, saving species, etc.—and then looks for a spectrum of persua-sive theories, as means, to secure those ends. And finally, the apparent hopelessness of ordering that very caboodle of practical ends and kit of theoretical means with a single comprehensive moral philosophy leads him on to his plea for pluralism and to challenge the very impetus to univocal theory construction.

To the worry that moral pluralism invites moral promiscuity, had Stone expressly confronted it, he might have replied, more or less as Hargrove does, that all moral philosophy presupposes persons of good will. Pluralism may supply a scoundrel with another sort of rationalization for ducking her responsibilities, but moral philosophy generally—monistic no less than pluralistic—is underdeterminate and, in the hands of a skilled, but unscrupulous, advocate can be made to justify all manner of action or inaction. (Didn't lesser Nazi war criminals at their Nüremberg trials hide behind Kant's noble notions of apodictic duty?) One might argue, by parity of reasoning, that the ethical lives of sincere persons of good will are proportionately enriched and empowered by moral pluralism, thus offsetting the invitation to abuse that pluralism inadvertently affords persons of less noble character.

Granted that moral pluralists may be sincere persons of good will, how *do* they decide between the inconsistent or contradictory indications of their several theories? Stone, of course, has thought about this too. He suggests we bring to bear a "lexical" procedure for reaching a decision. *Lexical*, in this context, is a euphemism for hierarchical ordering—prioritizing, if you will. Baldly put, what Stone suggests is this: We take our many moral "maps," "planes," and "frameworks" (our polyglot ethical systems or theories), lay them out over the "territory" (the problem, quandary, or conundrum) and, if they jibe, fine. If they don't, then we prioritize them.

But how? For pluralists there's no "master principle," no supertheory, by definition. His back against the wall, Stone frankly endorses appeal to what Regan (1983) calls "considered intuition," and to cultivated moral tastes, sensibilities, feelings, and "moral faculties." Wenz (1988) similarly, asks us to use unspecified "good judgment"; while Hargrove (1985), for his part, is simply willing to live with more of a mess than Stone or Wenz.

But what does that really tell us? When push comes to shove, how do we choose between theory A with its recommended course of action a, B with b, and C with c? Writes Stone (1987, 256),

[W]hen we turn to the selection of planes—what things [people, animals, plants, species], as bundled in what governance [utility-maximizing, person-respecting], count—we are removed to another jurisdiction in which our minds operate less by appeals to consistency than provocations of irony and humor. Here the dynamic involves the demonstration of buried contradictions in our lives, rather than of inconsistency among our ideas. Emotion has a more legitimate rein (or reign); suppressed feeling and insight are released and mobilized . . . [we] are less under the sway of the stuff we academics do than of literature, folk songs, war, art, landscape, and poetry. . . . Poetry and literature, obviously, are high forms of intellect; but rather than to derive "truths," they make them manifest.

The final resolution of the intractable dilemmas that will inevitably confront the moral pluralist, Stone (1987, 256) tells us, lies in "selecting a version of the world." Stone points in his final pages, in other words, to metaphysics. To "buy into" a "plane"—a set of ethically enfranchised entities (a "moral ontology"), as Stone revealingly calls such a set, and a "governance" (how exactly those entities are endowed with rights or equal consideration of interests, respect, or whatever)—is to buy into a worldview. When we are forced to choose between "planes," we make a metaphysical commitment as well as a moral choice.

But then the real work, the ethical *Grundlegung* should commence anew. We might think of our hard moral choices (in my opinion misleadingly mystified by Stone with his talk about intuition, literature, art, irony, humor, and such) as actually revelatory of the deeper—but because deeper less fully conscious—structures of our thinking. The task then becomes to call these organizing concepts up on the screen—to articulate in a more self-conscious and deliberate way the worldview, the metaphysics, which has rationally (we hope), but subconsciously, arbitrated among the divers moral "maps." However, once we have carried through on that project, the many "maps," and the whole apparatus of moral pluralism, become otiose. Some of the "maps" will be seen to assume untenable versions of the world or versions of human nature and we may readily consign them to the historical rubbish heap—along with "maps" to ferret out and punish blasphemy and hunt down and burn witches, which involve concepts like God's literal word and efficacious satanic rites (and verses), and other notions belonging to a version of the world that centuries of experience and critical thinking have, let's face it, invalidated.

Stone (1987, 256) seems to think, however, that such metaphysical questions lie beyond philosophical competence: "It is just that these 'big' questions lie outside the province of academic and legal philosophy, which are more at home working *within* or talking *about* planes." Here, finally, is the crux of what I think is wrong with moral pluralism. It severs ethical theory from moral philosophy, from the metaphysical foundations in which ethical theory is, whether we are conscious of it or not, grounded.

THE CASE FOR A UNIFIED MORAL PHILOSOPHY

Can ethics be so severed from moral philosophy, the metaphysical ground-work of ethical theories? The Medieval worldview seems to most latter-day Moderns to be a quaint anachronism and its associated moral "maps" to be curious—when they are not sinister—relics of a bygone mentality. But the Modern worldview is itself rapidly becoming history. How, there-fore, can we reject, out of hand, condemnations and death sentences for "blasphemy," witch hunts, and book burnings and continue uncritically to ascribe, in a pluralistic spirit, to equally—though more recently—ob-solete eighteenth-century moral theories like hedonic utilitarianism or "pure reason" Kantianism?

Why, more pointedly, we may ask, has Stone borrowed his "maps" and "planes" from the moral philosophies of Bentham, Mill, Kant, and other Modern philosophers, and from those of Schweitzer, Singer, Leopold, Taylor, and other contemporary philosophers, but neglected to borrow with equal alacrity from Medieval philosophers like St. Thomas, and St. Augustine, and ancient philosophers like Plato and Aristotle? Or, why do we not find "maps" and "planes" featured in *Earth and Other Ethics* taken from the Old Testament—say the Mosaic Decalogue—or from the Ko-ran? The answer is, I suggest, that Stone and most of us who are thought-ful enough to worry about the human treatment of whales, rain forests, and the ozone zone, do not buy into divine revelation of moral com-mandments or the independent existence of the Good (with a capital "G")—concepts that are among the various metaphysical background as-sumptions of Aquinas, Augustine, Plato, Aristotle, the late Ayatollah Ruhollah Khomeini, and the Reverend Jerry Falwell.

But then each of the Modern ethical systems that Stone so deftly employs in his pluralistic ethical tool kit also comes wrapped in its own metaphysical vestments. Consider the threadbare metaphysical cloth from which classical utilitarianism is cut. Utilitarianism assumes a radical individualism or rank social atomism completely at odds with the relational sense of self that is consistent with a more fully informed evolutionary and ecological understanding of terrestrial and human nature and with feminism. Bentham (1823, 12) could not have more clearly revealed his reductive assumptions when he wrote, "the community is a fictitious body composed of the individual persons who are considered as constituting as it were its members. The interest of the community then is what?—the sum of the interests of the several members who compose it."

Bentham, the founder of utilitarianism, also invests intrinsic value and disvalue exclusively in psychological experiences—pleasure and pain, in all their protean forms. Such a psychologized understanding of good and evil is historically linked with, if it does not literally follow from, the radical Cartesian split, ubiquitous in Modern philosophy, between subject and object, and the resulting alienation of the self from the "external world"—which includes our own bodies. "Sense data" and sensations are, from the prevailing Modern point of view, the nearest—and hence the dearest—realities. To employ Stone's several utilitarian "planes," therefore, involves buying into a vision of human (and animal) nature in which isolated egos (*subjects*-of-a-life) are imprisoned within alien mechanical objects (their bodies) and look fearfully out on a foreign "external world." The only "things" to which good and evil can attach, given such a worldview, are, naturally, positive and negative private *subjective* psychological states.

To adopt Kant's moral theory is to buy into a vintage European Enlightenment philosophy of human nature in which Reason (with a capital "R") constitutes the essence of "man," somewhat in the way that the "image of God" constitutes the essence of "man" in the biblical conception of human nature. It is revealing, I think, to note that Kant himself never considers the "marginal cases," which animal welfare ethicists routinely volley onto contemporary orthodox Kantians. He never seems to notice, in other words, that, by his principles, subrational human beings such as infants, imbeciles, and the senile would also be "mere things" (as he characterizes sentient animals lacking reason) and might be treated accordingly. That's not because Kant didn't think his theory through, but because he understood reason to be less an organic function or capacity than a kind of philosophically sanitized, Enlightenment equivalent of the *imago dei* inhabiting all human beings, quite irrespective of their functional rationality.

Now let's return once more to Stone's senator, a model moral pluralist, and consider a variation on Stone's description of her agile ethical experience. After "embracing utilitarianism" on a floor vote in the morning "deciding what sort of toxic waste program to establish," her staff reminds her that in the afternoon a vote will be taken on a Forest Service plan to "road" the Gila wilderness. Our senator has read *A Sand County Almanac* and added the land ethic to her moral repertoire. So, having given utilitarianism a turn in the morning, embracing the land ethic in the afternoon, she votes against the Forest Service. That means that over lunch she has blithely stepped out of the atomized, mechanical, and dualistic view of nature and human nature inspiring utilitarianism and into the organic, internally related, holistic view of nature and human nature animating the land ethic—a worldview in which human beings are not privatized pleasure-loving, preference-satisfying egos, but integrated plain members and citizens of social and biotic communities. Then, upon leaving the Capitol, she remembers that she has promised to help her son write a school essay that evening. So, tired though she may be with handling the public business all day long, during dinner she slips into a Kantian mode, and considers that a promise is a promise, and that (as Stone represents it at least) one should not use utilitarian cost-benefit analyses appropriate to funding toxic waste programs in deciding what to do in family affairs. So, thus buying into a Prussian view of ironclad categorical, apodictic imperatives, grounded in metaphysical Reason, she works past her bedtime editing her son's essay, "How I Spent My Summer Vacation."

Moral pluralism, in short, implies metaphysical musical chairs. I think, however, that we human beings deeply need and mightily strive for consistency, coherency, and closure in our personal and shared outlook on the world and on ourselves in relation to the world and to one another. Stone (1987, 256) is skeptical that Truth, with a capital "T," may be had in matters metaphysical: "No simple formula about truth is available when we ascend to the level of selecting a version of the world for scientific purposes, that is in deciding whether and in what form to posit matter, space, energy, time, and their relationships." I am no more sanguine than he, but I do think that we can expect to generate comprehensive conceptual systems which fully embrace our ever-growing body of empirical knowledge, scientific theory, and self-discovery. Although in many ways *Earth and Other Ethics* is a much better book than *Should Trees Have Standing?*, in the years between *Trees* and *Earth* Stone seems to have abandoned a project that I think it is more important now than ever to try to advance. In the earlier book he wrote,

The time may be on hand when these sentiments, and the early stirrings of the law, can be coalesced into a radical new theory or myth—felt as well as intellectualized—of man's relationships to the rest of nature. I do not mean "myth" in the demeaning sense of the term, but in the sense in which, at different times in history, our social "facts" and relationships have been comprehended and integrated by reference to the "myths" that we are co-signers of a social contract, that the Pope is God's agent, and that all men are created equal. . . . What is needed is a [new] myth that can fit our growing body of knowledge of geophysics, biology, and the cosmos. In this vein, I do not think it too remote that we may come to regard the Earth, as some have suggested, as one organism, of which mankind is a functional part—the mind, perhaps: different from the rest of nature, but different from the rest of nature as a man's brain is from his lungs. (Stone 1974, 51–52)

THE DISTURBING CONNECTION BETWEEN MORAL PLURALISM AND DECONSTRUCTIVE POSTMODERNISM

Absent such a comprehensive model to focus and order our competing moral concerns, we are left with kaleidoscopic and random, albeit enriched, moral lives—individually. Collectively, socially, we are left with irreconcilable factional disputes. Stone's happy-go-lucky moral pluralism, culturally generalized and interpreted, is allied with—if not equivalent to—deconstructive postModernism. Absent a comprehensive and culturally shared new myth, we are left with plural points of view, perspectives, multiple outlooks—each of which has an equal claim on "truth."

The "postmodern turn" in environmental philosophy has recently been taken by Jim Cheney (1989a, 1989b). Joining other ecofeminists running out to bark at Deep Ecology, Cheney snaps at Deep Ecology's "totalizing" vision—a vision not unlike Stone's regrettably abandoned one—which attempts to "colonize" other outlooks. By "totalizing," Cheney seems to mean comprehensive. By "colonizing" he seems to mean a claim to be the best available. Cheney employs these neologisms repeatedly and they have the distinct ring of an argot or cant. This is the closest Cheney (1989b, 310) comes to defining them: "One form that understanding can take is that of the construction of a totalizing theory designed to assimilate the other into a unifying conceptual framework. . . . One of the functions of a totalizing theory is to rationalize the 'colonizing' of the other, the control of the other by means of control over naming." A metaphysical system that tries to embrace our ever-expanding human experience, to comprehend it, *and* to make sense of it, is part of the problem, Cheney thinks, not the solution. In any case, comprehensive system building, Cheney also seems to think, is a decidedly Modern preoccupation. With the "demise of modernism" there has occurred a "shattering into a world of difference, the postmodern world" (Cheney 1989b, 302).

"Postmodernism" is a term associated with two very different things. One we might call "constructive" postModernism, following Frederick Ferré (1996b). Modern natural philosophy, essentially classical mechanics, has been overturned by the New Physics. Everything else Modern—capitalism (and anticapitalist Marxism) in economics, utilitarianism in ethics, the social contract theory in political philosophy, etc.—that had orbited Modern natural philosophy, has been left without a center or a foundation. We live in a time not unlike Plato's or Descartes's. The old order has passed, but the new one has not yet arrived. For Plato the old order was the Homeric-Hesiodic world; for Descartes, it was the Aristotelian-Thomistic cosmos; for us it is the Cartesian-Newtonian universe. In our time, the contemporary academic and legal philosophers "working within and talking about planes," as Stone put it, are like the poets and rhapsodes scorned by Plato, and the Schoolmen contemned by Descartes—an army of craftspersons working frantically to keep a crumbling old edifice (to employ Descartes's architectural metaphor) in some semblance of repair.

In the Ferréian sense of the term, "postModernism" is a place marker. While we revolutionary philosophers turn to the task of razing the old structures and rebuilding a new metaphysics from the ground up—by distilling the abstract ideas out of quantum theory and ecology, as Descartes distilled the abstract ideas out of Copernican astronomy and Galilean mechanics—and while we remodel, accordingly, the satellite areas of philosophy, like ethics and political theory, we call this interlude "postModernism," since all we know for sure is that Modernism is dead (though not gone). We can't be quite sure yet what Modernity's successor will turn out to be, so we remain cautious and wait for "Organicism" or "Systems Theory" or some such label to take hold.

The other sense of "postmodernism," following such thinkers as Jacques Derrida (1981) and Richard Rorty (1979), is exclusively deconstructive—and essentially nihilistic. For the constructive postModernists the fractured present is an existentially distressing moment, but a moment of great creative intellectual opportunity—exhilarating, exciting, and stimulating. Deconstructive postModernists, on the other hand, are content to deconstruct the old texts and declare that there will be no new master narratives, no new *New Organons*, *Meditationses*, or *Principias* to set the course for generations to come. We don't just need a *new* metaphysics, they seem to think, we need to get off the metaphysics treadmill altogether; we don't just need to reorganize our world*view*—to respond to and accommodate fundamental changes in natural philosophy—we need to see (oops, realize, rather) that a "view," a "vision" of any sort is a Modernist hang-up.

Cheney's references to Deep Ecology's metaphysical pretensions and vision-constructing aspirations drip with contempt. "Why would it occur to one," Cheney (1989b, 301) writes, "that alienation is to be overcome by, of all things, metaphysics, by the empathetic internalization of a highly abstract, humanly constructed *vision* of wholeness, connectedness, and health." It seems that like Ronald Reagan, who consigned "liberal" to the dictionary of dirty words, Cheney wants us to smirk at the Deep Ecologists' innocent description of their "vision."

Who knows whether future postModern philosophy will be constructive or deconstructive? But if deconstructivism is the wave of the future then we should not call it "postModernism," but "post-Western civilizationism," since metaphysics and comprehensive intellectual system building, with natural philosophy at the core, go way back in the Western tradition, considerably further back than the Modern period.

The impetus to deconstructive postModernism is largely political. But its argumentative fulcrum is epistemological. We have given up on Truth (with a capital "T"). To mirror nature with the mind has been a common ambition of philosophers from Thales to Russell in the Western tradition. Past Western philosophers hoped to arrive at and guarantee the truth by inductive/empirical methods, or by deductive/rational methods, or by a judicious combination of the two. Through centuries of error, they kept the faith that we would eventually arrive at a conceptual model that would correspond, point for point, to Reality (with a capital "R"). That dream has become more elusive now than ever. Newton seemed at last to have grasped Reality by the tail and to have put a lock on Truth. But then along came Planck, Einstein, and finally Heisenberg. Uncertainty is now a cornerstone of foundational physics.

Grant skepticism the freest rein. Must we, therefore, accede to nihilism and relativism, as the deconstructive postModernists seem to think? Not necessarily, I would argue, since though we may not hope to marry Truth to Reality, we may hope to find an intellectual construct that comprehends and systematizes more of our experience and does so more coherently than any other. That's exactly what Stone meant in *Trees*, I think, when he urged us not to make a final assault on Reality and Truth, but to seek a new "*myth*"—one "that can fit our growing body of knowledge."

But such an honest and reasonable compromise between old-fashioned truth seeking and nihilism is politically suspect. According to Cheney it represents a last ditch effort to "colonize" "other" points of view, though he wouldn't want to own the visual metaphor. There is no one true view. Hence, everyone is entitled to her own myth, one that grows out of her own personal experience, however limited and uninformed it may be. We require a "politics of difference" in which truth (with a small "t") is reached by "social negotiation," not "colonization."

To my knowledge none of the philosophical Deep Ecologists who are the targets of Cheney's attack has proposed conversion to Ecosophy T or Ecosophy S at sword point, as the colonizing Spanish spread Christianity, nor have they suggested that harmony with nature grows out of the barrel of a gun. It seems, rather, that they are guilty of assuming that people can agree about what is what—if they are willing to come up to speed on our growing body of knowledge and rationally think through how that knowledge may be integrated into a single coherent worldview. They have put their best foot (or feet) forward with Ecosophy T and Ecosophy S and I think that they are willing to argue these ecosophies on their merits. Why must we resort to *negotiation* between intractable parties when the hope of agreement remains? Why not listen to one another . . . and be open to *persuasion?*

Because, it seems clear from Cheney's paper, the ground rules for persuasion themselves are totalizing/colonizing. Our growing body of knowledge comes from science and "science has constructed itself in such a way that it has insulated itself from social negotiation" (1989b, 308). Never mind that science is an international activity, the hallmark of which is the falsifiable hypothesis and the repeatable experiment. Cheney even considers it to be politically suspect to suggest making *reason* an arbiter of what is worth believing and what isn't—since reason may be a colonizing device of patriarchy.

So, in the new Dark Ages of deconstructive *différance*, without even the minimum methodological agreements required for resolving differences of opinion by informed, reasoned argument, negotiation is our only recourse. Or is it? Mention of the Spanish conquistadores' technique for securing consensus reminds us that a far more likely option for a realpolitik of difference in a shattered and fragmented world is naked power—backed either by bullets or bucks. Why negotiate with someone with whom agreement is hopeless when you can have your own way—when the "other" can be bombed, terrorized, bought, pacified, or sweet-talked into submission?

A SINGLE MORAL PHILOSOPHY UNITING MULTIPLE MORAL COMMUNITIES

The moral pluralists' inability clearly to articulate a criterion for choosing among several inconsistent courses of action, indicated by several incommensurable moral theories, is not itself a terribly serious problem. (Monistic theories—Kant's notoriously, with its conflicting *categorical* duties—sometimes run aground on the same sorts of intractable practical contradictions.) Rather, in my opinion, it is a symptom of a deeper, more distressing malaise—the disengagement of ethics from metaphysics and moral philosophy. Hargrove (1985), for example, simply regards the recent emergence of environmental and animal welfare ethics to have proceeded from new "moral perceptions"—rather than from newly acquired cognitive lenses which have reorganized what our senses have perceived all along—as if suddenly we acquired keener senses for non-natural moral properties. The environment and animals have been around all along. I rather think that we now regard them as appropriate beneficiaries of ethics, not because we perceive something in them that we didn't perceive before, but because we better understand what and who they are in relation to what and who we are.

On the other hand, I completely agree with Stone, who is too kind to put it so flatly, that a monistic system like Paul Taylor's simply fails to integrate our many and genuinely diverse moral concerns. So how can we have our cake and eat it too? We must operate effectively within a multiplicity of moral spheres—family obligations, the duties associated with our professional lives, our public lives, our interspecies, and ecosystemic and biospheric relationships—each with its very different set of demands that often compete, one with another. At the same time we feel (or at least I feel) that we must maintain a coherent sense of self and world, a unified moral worldview. Such unity enables us rationally to select among or balance out the contradictory or inconsistent demands made upon us when the multiple social circles in which we operate overlap and come into conflict. More important, a unified worldview gives our lives purpose, direction, coherency, and sanity.

Stone's term *lexical,* for setting priorities among the multiple moral spheres through which we move, not only connotes an alphabetical hierarchy, it also connotes, ever so subtly, that such a hierarchy has a principle in a home-base or root notion. For what "lexical (in contradistinction to 'grammatical') meaning" means is the base or root meaning of a word (in contradistinction to the multiple but clustered meanings of its grammatical forms and variations). The base or root moral concept—which may serve as a univocal "lexical" root, with a multiplicity of "grammatical" permutations—is what Aldo Leopold (1949) called "the community concept." The version of the world or "myth" in which the community concept is embedded is provided by Charles Darwin's general evolutionary epic. In *The Descent of Man,* Darwin constructed a communitarian moral philosophy consistent with and embedded in the larger evolutionary worldview outlined in *The Origin of Species.* It goes something like this:

The protomoral sentiments of affection and sympathy (upon which David Hume and Adam Smith erected their moral philosophies) were naturally selected in mammals as a device to ensure reproductive success. The mammal mother in whom these sentiments were strong more successfully reared her offspring to maturity. For those species in which larger and more complex social organization led to even greater reproductive success, the filial affections and sympathies spilled over to other family members—fathers, siblings, grandparents and grandchildren, uncles and aunts, nephews and nieces, cousins, and so on.

Human beings evolved from highly social primates in a complex social matrix, and inherited highly refined and tender social sentiments and sympathies. With the acquisition of the power of speech and some capacity for abstraction, our ancestors began to codify the kinds of behavior concordant and discordant with their inherited communal-emotional bonds. They dubbed the former good and the latter evil. Ethics, thus, came into being.

As human gens began to merge to form tribes and social organization and relationships grew more varied and complex, the circle of morally enfranchised persons expanded apace and ethical prescriptions and precepts grew more varied and complex in response to and as a reflection of the newer, more varied and complex social structures. Capping off his description of this process, Darwin (1871, 100–101) wrote,

> As man advances in civilization, and small tribes are united into larger communities, the simplest reason would tell each individual that he ought to extend his social instincts and sympathies to all the members of the same nation, though personally unknown to him. This point being once reached there is only an artificial barrier to prevent his sympathies extending to the men of all nations and races. If, indeed, such men are separated from him by great differences of appearance and habits, experience unfortunately shews us how long it is, before we look at them as our fellow-creatures.

Ontogeny recapitulates phylogeny in our social lives and moral institutions as well as in our phenotypic growth and development. The primitive family, clan, and tribal communities, which Darwin imagines to have gradually evolved, did not simply disappear upon their merger into larger and looser social wholes. They remained intact and became, rather, encircled by these larger communal spheres. Not only do we still retain the more ancient bonds, we feel them to be stronger than those of more recently evolved associations. Correspondingly, we feel the mores of the more venerable and intimate communities to be more binding.

Darwin himself anticipated the recent layering on of the human-animal community orbit. Quite appropriately so, since it was he who first suggested that we conceptually reorganize contemporary animals as members of a wider community or kinship group (i.e., as beings descended along parallel evolutionary lines from common ancestors). "Sympathy beyond the confines of man," he wrote, "that is humanity to the lower animals, seems to be one of the latest moral acquisitions. . . . This virtue, one of the noblest with which man is endowed, seems to arise incidentally from our sympathies becoming more tender and widely diffused until they are extended to all sentient beings" (Darwin 1871, 101).

Half a century later, Charles Elton added the most recent addition to the nested social circles to which we now regard ourselves as belonging. Elton (1927) suggested that we conceive of ecological relationships as uniting plants, animals, soil, airs, waters, and so on into "biotic communities." Aldo Leopold (1949) simply plugged Elton's community concept in ecology into Darwin's analysis of the origin and evolution of ethics, and articulated a land or environmental ethic.

We have before us then the bare bones of a *univocal* ethical theory embedded in a coherent worldview that provides, nevertheless, for a *multiplicity* of hierarchically ordered and variously "textured" moral relationships (and thus duties, responsibilities, and so on), each corresponding to and supporting our multiple, varied, and hierarchically ordered social relationships. And so we can discard the competing and inconsistent metaphysics of morals—Kant's, Bentham's, and the lot—that make up the theoretical menagerie of moral pluralism and, in the last analysis, that only serve to obfuscate the actual basis of our multiple moral sensibilities, the interplay between them, and the lexical principles (the "second-order principles" elaborated in chapter 4) of their delicate arrangement.

I have more fully expounded this theory elsewhere, nor is this an appropriate occasion to recapitulate it or add to it (Callicott 1989; and here in chapter 4). Borrowing an image that seems to have been original with Richard Sylvan and Val Plumwood, I suggested that we graphically represent the expansion of our moral sensibilities from narrower to wider circles, not as Peter Singer (1982) would have us represent it, like the expansion of the circumference of a balloon, but like the annular growth rings of a tree (Routley and Routley 1980). In such a figure the inner rings remain visible and present and the outer are added on, each more remote from the center, from the moral heartwood.

The Hume-Darwin-Leopold line of social, humane, and environmental ethics—univocal in its worldview and moral philosophy, but multiple in its moral domains—has not been widely endorsed or even critically debated as an alternative to moral pluralism. This is probably because such a community-centered complex is rooted in a theory of moral sentiments. It thus got confused with emotivism, after the ascendency of logical positivism, and then associated with "rank relativism" (as Stone calls it). It finally went completely out of fashion in philosophy. Ethics grounded in a theory of moral sentiments emerged as a part of the romantic revolt against the apotheosis of reason in the Enlightenment and has recently survived primarily in the biological literature, having been established there by no less great a figure than Darwin. It has reemerged in contemporary sociobiology—which by itself makes such a theory a philosophical pariah.

Such a moral philosophy as I have here outlined is in one sense pluralistic; in another it is not. It does involve a multiplicity of overlapping and competing community-generated duties and obligations. To that extent, it is pluralistic. But it is not pluralistic *sensu* Stone (and Wenz and Brennan, for that matter), because it involves only one metaphysics of morals: one concept of the nature of morality (as rooted in moral sentiments), one concept of human nature (that we are social animals voyaging with fellow creatures in the odyssey of evolution), one moral psychology (that we respond in subtly shaded ways to the fellow members of our multiple, diverse, tiered communities and to those communities per se). Certainly, it does not suggest that we follow Kant here, Bentham and Mill there, Singer and/or Regan yonder, and Leopold at the frontier. It posits a single coherent strand of moral thought: David Hume and Adam Smith set out its elements in the eighteenth century, Charles Darwin grounded them in an evolutionary account of human nature in the nineteenth, and Aldo Leopold (making moral hay of Charles Elton's ecological paradigm) provided its outermost "accretion" in the twentieth.

9

Moral Monism in
Environmental Ethics Defended

In *Earth and Other Ethics*, Christopher D. Stone (1987) argues that our many moral concerns—for fellow human beings, for sentient animals, and for the environment—cannot be embraced by a single ethical theory. He therefore recommended moral pluralism. In trying to do the right thing in each domain of our ethical lives, we should be guided by the available theory that seems most applicable. For example, public policy might best be decided by the principle of utility; interpersonal relationships might best be guided by the categorical imperative; personal habits might best be regulated by the golden mean; and so on. Though Stone (1987, 133–34) uses the term "plane" instead of "theory," it is clear from how he defines planes—as "intellectual frameworks" which include an "ontological commitment" and "rules" of conduct—that by planes he refers to what are more commonly called ethical theories.

In "The Case against Moral Pluralism," I argued that moral pluralism, so understood, was intolerable (chapter 8). First, an agent would have no means of deciding between them when two or more theories (or "planes") yield contradictory practical indications. For example, animal rights would prohibit controlling deer populations by means of hunting,

171

while the Leopold land ethic would not only permit it, but require it. Thus, a pluralist would at once have to oppose deer hunting and warmly endorse it. Second, an unscrupulous agent might be tempted to choose the theory that was most convenient or self-serving. For example, animal liberation would censure doing nothing, when one could do something, to save the life of a wild animal in distress or to end its life painlessly. But if one did not want to bother, inaction, in such circumstances, might be rationalized as consistent with environmental ethics. John Stuart Mill ([1874] 1969, 376), incidentally, worried about this problem with pluralism. "The people of this generation," he wrote, "do not commonly . . . own . . . binding allegiance to any standard, but live in a kind of confusion of many standards; a condition not propitious to the formation of steady moral convictions, but convenient enough to those whose moral opinions sit lightly on them, since it gives them a much wider range for defending the doctrine of the moment."

These two problems with moral pluralism, however, are not decisive. Contradictory practical indications sometimes arise within univocal ethical theories—Kant's notoriously. And all ethics presuppose that agents act with good will. Much more serious is a third problem with moral pluralism. Ethical theories are embedded in moral *philosophies*; and for a single agent to decide public policy by the principle of utility, to act in his or her interpersonal relationships according to the categorical imperative, to regulate his or her personal habits by the golden mean, and so on, would require that agent either simultaneously to hold mutually contradictory moral philosophies or to put on and take off mutually contradictory moral philosophies with the same ease and frequency as he or she changes clothes.

When an agent adopts an ethical theory, an ethical "intellectual framework" as Stone defines his neologism, he or she adopts a moral psychology, a notion of the supreme good, a criterion of moral considerability, among other foundational ideas. Facilely becoming a utilitarian for this purpose, a deontologist for that, an Aristotelian for another, and so on, implies either that the pluralist simultaneously hold all the contradictory foundational ideas supporting each theory, or first affirm one set, then reject it in favor of another, and then reject that set for yet another, only to return to the first later, back and forth, round and round. A mature moral agent, I submit, wants a coherent outlook—the one that seems true. He or she cannot comfortably live in a perpetual state of self-contradiction or as the philosophical equivalent of an individual with a multiple personality disorder.

A THEORETICALLY COHERENT ALTERNATIVE TO MORAL PLURALISM: MULTIPLE COMMUNITARIANISM

But how can we deal with our many and very different moral concerns without resorting to pluralism? I suggest that we adopt a form of communitarianism instead. At once, each of us is a member of a family, a civic society, a nation state, the global village, Midgleyan "mixed communities" (that include domestic animals), and local, regional, and global biotic communities. Each of these memberships generates peculiar duties and obligations. Thus, we can hold a single moral philosophy and a univocal ethical theory, but one that provides for a *multiplicity* of community memberships, each with its peculiar ethic. The ethical obligations generated by our many community memberships often conflict, but, since all our duties—to people, to animals, to nature—are expressible in a common vocabulary, the vocabulary of community, they may be weighed and compared in commensurable terms.

Let me illustrate first in context of the familiar realm of social ethics and then in context of the novel realm of environmental ethics.

One has special duties to one's children—to feed, clothe, shelter, and educate them, to shower them with love and affection. These radical obligations have arisen because the family is the most venerable and intimate community to which one belongs. One also has duties, generated by the much more recently emerged "community of nations" and "global village," to help relieve starvation among people half way around the planet. If one's means are limited, these duties may come into conflict. But communitarianism allows one to weigh one's duties on a single scale, calibrated in a single metric, and attempt to balance them fairly. Thus, in the case at hand, one might reasonably conclude that one ought to give one's children fewer or less expensive presents at Christmas in order to make a modest contribution to Oxfam. On the other hand, if one were sorely impecunious and faced the choice of spending one's last dollar buying food for one's own children or buying food for a child in Somalia, then of course the obligation to one's own children would take precedence.

We sympathize with our fellow citizens in the Pacific Northwest whose livelihood depends upon logging and milling old-growth timber. Yet we have learned that we are citizens not only of a nation state, but also of hierarchically ordered biotic communities. In the words of Aldo Leopold (1949, 109), "this new knowledge [has] given us a sense of kinship with fellow-creatures; a wish to live and let live; a sense of wonder over the magnitude and duration of the biotic enterprise." Membership in this larger biotic community generates duties to preserve the old-growth forest ecosystem and the endangered species, such as the northern spotted owl, that depend upon it. Our duties to the local people whose way of life is destroying the forest would take precedence over our duties to less closely related life forms and more diffuse and tenuous biotic communities if the choice were between cutting down all the trees and cutting down all the local people. But that is not the choice we face. Rather, the choice is between temporarily preserving, on the one hand, an ephemeral human lifestyle that is doomed in any event, and, on the other, preserving in perpetuity an ecosystem and the species that depend upon it. Things being what they are, our duties to preserve endangered species and the health and integrity of the mature Douglas fir ecosystem by banning further logging of old-growth forests in the Pacific Northwest weigh in more heavily. And we can compensate the affected human beings by supporting job retraining programs, start-up funds for new businesses, and the like.

PLURAL PRINCIPLES AND *INTRA*- VERSUS *INTER*PERSONAL PLURALISM

Please note that in these illustrations I do not insist upon deriving our duties to family members and foreigners, to our fellow Americans and the old-growth forests from a single "master principle"—Leopold's summary moral maxim—similar to Mill's principle of utility or Kant's categorical imperative. Rather, I argue for a single moral *philosophy*—duties and obligations generated by community membership and grounded in a variety of distinctly moral sentiments—not for a single *principle* of conduct (although, to be sure, the two second-order principles, developed in chapter 4, are implicitly at play here).

Nor do I wish to impose a communitarian moral philosophy and an associated theory of moral sentiments on anyone else by any force other than the force of argument. I am fully committed to moral pluralism in another sense. I uphold everyone else's right to explore or to adopt a moral philosophy and ethical theory that seems persuasive to them. In other words, while I find *intra*personal pluralism objectionable for the reason stated, I am wholeheartedly committed to *inter*personal pluralism. Indeed, for persons of good will who still find intrapersonal pluralism tenable— the principal reason I have given for thinking otherwise notwithstand- ing—I uphold their right to choose to suffer from the intellectual equiva- lent of a multiple personality disorder if that is what they think is best for them. Philosophy, including ethics, can flourish only if a variety of points of view may be freely expressed and debated. Just as essential, on the other hand, to the flourishing of philosophy, is a complementary commitment to reasoned persuasion. Intelligent people of good will should eventually reach agreement if they take the time to thrash out their initial differences (chapter 5). Deconstructive postmodern *différance* is also, in my opinion, untenable—because its endpoint is the doctrine that might (power), not argument, determines what is right.

Of all those who have reacted to my case against moral pluralism, Peter Wenz has been the most understanding. But because I do not insist that a single moral *principle* can adequately guide our actions in every cir- cumstance, he thinks that the view that I defend is intrapersonally plural- istic, despite my protestations to the contrary. I really advocate "moderate [intrapersonal] pluralism" according to Wenz (1993, 72) in "Minimal, Moderate, and Extreme Moral Pluralism," because I employ "many moral principles, and they are not all derived from a single, master principle. Some moral principles concern which [community] relationships are more important than others, [for example,] parenthood more than friendship, friendship more than citizenship, etc. Other principles . . . are used to identify when the normal priorities do not apply, [for example,] when citizen obligations override familial duties. . . ."

This suggests a formalization of the process of weighing and balanc- ing the various duties and obligations generated by our many community memberships with which I myself feel a trifle uncomfortable (though some- thing approaching such a formalization is set out in chapter 4). Be that as it may, the main fault that I find with Wenz's otherwise fair and well-informed discussion is his assumption that what is at issue is pluralism at the level of principle instead of pluralism at the level of theory. Wenz (1993, 72) is quite right to say that "Callicott neither presents, nor claims to possess, any master rule or principle from which one can deduce uniquely correct moral conduct in situations of moral conflict" (although the two second-order principles elaborated in chapter 4 come close). What I do present and claim to possess (without qualification) is a univocal moral *philosophy* and associated ethical *theory*. Rather, the sort of pluralism to which I object is the sort that Stone advocates—and that Wenz calls "extreme pluralism"—in which an agent becomes a utilitarian in one situation, a deontologist in another, an emotivist, in a third, and so on. As a moderate moral pluralist, Wenz (1993) too claims to have a "single theory"—a pluralistic theory. But just what the elements of that theory are—just what moral psychology Wenz endorses, what value theory he holds, what notion of the good he commends, etc., and why—Wenz never discloses.

G. E. VARNER ON HOLISM AND PLURALISM
IN ENVIRONMENTAL ETHICS

Unlike Wenz, G. E. Varner has focused on what is in fact at issue in the debate started by Stone and joined by me—"extreme pluralism," intrapersonal pluralism at the level of theory. The pluralism that Varner endorses "acknowledges distinct, theoretically incommensurable bases for direct moral consideration" of various entities such as human beings, animals, plants, nations, species, ecosystems, and the biosphere.

   Saying that he "cannot go into the details of [the] argument here" in "No Holism without Pluralism," Varner (1991, 179) simply declares that the sort of univocal communitarian ethical theory that I recommend cannot provide direct moral consideration both for individuals, such as human beings, animals, and plants, on the one hand, and wholes such as nations, species, ecosystems, and the biosphere, on the other: "If it is plausible to say that ecosystems . . . are morally considerable . . . it must be for a very different reason than is usually given for saying that individual human beings are directly morally considerable" (Varner 1991, 179). As Wenz (1993, 73) points out, "Varner merely refers to reasons that are *usually* given for maintaining that people are morally considerable. Whatever these usual reasons are, they may or may not be Callicott's. Thus, Varner cannot claim to have shown that Callicott's basis for maintaining that people are directly morally considerable is incommensurable with Callicott's basis for according direct moral consideration to biotic communities."

The bases to which I appeal for according moral considerability to human beings, on the one hand, and to ecosystems, on the other, *are* different. But they are *not* incommensurable. The common denominator is the community concept. In my opinion, the moral considerability of the fellow members of our various human communities, is ultimately grounded in certain moral sentiments—altruistic love, sympathy, charity, and a sense of fairness, among others. The moral considerability of ecosystems is ultimately grounded in other, very different moral sentiments that have, as their object, the community as such—respect, loyalty, patriotism, group pride, a sense of team spirit.

In the familiar social sphere we weigh and balance our duties to fellow members and our duties to communities-as-such all the time. To take an example that is painfully familiar to all us tenured academics, one's sympathy for a less-than-brilliant probationary member of one's department may conflict with one's loyalty to the department as such and one's pride in its tradition of excellence when one must vote on that member's retention or tenure. Assessing one's duties to such a colleague as an individual in accordance with one theory, say Kant's, and one's duties to one's department in accordance with another theory, say Plato's, would leave one with an unresolved conundrum. Again, a principal reason for wanting a single ethical theory is to express conflicting obligations in commensurable terms so that they can be weighed one against the others. But nowadays, such a theory must be sufficiently general and comprehensive to reach the new ethical quandaries posed by emergent interspecies and environmental moral concerns.

THE ANALOGY BETWEEN PLURALISM IN SCIENCE AND PLURALISM IN ETHICS CRITICIZED

Wenz (1993) points out that Stone's argument for intrapersonal pluralism rests on a faulty analogy between science and ethics. The same faulty analogy, incidentally, vitiates the argument for intrapersonal pluralism proffered by Andrew Brennan (1992). The sciences, Stone and Brennan think, can be compartmentalized. Ecology, for example, can be pursued without reference to astrophysics. But as far as I am aware, the sciences—with one outstanding exception—are mutually consistent and together paint a coherent portrait of nature. To take a case in point, my fundamentalist students have tried to discredit the theory of evolution by claiming that a purely natural, evolutionary account of self-organization in nature would violate the second law of thermodynamics. Instead, they believe, the manifest organization in nature can only be accounted for by a supernatural power—God—that could defy entropy. I omit the refutation of this fallacious argument. My point is that the sciences, though compartmentalized, are hierarchically ordered and mutually consistent: the theory of evolution is not contradicted by thermodynamics; and, though ecologists may never need to consult astrophysics in conducting ecological research, the path from astrophysics to ecology, as from thermodynamics to evolution, in the hierarchy of sciences may be easily traced. The one exception to this state of affairs in science is the inconsistency of quantum mechanics and the general theory of relativity. And in the face of this inconsistency, the response of the scientific community is not "scientific pluralism," the declaration of this inconsistency to be insurmountable and the affirmation of it as a good thing. Rather, the inconsistency between quantum mechanics and the general theory of relativity is regarded as indicative of a flaw in one or the other or both domains of theory. Thus, a contemporary physicist can aspire to no greater achievement than to "quantize gravity."

As Leopold (1942, 487) notes, "All the sciences and arts are taught as if they were separate. They are separate only in the classroom. Step out on the campus and they are immediately fused. . . . What are the sciences? Only categories for thinking. Sciences can be taught separately, but they cannot be used separately, . . ." As Wenz sagely points out, one's moral life is analogously integrated, and often cannot be compartmentalized. Duties to friends and strangers, to institutions and abstractions, to animals and to the biosphere may all come into play simultaneously. Hence we must be able to think about them coherently, something we cannot do if we think of the categorical imperative as governing our relationships with friends, the Golden Rule as governing our relationships with strangers, the principle of utility as governing our relationships with animals, and so on. While the generalized version of utilitarianism and deontology proposed by Peter Singer (1977) and Paul Taylor (1986), respectively, can embrace sentient animals and all living things, respectively, they cannot embrace irreducible environmental wholes such as species and ecosystems. A communitarian moral philosophy such as I espouse can. And that, I think, is a good reason for anyone concerned about animals and plants, species and ecosystems, as well as about people, to accept it. Another reason for accepting it is that it is informed by a contemporary understanding of ourselves and the world we inhabit.

INTRAPERSONAL PLURALISM AND
INTERPERSONAL PLURALISM ONCE AGAIN

In setting out and vigorously defending a communitarian moral philosophy to ground a coherent environmental ethics, Anthony Weston (1992, 333) seems to think that I wish prematurely to shut off further discussion and development of the field:

J. Baird Callicott . . . insists that we attempt to formulate, right now, a complete, unified, even "closed" (his term) theory of environmental ethics. Callicott even argues that contemporary environmental ethics should not tolerate more than one basic type of value, insisting on a "univocal" environmental ethic. In fact, however, . . . originary stages are the worst possible times at which to demand that we all speak with one voice. . . . The necessary period of ferment, cultural experimentation, and thus *multi*-vocality is only beginning.

Weston here mistakes the kind of moral pluralism against which I object, *intra*personal pluralism, for the kind that I warmly endorse and encourage, *inter*personal pluralism. For the reasons that I have given, I think that each of us should think through complex and multifaceted moral problems in coherent, mutually consistent terms, not adopt Aristotle's system on this occasion, Kant's on another, and Bentham's later in the day—systems that are mutually contradictory and that rest upon obsolete philosophical foundations. I am doing my best to articulate a coherent ethical theory, embedded in a "true" moral philosophy, capable of ethically enfranchising people, animals, and the environment. I am delighted that Holmes Rolston III (1988), Warwick Fox (1990), and Lawrence Johnson (1991), among others, are doing so as well and doing so very differently than I. Each of these environmental philosophers also offer "closed" moral philosophies, in the sense that they too try to tie up all the theoretical loose ends and deal with all the relevant issues. Rather than to close off further discussion, certainly I wish to keep the interpersonal debate going. Each philosopher's struggling to articulate a coherent ethic that is consistent with our current understanding of ourselves and the world we inhabit may not be the only way to explore nascent values, but it is certainly one way that has, in the past at any rate, proven to be enormously fecund. Pluralism *sensu* Stone actually seems more likely to close off further discussion. While a monistic ethicist pushes moral philosophy on into uncharted territory, an intrapersonal pluralist is content instead to select—off the rack, so to speak—an intellectually obsolete theory that seems best tailored to fit the practical problem of the moment. By pushing the envelope of moral philosophy, the monist provokes debate. Thus a dialectical conversation ensues, as it has in environmental ethics over the past quarter century, and moral philosophy develops exponentially. Pluralism serves to stifle this fertile debate and dialectical development.

By his own account, Weston (1992, 325) raises "very large questions of method." He seems to find fault with the very methods of moral philosophy. He calls for a long period of experimentation, during which new values evolve, before philosophers try to systematize them. As a precedent, he draws our attention to the gradual emergence of the ethics of persons and the associated concept of human rights. At the dawn of the Modern period, a new rhetoric began to take shape, in theology, in politics, in economics. But Weston omits to note that important contributors to the birth of these new notions were the systematic (and often dogmatic) philosophers of the period, such as Hobbes and Locke (chapter 2). Weston's pluralism, ironically, seems not to extend to method. He seems to want those of us who are struggling to articulate, ground, and systematize new values to desist and instead engage in *practices*, such as creating "ecosteries" (by analogy with monasteries), quiet places where one can immerse oneself in "natural settings" and "reinhabit" them (Weston 1992, 334–35). Personally, I think that this is a wonderful idea, but why does Weston advocate it as an alternative to rather than a complement of systematic environmental philosophy?

Like Weston, Hargrove (1993) seems to think that I am not supportive of interpersonal moral pluralism—each philosopher working toward his or her own univocal moral theory and non-philosophers choosing to guide their actions by the one that seems most persuasive to them. I do not claim, as he suggests, that my communitarian theory embraces or absorbs Rolston's theory, or Taylor's, or that of any other monistic environmental ethicist. I argue rather that mine is not only different from, but better than theirs. And I am prepared to listen to their counterarguments and be persuaded by one or the other of them if, upon rational reflection, they seem to me to be right.

Like Wenz (1993), Hargrove (1993) argues that I am an intrapersonal moral pluralist in spite of myself. In an early essay, I did try to cleanly distinguish between environmental ethics and animal liberation/rights (Callicott 1980). But I did not, as Hargrove insinuates, suggest that one should adopt Singer's or Regan's theory to guide one's actions in relation to animals and Leopold's theory to guide one's actions in relation to endangered species and to ecosystems. I argued instead that animal welfare ethics should be rejected, because they are uninformed by ecology and incompatible with environmental values, and that all our actions should be guided by a single moral principle, the summary moral maxim of the Leopold land ethic—even our actions in relation to other people. Of course, such extreme monism, monism at the level of principle, yielded repugnant misanthropic indications, and thus was utterly unacceptable. Chastened by William Aiken, Tom Regan, and others, I later argued, as I am arguing now, that the Leopold land ethic is part of a family of theoretically unified communitarian ethics (Callicott 1987, and here in chapter 4). And I attempted to show how our duties and obligations to domestic animals, as well as to other human beings, could also be grounded by a communitarian theory (Callicott 1988).

Hargrove insists that I can acknowledge duties to human beings and other animals because—as members of our various human communities and the mixed human-animal community, so engagingly characterized by Mary Midgley (1983)—they elicit our sympathy, but not to wild animals and plants, because they do not elicit our sympathy. Hargrove seems to forget that, if we can believe Leopold, wild animals are members of the biotic community. And, according to Leopold (1949, 204), the land ethic "changes the role of Homo sapiens from conqueror of the biotic community to plain member and citizen of it. It implies respect for his *fellow members*, as well as for the community as such." Thus, we may well feel sympathy for them too. But just as we do not have the same obligations to strangers as we do to family members, or the same duties to domestic animals as we have to our fellow human beings, neither do we have the same duties and obligations to wild animals as we have to domestic ones. Our various human communities, the mixed community (*sensu* Midgley), and the biotic community all generate different duties and obligations.

Worst of all, however, is the way Hargrove has narrowed down to sympathy the various moral sentiments in which I suggest that our various duties and obligations to our various fellow members and communities as such are ultimately rooted. Immediately after quoting a passage from my paper, "Animal Liberation and Environmental Ethics: Back Together Again," in which the word *sympathy* does not occur, Hargrove (1993, 4) writes, "the introduction of sympathy provides 'a common theoretical umbrella.'" And throughout his paper, he cavalierly refers to my "sympathy theory." When using a theory such as I sketch to decide which set of our duties and obligations—to people, to animals, and to the environment—takes priority over the others, Hargrove (1993, 8) writes, "Presumably, a moral agent would check to see whether he or she was supposed to have a lot of sympathy for the object of concern . . . a little . . . or none." This is purely an invention on Hargrove's part and, if I may say so, it is utterly irresponsible of him to attribute such notions to me without any basis in anything that I have written.

Sympathy is but one moral sentiment among many. It can extend only to individual human beings and sentient animals, hardly to plants, and certainly not at all to species, ecosystems, and other wholes. We have duties and obligations that are well acknowledged not only to our fellow citizens, but to our countries—which are communities "as such," not plausibly reduced to their members severally. When one presses a dollar bill into the hand of a homeless person, one may do so because one feels sympathy for that person. But in time of war when one leaves one's spouse and children and risks extreme danger and death for one's country, one could hardly say that one does so because one feels more *sympathy* for one's country than for one's family members. One feels, rather, group pride, patriotism, loyalty, indignation at aggression, and so on. Along with respect, these are the sort of moral sentiments in which, according to my proffered communitarian theory, the moral considerability of wholes—including species as such and the biotic community as such—is grounded.

To this, Hargrove could say, I suppose, that I, the professed moral monist, am really a pluralist after all because I recognize a multiplicity of moral sentiments. But this again is to misidentify the sort of pluralism with which I take issue. I am not opposed to pluralism at the level of principle, or to pluralism at the level of sentiment, or to interpersonal pluralism, but intrapersonal pluralism at the level of theory and of moral philosophy. Why? Because, in sum, the popular ethical theories that we have inherited from the past and that the intrapersonal pluralist blithely applies, one in this circumstance, another in that, and so on, are embedded in mutually contradictory moral philosophies, most of which have been invalidated by our ever-growing body of empirical knowledge, scientific theory, and self-discovery.

PART IV

NATURE'S INTRINSIC VALUE

Genesis and John Muir

LYNN WHITE JR.'S INFLUENCE ON ENVIRONMENTAL ETHICS

In "The Historical Roots of Our Ecologic Crisis," published in *Science* in 1967, Lynn White Jr. laid the blame for the "environmental crisis"—which had dawned on public awareness earlier in the same decade—at the door of the Judeo-Christian worldview. White is a distinguished, authoritative professor of Medieval church history and his infamous analysis was published in the organ of the American Association for the Advancement of Science, the most prestigious scientific journal published in the United States. Hence, "The Historical Roots of Our Ecologic Crisis" was widely read and broadly influential. It was subsequently reprinted in practically every one of the umpteen thousand anthologies on the environmental crisis published in the decade following its appearance in *Science*, thus multiplying its already large audience and magnifying its already considerable influence.

White focused on the environmental attitudes and values set out in Genesis and how they might have fostered ill-treatment of nature in Christendom through the ages. He argued, in effect, that since it is written in Genesis that human beings alone among creatures were created in the image of God and given dominion over nature and charged to subdue it, that Jews and Christians, taking this message to heart, attempted to live by its light. They regarded themselves as beings apart from the rest of nature, licensed by God to rule over it and bend it to their purposes. After two thousand years of putting this vision of the human-nature relationship into practice with increasing success, the twentieth century's technological wonders *and* the twentieth century's environmental crisis are the end results. Thus, White concluded, we must either jettison our Judeo-Christian heritage or substantially refigure its fundamental God-humanity-nature relationship if we hope to solve our environmental problems.

Of course, Scripture has a wonderful quality that I would characterize as creative ambiguity. Its words mean different things to different people in different circumstances. White's interpretation of what Genesis has to say about the proper relationship between people and nature is just that— an interpretation. It has subsequently come to be known as the "mastery" or "despotic" interpretation. Other contemporary professors of religion and theology, no less distinguished and authoritative than White, read the environmental message of Genesis in quite another way. In their view, the unique status of human beings among all God's creatures confers unique responsibilities, as well as unique rights, upon people. Among these responsibilities is to care for the rest of God's creation and to pass it on, in as good or better condition than it was received, to future generations. In giving us dominion over nature, God did not intend for us to enslave it or to do with it what we pleased. Rather, God intended for us wisely to manage or govern the creation that remains God's, not ours. We are God's "stewards" of creation—the caretakers of nature—not nature's new owners.

The reaction to White's despotic interpretation was so swift and came from so many quarters that no one person can be credited with formulating this alternative reading, which is now known as the "stewardship" interpretation. Since the late sixties and early seventies there have emerged no essentially new interpretations of the environmental attitudes and values in Genesis. One could either adopt the mastery interpretation or the stewardship interpretation, both of which put human beings in a dominant relationship to nature. Here, I offer a third interpretation of the controversial texts which was suggested to me by some remarks of John Muir, the great nineteenth-century preservationist. In the citizenship reading of Genesis that I here propose, human beings are intended to be "plain members and citizens" of nature, as the great twentieth-century American conservationist Aldo Leopold (1949, 204) put it in his famous "The Land Ethic," neither its tyrannical masters nor benign, managerial stewards.

Whatever the merits of Lynn White Jr.'s manifest argument (which I take up in due course), the subtext of his notorious article implicitly set the theoretical agenda for a future environmental philosophy (Hargrove 1986). Broad patterns of human behavior do not arise in an intellectual vacuum, White reminded us. Adequately to understand the environmental crisis, we must first dig up and critically evaluate the ideas of nature, human nature, and the proper relationship between people and nature embedded in our inherited worldview. They provide a theater for our actions, an archetypal image or ideal of what it means to be human, and the associated values that we human beings aspire to realize. White (1967, 1204, emphasis added) writes, "Unless we *think* about fundamentals, our specific measures may produce new backlashes more serious than those they are designed to remedy . . . unless we *rethink* our axioms." And he writes, "What people do about their ecology depends on what they *think* about themselves in relation to things around them; human ecology is deeply conditioned by *beliefs* about our nature and destiny" (White 1967, 1205, emphasis added). And again, "What we do about our ecology depends on our *ideas* of the man-nature relationship; more science and more technology are not going to get us out of the present ecologic crisis until we find a new religion or *rethink* our old one" (White 1967, 1206, emphasis added). And yet again, "We must *rethink* and refeel our nature and destiny" (White 1967, 1207). Finally, after ruminating on the complex relationship between attitudes and values, on the one hand, and behavior, on the other—a cryptotheme or subtext of "Historical Roots"—White (1973, 58) concludes, in a follow-up essay, "And so one might comment indefinitely, but in the end one returns to value structures"—as providing the best insight into a culture's behavior patterns. In short, the dire exigencies of the environmental crisis mandate radical change in broad patterns of human *behavior* in respect to nature; but, White insists, the way we act is conditioned by the way we *think*. Hence the fundamental questions are these: What ideas of nature, human nature, and the relationship between the two inspired our behavior toward nature in the past?; and What ideas of nature, human nature, and the relationship between the two might we postulate to facilitate a lasting rapprochement between people and the natural environment?

So stated, the dual *problematique*—critical and speculative—of environmental philosophy seems clear and direct. But such a simple statement of the enterprise skates blithely over not just a few patches of thin ice. Though certainly ideas influence behavior, obviously they do not determine it. People do, after all, behave in ways that run contrary to their professed beliefs, ideals, and values. And, given the inertia of habit, can changed beliefs, ideals, and values actually bring about changed patterns of behavior (Tuan 1968, 1970)?

Supposing these queries may be favorably resolved (Callicott & Ames 1989), how does one create new ideas of nature and human nature, and envision a more harmonious relationship between the two? May we philosophers just dream them up out of the blue, or must we somehow distill an ecophilosophy and -ethic from the relevant sciences (chapters 5 and 15)? Once formulated, how does a new paradigm trickle down into the popular worldview (chapters 2 and 3)? Is there, indeed, a collective mind, a Zeitgeist?

Not only is the forward-looking, speculative phase of environmental philosophy fraught with problems, so is the backward-looking, critical phase. Lynn White Jr. seized upon the most visible, the most evident, of our intellectual legacies. The Judeo-Christian cognitive complex is publicly confessed, literally, by a significant proportion of Western peoples in institutional settings—churches, synagogues, and temples. But a powerful secular cognitive complex is also ambient in our midst, the Modern scientific worldview, as it might be called, that is rarely publicly confessed, but is routinely publicly *pro*fessed, also in institutional settings—schools and universities. Moreover, technological manifestations of the scientific worldview are ubiquitous in our day-to-day lives (chapter 3).

White (1967, 1206) suggested that the latter is a product of the former, that science and technology grew, historically, out of the Judeo-Christian worldview: "The consistency with which scientists during the long formative centuries of Western science said that the task and the reward of the scientist was 'to think God's thoughts after Him,' leads one to believe that this was their motivation." I have no quarrel with his historical argument, as far as it goes, but what he fails to note is that the cognitive stock in trade of Modern science, as opposed to the warrant for undertaking it, is of Greek philosophical, not biblical religious provenance. Newton and other seventeenth-century scientists may have been inspired by belief in a transcendent creative deity and the *imago dei* to try to "think God's thoughts after Him," but the details of the Creator's supposed thoughts were inspired by Pythagoras and Democritus, not Moses and Paul. In my opinion, the more culpable conceptual roots of our ecologic crisis are traceable to the intellectual legacy of Greek natural philosophy—which may have insidiously influenced the environmentally controversial parts of Genesis (as I explain subsequently)—not the un-Hellenized intellectual tradition of the ancient Hebrews (Hargrove 1989).

It is well to remember that Lynn White Jr. (1967, 1207) describes himself in "Historical Roots" as a "churchman," and that while he believes that "since the roots of our trouble are so largely religious, the remedy must also be essentially religious, whether we call it that or not," the religious remedy that he recommends is Judeo-Christian. Rejecting Zen Buddhism and other exotic alternatives fashionable in the then new, growing, and (to some) threatening American "subculture," White suggests reviving Franciscan doctrines—"recessive genes," as it were, in the Judeo-Christian pool of ideas, "which in new circumstances may become dominant genes," as he put it in his follow-up essay, "Continuing the Conversation" (White 1973, 61). Lynn White Jr.'s seminal article, nevertheless, provoked a veritable tidal wave of apologetic literature defending the environmental attitudes and values of the Judeo-Christian worldview that he seemed so casually and carelessly to excoriate. In a short essay, the principal purpose of which is to fill a small empty niche in this apologia, I cannot begin to survey the resulting flood. I hazard to say, however, that by far the main stream of this literature has followed the channel White first cut, and focused on the Big Picture found in the first two chapters of Genesis relating God, humanity, and nature. And by far the greatest volume of this literature develops, in one way or another, the stewardship alternative to the despotic interpretation that Lynn White Jr. constructed of those crucial passages (Attfield 1983; Barr 1972; Black 1970; Fritsch 1980; Schaeffer 1970).

THE JUDEO-CHRISTIAN STEWARDSHIP
ENVIRONMENTAL ETHIC—ITS VIRTUES EXTOLLED

I think that those who have argued that the stewardship interpretation is better supported by the text than White's despotic interpretation have entirely won their case. And as one who has struggled for two decades to formulate a persuasive and adequate secular environmental ethic, I would like further to say that the Judeo-Christian stewardship environmental ethic is especially elegant and powerful.

As Tom Regan (1981, 20) forcefully put it, we environmental philosophers have sought to formulate "an ethic *of* the environment," not "an ethic for the *use* of the environment," a genuinely "environmental ethic" not "a 'management' ethic." And, as Regan (1981) also forcefully argued, the sine qua non of such an ethic is some plausible theory of intrinsic value or inherent worth for nonhuman natural entities and nature as a whole—value or worth that they own in and of themselves as opposed to the value or worth that they have for our use.

Little unambiguous progress has been made on that problem in the secular arena. On the other hand, the Judeo-Christian stewardship environmental ethic provides for the intrinsic value of non-human natural entities and nature as a whole simply and directly. Either by the act of creation or by a secondary fiat—surveying the result, as Genesis (1:10–31) reports, and declaring it to be "good"—God conferred intrinsic value on the world and all its creatures. Technically put, in the stewardship environmental ethic, God represents an objective axiological point of reference independent of human consciousness.

Those secular environmental ethicists who have managed theoretically to broker—how plausibly is another matter—intrinsic value or inherent worth for nonhuman natural entities and nature as a whole, then face the opposite problem of having too broadly distributed too much of a good thing. If every living being, as some have argued (Goodpaster 1978; Rolston 1988; Taylor 1986), is intrinsically valuable, then how can we human beings legitimately consume nonhuman natural entities in pursuit of our own interests? After all, we must eat something. People cannot live like the lilies of the field, on sunshine, water, air, and lifeless soil. And people must have houses, and clothes, and books, etc.—all of which have to be appropriated either directly from other living beings or mined at the expense of their resources and habitats.

These same secular environmental ethicists have met this problem with an elaborate set of hedges, designed consistently to rescue the practicability of their theories (Taylor 1986, chap. 6). But it all seems forced and ad hoc. The Judeo-Christian stewardship environmental ethic, on the other hand, addresses this problem with the same simplicity and directness as it addresses the first. In Genesis (1:24), it is clear that God is creating species, not specimens: "And God made the beast of the earth *after his kind*, and cattle *after their kind*, and everything that creepeth upon the earth *after his kind*: and God saw that it was good."

Moreover, the creation, as portrayed in Genesis (1:20–22), is replete and teeming with life: "And God said, Let the waters bring forth abundantly the moving creature that hath life, and fowl that may fly above the earth in the open firmament of heaven. And God created great whales, and every moving creature that moveth, which the waters brought forth abundantly, after their kind, and every winged fowl after his kind: and God saw that it was good. And God blessed them, saying, Be fruitful and multiply, and fill the waters in the seas, and let fowl multiply in the earth."

People have the right to harvest the surplus. Being created in the image of God burdens us human beings with certain responsibilities, to be sure. That is the essence of the stewardship reading. But let's not forget that the *imago dei* also confers on us certain complementary privileges. Hence, we are entitled to the usufruct of our dominion so long as we rule it benignly and do not draw on its capital reserves. Humanity has an asymmetrical relationship with other creatures. They have no obligations in respect to us as we do in respect to them, but then we have rights in respect to them that they do not have in respect to us.

During its first two decades, environmental philosophy has been somewhat bellicose, each thinker proclaiming the superiority of his or her particular line of criticism and speculative reconstruction over all the others. I think such internecine conflict was a natural concomitant of the exuberance and sense of purpose characteristic of a new, morally charged field of study. More important, I think it was necessary clearly to define a variety of points of view and approach. But as the field has matured and settled, such truculence, once both natural and necessary, now appears increasingly both unbecoming and counterproductive. I think we need to rebuild burned bridges better to serve our common and very serious practical purpose. The Judeo-Christian stewardship environmental ethic, accordingly, should get the intellectual respect it so very properly deserves. It has much greater potential than so far tapped to enlist the support and energies of a sizable segment of the public on behalf of environmental concerns. For the very large community of people who accept its premises—who believe in God, divine creation, a preeminent place and role for human beings in the world, and so on—it represents, in my opinion, the most coherent, powerful, and practicable environmental ethic available.

That having been said, I turn now to my main business here—which is to sketch a third, far more radical reading of the environmental implications of Genesis. This interpretation of the third kind was suggested to me by some remarks of John Muir.

MUIR'S CITIZENSHIP READING OF GENESIS

Muir's nascent environmental ethic rests, according to received intellectual history (Nash 1967, chap. 8), on a refined romantic aesthetic, and a mannerized transcendental theology, ontology, and axiology borrowed from Henry David Thoreau and especially from Ralph Waldo Emerson via Jeanne Carr. The bulk of Muir's writings supports such a framing of his ideas, but it leaves out of account a more thoroughly nonanthropocentric (or even anti-anthropocentric) dimension of his thought, which was rooted, surprisingly—and, some may think, paradoxically—in his youthful Christian tutelage.

As it seems to me, transcendentalism is in the last analysis a kind of ethereal humanism. And Stephen Fox (1981, 51) insists that after his exposure to Eastern-influenced transcendentalism, Muir "stepped, unequivocally and permanently, outside the Christian tradition." More recently, Donald Worster has gainsaid this overly neat reading of Muir's mind. "Some writers," whom Worster (1988, 268) does not name, "have seen in this emergent Muir . . . a repudiation of . . . his Scotch Presbyterian background. [But] there was a harshly negative side to Muir's vision, a disgust for human pretensions and pride that ran very close to misanthropy."

If so, Muir's misanthropy was always tempered by humor and good taste. But in any event, Muir's father, Daniel, was a religious psychopath, a Bible-reading child-beating sadist, who forced his son John to commit to memory all of the New Testament and most of the Old (Cohen 1984; Fox 1981; Muir 1913). Therefore, we may be confident that Muir knew his Scripture and was well acquainted with the biblical worldview. However thorough and complete was Muir's eventual conversion from

Presbyterianism to transcendentalism, Muir at age thirty—before he had ever set foot in the Range of Light—cast his first sustained thoughts about the human-nature relationship in the more conservative and pedestrian concepts of the Judeo-Christian worldview. "The earliest product of his pen," in the words of his editor, William Frederick Badè (1916, xxv), was a journal, written during 1867–68, and posthumously published in 1916 under the title *A Thousand Mile Walk to the Gulf*. As Muir was addressing no one but himself, we have, in this work, a most intimate and candid record of his earlier ideas.

Muir himself gave no rubric to his eccentric interpretation of Genesis and his corollary radical environmental ethic forged from Judeo-Christian ideas. In deference to Aldo Leopold (1949, 204), whose secular "land ethic" would similarly exchange Homo sapiens' "conqueror role" in respect to the "biotic community," not for the role of viceroy or steward, but for that of "plain member and citizen," I call it the "citizenship interpretation."

Aldo Leopold himself, incidentally, has very little directly to say on the subject of biblical attitudes and values respecting nature, but what he does say anticipates White's despotic reading: In the foreword to *A Sand County Almanac*, Leopold (1949, viii) comments that "conservation is getting nowhere because it is incompatible with our Abrahamic concept of land. We abuse land because we regard it as a commodity belonging to us." Such was the patriarch Abraham's view, he unmistakably implies. "When we see land as a community to which we belong," Leopold (1949, viii) goes on to say, turning the despotic view inside out, "we may begin to use it with love and respect." In "The Land Ethic," Leopold (1949, 204–5) refers to Abraham again, this time in terms even more explicitly foreshadowing White's despotic reading: "Abraham knew what the land was for: it was to drip milk and honey into Abraham's mouth. At the present moment the assurance with which we regard this assumption is inverse to the degree of our education." This remark follows right on the heels of Leopold's envisioning the ecology-driven shift, just noted, from Homo sapiens' traditional conqueror role in the land community to that of plain member and citizen.

Muir, similarly, was well aware that a despotic attitude toward the environment was generally assumed to be supported by Scripture. But rather than concur with such a reading, abandon the tradition, and look for other metaphysical grounds to support an environmental ethic, as Leopold does, Muir takes the argument straight to the Despotarians' turf and argues for human citizenship in nature squarely on biblical principles. Muir (1916, 136–37) begins with an aggressive send-up of the conventional despotic reading:

> The world we are told was made especially for man—a presumption not supported by all the facts. A numerous class of men are painfully astonished whenever they find anything living or dead, in all God's universe, which they cannot render in some way what they call useful to themselves. They have precise and dogmatic insight into the intentions of the Creator. . . . He is regarded as a civilized, law-abiding gentleman in favor of either a republican form of government or of a limited monarchy; believes in the literature and language of England; is a warm supporter of . . . Sunday schools and missionary societies; and is as purely a manufactured article as any puppet of a half penny theater.
>
> With such views of the Creator it is, of course, not surprising that erroneous views should be entertained of the creation. To such properly trimmed people, the sheep, for example, is an easy problem—food and clothing "for us," . . .

Muir (1916, 137–38) goes on to indulge his irritation at popular anthropocentrism by running through a random list of alleged God-given natural utilities. For example, "in the same pleasant plan, whales are store houses of oil for us, in lighting our dark ways until the discovery of the Pennsylvania oil wells." Most amusing, "hemp," he writes, "to say nothing of the cereals, is a case of evident destination for ships rigging, wrapping packages, and hanging the wicked." He finishes his miscellany of divine provisions for man with mention of cotton, iron, and lead, "all intended for us."

Muir (1916, 138) then returns to "the facts," and rhetorically poses the following countercases to these "closet researches of clergy": "How about those man-eating animals—lions, tigers, alligators—which smack their lips over raw man? Or about those myriads of noxious insects that destroy labor and drink his blood? Doubtless man was intended for food and drink for all these?"

In this masterpiece of theological satire, Muir (1916, 138) imagines the horrified reply of the unnamed "profound expositors of God's intentions": "Oh, no these are unresolvable difficulties connected with Eden's apple and the Devil." After rehearsing a few more countercases—poisonous minerals, plants, and fishes—and pointing up the fact that "the lord [with a small 'l'] of creation," viz., "man," is "subjected to the same laws of life as his subjects," Muir expounds an alternative environmental theology. But it is not by any stretch of the imagination a variation on the stewardship theme:

> Now, it never seems to occur to these far-seeing teachers that Nature's object in making animals and plants might possibly be first of all the happiness of each one of them, not the creation of all for the happiness of one. Why should man value himself as more than a small part of the one great unit of creation? And what creature of all that the Lord has taken the pains to make is not essential to the completeness of that unit—the cosmos? The universe would be incomplete without man; but it would also be incomplete without the smallest transmicroscopic creature that dwells beyond our conceitful eyes and knowledge. (Muir 1916, 139)

Notice that Muir here seems intentionally to mix his worldviews. He writes "Nature's object" not "God's object," but in the same sentence he also writes "the creation of all" not "the evolution of all." In the next sentence he names "the Lord" as maker of "the cosmos" which then immediately becomes "the universe." He appears, in other words, to be deliberately rereading Genesis in the light of modern science. This impression is certainly confirmed as his exposition continues,

> This star, our own good earth, made many a journey around the heavens ere man was made, and whole kingdoms of creatures enjoyed existence and returned to dust ere man appeared to claim them. After human beings have also played their part in Creation's plan, they too may disappear without any general burning or extraordinary commotion whatever. (Muir 1916, 140)

Muir wrote this, we should remind ourselves, less than a decade after the publication of *The Origin of Species*. Equally remarkable, twenty years before ecology had a name and separate identity as a science, he also wrote, "the antipathies [predator-prey relationships] existing in the Lord's great animal family must be wisely planned, like balanced repulsion and attraction in the mineral kingdom" (Muir 1916, 98). However informed by a whole 'nother way of comprehending the facts, Muir (1916, 98–99, 139) cements his citizenship reading of the place God intended for humankind in nature with a more specific and direct allusion to particulars of the creative events in Genesis:

> From the dust of the earth, from the common elementary fund, the Creator has made *Homo sapiens*. From the same material he has made every other creature, however noxious and insignificant to us. They are our earth-born companions and fellow mortals. . . . Doubtless these creatures are happy and fill the place assigned them by the great Creator of us all. . . . They, also, are his children, for He hears their cries, cares for them tenderly, and provides their daily bread. . . . How narrow we selfish, conceited creatures are in our sympathies! How blind to the rights of all the rest of creation! With what dismal irreverence do we speak of our fellow mortals! They . . . are part of God's family, unfallen, undepraved and cared for with the same species of tenderness and love as is bestowed on angels in heaven and saints on earth.

In comparison with Muir's citizenship rendering of the biblically ordained relationship of human beings to the rest of creation, the despotic and stewardship interpretations seem to differ only on the character of the archonship that God granted to humanity. Did God intend for us to be tyrant or regent? That we are lord and master of creation is not at issue. Muir, on the other hand, often writes "lord of creation" and "lord man" with evident contempt for the attitude to which such phrases allude. How, the question thus naturally arises, could Muir, a close, albeit forced, student of Scripture, have arrived at such a singular reading? I proceed to an examination of the text to see if it can support the spin Muir gives it.

THERE ARE ACTUALLY TWO GENESISES IN THE BIBLE

Lynn White Jr. not only set the agenda for subsequent environmental philosophy, he also set, it seems, a low standard of biblical scholarship for critically glossing the environmental message of Genesis. Writes White (1967, 105),

> By gradual stages a loving and all powerful God had created light and darkness, the heavenly bodies, the earth and all its plants, animals, birds, and fishes. Finally, God had created Adam and, as an afterthought, Eve to keep man from being lonely. Man named all the animals, thus establishing his dominance over them.

God planned all of this explicitly for man's benefit and rule: no item in the physical creation had any purpose save to serve man's purposes. And although man's body is made of clay, he is not simply part of nature: He is made in God's image.

I have by no means attempted to read systematically through all the apologetic literature amassed to counter this, the hard core of White's despotic reading, but most of what has casually scrolled across my screen conflates, with the same alacrity as White does here, the two very different geneses, Genesis-P and Genesis-J, that lie head to foot in the first pages of the Holy Bible.

White here begins with unmistakable allusions to the former (the creation of light and darkness, the earth and all its furnishings, and so on), then jumps over to allude to the latter (the creation of Adam and Eve and the naming of the animals), then jumps back to another allusion to the former (humanity's dominion), then jumps once again over to allude to the latter (Yahweh's forming Adam from dust), and comes to rest with a final allusion to the former (the *imago dei*).

With only slightly less redactive agility, most of the stewardship counterinterpreters begin by reminding us that the *imago dei* is a double-edged sword, and point out that God finds the creation to be "good" right off the mint. Little aid and comfort, incidentally, is given to the stewardship interpretation by repairing to the Hebrew words translated as "dominion" and "subdue." According to James Barr (1972, 61–62),

[T]here has indeed been in the modern exegetical tradition, especially when the image of God has been identified with man's dominion over the world, a tendency to dwell with some satisfaction on the *strength* of the terms. The verb *rada* "have dominion" is used physically of the treading or trampling down of the wine-press; and the verb *kabas* "subdue" means "stamp down." According to Black [1970, 37], it "is elsewhere used for the military subjugation of conquered territory, and clearly implies reliance on force"; "it is a very powerful expression of man's attitude toward the rest of nature, and suggests that he sees himself in a position of absolute command."

Nevertheless, the Stewardarians go on to insist that the initial ambiguity of the term "dominion," to define our God-given position in nature, is later unmistakably clarified by God's express declaration that Adam was put "into the garden of Eden to dress it and to keep it" (Gen. 1:16). We are created to be God's gardener, so to speak. This seems to be as clear an expression of stewardship as one could hope to find, they say. (Indeed it is the horticultural equivalent—eminently appropriate to a garden setting— of the pastoral metaphor etymologically built into the very term "steward- ship" itself, which comes from the Old English word *stïweard*, i.e., sty-ward.) As the coup de grâce, they argue that it was far from God's intention, in commanding us to have dominion and to "subdue"—a less ambiguous, more ominously tendentious term—the earth (and all its creatures), that we pollute, degrade, and destroy it (and them). Just as the vulgar Despotarians mocked by Muir, make convenient use of "Eden's apple," to explain the existence of natural evils, so the Stewardarians point out that environmental pollution, degradation, and destruction came to pass only after the "fall." Our environmental crisis is the eventual outcome of "origi- nal sin," the disobedience of Adam and Eve in tasting the fruit of the tree of the knowledge of good and evil, they argue. (Genesis, incidentally, no- where identifies the fruit of the tree of the knowledge of good and evil as apples.) For example, a most eloquent Stewardarian, Wendell Berry (1981, 268), writes, "The instruction of Genesis 1:28 was, after all, given to Adam and Eve in the time of their innocence, and it seems certain that the word 'subdue' would have had a different intent and sense for them at that time than it could have for them, or for us, after the Fall." Fallen and cursed, we have perverted this, God's "first," unnumbered commandment as we have all the ones in the Decalogue and elsewhere.

But even upon the most casual reading, one may notice that there are two entirely distinct—and entirely inconsistent—accounts of creation back and forth between which indiscriminately jump Genesis's despotic and stewardship interpreters alike. Chapter 1, verse 1 of Genesis begins with the famous first words, "In the beginning God created the heaven and the earth." There follows an account of creation consuming six days in which the order of the creation proceeds rationally—from a modern point of view, at any rate—even in a sense, scientifically. First, light was created (Gen. 1:3). (As in contemporary big bang cosmology, at first it was all flash and no substance.) Then the watery void was divided by a firmament (Gen. 1:7). On the third day, the dry land was gathered together and the plants created (Gen. 1:9–13). On the fourth, the sun, moon, and stars were hung in the firmament (Gen. 1:14–19). On the fifth and sixth, ani- mals and people were created, respectively—in the case of the latter, both male and female together, *n. b.*—(Gen. 1:20–27). Then there follow the passages—the *imago dei*, dominion, subduction, etc.—which have so exercised environmentalists (Gen. 1:26–28). Penultimately—and of special interest to animal liberationists, who have also latterly gotten into the Genesis-interpretation act—God prescribes a vegetarian diet for both people and beasts suggesting a divine intent to ordain a world not only without environmental pollution, degradation, and destruction, but a world without any interspecies bloodletting at all, on however sustainable a basis (Gen. 1:29–31). Finally, on the seventh day God rested and commemorated the cessation of labor by establishing every subsequent seventh as a Sabbath (Gen. 2:1–3).

However, with chapter 2, verse 4, everything seems to begin again, thereupon to follow an entirely different scenario: "These are the generations of the heaven and the earth in the *day* [singular] that the Lord God made the earth and the heavens." Now comes a story in which first a particular man, Adam, is created (Gen. 2:7). Then an arboreal garden—an agroforest permaculture, as it were—is planted for him to tend (Gen. 2:8–9). Next come the animals (Gen. 2:19). Then, lastly, a woman, Eve, is created (Gen. 2:21–22)—a mere "afterthought," as White provocatively (and irreverently) puts it.

Nearly three centuries of scholarly reflection and research have revealed that Genesis, as we have received it, is woven from three narrative strands, conventionally labeled J, P, and E, for the Yahwist, Priestly, and Elohist sources, respectively (Weiser 1961). The Priestly narrative comes first in the order of presentation, but is last in order of composition—composed, most scholars agree, during the fifth century B.C.E. (Weiser 1961). The Yahwist narrative—of which the garden-of-Eden account of creation is a part—is half a millennium or so older, composed in the ninth or tenth century B.C.E. (Weiser 1961). (The Elohist source does not figure in to the central texts with which environmentalists have been principally concerned and so for my purposes here can be passed over without further comment.)

SIMILARITIES BETWEEN GENESIS-P AND PRE-SOCRATIC GREEK NATURAL PHILOSOPHY

The great Cambridge classicist F. M. Cornford has pointed out the remarkable similarity between the fifth-century Genesis-P and sixth- and fifth-century pre-Socratic Greek natural philosophy. According to Cornford (1952, 200), in the most recent biblical version of creation, "the action of Elohim has become extremely abstract and remote. . . . The whole account becomes a quasi-scientific evolution of the cosmos. The process is the same as in the Greek cosmogonies—separation or differentiation out of primitive confusion."

Like the Milesians, the author of P represents the cosmos to have arisen from a primordial lawless unity, and like Thales more especially, he identifies that unity with water. That everything might be made of water, and that there are waters above as well as below may have followed "logically" from reflection on the fact that both the sky and the sea are blue and that water falls from the sky. And just as Anaximander has the world order come into being by a process of division, a "separating out," of opposites contained in the urstuff, so the author of P represents Elohim to have effected creation first by a division of opposites: "God divided the light from the darkness"; God called the "firmament"—corresponding to Hesiod's "chaos" (which means "gap" in Greek, not "confusion")—into being to "divide the waters from the waters"; and finally, from the salt waters of the sea, which had been divided by the firmament from the sweet waters of heaven, God separated off the dry land (Gen. 1: 4–6). Then, in the order, more or less, that Darwin (anticipated by Anaximander of Miletos and Empedocles of Acragas in the sixth and fifth centuries B.C.E.) represents organic beings actually to have arisen, God creates plants, animals, and Homo sapiens.

Read as a rational cosmology, Genesis-P resembles contemporaneous Greek cosmologies, virtually point for point. Heaven is a star-studded leaky vault made of fresh water, held up by an airy bubble or "firmament." It arches over a disc-shaped Earth, which is surrounded by a "river" (as the contemporaneous Greeks thought of it) of salty Ocean. Even three of the four Greek elements, water, air, and earth, are unmistakably present in Genesis-P, expressly represented by the characteristic fauna which move in or on each—swimming whales and fish, flying birds, and creeping beasts and cattle, respectively. And the simultaneous tendency of Greek philosophy toward humanism—"man is the measure of all things," etc.—is also clearly evident in Genesis-P. Indeed, P's Hebrew analog of Hellenic humanism—the *imago dei*, dominion, and subduction—is precisely what all the environmental fuss has been about.

There is something impertinent, I dare say, in the compiler(s) of the Old Testament putting the more recent account of creation before the more ancient one. Uncritical readers, by far the majority of readers, piously believe that the whole Bible proceeds from one divine source—that it is all literally the Word of God. And, moreover, most readers also piously believe that the Pentateuch, the first five books of the Bible, was transcribed by one human secretary, as tradition alleges, namely Moses. Naturally, therefore, most readers strive consciously or unconsciously for consistency in what they read. Thus, given the dyschronological order in which the two geneses are arranged, the more ancient is read in the light of the more modern. To get a fresh reading, therefore, of the original, the more venerable Yahwist version of creation—and the Genesis, moreover, to which Muir alludes exclusively—I suggest that we set aside the Hellenized upstart, the Johnny-come-lately Priestly version of creation, try to forget all about it, and see what the older Yahwist text has to say standing alone.

NATURE AND HUMAN NATURE IN GENESIS-J

First, as Artur Weiser (1961, 73) comments, in J "the primeval condition of the world before the creation . . . is pictured . . . as a desert"—a far more appropriate image of primal homogeneity for the Sinai-sobered Hebrews than the watery *apeiron*, an image natural and appropriate to the coastal Ionian philosophers, from whom the author of P seems heavily to have borrowed. A mist watered the whole face of this barren ground and Yahweh formed a man from the mud thus made and breathed into his nostrils the breath of life (Gen. 2:6–7). As Weiser (1961, 73) also comments, in sharp contrast to the formal style of P, "Gen. 2: 4ff . . . tells the story in a lively and vivid fashion."

The "breath of life" is a divine essence and may prefigure the *imago dei* of the more sophisticated version that will have come along in another four or five hundred years. Jeanne Kay (1988, 314), comments that "The Hebrew word *nefesh* is used in the Bible both for the human spirit and also for animal spirits. . . . *Ruach*, meaning wind, spirit, or breath, is the source through which God animates all life." However, later in the day, when the animals are created—though God also forms them, working with mud, in the same lunch-bucket style—no mention is made of God's breathing into them the breath of life (Gen. 2:19). In his brief gloss, Muir ignores this difference and stresses instead the "dust of the earth, . . . the common elementary fund" from which "the Creator has made Homo sapiens" and "every other creature." Still, I think Muir is right to insist that in this text, at least, one finds a much closer communion between us and the earth and the animals than the Despotarians (and Stewardarians as well) admit. Certainly one finds in J a much greater commonality among all creatures than in the canonically earlier, but temporally later account.

Apparently thinking of Genesis as a composite whole, White (1967, 1205) remarks that "man shares, in great measure, God's transcendence over nature." That is certainly a fair inference from P, but the measure is inverted in J. In Hebrew, the word *adamah* means "earth." Thus, the man's very name, Adam, assimilates him to the earth. John S. Kselman (1985, 12) comments that "a number of scholars have proposed that the noun *adam*, 'man,' does not only indicate 'humankind' but, in a number of instances, is a masculine variant . . . of the feminine form of *adamah*." Setting aside such linguistic arcana, as E. A. Speiser (1964, 16) comments,

[I]n *adam* "man" and *adama* "soil, ground" there is an obvious play on words, a practice which the Bible shares with other ancient literatures. This should not be mistaken for mere punning. Names were regarded not only as labels but also as symbols, magical keys as it were to the nature and essence of the given being or thing. . . . The writer or speaker who resorted to "popular etymologies" was not interested in derivation as such. The closest approach in English to the juxtaposition of the Hebrew nouns before us might be "earthling: earth."

Phyllis Trible (1978, 77) also stresses the verbal association between Adam and the earth: "A play on words already establishes relationship between earth creature *(adam)* and the earth *(ha adama)*." *Adam* may, in fact, involve a triple word play, adding another layer of earthy association to the name. According to geographer Jeanne Kay (1989, 219), "the Hebrew cognate *adom* also means the color red, strongly suggesting a visual relationship [with] . . . the Mediterranean region's terra rosa soils."

After making a man—an "earthling" (à la Speiser) or "earth creature" (à la Trible)—God planted the garden of Eden. Is Eden a special place in the world or is it meant to signify the whole living, green earth? J's geography of Eden is as tantalizingly ambiguous as its anthropology, but the whole-of-nature reading is powerfully suggested. Eden lies in an "east-ward" direction (Gen. 2:8), but east of what we are not told. Other clues are more definite, however. Of the four rivers draining Eden the first seems to be the north-flowing Nile, "that compasseth the whole land of Ethio-pia" (or "Cush"); the fourth bears the name in King James's translation of J that it bears on maps today, the south-flowing Euphrates; and the third, Hiddikel, is the Tigris (Gen. 2:11–14). Eden, thus, seems to encompass the face of the earth from the Nile valley on the southwest to the region north of the Persian Gulf on the east—the entire known universe in the experience of tenth- or ninth-century Israelites. Eden, clearly (or at least as clearly as myth will allow), is nature primeval.

As Yahweh's breathing into Adam the breath of life in J may prefigure the *imago dei* in P, so the fact that in J Yahweh also "put him into the garden to dress and keep it" may prefigure humanity's dominion over nature—later expressly developed in P. Dominion over nature in P may be further prefigured in J by the privilege God grants Adam to name the animals, "thus establishing his dominance over them," as White puts it, assuming the same primitive logomancy just explained by Speiser (Gen. 2:19–20).

But, as in the case of our transcendence over nature, so in the case of our dominance, the measure is far less in J than in P. To be sure, Adam may name the animals and thus control them, but why were they created? "And the Lord God said, It is not good that the man should be alone; I will make an help meet for him," answers the text (Gen. 2:18). They were created, as Muir somewhat recklessly put it, to be our "earth-born com-panions and our fellow mortals." Actually, they were created as *candidates* for companion-to-Adam, a niche that Eve was finally to fill. Though Muir exaggerates, his point is, nevertheless, essentially well taken. Even though no proper companion for the man was found among the animals, the mere idea that Yahweh and Adam might look among them for one sug-gests once more that people were intended to share a lot in common with other creatures rather than to share "in large measure" God's transcen-dence over creation.

There follows then the account of how Yahweh made a woman from one of Adam's ribs, having caused a deep sleep to fall upon the first earth creature. Of course, this account does go out of its way to reverse the ordinary birth relationship in which the male is born from the female. Woman in J is born from Adam, thus establishing the dominance of the male over the female—just as in the immediately preceding episode the dominance of people generally over the animals was established. Lynn White Jr. mentions this episode in Genesis, I speculate, to ally feminist with environmentalist enmity against the text. Leaving it to my feminist colleagues to critique, I shall say no more about that unnatural first human birth, so as not to digress any further from the central environmental theme of this discussion. Instead, I move straight on to the fulcrum of Muir's citizenship interpretation, the meaning of the knowledge of good and evil.

THE KNOWLEDGE OF GOOD AND EVIL—WHAT IT IS NOT

The mysterious tree of the knowledge of good and evil is first mentioned along with the all-too-symbolically-transparent tree of life as being among the other good and pleasant trees in the midst of the garden (Gen. 2:9). It is mentioned again, just before the creation of the animals, and the man is expressly forbidden to eat of it, on pain of death (Gen. 2:17). As soon as the woman has been created, married off, and settled in, it returns to center stage (Gen. 3:1–3).

We need not tarry over the familiar story of the temptation. The subtle serpent beguiled the woman, who ate of the fruit of the tree of the knowledge of good and evil. She didn't die—not forthwith at any rate. And she found the woeful tree to be as good for food and pleasant to the eyes as the other trees of the garden and desirable to boot to make one wise. So she also gave some unto her husband and he too did eat of it (Gen. 3:1–6). Exactly as the serpent promised, "the eyes of them both were opened" (Gen. 3:7).

And just what wisdom dawned on them?

"They knew that they were naked" (Gen. 3:7). That's it. That's the only noetic datum that the text says that they acquired. No other specific knowledge or wisdom is mentioned. We are left to wonder how this particular bit of knowledge is related to something so fundamental and general as the knowledge of good and evil. What's the connection?

In the popular mind, the knowledge of good and evil is inevitably equated with the knowledge of sexual congress. Certainly this hypothesis can be linked simply and directly with nakedness. Exposed genitalia arouse sexual desire. Immediately the man and the woman sew aprons of fig leaves to cover themselves (Gen. 3:7), adding credence to the vulgar view. The whole story, moreover, is erotically charged—we are given to imagine a perpetually youthful adult couple, both nude, who spend days without number in a lush, tropical garden with nothing to do but eat the mangoes, bananas, figs, pomegranates, and whatnot everywhere surrounding them, chat with Yahweh during His walks through the garden in the cool of the evening, . . . and entertain one another. Since Freud and Jung have made us so keenly aware that the serpent, who tempts the woman, is a patent phallic symbol in dream as well as myth, the coital gloss even seems "scientifically" supported by modern psychology.

But, despite all of this, knowledge of sexual congress cannot be the correct understanding of the knowledge of good and evil in Genesis-J, because the man and woman have already lawfully known one another— in the biblical sense of the term. For what else could be meant when it is earlier said, *before* they ate of the fruit of the tree of the knowledge of good and evil, that "therefore shall a man leave his father and mother, and shall cleave unto his wife: and they shall be one flesh" (Gen. 2:24)?

Having disposed of the vulgar interpretation, which equates good and evil with sex—as if chastity were all there is to morality, or as if sex not money were the root of all evil—let us consider a more general, if equally simple reading. Before eating of the fruit of the tree of the knowledge of good and evil, we might suppose that the first man and woman simply had no knowledge whatever of good and evil. That is, they were unable to distinguish right from wrong. If acquaintance with the distinction between good and evil, right and wrong, *simpliciter*, is what we are given to understand that the man and the woman acquired upon eating of the fruit of the tree of the knowledge of good and evil, then Yahweh is slandered by implication. For not having eaten of the fruit of the tree of the knowledge of good and evil, the man and the woman could not *know* that it was wrong, evil, to disobey Yahweh and eat of the fruit of the tree of the knowledge of good and evil. They would be caught in a double-bind, a "Catch-22," and Yahweh would be guilty of cruelly toying with them . . . planting (literally) a deadly trap for them . . . setting them up for a fall.

So, let us go back to the drawing board, and work with the scant— but, as we shall see, entirely sufficient—information that we are given to discover the true and profound meaning of this mysterious knowledge.

ANTHROPOCENTRISM AND THE
KNOWLEDGE OF GOOD AND EVIL

The serpent says that the knowledge of good and evil is a divine perquisite: "and ye shall be as gods, knowing good and evil" (Gen. 3:5). As it turns out, the serpent did not lie about that either. Yahweh confirms it. Apparently addressing other gods in the neighborhood, Yahweh says, "Behold, the man is become one of us, to know good and evil" (Gen. 3:22)." Of J, Weiser (1961, 103) remarks, "individual passages"—these, for example— "still enable its original polytheistic mythology to be recognized." And so that man not become a god in fact, as well as in pretense to an exclusively divine wisdom, i.e., "lest he put forth his hand and take also of the tree of life, and eat, and live forever, . . ." Yahweh "sent him forth from the garden of Eden to till the ground from which he was taken" (Gen. 3:22–23).

Putting the two clues together—(1) the phenomenological discovery that the first couple made upon eating the fruit of the tree of the knowledge of good and evil, viz., that they were naked, and (2) that the knowledge of good and evil is properly a divine not a human knowledge—I suggest that the knowledge of good and evil means neither knowledge of sexual congress, certainly, nor the simple knowledge of the difference between right and wrong, but the power to *judge*, to *decide*, to *determine* what is good and what is evil *in relation to self*. When the author of J says "they knew that they were naked," we may understand that to be just a graphic way of saying that they became *self*-conscious, *self*-aware. That information, which a moment ago seemed so particular and trivial, *is* just the knowledge of good and evil—if not the whole of the knowledge of good and evil, then the foundation for all the rest. For once aware of themselves, they may treat themselves as an axiological point of reference. Indeed, the text suggests by its very silence on any alternative to Yahweh's banishment, or any compromise, and by the finality of that banishment, that once aware of themselves they *will* inevitably treat themselves as an intrinsically valuable hub to which other creatures and the creation as a whole may be referred for appraisal. Self-consciousness is a necessary condition for self-centered-ness, self-interestedness.

Yahweh, it seems, cares for the creation as a whole. J's idyllic descrip-tion of Eden, the delight that Yahweh evidently takes in the garden, the fact that it was created not for us, but we for it, "to dress it and to keep it," all subliminally indicate that Yahweh's concern is for the whole of nature and for each of its parts equally, not for people alone or even for people especially. At any rate, that is exactly how Muir reads this text. Once again:

Why should man regard himself as more than a small part of the one great unit of creation? And what creature of all that the Lord has taken the pains to make is not essential to that unit—the cosmos. The universe would be incomplete with-out man; but it would also be incomplete without the smallest transmicroscopic creature that dwells beyond our conceitful eyes and knowledge.

Taking courage from Muir's insight, we may fill in explicitly what he finds unmistakably implied. Once human beings became self-aware and therefore self-centered, they began to size up the creation in relation to themselves. Some of the things that Yahweh had created people declared "evil" weeds and vermin—nettles and poison ivy; mosquitoes, wolves, bears, and the like—and put them on an agenda for extermination. In the inimitable words of Muir (1916, 141), "all uneatable and uncivilizable animals, and all plants which carry prickles, are deplorable evils which . . . require the cleansing chemistry of universal planetary combustion." On the other hand, the edible plants and tamable animals are pronounced "good," and they are cultivated and encouraged.

The gnarly curses that Yahweh imposes upon Adam and Eve, it seems so harshly and remorselessly, represent and epitomize, in the powerful and subliminal symbolism typical of mythopoeia, the inevitable alien-ation from nature that necessarily attends anthropocentrism. If the part would separate itself from the whole, and parse the whole into good and evil categories in relation to self-interest, then the part, by that very act, disrupts the harmonious life of the whole.

ANTHROPOCENTRISM AND YAHWEH'S CURSES

First, there will be enmity between human beings and the lower animals, represented by the serpent (Gen. 3:14–15). What could be a clearer indication of the rupture of a harmonious world?

Second, for women, childbirth—natural and easy for all other species—shall be unnaturally labored and painful (Gen. 3:15).

Third, for men, work becomes necessary. Animals live, as Adam and Eve once did, on what nature freely provides. With the emergence of anthropocentrism, agriculture comes into being, and with it, thorns, thistles, and sweat (Gen. 3:17–19). As agro-ecologist Wes Jackson (1987, 6, 64) remarks, "The Fall, at least as Christians have understood it from Hebrew mythology, can be understood in a modern sense as an event that moved us from our original hunting-gathering state, in which nature provided for us exclusively, to an agricultural state, in which we took a larger measure of control over our food production, changing the face of the earth along the way. . . . I suspect that agriculture is at the core of the Fall."

Agriculture is indeed a central and ambivalent preoccupation of J. In the beginning, the dusty chaos was barren for two reasons: because "the Lord God had not caused it to rain upon the earth and there was not a man to till the ground" (Gen. 2:5). Yahweh put the earthling "into the garden of Eden to dress it and to keep it"—a further allusion to cultivation of a kind. But upon being banished from the fruity forest, people afterward must eat "the herb of the field" (Gen. 3:18). The light pruning and raking implied in dressing and keeping God's permaculture is, accordingly, exchanged for heavy and coercive field work. Genesis-J thus insightfully unites labor-intensive agriculture and anthropocentrism. The connection is this: Farming begins precisely when the "good" plants are favored and cultivated. The ordinary course of nature must be opposed. One gets one's bread thereby, but it takes work. You have to plow the ground, hoe the "weeds," and battle the "pests." It also insightfully unites agriculture and an increase in human fertility: Yahweh says to Eve, "I will greatly multiply thy sorrow *and thy conception*" (Gen. 3:16, emphasis added).

And if all that were not a clear enough indication that original sin is just anthropocentrism itself and the inevitable alienation from nature that it brings in its train, the author of J represents Yahweh to expel Adam and Eve from Eden, from nature altogether. From the point of view of my earlier geographical interpretation, this expulsion is not literally to another locale; it represents, rather, the abandonment of Homo sapiens' intended ecological "place" in nature.

Finally, God imposes the death sentence upon Adam and Eve for their disobedience. Death, I think, is clearly but subtly connected to self-consciousness—as a matter of logic. A conscious, but not *self*-conscious being lives in the eternal present. She remembers no personal past, and dreads no future end to her personal existence. No self-consciousness, no experiential identity as a continuous being, no personal death.

Of course, I do not mean to suggest that other animals, if indeed they lack self-consciousness, and the ancestors of Homo sapiens do not and did not die, organically speaking. I mean that they do not and did not die phenomenologically speaking. Before eating the fruit of the tree of the knowledge of good and evil, man and woman were naked, but did not *know* that they were naked. Similarly, before eating the fruit of the tree of the knowledge of good and evil, they died, but they did not *know* that they died.

Eventually, "men began to multiply on the face of the earth" (Gen. 6:1). Yahweh remarks, "My spirit shall not always strive with man. . ." (Gen. 6:3). Indeed, so out of hand had become anthropocentric, agricultural humanity that "it repented the Lord that he had made man on the earth, and it grieved him at his heart. And the Lord said, I will destroy man whom I have created from the face of the earth; . . ." (Gen. 6:6). Fortunately for us, however, "Noah found grace in the eyes of the Lord" (Gen. 6:8). Yahweh did not destroy us altogether, but seems to have hoped, after cleansing everything by means of the flood, to make a new beginning with the righteous Noah and his seed. Apparently, however, there was no way to restore us to our previous animal-like innocence and integration with the rest of creation. Once we had tasted the fruit of the tree of the knowledge of good and evil, there was no possibility of a return to Eden.

THE ATAVISM OF GENESIS-J

Stepping back from the details of this most remarkable narrative, one may sense here deep racial memories and a nostalgia for a past that, by the time

J was composed, three thousand years ago, is only dimly visible—as through a glass darkly. J seems openly to lament the Neolithic revolution, the shift from foraging to agriculture that had befallen evolving Homo sapiens some seven millennia beforehand. If the Nile is not the modern name of the River Gihon, if Cush has been misrendered, "Ethiopia" by King James's scholars, and if, therefore, Eden is to be understood as a place in nature, not nature as a whole, a place eastward of Palestine, then J even seems also to have pinpointed the exact location of the baleful origins of agriculture—Mesopotamia, the Tigris and Euphrates valleys. It regards an agricultural modus vivendi as a cursed way of life and marks the dawn of the Neolithic as the point of departure for an upwardly spiralling human population and a multitude of human troubles. It accurately, if in a foreshortened fashion, suggests that Homo sapiens' earliest ancestors dwelt in a tropical forest and fed on fruit. It yearns for a return to that simian life of unselfconscious, guiltless ease and absorption. Then, there was no death, in a sense, because there was no self-awareness. And, in a sense, there were not many people, only two, a generic, earthy everyman and everywoman, for the same reason. Perhaps this latter point warrants a brief explanation.

As a philosopher I have always had a problem understanding the Hindu doctrine of reincarnation. For if one does not remember one's former life (or lives) then how is one's present self any more identical with one's former self (or selves) than with other past centers of consciousness? "I" live for a while, let's say during the eighteenth century, and die. Then, I am born (again?) during the twentieth, the person who is the author of this book. One continuous series of phenomenological events ends and, two hundred years later, another begins. Absent self-consciousness uniting "my" past life and my present one, then how am I identical with one eighteenth-century person rather than another? Ah, but absent self-awareness how am I identical with my "own" (as I can say only because I am self-conscious) immediate past, present, and future; or different from the past, present, and future of some other conscious being? No self-consciousness, no experienced identity as a continuous being, no phenomenological difference between me and you.

However that may be, J is, in a word, atavistic. It suggests that salvation lies in an evolutionary reversal—but bars the way back with cherubim and a flaming sword. It urges a return to innocence, to immersion in nature—but provides no recipe for fulfilling that longing. The environmental ethic that it seems to suggest, given how far we have "progressed," appears impractical to all except a few scattered earth-hippies stuck in the 1960s. It seems to recommend that we lose our*selves*; quit work; go back to the jungle; take off our clothes; get naked; don't worry; be happy; don't hassle the animals; live on fruit and other forage; have fewer children (as a consequence perhaps of a low-fat diet); and just do what comes naturally. One may notice, I think, in Muir's accounts of his wilderness adventures a striving for just this style of life.

In addition to the sheer impracticability of the apparent retrogressive orientation of the citizenship environmental ethic, one might argue that there lurks a glaring formal contradiction at its core. We have tasted the forbidden fruit. The effects of its esters are irreversible. Try as we may, we cannot return to Eden. After all, even Muir came down from the mountains, married, farmed, raised children, and wrote books.

But perhaps, invoking a helical historical image borrowed from W. B. Yeats, we can return to Eden at a higher level of consciousness, a level of consciousness that does not negate, but transcends self-consciousness. Arne Naess and his followers have propounded just this idea—albeit without reference to the fruit of the tree of the knowledge of good and evil—in their concept of the "ecological self" or "Self- [with a capital 'S'] realization." Writes Naess (1987, 40), "It seems to me that in the future more emphasis has to be given to the conditions under which we most naturally widen and deepen our 'self.' With a sufficiently wide and deep 'self,' *ego* and *alter* as opposites are stage by stage eliminated. The distinction is in a way transcended."

Thus our damned self-consciousness, lamented by J, might be less overcome by self-abnegation, by a return to simple consciousness, than transcended by Self-realization, *sensu* Naess. Naess's idea is captured concretely and graphically by Australian environmental activist and Deep Ecologist John Seed in respect to an appropriately Edenic setting. After quoting the passage from P (Gen. 9:2), quoted here two paragraphs below, Seed (1985, 243) writes, "As the implications of evolution and ecology are internalized . . . there is an identification with all life. . . . Alienation subsides. . . . 'I am protecting the rainforest' develops to 'I am a part of the rainforest protecting myself.'" Seed goes on to say, "I am that part of the rainforest recently emerged into thinking." But in light of these investigations here we might want to say rather, "I am that part of the rainforest recently emerged into thinking . . . and more recently still that part of the rainforest gone beyond egoistic thinking to a wider sense of self."

In any case, we can well imagine that literate, progressive, fifth-century Hebrew priests were mortified by the melancholy primitivism and atavism in J and—with the alternative to its hopeless nostalgia offered by Deep Ecology some two and a half millennia off in the future—deliberately constructed P to amplify the slightest distinctions between Homo sapiens and the other creatures drawn in J. That P was written deliberately to off-set the implications of J is argued by Richard Elliott Friedman (1987) in *Who Wrote the Bible?* Thus, the author of P might make it seem to be God's intent all along that people be a case apart from the rest of nature, and that people were in fact given dominion over and charged to subdue the earth and fill it from pole to pole and ocean to ocean with our own species.

Evidence of such deliberate tampering comes in chapter 9 of Genesis when, after the flood abates, the anthropocentrism of the author of P appears again, this time more militant than ever: "And the fear of you and the dread of you shall be upon every beast of the earth, and upon every fowl of the air, upon all that moveth upon the earth, and upon all the fishes of the sea" (Gen. 9:2). Exploiting the new deal that God cuts with humanity after the watery decimation, the author of P seems quite consciously to recall and then to countermand the God-given pre-fall and pre-flood human dietary regime: "Every moving thing that liveth shall be meat for you; even as the green herb have I given you all things" (Gen. 9:3). Thus he justifies carnivory. In sum, P, one might say, makes a virtue of anthropocentrism, the very thing that J condemns as original sin.

One might also better understand the militant anthropocentrism of modern Despotarians. As Muir (1916, 139) remarks, "the fearfully good, the orthodox, of this laborious patch-work of modern civilization cry 'Heresy' on every one whose sympathies reach a single hair's breadth beyond the boundary epidermis of our own species." Perhaps they sense that a tide of antianthropocentrism wells just beneath the surface of Scripture and must be diked up lest it spill out and run riot. Now perhaps we can better understand why, moreover, the priestly compiler of the Old Testament did not simply slip the progressive and humanistically oriented version of creation in after—but put it instead in front of—J. Friedman

(1987) argues convincingly that the "redactor" was Ezra, an Aaronid priest working in and on behalf of the priestly source. Doubtless he wanted P to blunt J's atavism and craftily redirect its original nostalgic sentiment and primitivistic passion toward something that he regarded as more progressive and forward-looking—agriculturally based civilization.

A CONTEMPORARY CITIZENSHIP JUDEO-CHRISTIAN ENVIRONMENTAL ETHIC: A GLIMPSE OVER THE MOUNTAINTOP

Impatient with both the narrow textual focus and the anachronistic odor of the whole debate provoked by Lynn White Jr., Jeanne Kay (1988, 311) complains about the distortion we risk in "viewing Iron Age beliefs through modern environmental lenses." Reviewing the relevant texts in the whole Hebrew Bible, Kay (1987, 217, 227) concludes that primarily

> nature is God's tool of reward and punishment and its beneficence depends upon human morality. . . . A society which explains destruction of pasturage as the result of God's anger over idolatry or insincerity in temple sacrifices, rather than as the outcome of climatic fluctuations or overgrazing, may have little to offer modern resource management. Few environmentalists today believe [or will be persuaded by the Bible to believe] that environmental deterioration results from oppression of widows and orphans.

But Kay's excellent Old Testament historiography misses the point. Contemporary Jews and Christians, searching for meaningful advice about how to live in the world in which today they find themselves, will consult the Bible and will inevitably ponder what they read (in translation) in light of their contemporary concerns, their personal experience, and their own locale. And as to the disproportionate attention lavished on Genesis at the expense of the rest of the Bible in the contemporary debate about biblical environmental attitudes and values, not only is Genesis more explicitly concerned with setting out the Big Picture than other passages in the Bible, the fact that it comes at the very beginning also makes it a more important source for contemporary Judeo-Christian environmental attitudes and values than other biblical books: The slowest and least disciplined readers will have gotten through its first few chapters, even if they go no farther with their sacred studies.

The despotic, stewardship, and citizenship models are all, in a sense mythic, not scholarly interpretations. Though the work of historians of ideas and Biblical scholars may be of use in their development, they are not intended to reveal what the Bible actually said in an archaic language to its ancient audience about the proper human relationship to nature. Lynn White Jr., rather, intended to explore how the Bible may plausibly have been read in the late Medieval, early Modern, and Modern West to inspire and justify massive technological transformations of the environment. As Roderick Nash (1988, 89) notes, "White knew that the relevant question was not, what does [the Bible] mean but what did it mean to a particular society at a given time and place?" And the proponents of the stewardship interpretation argue that however Scripture may have been used in the past to motivate and justify human tyranny over other creatures and nature as a whole—all in the name of human progress—it can very plausibly be made to say to us, here and now, that we ought to govern nature with humility, care, and responsibility.

For more radical environmentalists who feel no more comfortable with the managerial anthropocentrism of the stewardship reading, however benign, than with the defiant human chauvinism of the despotic reading—but who still relate to Scripture—I resurrect and reconstruct here Muir's hitherto unheralded and incompletely developed citizenship model.

So just how can we live in the light of the Judeo-Christian citizenship environmental ethic? We cannot go back to Eden—to foraging and to simple animal consciousness—as I just pointed out, but we can hope, individually and collectively, to transcend self-centeredness and achieve deep ecological Self-realization. Attempting to translate that stance toward nature into action in the world, however, may lead to contradictions of another sort. How can we resolve what seem to be the irreconcilable conflicts of interest that exist in a world in which the divine injunction of P—that people seize dominion over the earth and subdue it and that we be fruitful and multiply—has been at last fulfilled? Can we, at this late date, afford to open our eyes to "the rights of all the rest of creation," as Muir calls on us to do, while, in a global village already bursting at the seams and still growing exponentially, meeting basic human needs and vouchsafing basic human rights continue to elude our efforts?

Contemporary environmentalists and contemporary proponents of human economic development share a common understanding of the global environmental *problematique*, though they weigh in on opposite sides of the issue. As one economist (Baxter 1974) put it, notoriously, there are people and penguins and when push comes to shove human rights take precedence over penguin rights. Environmentalists, on the other hand, see themselves as sticking up for the rights of penguins, mountain gorillas, timber wolves, and all the other threatened and endangered species in a swelling flood of humanity.

To resolve their conflict, environmentalists and proponents of human economic growth and development have basically agreed to zone the globe, roughly in proportion to the political clout each can command. Islands, large and small, of "habitat"—in the sea of humanity and humanity's warrens, roads, and domestic plants and animals—are reserved for the wild creatures. The large islands are called wilderness areas "where," in the words of the U.S. Wilderness Act of 1964, "the earth and its community of life are untrammeled by man, where man himself is a visitor who does not remain" (Nash 1967, 5). The smaller are called wildlife refuges, nature reserves, and national parks. This shared understanding of conservation rests on a shared philosophical assumption, viz., that people are a case apart from the rest of nature, and an even deeper shared metaphysical assumption, *viz.*, that the world is an aggregate, a mere collection or assortment, of separable parts.

The Judeo-Christian citizenship environmental ethic, however, challenges both of these assumptions. At the core of the citizenship interpretation of the Big Picture set out at the beginning of the oldest Hebrew sacred texts is the notion that people are created to be a part of, not to be set apart from, nature. The human/nature bifurcation—and, a fortiori, the bifurcation of human interests and the interests of all the rest of creation—was unintended by Yahweh. The very concept of conflicting and competing interests emerged, taking the citizenship point of view, from a presumptuous act on the part of the original human couple. As Modern secular ethicists urge us to exchange narrow, shortsighted self-interest for an "enlightened" self-interest, so a contemporary citizenship environmental ethicist might urge us to exchange Modern enlightened self-interest for a postModern "embedded" self-interest. And the central insight of ecology— the contemporary myth inspiring the citizenship reading of the ancient text—is that the world's myriad living beings do not exist in isolation from one another. We earth creatures are all enmeshed in a tangled web of life.

Although the web-of-life metaphor has become hackneyed, it seems, nevertheless, neither to have been well understood nor to have thoroughly percolated into the collective cultural consciousness. From an ecological point of view, as ecologist Paul Shepard (1969, 2) so beautifully expressed it,

[T]he self [is] a center of organization, constantly drawing on and influencing the surroundings, whose skin and behavior are soft zones contacting the world instead of excluding it. . . . Ecological thinking . . . requires a vision across boundaries. The epidermis of the skin is ecologically like a pond surface or forest soil, not a shell so much as a delicate interpenetration. It reveals the self as ennobled and extended rather than threatened as part of the landscape and the ecosystem, because the beauty and complexity of nature are continuous with ourselves.

Shepard (1969, 3) goes on to endorse Alan Watts's felicitous phrase, "the world is your body." And, complementarily of course, each of us is the world: the focus of a unique concatenation of relationships with all the other foci—the "knots in the biospheric web of relations," as Arne Naess (1973, 95) put it.

Self-realization, so understood, leads us, then, to reframe our practical environmental problems. Framing our most important latter-day existential dilemma as human rights versus the rights of nature, indeed, is part of the problem, not a correct statement of the problem. To think in terms of multiple centers of sharply defined, exclusive, and competing interests in a zero-sum struggle for life, from a deep ecological point of view, is like thinking of the parts of our bodies in a similar way. We do not pit the rights of the heart against the rights of the liver or the rights of the hands against the rights of the feet. From an ecological point of view, it makes as little sense to pit the rights of people against the rights of other creatures and of nature as a whole. Pursuing Self-realization and adopting its corollary embedded self-interest approach to problem solving leads us instinctively to avoid simply assuming a zero sum and to look first for a win-win solution when human aspirations confront environmental and ecological exigencies.

Rather than thinking, therefore, of the planet as divided into ever-expanding human economic development zones—assumed to be inevitably environmentally destructive—and ever-shrinking wilderness areas and biological *refugia*, let us think instead about creating a garden planet. We can no more recreate the original garden of Eden than we can recover our aboriginal unselfconsciousness. But we can try to live harmoniously in and with nature—not by reverting to a condition of preagricultural savagery, but by employing all of our postindustrial technological ingenuity and ecological understanding to create an environmentally benign sustainable civilization (chapter 18).

Don't get me wrong. I support—with both purse and pen—wilderness zones and wildlife reserves as ardently as any environmentalist. But I think that *in addition to* dedicating tracts of land for the exclusive habitation of other species, both plant and animal, we might also envision and then attempt to create patterns of human development and styles of life that are adapted to the natural ecosystems in which they are enmeshed. It is possible, in principle, for human economic activities to be compatible with ecological diversity, integrity, and beauty. Not only that, it is possible, in principle, though it seems like heresy for an environmentalist to say so, for human economic activities to enhance natural ecosystems. Yea, verily I say unto thee that we can enrich nature, while enriching ourselves. Surely we can envision and work to create an eminently livable, systemic, postindustrial technological society well adapted to and at peace and in harmony with is organic environment. Can't we come to value a plethora of useless products and needless gadgets less and natural aesthetic, intellectual, and spiritual bounty more? A civilized, technological humanity can live not merely in peaceful coexistence but in benevolent symbiosis with nature. Is our current mechanical technological civilization the only one imaginable? Is the nature preserve the only way we can effect conservation? Aren't there alternative technologies? Can't we be good citizens of the biotic community—drawing an honest living from nature and giving back as much or more than we extract? We cannot find God's paradise lost and return to a state of innocence among its trees, but perhaps we can cooperate with nature to transform the industrial wasteland into a healthy, self-sustaining planetary garden of which we can be proud.

11

Rolston on Intrinsic Value:
A Deconstruction

THE CONCEPT OF THE INTRINSIC VALUE OF NATURE
IN ENVIRONMENTAL PHILOSOPHY

Despite its broad audience appeal and the wide variety of topics it covers, *Environmental Ethics* by Holmes Rolston III (1988) is driven by a rather narrow, and somewhat technical, concern in the young, controversial, and—from a professional point of view—still marginal subdiscipline of environmental philosophy. Rolston's greater audience, he must have felt, would not be interested in the principal personages and historical details of the scholarly debate (which I summarize in the paragraphs that follow) and so he keeps them mostly offstage. But to his colleagues in the field, it should be abundantly clear that in *Environmental Ethics*, Rolston relentlessly pursues what has emerged as the central theoretical quest of environmental philosophy—intrinsic value for nonhuman natural entities and nature as a whole. His book is subtitled "duties to and values in the natural world." But as Rolston sets things up, we have duties to the natural world only to the extent that we may find values in it. Hence, since the former rest on the latter, the latter are what ultimately matter. It would not be inaccurate to say that *Environmental Ethics*, the book, is a monument to a single general idea—nonanthropocentric and nonanthropogenic objective, intrinsic value in nature.

The first papers in environmental ethics by professional philosophers appeared in 1973. In "Is There a Need for a New, an Environmental Ethic?" Richard Sylvan claimed in effect that what he called "dominant Western ethical traditions" provide only instrumental, not intrinsic, value for non-human natural entities and nature as a whole (Routley 1973). To demonstrate his point, in a rough and ready way, Sylvan concocted a thought experiment in which the "last man . . . lays about him eliminating, as far as he can, every living thing, animal or plant. . . . What he does," Sylvan argued, "is quite permissible according to [the] basic [human] chauvinism" characteristic of the dominant traditions (Routley 1973, 207). Arne Naess's 1973 paper, "The Shallow and the Deep, Long-Range Ecology Movement: A Summary," was less focused on ethics than Sylvan's, but Naess (1973, 95–96) does remark (incorrectly, as my experience suggests) that "the ecological field-worker acquires a deep-seated respect, or even veneration, for ways and forms of life . . . that others reserve for fellow-men." And the first "plank" of the "platform" for the Deep Ecology movement, which Naess coauthored with George Sessions, declares the intrinsic value of "nonhuman life on Earth" (Devall and Sessions 1985, 70.) In "Is There an Ecological Ethic?," the first paper in environmental ethics by an American professional philosopher, Rolston (1975) himself insisted that a proper ecological ethic rested on finding "good," "worth," "value" in nature. Rolston (1986) pursued this goal in a series of subsequent papers. Tom Regan (1981) supplied the sharpest possible definition of the issue. He distinguished between a "management ethic," "an ethic for the *use* of the environment," and a genuine environmental ethic, "an ethic *of* the environment," and reiterated in no uncertain terms, Sylvan's, Naess's, and Rolston's intimations that such an ethic turned crucially on finding objective "intrinsic worth" in nature: "The development of what can properly be called an environmental ethic," he wrote, "requires that we postulate inherent value in nature" (Regan 1981, 34). In my own papers, going back to 1979, I have also affirmed the importance of the value question in environmental ethics and early on endorsed the postulate of nature's objective, intrinsic value (Callicott 1989).

There have, however, been dissenters. Bryan Norton, for example, has attacked the anthropocentric/nonanthropocentric, instrumental/intrinsic distinctions as otiose (1986). Norton (1989) points out that whether rain forests are intrinsically valuable or instrumentally valuable the practical consequences are the same, viz., that we ought to work to save them. The philosophical debate is merely academic—in the worst sense of the word—and needlessly divisive, Norton (1989) charges. Further, environmental philosophers alienate themselves from the "real world" of environmental affairs (prominently inhabited, in Norton's view, by environmental lobbyists in Washington, D.C.) because of our interminable bickering about such abstruse problems, without apparent practical moment. Theoretically, Norton (1989) defuses the issue with a neopragmatist gloss. If two theories "converge" on the same practical payoff, they differ only verbally. Of course I thoroughly disagree (chapter 12), and I am grateful to Rolston for reaffirming the centrality of the question of intrinsic value in nature for environmental ethics. With Rolston's book now at the forefront of the field, the problem of whether or not nature possesses intrinsic as well as instrumental value and the problem of the ontological status of values are thrust once more to the foreground of debate.

OBJECTIVIST AND SUBJECTIVIST ACCOUNTS OF INTRINSIC VALUE IN NATURE

Rolston stands tall, among a handful of other environmental philosophers, in holding, without qualification, that intrinsic value actually exists *objectively* in nature. Suppose all consciousness were obliterated at a stroke. Some kinds of value, nevertheless, would remain in the natural world, according to Rolston. Among environmental philosophers, Robin Attfield (1981), Paul Taylor (1981, 1983), Peter Miller (1982), and the Deep Ecologists (Devall and Sessions 1985) seem sympathetic to this view. For his part, Regan (1981)—while he regards a persuasive theory of objective, intrinsic value to be the sine qua non of any true ethic *of* the environment—offers none himself and, moreover, doubts that any "rationally coherent" theory of intrinsic value for unconscious nonhuman natural entities and natural wholes can be achieved. After thinking very hard, during the mid-1980s, about the ontology of value finally I came reluctantly to the conclusion that intrinsic value cannot exist objectively (Callicott 1984). Sylvan in collaboration with Val Plumwood (Routley and Routley 1980), William Grey (Godfrey-Smith 1980), John O'Neill (1992), Robert Elliot (1992), and I have provided, however, *nonanthropocentric* value theories for environmental ethics without going off the deep end and claiming that such value may exist independently of subjects (Callicott 1989). Though the details of our theories differ, we all defer to the conventional Modern view that value always necessarily involves a valu*er* as well as a valu*ee*.

Subjects are valu*ers*. And we subjects are almost always also valu*ees* because we almost always value ourselves. But mere objects too are routinely valuees. There is nothing remotely controversial about this claim. We value our houses, our cars, and so on; we value works of art; we value, to be sure, nonhuman natural entities and nature as a whole. What is worth arguing, because it has not been so universally endorsed, is the proposition that nonhuman natural entities and nature as a whole may be valued not only for what they do for us, but—just as most of us value (at the very least) our children and other family members—they may also be valued for their own sakes as well. I try to pass this altruistic species of ascribed value off as "truncated intrinsic value"—since it is not a kind of instrumental value and instrumental and intrinsic value are usually paired as alternatives between which a middle is excluded (Callicott 1989). Truncated intrinsic value is the value we ascribe to something *for* itself even if it has—since nothing does, in my honest opinion—no value *in* itself. Rolston (1988) spurns such a compromise, even though he doesn't argue that it won't do all the axiological work of his own more problematic stance. He exposes such theories for what they really are—theories not of intrinsic, but of "extrinsic," value in nature. While such theories may be nonanthropo*centric*, they are nevertheless certainly not nonanthropo*genic*, or, more accurately, non*vertebra*genic, since nonhuman animals, all vertebrates at the very least, are conscious and therefore may be said, in the widest sense of the term, to value things. Rolston himself nobly holds out for objective, nonanthropocentric, and nonanthropogenic (nonvertebragenic), literally intrinsic values in the natural world. The anthropocentic-instrumental/nonanthropocentric-intrinsic distinction can get much more complicated than at first it seemed. In addition to my theory of anthropogenic but nonanthropocentric (truncated) intrinsic value, Eugene C. Hargrove (1989, 1992) has recently recognized a species of anthropocentric (and, a fortiori, anthropogenic) intrinsic value in the disinterested pleasure we take in natural beauty.

ROLSTON'S CORE THEORY OF OBJECTIVE
INTRINSIC VALUE IN NATURE

How does Rolston manage to defend his simple but radical position on intrinsic value? As I began by saying, that is the burden of practically the whole of Rolston's book. His philosophical style is artful, seductive, and persuasive. His arguments are many and ingenious. Cumulatively, his labyrinthine argumentation is overwhelming. Here, I can hardly hope to evaluate each of Rolston's arguments in his *Environmental Ethics* for objective, intrinsic natural value. However, running through them all I think I discern Ariadne's thread in a concept broached and eventually abandoned by Regan (1976), but later defended by Attfield (1981, 1983) and Taylor (1981, 1983, 1986). Ignoring the twists and turns of each byway, let me summarize what I understand to be the main avenue of Rolston's approach and then see if it conducts us safely to the sanctum sanctorum of environmental philosophy or . . . to a cognitive cul-de-sac.

Rolston (1988, 101) points out that all organisms defend their "own kind as a good kind." By this he means that all organisms—even plants, which to the untutored eye seem so passive—actively defend their lives, and strive to propagate their own species. Animals obviously flee or fight actively when threatened, and struggle—some epically— to reproduce. Plants quietly compete for light and space; they synthesize complex allelopathic chemicals which can poison the roots of a pushy neighbor, or kill or discourage any animals that would eat them; and they invest considerable energy in the production of flowers, nectar, pollen, and seed. Each organism has a telos, a built-in end. In the terminology of Taylor (1986), each is a "teleological-center-of-life." Thus, each is an end-in-itself. Each, therefore, has a good of its own. What else does it defend? That all organisms are ends-in-themselves with goods of their own may be what we choose to mean by saying that they are intrinsically valuable.

The environmental ethic that Taylor constructs around this concept is almost classical in its univocal formality. According to Taylor (1986), being a teleological-center-of-life (and thus an end-in-itself) is the necessary and sufficient condition for possessing inherent worth and enjoying moral considerability. Hence, for Taylor, all living beings—plants, animals, and humans—are of *equal* intrinsic value, and nonliving things (such as the atmosphere and ocean), wholes (such as species and ecosystems), and geological and evolutionary processes (such as outgassing and natural selection) have *no* intrinsic value at all. Taylor correctly styles his environmental ethic, "biocentrism": it is literally and univocally life-centered.

The environmental ethic that Rolston (1988) constructs around this concept is far more subtly shaded. Sentient animals *feel* the good that they defend. And that has to be worth something—a value bonus, as it were. And human beings are *self-aware*, and therefore reflexively conscious of the good that they both feel and consciously and unconsciously defend. That is worth a great deal more. So Rolston forthrightly posits a hierarchy (although he doesn't call it that) of intrinsic value in nature and defends a pecking order (nor does he call it that either) in nature, with humans in their traditional place at the top. We can, thus, in good conscience, according to Rolston (1988), hunt and kill and eat animals and use plants in all sorts of ways—provided we respect these other forms of life and do not endanger or exterminate species or lay waste to ecosystems. Robin Attfield (1981) proposes a similarly graded system of intrinsic value in nature, though he does not extend his to wholes—as Rolston does—nor is his argument as biologically rich and subtle as Rolston's.

Species and ecosystems also, *pace* Taylor and Attfield, possess Rolstonian intrinsic value. Each organism "re-presents" its species. Each is a token of its type. Its type is indeed its telos, just as Aristotle would have it. Each strives to be good-of-its-kind, and some succeed better than others. Remember Rolston's key formula with which I began this summary, and to which he himself returns again and again: all organisms defend their "own kind as a good kind." Hence kinds—species—also have intrinsic value. Ecosystems are the matrix in which each kind comes to be what it is. If each organism defends its own kind of good, then the system, the landscape, into which that good fits—like a piece of a picture puzzle—is also arguably good. Rolston notes that in ecosystems a lot of "pushing and shoving" goes on. This pushing and shoving is exactly what has sculpted—physiologically as well as anatomically, psychologically as well as morphologically—the complex organisms that defend their own kind of good. Indeed, ecosystemic complexity, as Paul Shepard earlier emphasized, is reflected in our own powers of abstract thought, self-consciousness, and moral responsibility (1978). If these attributes are morally valuable—as most Western moral philosophies, one way or another, insist—then some of that value should rub off on the system that brought them forth.

Following this line of argument, Rolston (1988) is led to assert the intrinsic value of elemental natural processes, going all the way back to the big bang. These processes—including the forging of all the other elements out of hydrogen in the core of large stars, the formation of planets, and the spontaneous synthesis of ever more complex chemical compounds at Earth's surface—led up to the emergence of living beings. Just as sentience and self-consciousness receive value bonuses, added to their basic value as organic ends-in-themselves, according to Rolston's accounting, so these infra-living processes, as necessary conditions for the emergence and continued existence of intrinsically valuable life, receive a value dividend, so to speak.

The metaethics to which Taylor and Rolston variously subscribe is Kantian at its core. Organic beings have built-in *teloi*. Therefore each is a conative end-in-itself. Therefore each has intrinsic value. That fact generates duties. We may have no affection for them, but we are logically compelled grudgingly to grant such beings (and, in Rolston's case, species, ecosystems, and "projective" elemental nature) moral considerability. Why? Because the value that I accord myself—which I demand that others respect and which I categorically defend—rests, in the final analysis, upon the *same* ground. And if I am to be logically consistent in claiming intrinsic value for myself, because I am an end-in-myself, I must extend the same respect that I have for myself—and that I demand from others—to those others whose value turns on the same thing as my own. Of course Taylor and Rolston conveniently forget that Kant, for whom the ground is reason, allows that the *value* of reason depends ultimately upon the value *ascribed* to herself by a rational being. In a crucial passage, Kant (1959, 47, emphasis added) writes, "The ground of this principle [the categorical imperative] is: 'rational nature exists as an end in itself.' Man necessarily *thinks of* his own existence in this way; thus far it is a subjective principle of human action." In Kant's view this subjective principle becomes (relatively) "objective" by generalization, viz.: "Also every other rational being *thinks of* his existence by means of the same rational ground which holds also for myself; thus it is at the same time an objective principle from which, as a supreme practical ground, it must be possible to derive all laws of the will" (Kant 1959, 47, emphasis added). Kant himself, it is important to recognize, worked within the Modern metaphysical parameters set out by Descartes and Galileo and avoided committing what would later be called the naturalistic fallacy. Taylor and Rolston seem to forget that in all ethics explicitly or implicitly cast in the Kantian mold, a relatively objective principle is reached by generalizing a merely subjective one. Thus, the rug is pulled out from under such a generalization attempting to reach organisms that are not subjective (as well as objective), beings that do not *"think of"* or *subjectively experience* their own being "in this way." But even if we agree with Rolston that a behavioral analog to a rational being's valuing herself can be found in a living being's "defending its own kind as a good kind," one might recoil—that's my reaction, anyway—from this Prussian emphasis on duty, derived from a cold generalization of egoism, as Kenneth Goodpaster (1979) observed. Why? Because it is incongruent with one's experience of natural value—it is with my own, anyway—and prefer an approach to ethics based as much on feeling as reason and communal bonds as apodictic duty.

OBJECTIVE INTRINSIC VALUE AND THE
METAPHYSICAL FOUNDATIONS OF MODERN SCIENCE

Quite apart from the vagaries of personal moral experience and ethical taste, while Rolston's general argument for literally intrinsic value in nature is studded with evolutionary and ecological facts and theories, it remains—when all is said and done—painfully inconsistent with the most fundamental tenets of the Modern scientific worldview. Let me hasten to say that to his credit Rolston never once appeals to transcendent axiological principles—to God, for example, as an independent axiological point of reference, or to a Platonic form of the Good. His insistence upon objective value is not inconsistent with the fundamental tenets of the Modern scientific worldview in *that* way, i. e., in the same way as, say, "creation science" is. On the contrary, Rolston prosecutes his argumentation, a many-splendored thing, for objective, intrinsic value in nature strictly on conventional naturalistic grounds. But there's the rub. The pounding incoming waves of Rolston's scientifically informed arguments for objective, intrinsic value in nature, run counter to the ground sea of the metaphysical foundations of Modern science—which he unquestioningly assumes and even explicitly affirms. The shear force between surface argumentation and conceptual substrate effectively deconstructs Rolston's text.

Relevant to the matter at hand are the metaphysical foundations of Modern science, *sensu* Burtt (1954). The first and most fundamental is the Cartesian split between the *res extensa* and the *res cogitans*—between extension and thought, matter and mind, object and subject. The second is the Galilean distinction between primary and secondary qualities (as John Locke, the self-described underlaborer to the great Isaac Newton, called them). The former are objective properties of the extended things (objects); the latter are dependent for their existence on thinking things (or subjects). The third is the derivative Humean distinction between fact and value—which simply extends the object-subject/primary-secondary parsing of empirical qualities on to value qualities (chapter 5). Therefore, objective nature, *classically conceived*, is, in itself, neither green nor good. Value, like color, is observer dependent, subjective in provenance. A value-neutral nature is, therefore, less a dogma of the Modern scientific worldview, as Rolston tries to stigmatize it, than an immediate inference from the institutionalized metaphysical foundations of Modern science.

Hence, the only way that Rolston could really convince us that value exists independently in the natural world would be to provide a persuasive alternative to the integral set of Cartesian-Galilean-Humean assumptions that render the subjective provenance of value so fundamental to the Modern scientific outlook (Miller 1989). Thus I was especially interested to encounter the word *metaphysics* in the peroration to the climactic chapter, entitled "Natural Value," in *Environmental Ethics*, and the promise of a discussion of "the nature of nature," "our concepts of nature," "our notion of the kind of universe we live in," "our model of reality" (Rolston 1988, 230–31). But in the paragraphs that followed, this grand prospect was scaled down from an alternative meta*physics* to a "meta*ecology*" that "finds unity, harmony, interdependence, creativity, life support, conflict and complement in dialectic, stability, richness, community" all in the terrestrial environment (Rolston 1988, 230ff.).

Yes! To be sure! I too disinterestedly value (verb transitive) all these things considered both separately and synergistically. But the universe in which we live is much larger than the infinitesimally small, albeit near, corner of it described by ecology, and the findings of ecology conventionally are interpreted within our larger, more universal model of reality.

Rolston does, of course, duel the Humean fact-value mode of dualism—that is one way of describing the major preoccupation of his book. But he does not take up arms against the Cartesian object-subject duality—the very castle keep of the subjectivity of values—in respect to which the Humean fact-value dichotomy is but a footnote. That remains an altogether unchallenged substrate of his dissertation. Nor does he challenge the Galilean mode of dualism, the primary-secondary quality distinction. On the contrary, he explicitly affirms it: "The greenness of the tree," Rolston (1988, 113–14) writes,

is in my head, but it looks as though the tree is green. Out there are only electromagnetic waves of 550 nanometers. The greenness is projected, manufactured in my head and apparently hung on the tree. . . . [Actually] the "projection" is better called a "translation." . . . The tree is *sending* and the human *receiving*. The human is not doing any sending, nor the tree any receiving. The incoming signals are "translated" as green and so the tree appears green. In one sense this is an illusion; in another it is not. There is no experience of green in the tree, but there is ample reality (radiation) out there, behind and exciting my experience.

Rolston's purpose in rehearsing this conventional Modern scientific ontology of primary and secondary qualities is to argue that the value qualities we find in nature (beauty and goodness) should not be understood to be even more ephemeral "tertiary" qualities—as Samuel Alexander (1968), adapting Locke's terminology, called them—requiring the existence of a subject for their actualization. We are to understand, rather, that while the greenness (the qual, not the radiation) of the tree exists only in the mind of the beholder, the moral and aesthetical value of the tree is really out there—no less categorically objective than the electromagnetic waves of precisely 550 nanometers—irrespective of the existence or nonexistence of minds and beholders. But for all Rolston's subtlety of argument, the strength of the undertow of the standard paradigm pulls it down. As long as he grants that there are independent ("freestanding") objects and correspondingly independent subjects, and primary qualities and secondary qualities—and these basic, essentially conservative presuppositions are never mooted in his book—all the argument in the world to the effect that goodness is more objective than greenness is going to look like a magic show, brought off with smoke and mirrors.

Let me note here a seemingly trivial, but I think telling symptom of this inconsistency between wave motion (Rolston's indefatigable scientifically informed argumentation for objective, intrinsic value in nature) and ground sea (the metaphysical foundations of Modern science). E. O. Wilson pays tribute to Rolston's book on the back cover, and Rolston pays tribute to Wilson within—as entomologist and species conservationist. But Rolston never once mentions sociobiology, the "new synthesis" for which Wilson is philosophically notorious and of all the things for which Wilson is acclaimed, the thing most germane to ethics. Indeed, in *Environmental Ethics*, Rolston never discusses the biological construction of ethics, period. Sociobiology is the most recent development in a natural history of ethics going back to Darwin (chapter 6). So here is a mystery: In a 391-page book about why we ought to embrace a biologically informed ethic and biologically oriented duties, we look in vain for support from classical and contemporary biological theory about the nature, origin, and evolution of morality. Why? Because classical and contemporary biological thinking about ethics is conducted within the parameters of the Modern scientific world view and therefore supports an environmental ethic based on an understanding of value that, though nonanthropocentric, is nakedly and unabashedly subjective and "vertebragenic," if I may employ this coinage.

POSTMODERN SCIENCE AND THE
INTRINSIC VALUE OF NATURE

Now I have been careful to say throughout that it is the metaphysical foundations of *Modern* science that shut down all arguments for objective, intrinsic value before they can get off and running. But we live in the postModern period. The Modern scientific worldview is obsolete. Hence, there is open to Rolston an alternative to the Cartesian and Galilean metaphysical assumptions that he uncritically accepts and ingenuously reasserts, an alternative that is consistent—indeed more consistent, since more up to date—with the scientific naturalism to which he so rigorously and admirably hews.

As science looks deeper and deeper into the farthest reaches of space and time and into the finest structures of matter, it becomes more and more apparent that knowledge is fundamentally physical—not an attribute of a nonphysical substance, the Cartesian thinking thing or passive sapient subject. Energy is, among other things, information; and information is energy. For empirical information to be collected, in other words, energy must be exchanged between the observer and the observed. Light or other electromagnetic radiation, sound or other mechanical energy, and the like must flow from the thing observed to the observer to be registered by our senses or by apparatuses—such as photographic plates, cloud chambers, or Geiger counters—that serve as sensory surrogates or extensions. Thus Descartes's *res cogitans*, his independent subject, is necessarily sucked into the *res extensa*, the physical realm.

Moreover, because energy does not increase and decrease continuously but in multiples of a least quantum of energy, measurement of phenomena like electrons, with mass-energy equivalents near the value of the quantum, unavoidably disturbs them. In contemporary physics, therefore, just as knowledge is physicalized, physical reality is correspondingly idealized. The act of observing changes the observed phenomena; to know nature—at least at the subatomic level—is to affect it, to participate in shaping its being. If, moreover, we rule out of scientific court any ontological claim that is in principle unverifiable—and that, after all, is how science distinguishes itself from pseudoscience, mysticism, and religion—then, an independent ultimate physical reality becomes no less problematic than an independent, irreducible psychic reality. We cannot know, for example, both the precise location and precise state of motion of an electron. We can know the one precisely and nothing of the other, or we can know both imprecisely. We cannot therefore say, without crossing the line between science and faith, that an electron actually has both a precise location and a precise state of motion. If we don't want to make Newtonian ontology a tenet of Modern physical religion, we must rather say that in choosing to know its location and not its state of motion we choose an actual reality for it and that before our observation, as a discrete object in space and time, it enjoyed only a *potential* existence.

There are a number of respectable metaphysical interpretations of quantum physics from which an environmental philosopher seeking to overcome the Modern normal fact-value dichotomy might choose. Most of these portray ultimate physical reality, as indirectly we experience it, to be a marriage between subject and object. From the point of view of the metaphysical foundations of postModern science, therefore, *all* natural properties—quantitative, qualitative, and axiological—exist only potentially on the side of erstwhile objects and are actualized only upon interaction with erstwhile subjects. (I carefully say "on the side of" and "erstwhile" here to emphasize that, whatever interpretation of quantum theory one chooses, the Heisenberg uncertainty principle is unimpeachable, and therefore object and subject cannot be so clearly and distinctly separated in the metaphysical foundations of the New Physics as they were in those of the old. There is one reality, with objective and subjective poles.)

But such *potential* instrumental and intrinsic values in nature—neither more nor less real than colors and states of motion—awaiting actualization by a conscious physical subject are not good enough for Rolston. No, he must go the whole nine yards and put a freestanding natural being's state of motion *and* intrinsic value in space and time, on the objective side of the Cartesian divide, and its color in a perceiver's sensorium, on the subjective side! The inertia of the unchallenged Modern framework—subjects and objects, primary and secondary qualities, facts and values—undercuts Rolston's multiple moral arguments, however one may assess the validity of each, and one has to go back to the book time and again to reread the text as a talisman against doubt and disbelief.

Rolston never considers a value theory for environmental ethics based upon and inspired by quantum physics in the book, *Environmental Ethics*, but in the pages of *Environmental Ethics*, the journal, he has recently written, "if quarks exist, the Yellowstone ecosystem is made of quarks, but the levels are so vastly different that we cannot generalize from observer dependent phenomena in quantum physics to the relation of the human self to the Yellowstone ecosystem. If there is interdependence in an ecosystem that funds ethics, this will have to be shown without benefit of physics" (Rolston 1989, 260).

Quantum physics and ecology are, in fact, remote from one another on anyone's continuum of sciences, and I am glad to have this opportunity to point out that I do not imagine that we might trace quantum uncertainties from quarks to subatomic particles to atoms to molecules to proteins to cells to multicelled organisms, populations, ecosystems, and the biosphere. In other words, I do not mean to suggest that, since bears are made of electrons, we cannot, in principle, definitely discover both the position and state of motion of the grizzly stalking us in the Yellowstone.

Rather, I mean to suggest that the New Physics might in future play an architectonic role in our global thinking about nature (and human society), just as the old physics did in the past (and, though its grip is slowly slipping, as it continues to do in the present). Alan E. Wittbecker (1990, 279) has also misrepresented the connection I draw between quantum theory and ecology: "Nevertheless, physics and ecology cannot be equated, as Callicott . . . tries to do. Ecology has principles that cannot apply to particles." He might have added that quantum theory has principles (uncertainty, for example) that cannot apply to organisms or ecosystems. But I do not "equate" ecology and quantum physics, I only compare them. Nor do I derive the former from the latter. I find, rather, that, in some respects, they are conceptually analogous.

Let me briefly explain. Physics has historically provided for the other sciences—social as well as natural—a paradigm, *sensu* Kuhn (1961) via Capra (1982). Darwin's theory of evolution brought biology into step with the Newtonian paradigm, not because Darwin attempted to explain, say, phenotypic variation by deduction from Newton's laws of motion, but because his theoretically pivotal concept of natural selection provided a metaphorical "mechanism" for the ateleological temporal efflorescence of natural kinds. And Thomas Hobbes's and John Locke's variations on the "state of nature" theme have dominated Modern Western social thought for so long because the picture they drew of insular, single-mindedly selfish individuals, chaotically bouncing around in a political power vacuum, was an analog in moral philosophy of the prevailing mechanical model of nature in natural philosophy. In the social analog of the Newtonian universe, people are, as it were, social atoms, propelled along a straight line by a force—their egoistic impulses—analogous to inertial momentum in physics. They might be deflected from their acquisitive vectors only by collision with other social atoms or by influence from some social analog, like tax incentives, of a physical force, like gravity. Adam Smith has emerged in Modernist mytho-historiography as the Robert Boyle of the social sciences who, in the *Wealth of Nations*, provided the gas laws for political economy.

In suggesting here that the atomic social theories of Hobbes and Locke and the allied economic theory attributed to Smith owe something to Isaac Newton and the giants upon whose shoulders he stood, I do not mean to imply that Hobbes, Locke, and Smith attempted to *deduce* their ideas from Newton's laws of motion any more than did Darwin. Rather, I mean to suggest that these Modern social theories were appealing and persuasive because they provided an *analog* in moral philosophy to the then new and exciting picture of nature emerging in natural philosophy. As the New Physics supplants the old, like the old, we may expect (as well as hope) that it will serve as a model for all the rest of our thinking. Ecology, happily, is ripe—not for reduction to the New Physics, certainly— but for logical and structural *comparison*, because of its emphasis on relationships and corresponding de-emphasis on separable substances, as I have elsewhere attempted to argue in some detail (chapter 15). If I may put it so, ecology intellectually resonates with the New Physics. Therefore, I think, a value theory *inspired by* and conceptually *analogous to*, but by no means reduced to or derived from, quantum physics is particularly congenial to an ecologically informed environmental ethic.

A NONANTHROPOCENTRIC VALUE THEORY FOR ENVIRONMENTAL ETHICS CONSISTENT WITH MODERNISM

Let me conclude by saying that I applaud Rolston's heroism, industry, and ingenuity in defending an unadulterated and uncompromising theory of nonanthropocentric objective, intrinsic value in nature. At least while I'm in the tent and he's in the pulpit, I myself am a born-again believer. But just in case his arguments fall on deaf ears or dissipate in the hard light of the Modern afternoon, I shall continue to defend his flanks with another stratagem.

We live during a period of millennial change in the Western worldview—a revolutionary time, intellectually speaking, not unlike Plato's and Descartes's. One worldview, the Modern mechanical worldview, is gradually giving way to another. Who knows what future historians will call it—the organic worldview, the ecological worldview, the systems worldview . . . ? (Since we don't know now what it will become we call it "postModernism" while we wait for it to take more definite shape.) I have tried to develop alternative nonanthropocentric value theories consistent with the metaphysical foundations of the old and the new world views, respectively. I have just indicated how a nonanthropocentric value theory consistent with the new paradigm might be constructed, but I also think it is important to offer a less elusive, tide-bucking nonanthropocentric value theory than Rolston's, based upon Modernist orthodoxy, for unregenerate Modernists, to whom values in nature without valuers seems less a heresy than an oxymoron.

The classical (Darwin's own) and contemporary (sociobiological) natural history of morals affirms the existence of distinct social instincts and sympathies, not only among human beings but among many social mammals. (Incidentally, Rolston, for all his biological enlightenment, quaintly insists throughout his discussion that humans alone in the natural world are moral beings. What about the intraspecies morality of elephants, wolves, cetaceans, gorillas, and other highly social beasts?) We quintessentially social, human animals are endowed with a well-developed capacity for love and a genuine selfless concern for the welfare of others and for the commonweal per se—because we survive, flourish, and reproduce more successfully in a social matrix than as solitaries, according to Darwin's classical account, or because natural selection has favored altruistic dispositions that promote the welfare of proximate conspecifics (who were, until recently, almost always close kin), according to the contemporary sociobiological account. These inherited social instincts and sympathetic dispositions are genetically underdetermined and await information by culture for their eventual expression—somewhat like our capacity for speech and a disposition to talk, which we also inherit, but for the realization of which we must be informed by a specific culture's peculiar language. The moral sentiments, as Darwin called them, have been cast more widely as societies have grown in membership and complexity. "His sympathies," Darwin wrote of progressively socialized Homo sapiens, "became more tender and widely diffused, extending to men of all races, to the imbecile, maimed, and other useless members of society; and finally to the lower animals." After approvingly quoting these lines from *The Descent of Man*, in "Is There an Ecological Ethic?" Rolston wrote (1975, 109): "[A]fter the fauna, can we add the flora, the landscape, the seascape, the ecosystem? There would be something magnificent about an evolution of conscience that circumscribed the whole."

Indeed there would. Modern evolutionary and ecological biology enable us to perceive nonhuman natural entities as our kin and terrestrial nature as a whole as our extended family or community. We can, as Rolston (1975, 109) said in his first paper, "be drawn to them in love." But after

Rolston's thinking matured and solidified (not to say "rigidified"), this disarmingly simple, tender *Modern* theory of disinterested extrinsic value distilled from our humanly refined animal sentiments has been purged from Rolston's philosophy. His present thesis demands that we respect nature for the values that are there; it does not draw us into a love affair with her. Maybe that's a good thing. But in case some hardheaded (but softhearted) Modernists just cannot bring themselves to believe that values can exist without valuers, it is worth keeping in mind that there is another axiological path—consistent with *Modern* science—to what Rolston calls a "primary," a nature-regarding environmental philosophy.

Intrinsic Value in Nature:
A Metaethical Analysis

TWO PROOFS FOR THE EXISTENCE OF INTRINSIC VALUE

The Phenomenological Proof

Edwin P. Pister, a now-retired Associate Fishery Biologist with the California Department of Fish and Game, worked long and hard to save from extinction several species of desert fishes living in small islands of water in an ocean of dry land. He and his allies took the case of the Devil's Hole pupfish—threatened by agrobusinesspersons pumping groundwater for irrigation—all the way to the United States Supreme Court; and won (Pister 1985).

Pister was often asked—not only by laypersons, but by incredulous members of his own department (dedicated as most were to providing anglers with game fish)—What good is it, anyway? The question presupposed that a species has no claim to existence unless its members have some utility, some *instrumental* value. For years he struggled to answer that question on those terms. Clearly, thumb-sized desert fishes living in pools of water no bigger than a stock tank would never provide sport or meat. The Devil's Hole pupfish can dwell, however, in water several times more saline than seawater. Perhaps the secrets of its remarkable kidney could be used in treating people with renal disorders (Pister 1985).

But *speculative* utility, the *possibility* that desert fishes might prove to have some instrumental value, was not the reason that Pister so ardently dedicated himself to their preservation. He felt a *moral* responsibility to save them from extinction. Whether they had instrumental value or not, they had, Pister believed, *intrinsic* value. But this "philosophical" concept was hard to explain to colleagues and constituents. As one put it, "When you start talking about morality and ethics, you lose me" (Pister 1987, 228). Finally, Pister found a way to put the concept of intrinsic value across clearly. To the question *What good is it?* he replied, *What good are you?*

That answer forces the questioner to confront the fact that he or she regards his or her own total value to exceed his or her instrumental value. Many people hope to be instrumentally valuable—to be useful to family, friends, and society. But if we prove to be good for nothing, we believe, nevertheless, that we are still entitled to life, to liberty, to the pursuit of happiness. (If only instrumentally valuable people enjoyed a claim to live, the world might not be afflicted with human overpopulation and over-consumption; certainly we would have no need for expensive hospitals, nursing homes, prisons, and the like.) Human dignity and the respect it commands—human ethical entitlement—is grounded ultimately in our claim to possess intrinsic value.

Call this the phenomenological proof for the existence of intrinsic value. The question *How do we know that intrinsic value exists?* is similar to the question *How do we know that consciousness exists?* We experience both consciousness and intrinsic value introspectively and irrefutably. Pister's question *What good are you?* simply serves to bring one's own intrinsic value to one's attention.

The Teleological Proof

Richard Sylvan and Val Plumwood offer another—in this case, teleologi-cal—proof for the existence of intrinsic value (Routley and Routley 1980). Tools—such as shovels, wrenches, and screwdrivers—exist. And tools are paradigm cases of things that have instrumental value. Indeed, if tools had no instrumental value they wouldn't exist. Shovels, in other words, would not have been invented except as instruments for digging, or wrenches and screwdrivers except as instruments for turning bolts and setting screws. And since such things exist by artifice, not by nature, if they had not been invented they wouldn't exist.

According to Sylvan and Plumwood, the existence of instrumental value entails the existence of intrinsic value: "Some values are instrumental, i.e., a means or an instrument to something else that has value, and some are not, but are noninstrumental or intrinsic. Some values at least *must* be intrinsic, some objects valuable in themselves and not as means to other ends (Routley and Routley 1980, emphasis added).

The argument is enthymemic here, but appears to be analogous to Aristotle's at the beginning of the *Nicomachean Ethics* for something—human happiness, Aristotle believed—that is an end in itself. The existence of means, in short, implies the existence of ends. Though one means may exist for the sake of another—say, a forge for the making of shovels—the train of means must, Aristotle argued, terminate in an end which is not, in turn, a means to something else: an end-in-itself. Otherwise the train of means would be infinite and unanchored. And since means are valued instrumentally and ends-in-themselves are valued intrinsically, if ends-in-themselves exist—and they must if means do; and means do—then intrinsic value exists.

THE INTRINSIC VALUE OF NATURE: MORAL TRUTH AND PRAGMATIC EFFICACY

In addition to human beings, does nature (or some of nature's parts) have intrinsic value? That is the central *theoretical* question in environmental ethics. Indeed, how to discover intrinsic value in nature is the defining problem for *environmental* ethics. For if no intrinsic value can be attributed to nature, then environmental ethics is nothing distinct. If nature, that is, lacks intrinsic value, then environmental ethics is but a particular application of human-to-human ethics (Routley 1973; Rolston 1975; and Regan 1981). Or, putting the same point yet another way, if nature lacks intrinsic value, then *nonanthropocentric* environmental ethics is ruled out.

The Convergence Hypothesis

Bryan Norton (1992) fairly asks why we should want a *distinct* nonanthropocentric environmental ethic. There is the intellectual charm and challenge of creating something so novel. And that, combined with a passion for championing nature, is reason enough for me, a philosopher, to search for an adequate theory of intrinsic value in nature. But so personal, so self-indulgent a reason is hardly adequate. What can a nonanthropocentric environmental ethic *do* to defend nature against human insults that an anthropocentric ethic cannot?

Nothing, claims Norton (1991), if we take human interests to be sufficiently broad and long. Nature serves us in more ways than as a pool of raw materials and a dump for wastes. It provides priceless ecological services, many of which we imperfectly understand. And, undefiled, nature is a source of aesthetic gratification and religious inspiration. When the interests of future generations (as well as of present persons) in the ecological services and psycho-spiritual resources afforded people by nature are taken into account, respect for human beings (or for human interests) is quite enough to support nature protection, Norton argues. Thus anthropocentric and nonanthropocentric environmental ethics "converge"; that is, both prescribe the same personal practices and public policies (Norton 1991).

But do they? The most pressing environmental concern of the waning twentieth century is the erosion of nature's biological diversity. Edward O. Wilson estimates that the current rate of anthropogenic species extinction is 1,000 percent to 10,000 percent the normal "background" rate (Wilson 1988). Several episodes of abrupt, mass species extinction occurred previously in the biography of Planet Earth (Raup and Sepkoski 1984). But none are believed to be attributable to an organism run amuck—certainly not to an organism capable of moral choice (Raup 1988, 1991). Is the current tide of species extinction inconsistent with human interests, however wide and long we make them out to be?

David Ehrenfeld (1988) for one, doubts it. Probably endangered species—such as the Bengal tiger and African elephant—that conservation biologists call "charismatic megafauna" would be sadly missed by future generations of Homo sapiens if the present generation allowed them to become extinct. And for just that reason there is a good chance that many such species will survive the holocaust. But, as Ehrenfeld (1988) points out, the brunt of the human assault on nature is borne by species that are not charismatic. In fact, most are insects, creatures more usually feared and loathed than admired by human beings. Nor is it likely that most of the species at risk of imminent extinction will prove to be raw material for useful products—such as medicines, fuels, fibers, foods, or feeds. Moreover, as Ehrenfeld (1988, 215) notes, "the species whose members are the fewest in number, the rarest, the most narrowly distributed—in short, the ones most likely to become extinct—are obviously the ones least likely to be. . . ecologically influential; by no stretch of the imagination can we make them out to be vital cogs in the ecological machine." The aforementioned Devil's Hole pupfish is a case in point. If it goes extinct the biosphere will be poorer, but will function not one iota less serviceably.

Norton's stretching of human interests, however, goes beyond goods, services, and the charismatic megafauna (and flora, such as the giant sequoia and Douglas fir) that excite popular natural aesthetic sensibilities. Those people who have what Aldo Leopold (1953, 149) called "a refined taste in natural objects" may "value the wonder, excitement, and challenge [presented to the human mind] of so many species arising from a few dozen elements of the periodic table," as Ehrenfeld (1988, 215) puts it. We might call that the "scientific" or "epistemological" utility of other species. Beyond even that, Norton finds a "moral value" in noncharismatic species. But it is a curious sort of moral value similar to the moral value that Immanuel Kant, notoriously, found in refraining from cruelty to animals. According to Norton (1988, 201), "Thoreau . . . believed that his careful observation of other species helped him to live a better life. I believe this also. So there are at least two people, and perhaps many others, who believe that species have value as a *moral* resource to humans, as a chance for humans to form, re-form, and improve their own value systems."

Let us grant the truth of Norton's "convergence hypothesis." All species severally and biodiversity globally can be embraced by an anthropocentric environmental ethic. From that does it follow, as Norton claims, that the attribution of intrinsic value to nature in environmental ethics proper is a pernicious redundancy? A sufficiently widened and lengthened anthropocentrism can do all the moral work that attributing intrinsic value to nature does. That's the redundancy claim. And trying to attribute intrinsic value to nature only stirs up contention among environmentalists, which the antienvironmental forces can exploit on the military principle of divide and conquer. That's the perniciousness claim. The more conventional, the more conservative approach of limiting intrinsic value to human beings is, therefore, the more *pragmatic* approach. If providing suasive theoretical support for private environmental practice and public environmental policy is, after all, the raison d'être of environmental ethics, then environmental philosophers should abandon the theoretical search for intrinsic value in nature.

However, Norton, I think, has overlooked two points: one pragmatic, the other a matter of, shall we say, moral truth.

Moral Truth

To take the latter first, one wants to offer the right reasons for doing the right thing—as well as to get the right thing done—irrespective of pragmatic considerations. The agony of the American Civil War might have been avoided if Abraham Lincoln and his fellow abolitionists had just argued for an end to slavery on economic instead of on genuinely ethical grounds. Lincoln might have persuaded Southern plantation owners to voluntarily, even gladly, free their slaves, because to do so would be in the planters' enlightened self-interest. Hired laborers can be laid off during slack seasons, while slaves must be fed, clothed, and sheltered year-round. The high "security" costs of slave owning—the costs of confining slaves, overseeing and guarding them while they work, catching runaways, and protecting oneself, one's family, and one's property from attack by mutinous slaves—could be saved. And so on and so forth. And if that were not argument enough, Lincoln might have pointed out that freeing their slaves would present Southern slave owners a chance to form, re-form, and improve their own value systems. Abolition could be a moral *resource*. (Think for a moment about the repugnance of that argument.)

Let me hasten to say that there's nothing wrong with giving instrumental reasons, ancillary to the right reasons, for doing the right thing. Human beings, we believe, have intrinsic value. Therefore, we think that to enslave human beings is wrong. And besides, slavery is economically backward. Similarly, other species, we are beginning to believe, are also intrinsically valuable. Therefore, to render other species extinct is wrong.

And besides, we risk injuring ourselves and future generations of human beings in a wide variety of ways if we do not vigilantly preserve other species.

The Burden of Proof

Moreover, granting intrinsic value to nature would make a huge practical difference. Were we to do so, the burden of proof would be lifted from the shoulders of conservationists and shifted onto the shoulders of those who, pursuing other values, are—intentionally or unintentionally, knowingly or inadvertently—destroying nature.

Warwick Fox (1993) has developed this—the pragmatic—point most fully and clearly. He begins by noting that having intrinsic value does not make its possessor "inviolable." As pointed out in the previous section of this chapter, human beings claim to be intrinsically valuable. But acknowledging that claim does not entail that the life, the liberty, the opportunity to pursue happiness of every human being on every occasion ought not be eclipsed by some superior, opposing, and inconsistent value. Felons are rightly deprived of their liberty; sometimes of their lives. Though there is a sizable pacifist minority, a majority of decent people think that to put at risk the lives of innocent young men and women to defend their countries against aggression is morally permissible. A narrow majority of Americans even believed that, during the recent Persian Gulf war, we rightly risked—and in thousands of instances actually sacrificed—the lives of innocent Iraqi citizens as well as Iraqi soldiers and the soldiers of many industrial nations merely to keep down the cost of energy and to disabuse a tyrant of his delusions of grandeur.

However, when an intrinsically valuable human being is deliberately deprived of his or her liberty or life, or deliberately put in harm's way, we believe that, to be consistent with human-to-human ethics, *sufficient justification* for doing so must be offered. Thus, trials are conducted, evidence is presented and weighed, and grave verdicts are rendered, before a person may be imprisoned or executed; and public debates are held over the course of many days, before soldiers may be sent into combat. But, as Fox (1993, 101) points out, since

the nonhuman world is only considered to be instrumentally valuable then people are permitted to use and otherwise interfere with any aspect of it for whatever reasons they wish (i.e., no justification for interference is required). If anyone objects to such interference then, within this framework of reference, the onus is clearly on the person who objects to justify why it is more useful to humans to leave that aspect of the nonhuman world alone. If, however, the nonhuman world is considered to be intrinsically valuable then the onus shifts to the person who wants to interfere with it to justify why they should be allowed to do so.

Since old-growth forests, for example, are not yet widely acknowledged to have intrinsic value, timber companies may fell them without first offering any justification whatever. If environmentalists want to stop the clear-cutting of dwindling old growth forests on public land (to say nothing of those on privately owned land) they have to go to court seeking a legal injunction. If, on the other hand, the intrinsic value of nature were widely acknowledged and legally institutionalized, then timber companies would have to go to court seeking permission to fell an old-growth forest—thus being burdened to offer sufficient justification—whenever they intended to do so. As Fox (1993, 101) notes, this would amount to "a revolution in the way we treat the nonhuman world that is comparable to the difference for humans between a legal system that operates on a presumption of guilt until innocence is proved beyond reasonable doubt and one that operates on a presumption of innocence until guilt is proved beyond reasonable doubt. The question of just where the onus of justification lies can be highly significant for the parties concerned!"

A MODERN THEORY OF THE INTRINSIC VALUE OF NATURE

So far, then, the following is certain: intrinsic value exists; enjoying widely acknowledged intrinsic value makes a big practical difference to someone's or something's moral status; and, therefore, providing theoretical grounds for according intrinsic value to nature (or some of its parts) is a worthwhile project—the principal, the defining project of environmental ethics. But just *what*, more precisely, is intrinsic value?

The term *intrinsic value* and the less-used alternative term *inherent worth* mean, lexically speaking, pretty much the same thing. *Merriam Webster's Collegiate Dictionary*, tenth edition, defines *intrinsic* thus: "belonging to the essential nature or constitution of a thing." And it defines *inherent* thus: "involved in the constitution or essential character of something . . . : intrinsic." The English word *value* comes from the Latin word *valere*, "to be worth, to be strong"; and *worth* comes from the Old English word *weorth*, meaning "worthy, of value." Lexically speaking, thus, to claim that the value (or worth) of something is intrinsic (or inherent) is to claim that its value (or worth) belongs to its essential nature or constitution.

Now, note that the above-rehearsed phenomenological and teleological proofs for the existence of intrinsic value do not prove that intrinsic value, *thus defined*—that is, lexically defined—actually exists. True, when, in response to the question What good are you?, one considers one's own value, some value remains when one subtracts one's instrumental value to family, friends, employers, and society from one's total value. But that residue of value may not necessarily be part of one's essential nature or constitution in the same way that having, say, a central nervous system is. And, true, the existence of instrumentally valuable means, such as tools, entails the existence of noninstrumentally valuable ends, such as tool users. But the value of those tool-using ends-in-themselves may not necessarily belong to their constitution or be among their essential characteristics in the same way that having, say, hands is.

Some properties of a thing may be intrinsic in the lexical sense of the word. The inertness of helium, for example, is a lexically intrinsic property of that element, as is the mass of a billiard ball. Bipedal locomotion, an opposable thumb, and language use are lexically intrinsic characteristics of human beings. But, *from the point of view of Modern philosophy*, value cannot be such a property or characteristic of a human being or of anything else. Why? Because the radical Cartesian distinction between subjects and objects is fundamental to Modernism; and the value of something, from the Modern point of view, is determined by the intentional act of a Cartesian subject respecting an object—be that "object" the subject him- or herself, another subject, or a Cartesian object proper (a physical object).

Let me explain. Some states of Cartesian subjects are intentional; that is, they necessarily relate to something other than themselves (often, but not always, to proper Cartesian objects, that is, to physical things). And some states are not intentional. A Cartesian subject, for example, can be in an emotional state—a state of depression, say—without reference to anything else. Thus emotions are not necessarily intentional. But other subjective states are necessarily intentional. Desire, for example, is necessarily for *something*, though not necessarily for a proper Cartesian object. A depressed Cartesian subject might desire, for instance, to be in another nonintentional subjective condition, such as a state of euphoria. Or Cartesian Subject A might desire Cartesian Subject B to be in a certain intentional emotional state, such as in love with A. But most of the intentions of everyday desires, at least in our materialistic Modern experience, are proper Cartesian objects—certain foods, drinks, clothes, houses, cars, appliances, jewelry. From the point of view of Modern philosophy, value is *conferred on* or *ascribed to* an "object" by an intentional act of a subject. In the Modern worldview, *value* is a verb first and a noun only derivatively. Among other things they do, subjects think, perceive, desire, *and value*. The intentions, the targets, of a subject's valuing are valuable, just as the intentions of a subject's desiring are desirable. If there were no desiring subjects, nothing would be desirable. If there were no valuing subjects, nothing would be valuable.

The ethically all-important distinction between instrumental and intrinsic value, can, nonetheless, be preserved within the metaphysical constraints of the Modern world view. Something (be it oneself, another Cartesian subject, or a proper Cartesian object) "has" instrumental value if it is valued instrumentally. And what does it mean to value things instrumentally? To value them as means to some end—shovels for digging, wrenches for turning bolts, slaves for work, prostitutes for sex, cattle for milk and meat, Madagascar periwinkles for making the anticancer drug vincristine, the Yellowstone National Park for viewing monumental scenery and natural wonders, oneself for being a productive member of society and a good parent. Something (be it oneself, another Cartesian subject, or a Cartesian object) "has" intrinsic value if it is valued intrinsically. And what does it mean to value things intrinsically? To value them for their own sakes, as ends in themselves.

So what, from a Modern point of view, does it mean to claim that *nature* has intrinsic value? Nature has intrinsic value when it is valued (verb transitive) for its own sake, as an end itself.

Now, valuers don't value things arbitrarily. We frequently give our fellow valuers reasons to value things instrumentally. Suppose, for example, that Valuer A is fixing to hammer to bits a cracked and leaky ceramic pitcher and mix the shards with the clay in her garden to condition the soil. Valuer B may point out to Valuer A that the cracked ceramic pitcher can still serve as a vase for dried wildflowers or, if beautifully made, as an objet d'art. Valuer B has, in effect, given Valuer A a reason to value the cracked ceramic pitcher instrumentally. And in our moral discourse, we frequently give our fellow valuers reasons to value things intrinsically. Abraham Lincoln and other abolitionists gave their fellow valuers reasons to value African American slaves intrinsically. Tom Regan and other animal rights advocates give their fellow valuers reasons to value animals intrinsically. A big part of the *normative* work of contemporary environmental ethics is to give our fellow valuers reasons to value nature intrinsically.

Part of the *metaethical* work of contemporary environmental ethics— the work of this essay—is to analyze the concept of intrinsic value in nature. And that work would at this point be finished except for two considerations. First, some philosophers working well within the meta- physical constraints of Modern philosophy claim that lexically intrinsic value exists in nature. They claim, that is, that intrinsic value is not merely conferred or ascribed by valuing subjects, but that it exists objectively. Second, the radical Cartesian distinction between subjects and objects that is fundamental to Modernism has been subverted, thus suggesting the possibility of constructing a postModern theory of intrinsic value in nature.

KANT ON OBJECTIVE INTRINSIC VALUE

Immanuel Kant, a thoroughly Modern philosopher, tried to draw a dis- tinction between objective and subjective values, without ignoring the Cartesian boundary between things subjective and objective. A close analy- sis of Kant's gambit may shed some light on claims by contemporary Modern philosophers to find objective intrinsic value in nature.

In the *Foundations of the Metaphysic of Morals* Kant writes,

Suppose that there were something the existence of which in itself had *absolute worth*, something which, as an *end in itself* would be a ground for definite laws. . . . Now, I say, man and, in general, every rational being exists as an end in himself and not merely as a means to be arbitrarily used by this or that will. . . . Such beings are not merely subjective ends—whose existence, as a result of our action, has a worth for us—but are *objective ends*, i.e., beings whose existence in itself is an end. . . . (Kant 1959, 46, emphasis added)

Schematically expressed, Kant seems to be asserting:

end in itself ⇒ objective end ⇒ absolute worth

But why are such beings—beings whose existence in itself is an end for them—*objective* ends? Such beings may value (verb transitive) themselves as ends in themselves—that is, they may value themselves intrinsically—but how does that make their intrinsic value *objective?* Kant seems to realize that he has explained nothing, so he goes on.

Man necessarily *thinks of* his own existence in this way; thus far it is a *subjective* principle of human action. Also every other rational being thinks of his own existence by means of the same rational ground which holds also for myself; thus it is at the same time an objective principle from which, as a supreme practical ground, it must be possible to derive all laws of the will. (Kant 1959, 47, emphasis added)

Kant does not here claim that the "absolute worth" (intrinsic value) of rational beings is straightforwardly objective—a (non-natural) property woven into their essential nature or constitution. Nor does he commit the naturalistic fallacy by arbitrarily (and self-servingly) asserting that rationality is a value-conferring property. One values (verb transitive) oneself intrinsically. "Thus far," Kant carefully notes, one's intrinsic value "is a subjective principle of human action."

Kant immediately claims, nevertheless, that it somehow becomes "objective" when one considers that others value themselves in the same way. Does the intrinsic value of a rational being magically get transformed from a subjectively self-conferred to an objective property, merely by this consideration? If so, How?

Two interpretations of this transmogrification of subjectively conferred intrinsic value into objective intrinsic value occur to me.

The first is that rationality is the same—in the strong sense of identical—in all rational beings. When it reflects on itself as an end itself, it reflects, perforce, on itself in all other rational beings. Maybe this is what

Kant means when he writes, "Also every other rational being thinks of his own existence by means of the same rational ground which holds also for myself." In other words, maybe for Kant, rationality is like a Platonic form or sort of like Atman-Brahman in the Advaita Vedanta Hindu tradition of thought. Perhaps there is, in reality, only one form of Rationality in all us rational beings, or only one Rational Being, residing in all us Homo sapiens.

But does that make its *value* objective? Suppose Rationality manifests itself in all rational beings and in them all it values itself. But its value still remains conferred by the intentional act of a (now supposed to be universal) self-valuing subject.

Or Kant might mean that when one realizes that others value themselves as one values oneself, then one transcends the limitations of one's subjectivity. The blinkers come off. The scales fall from one's eyes. A kind of community, the moral community, the "kingdom of ends" comes into view. This transcendence of subjectivity operationally, but not actually, objectifies the value of others. That is, to realize that other rational beings value themselves as one values oneself—to wit, intrinsically—provides *the functional equivalent* of an objective property available to disinterested observation. A rational being should be "an end for everyone because it is an end *for* itself" (1959, 47).

So unless I'm missing something, when we look closely at Kant's claim that the "absolute worth" (intrinsic value) of rational beings is objective, all we find is an *assertion* that it is, together with some interesting justificatory clues. But when we follow those clues up, they lead not to genuinely objective intrinsic value, but only to a universal self-valuing subject or to its functional equivalent. Perhaps Kant's intellectual descendents in environmental ethics can do better than the master himself.

THE BIOCENTRISTS ON OBJECTIVE
INTRINSIC VALUE IN NATURE

The transition from Kantian anthropocentrism (or, more precisely, ratiocentrism) to Kantian biocentrism begins with the question, Why should we rational beings value only ourselves and other rational beings intrinsically?

Because, Kant seems to assume, only rational beings are capable of self-valuing. Certainly, only rational beings are capable of transcending the limitations of their subjectivity, of realizing that others value themselves as one values oneself—to wit, intrinsically. And only rational beings are autonomous, capable of deriving moral laws from the supreme practical principle, imposing those laws on themselves, and freely choosing to obey. Only rational beings, in other words, are legislators in the kingdom of ends.

To possess "objective" intrinsic value then, according to Kant, seems to require that a being be capable of (1) valuing itself as an end in itself and (2) realizing that other beings value themselves in the same way.

But is the second qualification morally defensible? So what if a being that values itself intrinsically is not capable of realizing that others value themselves in the same way? Why shouldn't it also be an end for everyone who is able to transcend the limitations of subjectivity—because it is an end for itself? In effect, Kant requires that a being be able to requite respect in order to qualify for receiving it. That amounts to a reciprocity criterion for moral considerability: Only moral agents can be moral patients.

And that exposes Kant's anthropocentrism (ratiocentrism) to the Argument from Marginal Cases (Regan 1979). If we suppose that rationality is itself an observable capability of certain beings—not an Enlightenment equivalent of the biblical *imago dei*, possessed by all human beings irrespective of capacity—then we must admit that all human beings are not rational beings. And if not, they are, by Kant's clear reckoning "things" not "persons" and, therefore, "have only relative worth as means" (Kant 1959, 46). Kant's ethic would therefore seem to countenance painful medical experiments on prerational human infants, hunting nonrational human imbeciles for sport, and making dog food out of postrational elderly human beings, among other wicked and depraved things. One way to avoid such untoward consequences of Kant's ethical theory is simply to eliminate the reciprocity criterion for moral considerability and value intrinsically all beings that arguably value themselves intrinsically.

Albert Schweitzer

To my knowledge, the first Modern philosopher to take this course is Albert Schweitzer. According to Kant (1787), unknowable "noumena" lie behind all phenomena which we apprehend spatially and temporally, through our built-in "forms of intuition" and variously organized by our built-in "categories of understanding." Perhaps Kant thought of universal reason as one such noumenon, the same, identical thing in all rational beings. Arthur Schopenhauer (1961), the post-Kantian philosopher from whom Schweitzer takes his metaphysics, identified a single noumenon at the core of *all* phenomena—the will-to-live—which we neither perceive nor know, but of which we are sometimes vividly aware (like when our lives are threatened). According to Schweitzer ([1923] 1994, 67), "In me the will-to-live has become cognizant of other will-to-live. There is in it a yearning for unity with itself, a longing to become universal. . . . Is it the result of my having become capable of reflection about the totality of existence?"

Schweitzer, clearly working in the Kantian and post-Kantian tradition, seems to bid for objectivity through both the universality of the will-to-live and the reflective transcendence of subjectivity:

Just as in my own will-to-live there is a yearning for more life, and for that mysterious exaltation of the will-to-live which is called pleasure, and terror in the face of annihilation and that injury to the will-to-live which is called pain; so the same obtains in all the will-to-live around me, equally whether it can express itself to my comprehension or whether it remains unvoiced. Ethics thus consists in this, that I experience the necessity of practicing the same reverence for life toward all will-to-live as toward my own. Therein I have already the needed fundamental principle of morality. It is good to maintain and cherish life: it is evil to destroy and check life. (Schweitzer [1923] 1994, 66)

Paul W. Taylor

Not to demean his biocentric ethic, Schweitzer was an amateur philosopher, less sensitive to the metaphysical constraints of Modernism than a professional might be. Paul W. Taylor is usually thought to have himself been untroubled by the difficulty that troubled Kant in moving from subjectively conferred value to objective value and to have provided a Kantian theory of objective "inherent worth" (Taylor's preferred term) in nature uncomplicated by some obscure transition from subjectively conferred to objective intrinsic value (or inherent worth). But such is not so. Taylor, a thoroughly Modern philosopher, was troubled by this problem.

In his first essay on environmental ethics, he is quite clear that all "worth" (all value) is "ascribed" (conferred) by "valuers" (Cartesian subjects) "who must do the valuing":

We must keep in mind that inherent worth is *not* some mysterious sort of objective property belonging to living things that can be discovered by empirical observation or scientific investigation. . . . Nor is there a logical connection between the concept of a being having a good of its own and the concept of inherent worth. . . . In order to show that such an entity "has" inherent worth we must give good reasons for *ascribing* that kind of value to it (*placing* that kind of value on it, *conceiving* it to be valuable in that way). Although it is humans (persons, *valuers*) *who must do the valuing*, for the ethics of respect for nature, the value so ascribed is not human value. That is to say, it is not a value derived from considerations regarding human well-being or human rights. It is a value that is *ascribed* to nonhuman animals and plants themselves, independently of their relationship to what humans judge to be conducive to their own good. (Taylor 1981, 204)

In his book on environmental ethics, however, Taylor changes his mind. Inherent worth there *is* treated as "some mysterious sort of objective property belonging to living beings." It is mysterious because Taylor distinguishes (1) "the concept of inherent worth" from "the concept of the good of a being" and (2) from the concepts of "intrinsic value" and "inherent value," both of which, he acknowledges, are "ascribed" (conferred) by valuing subjects. Avoiding the Scylla of the naturalistic fallacy by drawing the first distinction and the Charybdis of subjectivity by drawing the second, he sails off into unfathomable waters.

First, Taylor (1986, 71–72) avoiding the naturalistic fallacy:

The concept of inherent worth must not be confused with the concept of the good of a being. To bring out the difference between them, consider the logical gap between the fact that a being has a good of its own (an is-statement) and the claim that it should or should not be treated in a certain way (an ought-statement). One can acknowledge that an animal or plant has a good of its own and yet, consistently with this acknowledgment, deny that moral agents have a duty to promote or protect its good or even refrain from harming it.

According to Taylor, inherent worth bridges the is/ought or fact/value dichotomy—which was first clearly articulated by David Hume (1739), but is a function of the Cartesian cleft between subjects and objects. His reasoning appears to be purely Kantian: If we can successfully objectify "inherent worth" then statements about the *value* of beings that have it will be "is-statements." Fact and value will be welded together and we can thus move validly from "is-statements" to "ought-statements." Schematically expressed:

good of its own ⇒ inherent worth ⇒ duties to it

Now, here is Taylor defining two types of subjectively conferred value:

(a) *Intrinsic value.* When human or other conscious beings place positive value on an event or condition in their lives which they directly experience to be enjoyable in and of itself, and when they value the experience (consider it to be good) *because* of its enjoyableness the value they place on it is intrinsic. . . .

(b) *Inherent value.* This is the value that we place on an object or a place (such as a work of art, a historical building, a battlefield, a "wonder of nature," or an archeological site) that we believe should be preserved, not because of its usefulness or commercial value, but simply because it has beauty, or historical importance, or cultural significance. . . . Besides works of art, natural wonders, historical monuments, and other inanimate objects, . . . wild animals and plants may also have inherent value to people. But it is to be observed that, whatever the basis of the inherent value placed on something may be, whether aesthetic, historical, cultural, or a matter of personal sentiment, wonder, or admiration, *the inherent value of anything is relative to and dependent upon someone's valuing it.* (Taylor 1986, 73–74)

The (ever-so-subtle) difference between intrinsic and inherent value according to Taylor is that the former characterizes the way we value our subjective experiences (for example, the *pleasure* that a work of art gives its beholder), and the latter the way we value objective *entities* (for example, the work of art itself). So far, so good. Taylor has not yet confronted us with a Modern mystery.

But what about "inherent worth" (as opposed to "inherent value")? Taylor (1986, 75) says that it "is to be attributed only to entities that have a good of their own."

Wait a minute. What does "to be attributed" mean here? That this kind of *worth*, no less than the three species of *value* (instrumental, intrinsic, and inherent) is conferred, ascribed, that is, *attributed* (verb transitive) to beings with a good of their own—such that were there no "attributers" (no attributing subjects), there would be no inherent worth? Or does it simply mean that we should reserve the *term* "inherent worth" for some sort of objective property of beings that have a good of their own? Apparently the latter, because Taylor goes on explicitly to say that a being's inherent *worth* does not depend on some valuer valuing it instrumentally or inherently, or some valuer valuing the experience of it intrinsically. Thus, in his own words from his earlier essay, Taylor leaves us in *Respect for Nature* with "some mysterious sort of objective property belonging to living things," for which he provides no justification whatever. Just like Kant, he is aware of the problem. And just like Kant, he simply asserts that beings that have a good of their own have inherent worth, which worth somehow exists objectively, that is, independently of any valuing subject. And just like Kant, he couches this assertion in some ambiguous—and therefore obfuscating—prose in an attempt to clothe its nakedness.

Holmes Rolston III

Perhaps Taylor cannot find a way to defend the objectivity of inherent worth in nature and finds himself reduced simply to asserting dogmatically that the worth of beings with a good of their own is independent of a valuing subject because he tends to think that only human beings are valuing subjects. Remember, in "The Ethics of Respect for Nature" he writes that "it is *humans* (*persons*, valuers) who must do the valuing." There he conflates human persons and valuers. In his book, when defining "intrinsic value," he writes "When human *or other conscious beings* place positive value [etc.]"—thus acknowledging that nonhuman valuing subjects may exist. But when he goes on to define 'inherent value,' he lapses into expressions that indicate that, once again, he is thinking only of human beings as valuing subjects: inherent value is the value "that *we* place on an object or place" because of what "*we* believe"; "wild animals and plants may also have inherent value *to people*"; inherent value "is relative to and dependent upon *someone's* [not something's] valuing it."

But if we could be convinced that all living beings are self-valuing then, by Kant's gambit, their value could at least be functionally equivalent to objective intrinsic value (now departing from Taylor's special sense of the term *intrinsic value* and returning to its standard usage in environmental ethics) if not actually objective. That is Rolston's ploy.

After Darwin, no great leap of faith is required to believe that other *conscious* beings—imbeciles as well as rational human beings, all other primates, all other mammals, perhaps all other chordates—may value themselves intrinsically. To the sort of conflation of valuers with human beings to which Taylor seems to be prone, Rolston (1994, 160) wryly retorts, "No doubt the lemurs will take a dim view of such a theory, since lemurs . . . value their own lives intrinsically for what they are in themselves. . . . Lemurs cannot self-consciously evaluate . . . but they can behaviorally demonstrate what they value."

Okay, sure. But how could all merely living beings be self-valuing? To be able to persuade us that they are is Rolston's particular forte.

The ingenious adaptations and survival and reproductive strategies of plants and other organisms that lack consciousness are of value to themselves. Such value is, to be sure, instrumental value. Some of these strategies—the edible casings of the seeds of angiosperms, for example—are also instrumentally valuable to human beings; and some nectar-rich flowers, for example—are also instrumentally valuable to certain kinds of bats, birds, and insects. But all such adaptations and survival and reproductive strategies are, first and foremost, valuable to the plants themselves whose devices they are. And by the teleological proof for the existence of intrinsic value, the existence of instrumental value implies the existence of intrinsic value.

Further, plants are not as passive as they appear. Most contend with rivals and struggle for sunlight. Many excrete allelopathic chemicals from their roots to discourage competitors. Some are even actively carnivorous. All reproduce themselves. Each has a good of its own. "A life is defended for what it is in itself, without further contributory reference. . . . That is ipso facto value in both the biological and philosophical senses, intrinsic because it inheres in, has focus within, the organism itself" (Rolston 1994, 173).

Now take a close look at what Rolston has done. A striving, self-valuing plant is an end in itself. It has a good of its own, in respect to which its various adaptations and survival and reproductive strategies are valuable to it. But it is not conscious. Hence, it cannot be true to claim that if all consciousness were annihilated at a stroke, all value would be annihilated with it. So, it turns out, after all, that value is not necessarily subjective in the sense that it depends for its existence on the intentional act of a Cartesian—that is, conscious—subject. But is Rolstonian intrinsic value fully objective?

Not quite. Suppose all life—unconscious as well as conscious—were annihilated at a stroke and only atoms and molecules existed, organized only into non-living entities like stars and rocks. In this circumstance, as Rolston admits, his argument for objective intrinsic value—which depends, like Kant's, on some sense of self-valuing—could not get off the ground. Even for Rolston, value remains a verb first, but the syntactical subject doing the valuing is no longer necessarily a psychological subject. Thus, Rolston manages to argue persuasively that intrinsic value in nature is not necessarily dependent on a conscious subject—certainly not on a human subject. But he has not shown that intrinsic value can exist independently of a self-valuing subject of some sort.

Rolston's achievement, nevertheless, is quite extraordinary. For without expressly challenging the broadly Modern metaphysical assumptions bequeathed to Western thought by Descartes, Rolston has freed intrinsic value from its dependency not only on a self-conscious human subject, but even on a conscious animal subject.

Rolston's nonsubjectivist (but not fully objectivist) theory of intrinsic value in nature, however, is no more adequate for environmental ethics than any other version of biocentrism. For, without further argument, we are left with an environmental ethic that directly enfranchises only individual organisms. But environmental concerns have little to do with the welfare of *individual* bugs, shrubs, and grubs, and a great deal to do with wholes (such as species and ecosystems) and with abiotic aspects of nature (such as the atmosphere and ocean).

Rolston (1994, 177) is aware of this limitation of biocentrism, and, to his credit, frankly acknowledges it:

Instrumental value uses something as a means to an end; *intrinsic value* is worthwhile in itself. A warbler eats insects instrumentally as a food resource; the warbler defends her own life as an end in itself and makes more warblers as she can. A life is defended intrinsically, without further contributory reference. But neither of these traditional terms is satisfactory at the level of the ecosystem. . . . We are no longer confronting instrumental value, as though the system were instrumentally valuable as a fountain of life. Nor is the question one of intrinsic value, as though the system defended some unified form of life for itself.

For this reason, I myself have opted not to try following Kant and his biocentric descendents—to conjure objective intrinsic value out of self-valuing subjects and our capacity to realize that others value themselves as we value ourselves. Rather, I have suggested we base environmental ethics on our human capacity to value nonhuman natural entities for what they are—irrespective both of what they may do for us and of whether or not they can value themselves. And this we can do regardless of the nature of the object of our intentional act of intrinsic valuation as long as we think we have good reasons to value it intrinsically. We can value species (such as the Devil's Hole pupfish), ecosystems (such as Cedar Bog Lake), the oceans, the atmosphere, the biosphere—all for what they are in themselves as well as for their utility.

Rolston (1988, 1994), I should hasten to add, supplements his biocentrism by introducing other types of value tailored to wholes: "systemic value" and "projective value." An analysis of these kinds of value, however, lies beyond the scope of this discussion.

TOWARD A POSTMODERN THEORY OF INTRINSIC VALUE IN NATURE

According to Rolston (1994, 193–94), "resolute subjectivists cannot be defeated by argument, although they can be driven toward analyticity. That theirs is a retreat to a definition is difficult to expose because they seem to cling so closely to inner experience. They are reporting, on this hand, how values always excite us. They are giving, on that hand, a stipulative definition. That is how they choose to use the word *value*."

I think that that is a mischaracterization. Those who insist that value is subjectively conferred do not merely stipulate a definition or make a personal terminological choice, they reflect, rather, a foundational tenet of Modernism. Rolston believes himself to offer an account of objective intrinsic value, and by his own understanding of the subjectivist alternative, he does so indeed. Subjectivists, Rolston assumes, believe that value, like a tickle, must be *experienced* to exist: No *experiencer* (no *conscious* subject), no feelings and no value. But as my analysis here indicates, value, from a Modern point of view, is not, primarily, a subjective *experience*, but a subject's *intentional act:* No *intending* subject, no value. Now some intentional acts, even those of highly evolved self-conscious subjects, may not be experienced as such. A philanderer, for example, may not realize that he loves his wife until she leaves him. The reason that Rolston's biocentric account of intrinsic value is so persuasive is precisely because nonconscious organisms can be plausibly portrayed as self-valuing beings, even though they can have no experience of doing so.

A postModern account of intrinsic value in nature is difficult to envision because we are still very much in a state of transition from Modernity to something else. What that something else may be, we cannot be sure; that's why we call this interregnum "postModernism," not something more definite and descriptive. But at the critical core of postModernism, whether approached from the perspective of the New Physics or from that of literary theory, is the decentering, the deconstruction of the Cartesian subject.

The Heisenberg uncertainty principle in the New Physics subverts the clean Cartesian cleavage between subjects and objects. On the one hand, the knowing subject is, so to speak, physicalized, objectified—since information can be registered only if energy is exchanged between object and knowing subject, and energy belongs on the object side of the Cartesian cleft. And, on the other hand, the known object is subjectivized— since a necessarily physical act of observation, in the subatomic domain, disturbs, changes the observed system. On this basis, I have elsewhere suggested a theory of intrinsic value in nature that makes value, like any other natural property, a potentiality to be actualized by a situated observer/ valuer (Callicott 1985). Intrinsic value is not wholly objective, according to such an account, but neither are the formerly "primary qualities," such as position and velocity. Bryan Norton criticizes this postModern account of intrinsic value in nature as still too overshadowed by the Cartesian distinction between subjects and objects (Norton 1992).

Rolston never describes himself as a postModernist. And his non-subjectivist account of intrinsic value in nature is, as this analysis shows, consistent with the foundational tenets of the Modern worldview, turning, as it does, on the (unconscious) intentional act of a self-valuing organism. But notice, in developing this account, Rolston has deconstructed the Cartesian subject. He establishes a continuum, a slippery slope, running from fully self-conscious human valuers to quasi-self-conscious lemur valuers to conscious but hardly self-conscious warbler valuers to utterly unconscious trillium valuers. Step by step, the subjectivity of the subject is eroded until, with plants, we reach self-valuing nonsubjects.

Not only does Rolston (1994, 173–74) deconstruct the Cartesian subject, the bigger story he tells—the story in which his account of intrinsic value is located—also decenters the deconstructed subject:

Things do not have their separate natures merely in and for themselves, but they face outward and co-fit into broader natures. . . . Intrinsic value, that of an individual "for what it is in itself," becomes problematic in a holistic web. True, the system increasingly produces such values with its evolution of individuality and freedom. Yet to decouple this from the biotic, communal system is to make value too internal and elementary. Every intrinsic value has leading and trailing *ands* ["ands" not "ends"] pointing to value from which it comes and towards which it moves. Adapted fitness makes individualistic value too system-independent. Intrinsic value is part of a whole, not to be fragmented by valuing it in isolation.

These and similar remarks in the same vein lead up to Rolston's account of "systemic" value. But they might also be, as I am suggesting now, a prelude to a postModern account of intrinsic value in nature. Rolston both deconstructs and decenters the Cartesian subject. First he erodes the subject's subjectivity to a vanishing point, then he takes the subject out of the center of the picture. The self-valuing organism is located in a context, outside of which it is meaningless.

Eventually the Cartesian subject—like Plato's form of the Good, or Aristotle's Active Intellect—will become a historical curiosity, having lost its grip on the Western mind. What will take its place we cannot now foresee, residing as we do at the cusp of two paradigms—the waning Modern worldview and the waxing embryonic one that so far has not yet sufficiently developed to have acquired a distinct identity.

PART V

ECOLOGICAL METAPHYSICS
IN AGRICULTURE, MEDICINE,
AND TECHNOLOGY

13

The Metaphysical Transition in Farming:
From the Newtonian-Mechanical
to the Eltonian-Ecological

AGRICULTURAL ETHICS AND AGRICULTURAL METAPHYSICS

Presently, a wide array of widely recognized ethical questions—human, humane, and environmental—swirl around Modern agriculture.

What right, for example, have farm workers and innocent consumers to be protected from harmful agricultural chemicals?; at what cost in increased food prices? What personal and public values are sacrificed on the altar of the supreme value of Modern agriculture—maximizing production? Is this trade-off defensible?; is it necessary? What injustices has the Green Revolution created or compounded in so-called developing countries?

Quite apart from the human health effects of dietary antibiotics and growth hormones, how much animal suffering are we willing to countenance in feed lots and battery sheds so that the overconsumption of cheap meat and poultry by relatively wealthy denizens of developed countries may be indulged? Only the most irritable nonanthropocentric ethicists have complained on moral grounds about the genetic manipulation of animals through traditional methods of selective breeding. But the technological quantum leap represented by contemporary genetic engineering also pushes the ethical questions surrounding our genetic interference with other species into an excited state: The difference between selective breeding and genetic engineering is of sufficient degree to constitute a difference in kind.

Throughout human history and prehistory, agriculture has been a transformative force on the face of nature, veritably geologic in scale. *Modern* agriculture has sped up and spread out that force. Early agricultural societies transformed a number of fertile but sensitive plains and valleys into deserts. Today, Modern agriculture is threatening not just regions with unstable loesses and/or marginal rainfall, but whole biomes, myriad species, and elemental planetary processes. Rain forest clothing poor soils is felled to create ephemeral pasturage for cattle; and after the three or four years it takes for the cleared land to be exhausted, it is abandoned and more forest is felled and burned. With the destruction of their rain forest habitat, endemic species are rendered extinct, perhaps to the tune of a million more or less by the end of the twentieth century. Not to mention the CO_2 forthcoming from burning trees to convert forest to pasture, methane from increasing millions of cattle contributes significantly to the total tonnage of greenhouse gases annually pumped into the atmosphere. Agricultural chemicals poison not only human farm workers and consumers, they also poison other, often more sensitive, living beings. Tractor-plowed and row-cropped soils blow and wash away. So . . . how about the effects of Modern agriculture upon wild plant and animal species, upon biotic communities, upon soils and waters, and upon the very atmosphere, the planet's thin, sensitive cell membrane? Is Modern agriculture environmentally unethical, or what?

I mention some of the more salient human, humane, and environmental ethical questions stirred up by Modern agriculture, certainly not to address them all, nor to provide them with a typology, nor even as a prelude to selecting one or two of them for a more in-depth analysis. Rather I wish to point out, simply by reciting them, that they are familiar; and I wish, further, to note that they are being systematically addressed by a cadre of competent professional social scientists and moral philosophers. Less familiar are the *metaphysical* questions surrounding Modern agriculture. I dwell on these in the remainder of this discussion.

To suggest that Modern agriculture may be metaphysically maladroit as well as morally malodorous may seem like saying that the square root of two is blue. While *agricultural ethics* is a perfectly intelligible combination of terms, *agricultural metaphysics* sounds like an oxymoron. What has agriculture got to do with so arcane and abstract a subject as metaphysics? The answer is "really quite a lot." How people go about producing food both reveals and reflects their worldview. Indeed, because food production is one among several absolutely fundamental and universal human activities it affords a particularly clear window into the ambient cultural mind.

COMPARATIVE AGRICULTURAL METAPHYSICS

To get a feel for how thoroughly embedded in metaphysical assumptions food production actually is, consider food production in cognitive cultures that are radically different from our own. Because the metaphysics of food production in such cultures is so foreign, it sticks out like a sore thumb.

For example, subarctic European, Asian, and North American aboriginal hunter-gatherers viewed their world as animated through and through by animal and plant spirits and by their spirit wardens. Therefore, in the famous words of anthropologist Frank Speck (1938, 260), writing of Algonkian hunting and gathering, "with these people no act of this sort is profane, hunting is not a war upon the animals, not a slaughter for food or profit, but a holy occupation." In the minds of these people successful food production depended much less on skill with the bow and arrow and other Stone Age hunting paraphernalia than on favor from the animal spirits and spiritual gamekeepers. Hunting technique consisted less in tracking, stalking, and shooting, than in divining, dreaming, conjuring, ritually consuming meat, and respectfully disposing of bones.

Equally revealing are the agricultural practices of our European forebears. Pre-Hellenic Minoan priestesses spilled the blood of sacrificial victims—human and animal—in springtime to symbolically fertilize Gaia, the great Earth Goddess, and induce her to bring forth grain. In the Dark Ages pagan planters walked behind naked virgins tossing seeds against their bare buttocks from whence they would fall into the vaginal furrows, later to come to term. Medieval horticulturalists planted root crops during the dark of the moon and leafy and fruiting crops during the time of the month when the moon is high and bright.

These and thousands of other quaint hunting, gathering, and horticultural practices reveal the penetration of the ambient ideas about the nature of nature into the production process. Nature will yield us food only if we understand how she works and thus how we can make her work for us. Since the animals are at least as psychologically sophisticated as we, we must communicate and reciprocate with them so that they will give us all that they have to give—their flesh and fur. Or since Earth is a Great Goddess we must properly serve her and offer her our very best and most precious as a sacrifice. Or since she is a fecund female presence we must cultivate her with sympathetic magic and symbolically inseminate her. Or since the seasons are tuned to the cosmic rhythms and portentous planets, we must read the signs and likewise attune our sowing and harvesting to the most propitious astrological windows of opportunity.

Now let's look at our own Modern agriculture with the critical eye of a cultural anthropologist of the future. What we find in Modern agriculture is the quintessential expression in food production of the prevailing Modern worldview, classical mechanics or Newtonian physics and chemistry. Soil is regarded as nothing but a physical substratum in which plants sit. Where I formerly lived in central Wisconsin (at the northern extent of the sand counties, the southern reaches of which were lyrically celebrated by Aldo Leopold in *A Sand County Almanac*), potatoes are planted in the virtually sterile glacial till. The soil is so poor, it's blonde. (Naturally, local boosters have dubbed the region "the Golden Sands.") Simple elements, called "nutrients"—nitrogen, phosphorus, and potassium—are spread on the sand. Six to ten feet below the surface lies a large aquifer, the now subsurface glacial Great Lake Wisconsin. Center pivot irrigation rigs— one-eighth mile of pipe on huge wheels circling around a well—pump it up and spray it on. Carbon dioxide is universally available in the atmosphere. The genetic information contained in the DNA molecules of the certified seed potatoes acts as a blueprint for the assembly, from these primary ingredients, of carbohydrates. Potato pests, fungi, and weeds are controlled by pesticides, fungicides, and herbicides broadcast from airplanes. And most of the farmers regularly dust and spray their fields just as they bathe on Saturday nights—whether they need to or not.

On this chemico-mechanical conception of growing food, a chemicomechanical conception of production technique is overlaid. Processes are reduced to their simplest elements as on an assembly line. Products are standardized; scale is magnified; and crops are specialized and monocultured. Food "processing" is automated. Green beans are also grown on the golden sands. Del Monte has a cannery there. The beans are harvested with combines and blown into dump trucks. At the cannery the trucks empty their beds and the beans are conveyed along on belts, washed, sliced, cooked, and canned—with chemical additives and preservatives—then boxed up and shipped out.

THE NEWTONIAN-MECHANICAL PARADIGM
IN AGRICULTURE CRITICIZED

Well, so what? Modern agriculture is *Modern* agriculture precisely because it is based upon and informed by Modern science. Vision-seeking, feather-shaking savages were simply deluded to think that bears, deer, and beaver are intelligent, in some ways superior, beings, who, only if properly cajoled, will voluntarily surrender themselves to the hunter's weapons. And lots of innocent blood was spilled in the erroneous belief that the Goddess won't give grain unless she is honored with the ultimate gift—the life of a young man in his sexual prime. And lots of virgins probably needlessly died of pneumonia after walking around naked on the damp soil all day in the chill air of spring. And lots of farmers wasted their time waiting for the moon to get right before planting their crops. We know better. The Modern worldview is true and the others that preceded it are false.

But can we be so cocksure? Mesolithic hunters, Neolithic, Bronze, and Iron Age farmers were just as sure that they were right about how the world worked as our USDA bureaucrats, land grant agronomists, county extension agents, and agribusinessmen and -women are today. How can anyone *know* that her mental image of reality—and that's all that our minds can generate—corresponds to reality as it actually is? Unfortunately we can never transcend consciousness and just somehow *have* reality as it actually is—so that we can stand back and compare our mental images with it. One way that we test the truth of our intellectual constructs is constantly to submit them to critical scrutiny. In science the critical process is called the experimental method and has become highly refined. Because it is self-critical in principle, the scientific worldview is epistemologically set off from all its predecessors. At a more practical level we test our reality models by seeing if they "work." We act upon our beliefs, in other words, and if things turn out as we expect, then our models are confirmed.

Modern agriculture passes neither test, neither reality check. Notoriously it's not working, at least not sustainably. And it is based upon a bankrupt metaphysics, a worldview that has not withstood critical scrutiny and that is, in fact, dead in pure science, even though it lives on in applied science.

Sure, we have plenty to eat, food is cheap, and there is still of a surfeit of grain. But . . . soil compaction, erosion, and loss of fertility; the foreseeable exhaustion of fossil fuels and fossil waters; agro-chemical pollution of air, surface, and ground waters, and food itself; cyclic outbreaks of pests and the ensuing dialectic of ever more toxic and intensively applied pesticides; the loss of genetic diversity and the loss of the wild ancestors and relatives of our cultivars; rural depopulation and disruption of rural patterns of life; the corollary loss of centuries of transmitted agricultural experience and knowledge, the desiccation, in short, of the culture of agriculture; concentration of land ownership and the proletarianization of farm labor . . . all bode ill for the sustainability of Modern agriculture.

And as to the bankruptcy of Modern agriculture's metaphysical motif, classical mechanics was reluctantly abandoned by science during the first half of the twentieth century. Way back in the very first decade of the twentieth century, Albert Einstein argued that Newton's concepts of absolute, empty, Euclidean container space and independent, equably flowing time were not consistent with the results of experiments more sophisticated than those Newton devised. Around the same time, a host of other scientists were discovering forces, like electromagnetism and radioactivity that could not be embraced by the conceptual repertory of classical mechanics. The fine structure of the physical world increasingly appeared more energetic than material, more fieldlike than granulated, more integrated than fragmented, more probabilistic than deterministic, more potential than actual.

A NEW ECOLOGICAL PARADIGM
FOR AGRICULTURE COMMENDED

Simultaneous with these revolutionary developments in physics were parallel, conceptually resonant, developments in biology. S. A. Forbes, F. E.

Clements, and H. C. Cowles discovered that plants were not arrayed upon the landscape like furniture in a room, each piece separate from and independent of all the others. Rather, they were structurally and functionally integrated—and thus related, they hypothesized, to one another more like the parts of an organism than the parts of a mechanism. As multicellular organisms had evolved from looser associations of single-celled organisms, so ecosystems (as they eventually came to be called), they argued, had evolved, similarly, from similar associations of multicellular organisms. At each more complex level of organization emergent properties—properties irreducible to and unpredictable from the properties of the previous level—appeared or emerged. The new science of ecology, they suggested, was the "physiology" of these tertiary organic wholes. These early ecologists may have overstated the degree to which ecosystems are integrated and unified (chapter 7), but they were onto something new and enduring. The terrestrial environment is more than a mere aggregate of parts; it is a hierarchy of self-organized systems.

Now, let me hasten to say that I am not for a moment suggesting that such elements as carbon, nitrogen, phosphorus, and potassium are discredited theoretical entities—like phlogiston or, to take a more recent example, like the luminiferous ether. Nor do I think that such elements are not really plant nutrients; nor do I think that, directed by their DNA, plants do not in fact synthesize complex organic molecules from elemental components. And certainly I am not suggesting that soil is not in fact a mechanical medium in which plants stand. Indeed, soil erosion, which I just mentioned as among the symptoms of a false philosophy of farming, is a textbook example of a mechanical process—moving molecules of air and water bumping and grinding, blowing and washing the soil away, bit by bit, just like so many tiny billiard balls being knocked off a pool table by other balls of various sizes violently striking them.

What I am suggesting, rather, is that, prior to the twentieth century, Modern science thought that reality was *exclusively* mechanical and chemical and, apparently blissfully unaware of revolutionary changes in science commencing at the beginning of the century, twentieth-century agronomists proceeded on the assumption that soil was *nothing but* a mechanical medium and that plants were *nothing but* complex assemblages of a few simple elements and that agricultural goals—increasing yields, controlling weeds, pests, and pathogens, maintaining fertility, and so on— could be achieved Cartesian-style, by finding a separate solution for each and summing the results. Wes Jackson (1987, 68) comments, in this connection, that "Cartesianism is not just a tool or method of investigation. It is a *commitment* to how things really are. As Levins and Lewontin say [in *The Dialectical Biologist*], 'the method is used because it is regarded as isomorphic with the actual structure of causation. The world is like the method.'"

Newtonian physics and chemistry adequately describe a middle range of reality. But below the atomic level there lie strata of organization which the concepts of Euclidean space, time, and moving, externally related material particles cannot comprehend. And above the biochemical level there also lie several strata of organization that are not adequately represented as externally related aggregates of externally related material particles. Subatomic structures are not composed of a variety of tiny elastic bee-bees or marbles, some of which orbit around others—like miniature solar systems—despite the physicists' bad habit of calling them "particles." Organisms are not intricate natural machines. And ecosystems are not aggregates of intricate natural machines haphazardly and chaotically bouncing around together.

Classical mechanics went out of fashion as an intellectual paradigm, *sensu* Thomas Kuhn (1961), in theoretical physics, but we are just beginning to hear its death rattle as a more general intellectual paradigm, *sensu* Fritjof Capra (1982), in other areas of our thinking. That classical mechanics has served as a paradigm for thinking in agriculture is hardly surprising since it has represented a model, a template, for thinking about any and everything.

For example, despite the fact that human societies are knit into seamless wholes, not only by ties of kinship and mutual dependency, but by such evidently and irreducibly emergent social properties as language and culture, the Modern mechanical mind portrays society as *nothing but* an aggregate of individuals—or social atoms. Appetite is the analog in social atoms of inertial states in physical bodies. Each individual, in other words, is portrayed ideally as relentlessly and "rationally" pursuing "preference satisfaction," i.e., headed on a straight course to the objects of its appetites unless deflected by outside forces—collisions with other social atoms or such analogs of gravitational and magnetic forces as tax incentives and interest rates. Adam Smith is lionized as the Robert Boyle of the social sciences who in *The Wealth of Nations* supposedly provided the social analog of the gas laws.

In Modern medicine, similarly, the body is regarded as *nothing but* an elaborate mechanism and disease is understood, reductively, as the malfunction of a part: the heart, liver, kidney, or whatever; or more reductively still, the malfunction of certain kinds of cells or defective molecules: genes, proteins, enzymes, etc. Cures are effected either by surgery, the most purely mechanical of Modern medicine's techniques—taken to ultimate expression in the recent phenomenon of organ transplants in which the surgeon, like an automobile mechanic, removes the defective part and replaces it with another from an "organ bank," the medical equivalent of a parts warehouse. Or sometimes cures are effected with site-specific or broadcast chemicals—the topical application, injection, or ingestion of drugs into the human body—which chemicals are conceived as working mechanically at the molecular level of bodily organization.

GENERAL FEATURES OF A SYSTEMS METAPHYSIC

What more, one may fairly ask, is an organism, a society, and an ecosystem than an aggregate of parts? To answer that each is a *system*, a functional whole, goes part of the way toward explaining the difference. But a machine—an automobile or combine—is also a whole, the coordinated function of which is fully reducible to the separate and independent functions of its parts.

There are four features of the waxing holistic systemic paradigm that mark it off from the waning reductive mechanical paradigm.

First, a genuinely systemic whole exhibits emergent properties—as aforementioned, properties that are neither reducible to nor predictable from the properties of the parts. Language, for example, though spoken by individuals, is a social phenomenon, inconceivable as an attribute of individuals in isolation from social intercourse—as Ludwig Wittgenstein's droll remarks on the inconceivability of a private language, a language that only one person speaks to herself, confirms. A unified consciousness, a self, is an attribute of individual multicellular organisms—totally unpredictable from a consideration of cells alone and, I might add, still a complete mystery for Modern reductive science. Plant succession is an example of an emergent property at the ecosystemic level of organization. Studying specimens of birch and aspen in isolation from biotic communities, botanists cannot predict that birch and aspen populations would be succeeded by stands of oak and maple in northern hardwood forests.

Even classically mechanical systems exhibit emergent properties. The fluidity of water is not predictable from studying water molecules in isolation. Indeed, the standard example of an emergent property is drawn from Newtonian chemistry: Chlorine, a halogen, and sodium, an alkaline metal, combine to form common table salt—sodium chloride—which has none of the noxious properties of its parts. If emergent properties are recognized—though perhaps not acknowledged as such—by mechanists in mechanical systems, then why should they not be recognized in organic and ecological systems? If it is evident that the properties of salt are irreducible to the properties of sodium and chlorine, then it should be equally evident that the properties of potatoes and other foodstuffs are not reducible the properties of their constituents (to starches, protein, oils, and vitamins) and that the properties of ecosystems are not reducible to the properties of their component species.

Second, a genuinely systemic whole exerts downward causation on its parts. A water molecule in a bathtub is identical to every other water molecule—to those in a tropical typhoon and to those in an arctic glacier. A new carburetor fitted on an old Pontiac will not be differently affected by its mechanical environment than an identical carburetor fitted on a new Chevrolet. But when an individual organism is located in a particular ecosystem, the resulting phenotype is shaped partly by its genes and partly by its environment. One cedar tree, for example, planted in poor, sandy coastal soil may be stunted, and misshapen by prevailing hard winds. Another, from the same parent stock, may grow tall and straight on the sunny, fertile inland side of the coastal range. One deer may grow strong and fat on mast, browse, and field corn; and old in the absence of predators and hunters. Another a few miles away, sired by the same buck, may be runty and succumb to winter starvation in marginal habitat. Or consider a person with Chinese genes born into an English-speaking cultural environment. As persons—that is, as human organisms in cultural context—a Chinese American and a Polish American have more in common than either has with Chinese in China or Poles in Poland.

Third, the parts of a genuinely systemic whole are systemically related. The fenders of an automobile can be replaced with a sleeker set, its two-barrel carburetor can be replaced with a four-barrel one, racing shocks can be installed, and so forth, with no effect on the radiator, piston rods, or manifold. But the slightest change in societies, organisms, and ecosystems can have catastrophic effects. To transplant a kidney, despite the mechanical inspiration of the surgical procedure, is not at all like replacing the clutch plates of a car. A car will not reject a new part, but an animal body may very well do just that. The untoward effects of introducing alien species into ecosystems—the rabbit into Australia, Johnson grass into North America, the mongoose into Hawaii, and so on—are notorious. When television was first introduced into society its untoward social effects were thought to be limited to an economic downturn in the motion picture industry. But the catastrophic systemic effects on society of something apparently so innocuous as television are vast, profoundly affecting everything from child development to electoral politics; and while some are obvious, others are so indirect, synergistic, and insidious as to be only problematically tracked back to television as effect to cause. In systemic wholes, indeed, cause and effect relationships are not limited, as they are on a billiard table model of reality, to one cause, one effect. The components of societies, organisms, and ecosystems are causally related to one another in multiple and interacting positive and negative feedback loops. Cause and effect relationships are often indirect, synergistic, and nonlinear (chaotic).

Fourth, the parts of a genuinely systemic whole are internally related. They are what they are because of their relationships with one other. On the mechanical paradigm, objects—things—are the primary realities and relationships are secondary, insubstantial, and ephemeral. On a billiard table, when a game is in progress, each ball remains impassive and permanent; only their spatial relations change. The fact that the three ball is behind the eight ball, in other words, makes no difference to its three-ball-ness. It remains the same three ball irrespective of its relationship with the eight ball or any other ball on the table. Similarly, a water molecule remains a water molecule as it passes through the hydrologic cycle, and its constituent atoms remain hydrogen and oxygen as they pass through the reduction and combustion cycle. If we picture reality as nothing but a hierarchy of machinelike assemblages of billiard ball-like elementary bodies, then we are likely to ignore or downgrade the relational ties that not only bind the parts of genuinely systemic wholes to one another, but that constitute the essence of each, that make each thing what it is, that give each part of an organic system its distinctive characteristics.

Persons in society are who they are because of their relationships with other persons. Had my parents decided, after conceiving me, to move to China, before I was born, and throw in their lot (and mine) with Mao Tse-tung's revolution, I would not be the person I am today. It is doubtful that I would have become a philosopher, most unlikely that I would have become an American university professor, and quite certainly I would not be thinking these thoughts—all of which constitute me. Species in ecosystems, analogously, are shaped, over time, by their relationships in biotic communities. Each brings a phylogenetic heritage to a multiply interactive environment. Grass and grazer, predator and prey, host and parasite coevolve. Contemporary and contiguous species in ecosystems are, therefore, mutually constitutive. They are adapted to and embedded in enormously complex contexts. Hence, organisms depend upon specimens of other, coevolved species to actualize their genetic potential. Taken out of those contexts and put in others, they may degenerate, or not survive, or may irrupt as pests. They may certainly not be depended upon to remain exactly the same—like a water molecule when taken out of the ocean into the air by evaporation or like a Toyota exported from Tokyo to Topeka.

ALDO LEOPOLD'S ANTICIPATION OF
A NEW PARADIGM IN AGRICULTURE

On 7 September 1989, the *New York Times* wrote an obituary for industrial—or, to cut more to the quick of its metaphysical foundations, what I have here called "Newtonian"—agriculture. The *Times* reports that a recent study by the Board on Agriculture of the U.S. National Academy of Sciences "was seeking to reverse federal policies that for more than four decades have been focused on increasing the productivity of crop and livestock farms principally through heavy use of pesticides, drugs, and synthetic fertilizers." According to the *Times*, the Academy study "is perhaps the most important confirmation of the success of agricultural practices that use biological interactions instead of chemicals." Dimly perceiving that the Academy's study signaled a change in the metaphysical ground sea of Western agriculture, the report observes that "farming methods shunning chemicals have been viewed as unorthodox and incapable of generating harvests that match those that are produced with chemicals." Empirical studies conducted by the National Academy indicate, on the contrary, that in fact alternative agricultural methods are capable of producing harvests that exceed those that are produced with chemicals. But to say that organic farming methods have been viewed as "unorthodox" rather than as "unscientific" suggests that the postModern agricultural paradigm shift, now given the imprimatur of the National Academy of Sciences, does not represent a backward turn from a scientifically informed agriculture to a prescientific vernacular agriculture, so much as it represents a turn from one scientific foundation and model for agriculture, the Newtonian-mechanical, to another, the Eltonian-ecological.

The ecological critique of industrial agriculture, recently advanced by Wendell Berry and Wes Jackson, and finally legitimized by the National Academy of Sciences, was begun by Aldo Leopold. Or if Leopold was not the first to criticize Modern agriculture from an ecological point of view, he was, to my knowledge, the first to realize that ecology was a subversive science—that it undermined the foundations of the mechanical worldview—and that it held profound implications for the future of farming. Leopold's translation of the ecological worldview into a vision of a whole, healthy, humane, and environmentally sound agriculture is only scarcely conveyed in his aforementioned slender volume of philosophical essays. It has been my pleasure and privilege to edit, with Susan Flader, a new volume of Leopold's unpublished and previously published but uncollected philosophical and literary papers, for the University of Wisconsin Press; and in some of them his ecological critique of the mechanical paradigm and its agricultural expression is especially pointed and acute.

In a 1938 lecture delivered in the castle keep of applied Newtonian science, the University of Wisconsin College of Engineering, Leopold (1991c, 252) remarked,

[T]he engineer is to me a symbol of the state of the public mind. . . . The engineer has respect for mechanical wisdom . . . he has disrespect for ecological wisdom. . . . [But] all history shows this: that civilization is not the progressive elaboration of a single idea, but the successive dominance of a series of ideas. Greece, Rome, the Renaissance, the industrial age, each had a new and largely distinct zone of awareness. The people of each lived not in a better, nor in a worse, but in a new and different intellectual field. . . . Engineering is clearly the dominant idea of the industrial age. . . . Ecology is one of the contenders for a new order.

In a lecture to the Chamberlain Science Club of Beloit College two years earlier (1936), Leopold applied directly to agriculture his keen sense that ecology represents a new "intellectual field" bidding to become a new reigning conceptual paradigm, a "new order." "Scientific wild life management," he said,

while far younger than scientific agriculture, has . . . forged ahead of it in one point of its philosophy: its recognition of invisible interdependencies in the biotic community. When some women's club protests against the "control" of game-killing hawks, or the poisoning of stock-killing carnivores, or of crop-eating rodents, they are raising—whether they know it or not—a new and fundamental issue in land-use. Agriculture has assumed that by the indefinite pyramiding of new "controls," an artificial plant community can be substituted for the natural one. There are omens that this assumption may be false. Pests and troubles in need of control seem to be piling up even faster than new science and new dollars for control work. (Leopold 1991d, 237)

Leopold may have been the first critic of Modern agriculture clearly to characterize it as "industrial" or factory-like and to predict its short tenure: about three-quarters of a century—if we can pinpoint its origins in the 1930s and, assuming that the agricultural policy shift recommended by the National Academy of Sciences is vigorously implemented, anticipate its demise in the early twenty-first century.

In "The Outlook for Farm Wildlife," Leopold (1945, 168) identified "an unresolved contest between two philosophies of farm life:

1. The farm is a food-factory, and the criterion of its success is salable products.
2. The farm is a place to live. The criterion of success is a harmonious balance between plants, animals, and people; between the domestic and the wild; between utility and beauty. . . . It was inevitable and no doubt desirable that the tremendous momentum of industrialization should have spread to farm life. It is clear to me, however, that it has overshot the mark, in the sense that it is generating new insecurities, economic and ecological, in place of those it was meant to abolish. In its extreme form it is humanly desolate and economically unstable.

These extremes will someday die of their own too-much, not because they are bad for wildlife, but because they are bad for farmers.

Succeeding industrial agriculture, Leopold envisioned a scientifically informed agro-ecology. To be sure, an agro-ecosystem is an artificial plant and animal community created to replace a natural one. But an agro-ecosystem is deliberately designed to imitate the structure of a natural biotic community. In general, an agro-ecosystem involves both lateral and vertical diversity. It consists of a wide variety of plant cultivars overlaid by a proportionate variety of domestic animals, topped by human beings at the apex of the tiered structure. Some of the plant crops are grown for human consumption and some for consumption by farm animals. In addition to meat, milk, and eggs, the animal members of an agro-ecosystem produce manure fertilizers for crops, thus replicating the nutrient cycle of natural ecosystems.

Further, an agro-ecosystem is feathered into the natural ecosystem. The two are integrated and mutually enhancing. Wild crops, such as game, fish, nuts, berries, fruits, fuelwood, and timber, are encouraged or managed in addition to domesticated crops. As Leopold the game manager frequently notes, wildlife thrives only where both food and cover are abundant. While climax temperate ecosystems may provide much cover, they may also provide little food. A rich and diverse wild community is not only compatible in principle with a rich and diverse cultivated community, the latter may substantially augment the former. A middle landscape of small-scale, information-intensive agro-ecosystems centered in and integrated with a variety of local, natural biotic communities could be, though it sounds like heresy to say so, actually an improvement on natural climax communities, by measures of ecological diversity, complexity, and health.

Leopold's vision of an agro-ecosystem was most fully expressed in an essay, "The Farmer as a Conservationist," published in *American Forests* in 1939 (and reprinted in *The River of the Mother of God and Other Essays*). His point of departure is the already fairly diverse and environmentally benign quarter-section Wisconsin dairy farm with its typical assortment of livestock, patchwork of pasture and hay and grain fields; its kitchen garden, fence rows, woodlot, pond, marsh, and creek. But contemporary stratagems for an agro-ecology may also depart from the opposite end of the wild-domesticated spectrum. One might begin, that is, not with a conventional agricultural system, like a traditional family dairy farm, and ask how it might be de-industrialized and reecologized; one might begin, rather, with a natural ecosystem and ask how it might be cultivated rather than converted. This is Wes Jackson's approach at the Land Institute. Working with native prairie flora, Jackson and his associates are attempting to create grain-bearing permacultures.

Or, one might simply select and encourage the utilizable native members of natural communities. Charles M. Peters, Alwyn H. Gentry, and Robert O. Mendelsohn (1989) report that the nuts, fruits, oils, latex, fiber, and medicines annually harvested from a representative hectare of standing rain forest in Peru is of greater economic value than the sawlogs and pulpwood stripped from a similar hectare—greater even than if, following clear-cutting and slash-burning, the land is in addition converted to an industrial forest monoculture or to a cattle pasture. They conclude that "without question, the sustainable exploitation of non-wood forest resources represents the most immediate and profitable method for integrating the use and conservation of Amazonian forests" (Peters et al. 1989, 656).

Careful forest husbandry might increase the frequency of those trees producing valuable commodities without substantially altering the global character of rain-forest ecosystems. Arturo Gomez-Pompa and Andrea Kaus (1988) have argued, on the basis of the greater incidence of trees bearing edible fruits than would occur naturally, that extant remnants of Central American rain forests may once actually have been part of an extensive Maya permaculture, though to the inexpert eye they seem pristine wilderness.

AGRICULTURAL METAPHYSICS THE KEY TO SOLVING THE PROBLEMS OF AGRICULTURAL ETHICS

Returning now to the previously sounded tide of ethical concerns swamping Modern agriculture, a paradigm shift in the metaphysics of agriculture—from the Newtonian to the Eltonian, from the mechanical to the ecological—may provide relief from these as well. Wes Jackson (1987, 75) points out that "the ecological worldview . . . will tell us that one thing done wrong can create numerous problems throughout a system."

But he also points out that "if something is done right, if something is done that fits, several problems are taken care of at once." This feature of systems thinking applies to agro-ecological ethics as well as to agro-ecology.

Agro-ecosystems practically by definition substantially reduce, if they do not eliminate altogether, the application of chemical fertilizers and pesticides, and thus they will make agricultural environments healthier places to work and their "organic" products safer to consume.

The reduction in scale and mechanization, and increase in diversity and complexity of agro-ecosystems will create jobs and help to resettle the American countryside after its depopulation following the industrial revolution in farming. A new culture of agriculture, based upon the vernacular organic agricultural systems of the past, but richly informed by science and especially by ecology, will evolve.

In developing countries, the reduction of inputs, scale, and the need for large, expensive machinery for tilling, cultivating, harvesting, and irrigating might create an economic regime favorable to small landholders and thus pave the way for a more democratic distribution of land.

The factory-style intensive rearing and genetic engineering of farm animals epitomizes the reductive, mechanical paradigm. In it animals are treated as meat, milk, and egg producing Cartesian automata and the production *problematique* is divided, following Descartes's discourse on method, into its simplest elements, linearly ordered, and integrally summed. Such methods would naturally be abandoned in a future agro-ecology, as animals are reintroduced into vertically integrated agro-eco-systems. The unconscionable increase in animal suffering attendant upon the recent emergence of the factory farm would be reversed and farm animals might be restored their rights of membership in the mixed human-animal communities that have existed and evolved since domestication was first undertaken.

Sustainably harvesting the natural wealth of foodstuffs, medicines, wood products, lacustrine and riverine fishes in standing rain forests, and developing tiered tropical gardens of banana, coffee, and coconut under the forest canopies might go a long way toward saving the world's species-rich belt of rain forest.

In general, a postModern agriculture embedded in and expressive of the emerging ecological worldview may be just what the doctor ordered for the multiplying moral maladies of a moribund industrial agriculture.

14

Environmental Wellness

I have heard that a greater percentage of the population of Wisconsin is
overweight than that of any other state. I have also heard that more alcohol is consumed per capita in Wisconsin than in any other state. Where I
used to live—Stevens Point, Wisconsin—there are far more taverns than
there are churches and filling stations put together. Come to think of it,
for most people in Wisconsin, Stevens Point is probably best known for
its beer, Point Special.

Nevertheless, Stevens Point, Wisconsin, claims to be the wellness capital of the world. And not entirely without reason. Besides the brewery—
which is very well and produces, incidentally, a very healthy product if
consumed in moderation—Stevens Point is home to the National Wellness
Institute and every summer a week-long wellness conference is held on
the campus of the local state university. The conference treats its participants not only to the usual keynote addresses, plenary speeches, concurrent sessions, and workshops; it also features "fun runs," bike tours, and
buffets of the healthiest, most palatable foods imaginable for breakfast,
lunch, and supper. During the rest of the year, between the local YMCA

and the campus wellness program, the town/gown community has access, at least, to all the information, inspiration, services, and facilities that anyone could possibly want in order to lead a hyper-healthy lifestyle. For example, I participated in a University of Wisconsin-Stevens Point employee wellness program, which consisted of various physical tests, a lifestyle questionnaire, a lecture on the latest dietary recommendations, and a personal consultation with a wellness-oriented physician. It refreshed my commitment to the basic elements of wellness—plenty of exercise and a largely vegetarian diet—and it inspired me to reach for higher levels of achievement in these fundamental areas.

Wellness, of course, comprises much more than these essentially physical disciplines. In addition to physical wellness, the National Wellness Institute has identified no fewer than six other dimensions of wellness. They are the emotional, intellectual, and spiritual dimensions, which, for the purposes of this essay, may be understood to be relatively personal, and the social, occupational, and environmental dimensions, which may be understood to be relatively relational. I say "relatively" because, though it is tempting to think of one's positive emotions, creative thoughts, and good character as being located deep within one's physical husk, a moment's reflection makes one realize that these inner attributes are evidently dependent on a range of things outside oneself. The various dimensions of wellness, in other words, are thoroughly interrelated. One cannot be emotionally well if one has unsatisfying social relationships; one cannot be intellectually well if one abuses alcohol or drugs; one cannot be physically well if one lives on a Love Canal or in Mexico City or in any other grossly polluted environment.

My subject here is this most external and public dimension of wellness, environmental wellness. If Stevens Point cannot also claim to be the environmental capital of the world, Pointers, as the locals call themselves, can legitimately boast about considerable renown in that area as well. The UWSP College of Natural Resources houses one of the largest undergraduate and master's level programs in environmental education in the country and more recently the Wisconsin Center for Environmental Education has been established on campus. UWSP also offers a major in environmental communication, a minor in environmental studies, and there, back in 1971, I designed and implemented the world's first course in environmental ethics.

But my purpose here is not to pitch either the Stevens Point campus or community. The only pertinent point to these observations about Point is that there, if anywhere, wellness and environment intersect.

THE IMPORTANCE OF ENVIRONMENTAL WELLNESS

I don't think that you need to be a rocket scientist to figure out that environmental quality, as I just mentioned, is essential to overall human health and well-being. The sight of a person jogging through smog-clogged city streets is as much a visual oxymoron as the sight of a person jogging along smoking a cigarette. An ersatz environment of metal, glass, concrete, and asphalt; congested automobile traffic; drugs, poverty, homelessness, and the street crime they breed—all these seriously compromise our physical, emotional, and spiritual wellness. Environmental wellness, in short, is a necessary condition for human health and well-being generally. We cannot pursue personal wellness unless we also work collectively and cooperatively to ensure an improvement in our natural and fabricated environments.

But neither is my purpose here to belabor the obvious. Nevertheless, I would like to state clearly and emphatically that if we are interested in being well, then we must do more than pay attention to eating right and working out, to the quality of our character and our relationships, to maintaining occupational satisfaction and intellectual stimulation in our personal lives, and so on. We have to work to prevent further environmental degradation and to restore the environmental quality that we have already allowed seriously to erode. We have considerable individual autonomy over things like diet and exercise, how we spend our leisure, who our friends are, where we live, and what kind of work we do. But the environment is a commons. To realize the environmental dimension of wellness will take collective effort and political resolve. We must demand that our local, state, and federal governments put environmental issues at the very top of the political agenda. The globally emulated and envied American way of life, to say nothing of our individual states of wellness, will be undermined more surely by stinking air, foul water, incessant noise, inhumane cities, pesticide-, herbicide-, fungicide-, and antibiotic-tainted foods, increased exposure to ultraviolet radiation, a countryside depauperate of its native flora and fauna, and all the other subtle and not so subtle environmental degradations, than by economic recession or higher taxes. That having been said, I would now like to draw upon my particular expertise as a philosopher and explore the conceptual relationship between wellness and environment.

THE WELLNESS MOVEMENT IS ANCILLARY TO
THE ENVIRONMENTAL MOVEMENT

To me it seems not at all accidental that the wellness movement appears to have come into being shortly after the environmental movement. The contemporary American environmental movement was born in the early 1960s and had become a formidable social force by the end of that decade. While I do not pretend to be anything more than an interested bystander and beneficiary of the wellness movement, certainly not its historian, as I recall it seems to have come along in the 1970s. Could this conjunction be a mere coincidence or does it reflect a cognitive influence running from the emergence of the new environmentalism to the new notion of wellness? Of course, I think that it is more than a coincidence.

Surely a big part of what happened to bring on the environmental crisis, first widely recognized to exist in the 1960s, was a quantum leap in the level of environmental insults coming immediately after World War II. The heavy industry that had been rapidly geared up for war against the Germans and Japanese was redirected to an undeclared war on the environment. Tank and armored truck manufacturers retooled to make tractors and other industrial farm implements that attacked the homeland with unprecedented violence. DDT was first developed and manufactured for delousing GIs; after the war it was marketed to farmers as a miracle pesticide. In contrast to its low-compression antecedent, the high-compression internal combustion engine, first developed for warplane motors, creates nitrous oxide; after the War the high-compression engine was installed in automobiles; and nitrous oxide became a principal ingredient of urban smog. In short, between 1945 and 1965, the height of the foreign Cold War, the environmental carnage of the domestic green war became detectable to the naked eye, the naked nose, and the naked lung.

But our minds are notoriously selective in receiving and processing information from our senses. I grew up in Memphis, Tennessee, and I remember swimming in the Mississippi River somehow oblivious to the fact that it had become, by the mid-1950s, virtually an open sewer. Today, below Memphis, I wouldn't so much as stick my toe in the river. The difference between my sensibilities now and then is not just a product of experience and caution coming with age. The main difference is that I, like many of us, have now come to see the world through a new set of cognitive lenses. Rachel Carson, Stewart Udall, Barry Commoner, and above all, Aldo Leopold have not only called our attention to a polluted, eroded, and tattered natural world, but have taught us to think about and thus to experience our world—and, as I shall shortly argue, ourselves— ecologically.

Thus, a second major factor in the advent of a broad public awareness that the environment was in crisis—in addition to the stark fact that it was in actual crisis due to the postwar explosion of violent and toxic mechanical and chemical technologies—was the popularization of ecology. Ecology is not just an arcane subdiscipline of biology. Like the theory of evolution, it is pregnant with vast philosophical implications. Indeed, ecology, along with the theory of evolution in biology and relativity and quantum theory in physics, is propelling a sea change in the Western world view, a paradigm shift, as the pundits of science and culture call it. I would go further still and suggest that ours could be one of those moments in history—fraught with equal measures of danger and opportunity, fear and hope—that come but rarely in human cultural development: a moment in history not unlike the Golden Age of Greece when Western art, literature, philosophy, and democracy were born; or Renaissance Europe when Modern science and technology began to take shape.

Ecology, as any good textbook in the subject will explain on the very first page, studies the relationships between organisms and the environment. The operative word in this textbook definition is "relationships." Traditional Western science was analytic and reductive. Divide and conquer was its motto. As a result the world was pictured as an aggregate of objects, the whole exactly equal to the sum of the parts. Things, material objects, were believed to be the ultimate realities. Relationships were insubstantial, ephemeral, shifting, and external to the being of autonomous things in their splendid isolation. The clockwork machine became the dominant metaphor for representing the world order. A machine is an assemblage, an aggregate of parts. The function of the whole machine—

be it an automobile, a corn picker, a chain saw, whatever—is an exact summation of the functions of its parts.

In emphasizing relationships, ecology reverses figure and ground. The relationships between and among objects are reified. An organism comes to be seen as a nexus in a network of relationships, not at all as an independent being or isolable entity. The natural world is bound together through these relationships into a seamless whole. An ecosystem is a great deal more than the sum of its biotic and abiotic parts. There's nothing, by the way, in the least mystical in the ecological idea that the whole is greater than the sum of the parts. What more to an ecosystem is there than its parts? The real relationships that bind the parts into a whole, that's what. The parts plus the constitutive relationships make up the whole. One could even say, again without any mystification, that the parts, the objects—the various organisms that compose the living world—are literally constituted by their relationships. Deer, for example, are the unique and beautiful animals that they are precisely because they have coevolved with the wolf and other predators and with various species of woody vegetation. Each animal and plant is literally shaped, sculpted, by its relationships with other, coevolved animals and plants and with the physical, chemical, and climatic characteristics of its environment. Through the lenses of ecology and its sister sciences—the theory of evolution in biology and relativity and quantum theory in physics—the world around is beginning to be seen as more like a vast organism than like a vast mechanism.

You and I are organisms. Our unified consciousness is irrefutable evidence that we transcend the sum of our parts and that our various parts are what they are because of their relationships with one another and with the emergent organic whole. Yet under the sway of the now obsolescing mechanistic model of reality, we allowed ourselves to become convinced, despite our experience of personal unity and wholeness, that we were in fact variously fragmented. We bought into the myth crafted by the "father of Modern philosophy," René Descartes, that all organisms, including our human bodies, were actually elaborate, intricately complex machines constructed by a divine Artificer of infinite intelligence. Unified human consciousness, Descartes argued, was due to an entirely different type of reality—an indivisible soul or spirit—inhabiting our essentially mechanical bodies, even though consciousness is so evidently, so palpably somatic. Descartes split us in two, into soul and body, and then Modern mechanico-chemical medicine went on to subdivide the body into its various organs and other parts, each with its specific and independent functions. It is staggering to realize the power of ideas, to realize that a dominant intellectual paradigm can utterly blind one to the nature of something so intimate as one's organically whole, unified psychosomatic being.

Hard though it may be to believe, we conceived illness to be the malfunction of a particular organ or the breakdown of some other bodily part. Wellness—though we didn't call it that—health was simply understood as the absence of illness. We went along eating our bacon and eggs for breakfast, burgers and fries for lunch, pork chops and mashed potatoes for dinner, smoking our cigarettes, lying around in the evenings and on weekends drinking our Pepsis or beer, munching our chips and dip, watching Milton Berle and Jackie Gleason, Jack Webb and Broderick Crawford on TV—and hey, if all the parts in our bodies were working we considered ourselves to be well. You know, if it ain't broke, don't fix it. Then when symptoms of illness showed up, we went to the doctor for repairs.

Unfortunately, this philosophy of medicine is not as far out of fashion as blue suede shoes and drive-in movie theaters. In spite of all the recent academic talk about the body as cultural text, most of us still conceive of our bodies as machines and our doctors as glorified mechanics. When the clutch starts to slip or the brakes start to squeak, we take the jalopy in for a clutch repair or a brake job. Similarly, when angina sets in, due to atherosclerosis, some of us take our bodies in for a multiple bypass operation. Or, some of us suppose that we can ruin our livers by excessive drinking, and just go get a transplant—which we conceive of as pretty much the same sort of thing as, having abused the automatic transmission in a Pontiac, taking it in for a replacement. Sure it costs money and you have to take the vehicle off the road for a little while, but when you get your car back or your body back, as the case may be, it should run as good as new.

Let this caricature of "Modern medicine" serve as a foil for the contemporary wellness approach to health. By contrast, a wellness-oriented person would consult his or her physician about risk factors for atherosclerosis long before its symptoms appear. If you are at risk for heart disease, a wellness-oriented physician, in sharp contrast to his or her "conventional" counterpart, would advise you to make radical changes in your diet—to eliminate all red meat, all saturated fats, and to eat instead grains, legumes, dark green vegetables, fresh fruits, and the occasional morsel of deep-sea fish. You would also be advised to stop smoking immediately, to increase your exercise, perhaps move if you live in a dirty, noisy, crime-ridden city, change jobs if your occupational stress is high, perhaps even get a divorce if you are a member of a dysfunctional family or involved in an abusive marriage. By-pass heart surgery would be indicated only as a last resort.

Now here I return directly to the first philosophical business at hand, an explanation of the virtual simultaneous emergence of the environmental movement and the wellness movement. Let's step back and note the general difference between the mechanico-chemical and the wellness medical philosophies. So-called "conventional" medicine regards health as the absence of illness, and illness as the malfunction of a part. To restore health is to fix or replace the defective part. Wellness medicine regards health as an optimum condition of the whole human organism and its maintenance as a way of life, expressly involving the social, cultural, and natural environments that constitute a person's life in the widest sense. *Wellness is, in short, an ecological understanding of human health.*

THE MICROCOSMOS AND THE MACROCOSMOS

In the Western intellectual tradition, the human body has always been understood as a microcosm, a world order in miniature. Ancient Greek science conceived the universe to be composed of four elements—earth, air, fire, and water. The universe was understood to be governed by a natural law of dynamic equilibrium holding each element in check as it struggled for dominance against the others. Ancient Greek medicine, analogously, conceived the body to contain four vital humors—blood, bile, urine, and phlegm. Illness occurred when one or another of these exceeded its proper measure and dominated the rest. Asclepius, Hippocrates, Galen, and the other physicians among the ancients returned their patients to health by restoring the natural balance among their bodily humors. If the blood had gotten out of hand and the patient were fevered and sanguine, then cooling and bleeding were indicated. If the problem were excessive phlegm—diagnosed, I suppose, by the patient's feeling phlegmatic—then warming and induced sneezing were called for.

Further, changes in our thinking about the macrocosm, the world order at large, are followed by changes in our thinking about the microcosm, the human body. Between the sixteenth and eighteenth centuries, ancient Greek science, which was consolidated by Aristotle, was supplanted by Modern mechanical science, which was consolidated by Isaac Newton. A corresponding revolution in medical theory followed, and the human body was represented reductively as a complex machine and doctors became mechanics. During the twentieth century, a second scientific revolution occurred, epitomized by ecology and the New Physics, and right now, as I write and you read, a corresponding revolution in medical philosophy is taking place—the wellness movement.

From a wellness point of view, the person is viewed as an organic whole, an integrated system that transcends the sum of his or her parts. The body is an ecosystem in miniature. Further, just as in ecology, the human organism is seen as embedded in a network of hierarchically ordered internal relationships, relationships that are not merely incidental or adventitious but that partly constitute the person him- or herself. As a microecosystem, that is, one cannot be adequately conceptualized in isolation from one's social and cultural environments nor from the environing macroecosystems, from natural ecosystems proper.

So, to address the question about the curious conjunction of the environmental and wellness movements in a summary way, I submit that the popularization of ecology by Leopold, Udall, Carson, Commoner, and others launched the environmental movement directly, and precipitated the wellness movement indirectly and subliminally. Through the lens of ecology, we started to see nature less as a vast mechanism and more as a vast organism. We began to see nature, in other words, as an integrated system of subsystems and to perceive the postwar mechanical and chemical assault on the environment as a distressing disturbance of its web-like structure of dynamic relationships. Ecology also enabled us to see ourselves in analogous terms, less reductively and mechanically and more holistically and organically, and as thoroughly embedded in our social, cultural, and environmental milieux. *Therefore, I submit, the wellness movement is nothing other than the ecologization of medicine.*

THE WILDERNESS PARADIGM IN CONSERVATION REAPPRAISED

So far, I have been reflecting on recent history. Here, let me turn to what's happening right now at the interface of ecology and medicine. At first the flow of influence and information ran from ecology and the environmental movement to medicine and the wellness movement. Now, the flow of influence and information is running from medicine and the wellness movement to ecology and the environmental movement. The philosophy of conservation, in particular, is undergoing a rapid maturation process and is currently looking to medicine for guidance. First let me trace the present drift in conservation thought and then suggest how ecological medicine—preventive medicine or "wellness" as we call it in Central Wisconsin—is helping to guide it.

Until recently, our classic benchmark of environmental quality was the wilderness ideal. Accordingly, it was believed, the best way to preserve nature, if not the only way, was to exclude all human economic activities from representative ecosystems and designate them as wilderness areas or conservancy districts. In them, some old-growth forests could remain standing, wild animals could have a little habitat, and so on. In effect, we attempted to achieve environmental conservation by zoning the planet into areas where environmentally destructive human economic activities—like logging, agriculture, industry, and real estate development—would be permitted and areas where such activities would be excluded. Several recent and not so recent realizations are undermining the wilderness philosophy of conservation.

First, at the practical level, this approach to environmental conservation is defensive and ultimately represents a losing strategy. The development-permitted zones greatly exceed the development-excluded zones in number and size. Only about 4 percent of the Lower Forty-eight is in a designated or de facto wilderness condition. More acreage of the contiguous United States is under pavement than is under protection as wilderness! As the human population and economy grow, the pressure on these ragtag wild areas becomes ever greater. In temperate North America wilderness reserves, national parks, and conservancy districts have become small islands in a rising sea of cities, suburbs, farms, interstates, and clear cuts. And they are all seriously compromised by human recreation and by exotic species colonization. Big wilderness has receded to the subarctic and arctic latitudes. And even these remote hinterlands are threatened by logging, hydropower schemes, oil exploration, and other industrial intrusions, not to mention the threats posed by global warming and by exposure to sharply increased levels of ultraviolet radiation. The wilderness idea, hopefully and enthusiastically popularized by John Muir's best-sellers at the close of the nineteenth century, has played itself out, here at the close of the twentieth, in the pessimism and despair of Bill McKibben's recent best-seller, *The End of Nature*. McKibben's thesis needs no elaboration by me because his title says it all.

Second, at the historical level, we are beginning to realize that wilderness is an ethnocentric concept. Europeans came to what they called the New World and since it did not look like the humanized landscape that they had left behind in the Old World, they thought that it was a pristine wilderness, where, as David Brower likes to say (tongue in cheek of course), the hand of man had never set foot. But the Western Hemisphere was full of Indians when Columbus stumbled upon it. In 1492, the only continental-size wilderness on the planet was Antarctica. The aboriginal inhabitants of North and South America, further, were not passive denizens of the forests, prairies, and deserts, they actively managed their lands— principally with fire. Some paleo-ecologists believe that in the absence of Indian burning, the vast, biologically diverse open prairies of North and South America would not have existed. The American heartland would have instead been grown over with brush. Nor would the North American forests have been as rich and diverse in the absence of the Indian's pyrotechnology.

Third, at the theoretical ecology level, ecosystems were once thought to remain stable unless disturbed; and if disturbed, to return eventually to their stable states, called climax communities. To be constantly changing and unstable is now believed to be their usual, rather than exceptional, condition. Thus, whether we human beings interfere with them or not, ecosystems will undergo metamorphosis. But wilderness preservation suggests freeze-framing the status quo ante, maintaining the way things were when the "white man" first came on the scene. Hence, the wilderness ideal, so interpreted, represents a conservation goal that would be possible to attain, paradoxically, only through intensive management efforts to keep things the way they were in defiance of nature's inherent dynamism.

Fourth, at the philosophical level, the wilderness idea perpetuates the pre-Darwinian myth that "man" exists apart from nature. Our oldest and most influential cultural traditions have taught us that we human beings are exclusively created in the image of God, or that we are somehow uniquely endowed with divine rationality. Thus we, and all the products of our essentially supernatural minds, were thought to exist apart from and over against nature. For a wilderness purist, encountering any human artifact (not his or her own) in a wilderness setting spoils his or her experience of pristine nature. But Darwin broadcast the unwelcome news that we self-exalting human beings are mere accidents of natural selection, no less than any other large mammal. We are one of five living species of great apes. We are, to put it bluntly, just big monkeys—very precocious monkeys, to be sure, but monkeys nevertheless. And everything we do—from bowling and bungee jumping to writing *Iliad*s and engineering space shuttles—is monkey business. For many people Darwin's news was bad news because it seemed to demean us and to undermine our noblest pretensions and aspirations. But in the present circumstances, I think it is good news. If we are a part of nature, then we have a rightful place and role in nature no less than any other creature—no less than elephants, for example, or whales, or redwoods. And what we do in and to nature—the transformations that we impose upon the environment—are in principle no better or no worse than what elephants, or whales, or redwoods, may do in and to nature.

ECOSYSTEM HEALTH AS A NEW STANDARD OF CONSERVATION

I say "in principle" because I certainly do not wish to leave anyone with the impression that I think that because we are just as natural as all other organisms, all the things we do in and to nature—all the changes that we impose upon the environment—are okay. They are not all okay. Indeed, most of them are very destructive.

We are prepared to acknowledge that other species may have either beneficial or harmful effects on the rest of nature. If, for instance, there were five billion elephants on the planet instead of five billion people (or remembering that an adult elephant is more than a hundred times heavier than an adult human, if there were as much elephant biomass as presently there is human biomass), then the planet Earth would still be in the throes of an ecological crisis. Elephants, in other words, can also be very destructive citizens of their biotic communities. On the other hand, the biomass of bees and other insect pollinators of plants presently is probably greater than the human biomass—I don't know, I'm not a biologist—and certainly the bee population far exceeds the human population, but the ecological effect of all these bees is totally benign.

So, if the ecological impact of the activities of bees and elephants can be either good or bad, then why can't the ecological impact of human activities be good as well as bad? Measured by the wilderness standard, *all* human impact on nature is bad, not because human beings are inherently bad, but because human beings are not a part of nature—or so the wilderness idea assumes. The new normative concept in conservation philosophy—and here I return directly to how the wellness movement is now influencing the environmental movement—is ecosystem health. Human activities, including human economic activities, that are compatible with ecosystem health are okay and those that compromise ecosystem health are bad. With such a standard of conservation in view, we can, in theory, have our environmental cake and eat it too. We can envision a sustainable civilization, understood as a complex of human institutions and technologies that is compatible with ecosystem health.

Persuasively articulating the concept of ecosystem health as a new standard of conservation is a task calling for the close cooperation of philosophers, ecologists, and medical theorists. The ecological application of the concept of health is especially appealing, from a philosophical point of view, because "health" is at once normative and descriptive. Health, that is, is unquestionably a good thing; except in the most unusual circumstances no one had rather be sick than well. And it is also an objective thing; medical science can specify indices of health—a body temperature of 98.6° F, blood pressure and heart rate within certain ranges, a cholesterol count of under 200, and so on and so forth. One can defy one's doctor and *believe* that one's high heart rate, blood pressure, and cholesterol count are healthy, but one will simply be wrong, mistaken.

Analogously, ecosystem health is a good thing and it is also, in principle, an objective thing. Ecological science can—though so far research is still in the initial stages—specify indices of ecosystem health. And if the congresswoman from Idaho claims that in her opinion monocultural stands of plantation forests are just as ecologically healthy as old-growth forests, or if a developer claims that a golf course is just as ecologically healthy as a wetland, they may simply be mistaken. The beauty of the concept of ecosystem health as a standard of conservation is that, unlike the wilderness ideal, it does not condemn *all* human modifications of nature as degradations, but at the same time it does not permit us to hold the opposite extreme view and regard any human modification of nature to be evaluated simply on the basis of human preference. I may prefer to eat meat and smoke cigarettes all day, but doing so is not good for my health. Similarly, as a society we may prefer to turn the landscape into one huge complex of industrial farms, tree plantations, cities, suburbs, shopping malls, ski runs, and golf courses, but such would not be good for the health of the biosphere and its component ecosystems.

Ecologists are just now coming to grips with the problem of setting out objective criteria of ecosystem health in dynamic, long-humanized landscapes. As a philosopher, I shall not presume to tread on their technical turf. However, I can summarize here what appear to be emerging as the principal norms of ecosystem health. Ecosystem health may be evaluated by reference to the following five criteria: biological productivity, local species diversity, global species diversity, genetic diversity within species populations, and ecological functionality.

How much biomass is a given ecosystem producing? What is the optimum productivity for such a system? Would one or another treatment increase or reduce its productivity?

How many species historically inhabit a given landscape? In what numbers? Would one or another modification increase or reduce species diversity?

How many native, unique, or endemic species inhabit a given landscape? In what numbers? Would one or another modification protect or replace more sensitive native species with weedy exotics? Or protect or threaten a given landscape's endemics? Would it increase or reduce their populations?

Genetic diversity is vital to the capacity of species populations to rebound from diseases and parasites and to withstand other environmental stresses. Also vital to a population's future is to have sufficient genetic diversity to evolve in response to changing environmental conditions. Would a proposed development imperil an ecosystems' species populations?

How well are the plant communities of a given landscape holding soil and retaining moisture? How well are they fixing nitrogen? How efficient are its pollinators in assisting plant reproduction? Its soil microbes in digesting detritus? How many trophic layers exist in it? How tangled and redundant are its trophic pathways? Would one or another modification improve or impair any or several of these functions? And these are just a few of the important ecological functions that might serve as criteria of ecosystem health that we could employ to assess whether or not a given human project was or was not consistent with biological conservation.

Work is proceeding rapidly on the frontiers of what is now called "clinical ecology." In February 1991, a symposium devoted to ecosystem health was convened by the International Society for Environmental Ethics at the annual meeting of the American Association for the Advancement of Science in Washington, D.C. Ecologists and economists as well as philosophers presented papers on that occasion which are now collected in a book, entitled *Ecosystem Health*, published by Island Press. In June 1994, the First International Symposium on Ecosystem Health and Medicine attracted more than a thousand participants to Ottawa. The leading ecologist in the new field of ecosystem health, David J. Rapport of the University of Guelph, began publishing a new quarterly, *Ecosystem Health,* in order to provide a clearing house for research in the field and a forum for discussion. In this effort, he is actively seeking input from the medical community to help guide both research and its practical application to biological conservation and sustainable development.

SUMMARY AND CONCLUSION

Let me sum up the principal points of this essay and then return to "the Point" (as my erstwhile Central Wisconsin town is known in its bioregion) by way of conclusion. In the wellness movement, environmental wellness is considered to be one of seven dimensions of wellness. But I believe that environmental wellness is more than just one aspect of wellness among others. The whole wellness movement was inspired, however subliminally, by the environmental movement and the popularization of ecology—because the wellness movement treats the body as a microecosystem embedded within a hierarchy of macrosystems, both cultural and natural. Thanks

to the wellness movement, the concept of health has been transformed
from the absence of disease to an optimum state of well-being. This positive idea has recently been analogically transferred back from the human
organism to the natural ecosystem as a general standard of biological conservation and sustainable development. Thus the term *environmental
wellness* may in future serve not only to identify one dimension of human
wellness, but to represent a much larger ideal of human harmony with
nature.

As we approach the twenty-first century, we need to be guided by a
vision of a whole and healthy planet that includes us as a positively con-
tributing part. I like to imagine what the world might be like if ecologic as
well as well economic feasibility were a criterion of sound land use. And
when I do, I try to start from a particular point (no pun intended) of
reference.

I would sometimes take a noon-hour walk in the UWSP nature reserve just north of the campus. The area was once a neglected feral wetland, haphazardly used as an outdoor laboratory by natural resources faculty and students. Then a big insurance company up and decided to build
a "world headquarters" structure nearby and wanted to mine it for sand
and gravel. We campus environmentalists put up a howl of protest, but to
no avail. The ugly gravel pit filled with water and soon became an artificial lake, its physiognomy hardly distinguishable from the natural lakes of
the region dug by the glacier. With the financial assistance of the company and generous donations from members of the community, the naked
lakeshore and surrounding acreage was landscaped—not with ornamen-
tals, but with the prairie, bog, and forest plants indigenous to Central
Wisconsin. Now, after twenty years of artful ecological restoration, it is a
thing of beauty and much healthier than it was when we tried to "save" it.

So far, the contiguous grounds of Sentry Insurance's world headquarters—which, though tastefully landscaped, more resemble a golf course
than a natural area—are ecologically discontinuous with the reserve. But
that could change and the company's lands could be ecologically integrated with the reserve. Next, one could imagine the deconstruction of
the strip development on the roads radiating out of town. Some communities in Wisconsin forbid tasteless urban and suburban sprawl by ordinance. So could Stevens Point. The community's rural matrix is a mix of
old-fashioned family dairy farms, an ecologically benign form of agricul-

ture (relatively speaking), and the exurban estates of the local gentry—not a bad point of departure for an ecotopian experiment in even more environment-friendly methods of farming the land and inhabiting the landscape.

As imagination transports me farther out in time and space, I try to envision what the world would be like if all agriculture were patterned on natural rather than industrial processes, if forestry and range management were based on ecology rather than agronomy, if solar replaced fossil fuel and nuclear technologies, if urban environments were humanized and well integrated into their natural matrices. Sitting by Jonas Lake in Schmeekle Reserve on a warm Indian summer afternoon in mid-October—with the fiery maples, golden birches, and russet oaks reflecting on the clear water rippled by the Canada geese stopping over on their way south—I can almost believe that we can really do it.

After the Industrial Paradigm, What?

THE INDUSTRIAL PARADIGM

In the 1960s the environmental crisis came to public attention. The environment was sending a message to Modern Western civilization. Operating on the assumption that the prevailing Modern worldview was true, we were receiving negative feedback in the form of undrinkable water and unbreathable air. Our civilization seemed on course to either a violent self-destruction through nuclear holocaust (the noisy crisis) or protracted self-destruction through environmental degradation (the quiet crisis, as President John F. Kennedy's secretary of the interior, Stewart Udall, dubbed it). What could we do about it?

In "The Historical Roots of Our Ecologic Crisis," an enormously influential paper first published in *Science*, the prestigious organ of the American Association for the Advancement of Science, and republished in dozens of hastily assembled environmental-crisis anthologies thereafter, historian Lynn White Jr. (1967, 1204) argued that "unless we think about fundamentals, our specific measures may produce new backlashes more serious than those they are intended to remedy." In that paper, White, whether he intended to do so or not, set a two-stage agenda for a future environmental philosophy. First, identify and criticize those aspects of our inherited worldview that have led us to a dysfunctional relationship with the natural environment; and second, identify and articulate a new worldview, pragmatically validated—a worldview, that is, that will enable us to live sustainably and symbiotically with nonhuman natural entities and nature as a whole. In effect, the environmental crisis raised again the big old questions posed by the ancients and in turn by the early Modern philosophers. What is the nature of nature? What is human nature? And what is the proper relationship between the two? The last of these questions, put in familiar, old-fashioned, albeit gender-biased terms, is What is man's place in nature?

White himself boldly set out, in the same paper, on the first stage of that agenda. In his view, the most salient historical root of our ecologic crisis is Genesis in which God creates nature as a profane artifact, creates "man" in His own image, gives people dominion over nature, and charges us to multiply and subdue the earth. In retrospect this analysis seems painfully naive. Genesis, apologists have since persuasively argued, if anything, implies that the human relationship to nature should be that of a steward, not that of a greedy and shortsighted tyrant (chapter 10). The environmental crisis, as White points out, is the direct effect of Modern industrial technology. The first, self-critical stage of environmental philosophy should focus on the set of ideas that fostered the industrial revolution and from there work our way back to its historical roots. Accordingly, the first question we should pose is, What is the industrial paradigm?

Let me begin by making clear to what the phrase *industrial paradigm* refers—as I understand it. As we all well know, "paradigm" is a highfalutin word derived from the Greek, *paradeigma*, meaning "pattern" in plain English. And as we all also well know—though his use of the term is alleged to be imprecise and ambiguous—it was commandeered by the Harvard philosopher of science Thomas Kuhn (1961) to refer to a general intellectual pattern or conceptual model of nature in science. In the history of astronomy, for example, one might identify at least three paradigms: the Eudoxian, the Ptolemaic, and the Copernican. So one very natural interpretation of the phrase industrial *paradigm* is this: the general conceptual model of nature in science which inspired and informed the Industrial Revolution and eventually Modern industrial civilization.

Of course, here I beg a chicken and egg question. Which came first, a new general conceptual model of nature in science or the autonomous emergence of a new way of manufacturing, transporting, marketing, and consuming artifacts, "products"? The question is a very complex historical one. It is also an ideological one.

According to White (1967, 1203), "Western Europe and North America arranged a marriage between science and technology, a union of the theoretical and empirical approaches to our natural environment. The emergence of the widespread practice of the Baconian creed that scientific knowledge means technological power over nature . . . may mark the greatest event in human history since the invention of agriculture."

Materialists are likely to object that the new science was an intellectual penumbra arising from, reflecting, and rationalizing the inevitable outcome—the Industrial Revolution—of the blind dialectic of European socioeconomic history and Western technology. And, surely, developments that were largely empirical and internal to the evolution of industry fed back into and informed science. For example, according to the biophysicist Harold Morowitz (1972, 152), "Thermodynamic theory had its beginnings in the industrial revolution and was therefore very closely related to the operation of the steam engine. Professor Lawrence Henderson used to comment that the steam engine did more for science than science ever did for the steam engine." But the reason that the posterior relationship of thermodynamics to the steam engine is noteworthy is that it is anomalous. The development of the mechanical paradigm in science antedated the emergence of mechanical technology on a massive scale. Crudely put, the scientific revolution of the sixteenth and seventeenth centuries preceded the industrial revolution of the eighteenth and nineteenth centuries. And in the industrial revolution, again crudely but not untruly put, the then new science informed technique. Therefore, the industrial paradigm is the same as the reigning paradigm in Modern science: classical mechanics.

And, as a matter of fact, from its beginnings in the eighteenth century to its endings in the twentieth, the industrial paradigm has been decidedly, nakedly mechanical. Think of the power weaving looms of the eighteenth century, the mills of the nineteenth century, the factories and assembly plants of the twentieth century. First the raw, wild kinetic energy of falling water, and later the potential energy in coal and petroleum were tapped, harnessed, focused, and translated into rotary and reciprocal motion—"work"—to push rods and turn gears that, with a deafening rattle and clatter, wove cloth, lathed wood, and forged and assembled more machines: Colt rifles, McCormick reapers, Ford motorcars, Whitney cotton gins.

The same mechanical motif that inspired the design of all such industrial behemoths and the many mechanisms—typewriters, automobiles, washing machines—manufactured in them, was soon extended to the *process* of manufacturing. Its ultimate expression is the assembly line, which divides the manufacturing process into a linear sequence of ordinally arranged tasks. The assembly line represents a direct transposition of the Cartesian method of division and aggregation from the realm of scientific epistemology to the realm of manufacturing technique.

And those who perform, over and over again, the monotonous tasks of a functionary on the assembly line themselves become components of the mechanical environment that they inhabit. During the forty hours a week that they labor in the factory, workers become robots of a sort. And, indeed, as industrial civilization evolves into something else—into what else we can only speculate—the robotic human workers are actually being replaced by robots proper.

THE RELATIONSHIP BETWEEN NATURAL PHILOSOPHY
AND MORAL PHILOSOPHY

The general conceptual model of nature in Modern science—classical mechanics—inspired and informed a social order that complemented, reinforced, and supported the mechanical regime in technique. Even though it is overused, there is no substitute for the concept of a "paradigm," a pattern, in trying to understand the rapid and remarkable social transformation that also characterizes Modernity. The same abstract pattern believed to be manifest in the natural macrocosmos was projected as well upon the social microcosmos. To better disclose the structural identity obtaining between mechanical natural science and technology, on the one hand, and Modern social theory and practice, on the other, I must state a few historical postulates.

The first is this. In the West, the history of philosophy begins with natural philosophy. Thales, according to Aristotle the first Greek philosopher, asked and tried to answer the question, Of what is the world composed?—a question that physicists still seek to answer with the aid of supercolliding superconductors. Soon thereafter, Heraclitus asked and tried to answer the question, What is the *logos*—the Law of nature, in other words—that governs the world and makes it an ordered, not a chaotic realm? And such pre-Socratic thinkers as Anaxagoras and Empedocles asked and tried to answer the question, What fundamental forces drive natural processes? Today, physicists have identified four such forces—the strong and weak nuclear forces, electromagnetism, and gravity—among all of which they hope eventually to reveal a unity. Thus, as we see, the first Western philosophers were preoccupied principally, if not exclusively, with questions about nature. And, while work to answer the questions they posed has not gone forward uninterrupted, from the sixth century B.C.E. right down to the present the questions themselves have remained exactly the same and each thinker who has seriously taken them up has built directly on the work of his or her predecessors in the tradition.

That leads to my second historical postulate. Theoretical science—science at the highest level of generality, not the detailed and routine day-to-day work of ciphers in the field or laboratory—is only a highly refined and unified form of what the ancients thought of as natural philosophy or what the early Moderns sometimes thought of as natural theology. Today, natural philosophy or theoretical science is unified by a common method, the inductive-hypothetical-deductive-experimental method; a common paradigm, which *was* classical mechanics and is now in a state of uncertainty; and a division of labor into subareas of inquiry, into astronomy, astrophysics, physics, physical chemistry, chemistry, biochemistry, biology, and the rest.

Finally, my third historical postulate is this. While we may agree with Aristotle that, though temporally prior, natural philosophy is not logically prior—that honor rightly belongs to metaphysics—nevertheless, all other branches of philosophy, including metaphysics, have adjusted and conformed themselves to the reigning paradigm in natural philosophy. Especially ancillary to natural philosophy has been moral philosophy, in the broad sense, the philosophy of things human—such as psychology, ethics, and political theory. And this should come as no surprise or stir up any controversy because one fundamental mode of thought in the West, ever since the ancients, has been to view the human realm as a microcosmos structurally identical to the natural macrocosmos.

There was no reigning paradigm in natural philosophy among the ancient Greeks. One powerful contender for intellectual hegemony, however, was atomism. If these historical postulates are illuminating, that Protagoras was from the same the city, Abdera, as were Leucippus and Democritus is no accident. Protagoras and his fellow moral philosophers, whom we unjustly stigmatize as "sophists," articulated an ancient version of the social contract theory of law. Central to that theory is the conception of human persons not as thoroughly embedded in and inconceivable apart from society, but as egoistic individuals.

The rapaciously self-seeking "individual" in the social contract's mythical "state of nature" is the social analog of the classical material atom. (Remember that the Greek word *atomos* means "indivisible." So when we speak of "individuals" in society we are speaking precisely of social atoms, but with a word derived from Latin instead of Greek.) Thomas Hobbes, a student of Greek literature, revived the social contract theory in the seventeenth century, just as the mechanical paradigm of early Modern science, one cornerstone of which is atomism, was taking shape—illustrating quite nicely my postulate that moral philosophy is paradigmatically ancillary to natural philosophy. As Protagoras is to Leucippus and Democritus, so is Hobbes to Descartes and Galileo. The elemental desires of which Hobbes speaks are the social analog of inertia in physics, impelling each social atom on a collision course with others, as he or she singlemindedly pursues of his or her own personal interests at the expense of others.

In the early Modern version of the social contract, the conventional laws of society artificially constrain and regulate the behavior of social atoms, just as the laws of nature were supposed to constrain and regulate the motions of the material atoms proper. The Robert Boyle of the social sciences was Adam Smith, who, in *The Wealth of Nations*, provides the social equivalent of gas laws—macroeconomic laws characterizing the statistical outcome of the economic analog of exchanges of kinetic energy when the social molecules collide in a free market, which is the economic analog of empty space.

So, to make a long story short, all the characteristic institutions of Modern industrial society, such as free-market economies, sovereign liberal democracies enacting laws regulating the conduct of individual citizens, bureaucratic organization at every level of government, and juridical systems protecting the equal rights of individuals under the laws—all, I say, are expressions of the industrial paradigm, no less so than industrial technology itself. And that paradigm, as already argued, is the same as the reigning paradigm in Modern science: classical mechanics. Outside the factory, no less than inside, mechanisms pervade industrial societies. Machines are everywhere—on the roads, in the houses, sometimes even in the very bodies of individuals. Further, we speak, quite precisely albeit metaphorically, of the machinery of justice; and anyone who has ever dealt with a bureaucracy well knows its impersonal, mechanical character.

Now, how can we account for the current malaise plaguing Modern industrial societies? Surely the causes are many and complex. The untoward environmental and ecological consequences of massive and ubiquitous industrialization are one obvious source of anxiety. The untoward social consequences of massive and ubiquitous industrialization—such as the increasing disparity between the rich and the poor, drug abuse, a high percentage of the population of the most militantly industrial nation in the world confined to prison—are another. Our social machinery—the courts, the schools, the welfare bureaucracies—are rusty, broken down, and overwhelmed. Probing a little deeper, however, there seems to have occurred a loss of faith in industrial civilization, a pervasive feeling of inauthenticity. Few really believe that our environmental and social problems can be solved by more industrialization or even better industrialization or by more or even better social machinery. Need for fundamental change is felt. The optimism of such keepers of the faith as the American neoclassical economists Julian Simon and Milton Friedman seems hollow, even absurd. If one hews to the same historical postulates, one must say that the deeper reason for a loss of confidence in industrial civilization is the demise of its paradigm, classical mechanics, in contemporary natural philosophy.

We students of the history of philosophy trace the beginning of Modern philosophy to the seventeenth century and identify Descartes as its father. And all Modern philosophy—the divers turns taken by such thinkers as Spinoza, Leibniz, Berkeley, Hume, and Kant notwithstanding (to say nothing of Hegel, Fichte, and Nietzsche)—orbits around Classical Mechanics, the dominant paradigm in Modern natural philosophy or science, according to my historical postulates. Certainly Descartes himself deliberately set out to reconstruct metaphysics and epistemology so as to accommodate and reflect the contemporaneous revolution in natural philosophy. And the moral philosopher John Locke was, in his own estimation, but an underlaborer to Newton. Of course there were skeptics, such as Hume. They were, nevertheless, critically reacting to some of the unproven core concepts of the mechanical philosophy, such as determinate causality. And romantics, such as Rousseau and Hegel, were reacting to the spiritual paucity of the mechanical philosophy. For all Modern philosophers without exception, the mechanical paradigm in natural philosophy was central—whether warmly embraced (as by Locke), critically undermined (as by Hume), or violently rejected (as by Berkeley). Therefore, the sudden demise of classical mechanics in natural philosophy dooms Modern metaphysics, epistemology, psychology, ethics, social and political theory, economics—in a word, it dooms the Modern period as we know it in Western civilization.

THE POSTMODERN PERIOD IN PHILOSOPHY

The term *postmodernism* refers to different phenomena in different disciplines. In architecture it refers to a kind of ornate eclecticism that has followed the heyday of the so-called international style. In the history of the visual arts, what we call "modern art" comes into being with Cézanne and gains ascendancy with the advent of cubism and then abstract expressionism. Therefore, in the visual arts the natural reference of *postmodernism* is to work that is self-consciously opposed to modern art. In literature, the modern novel came along after the Victorian novel. So in literature, as in painting, modernism is more or less confined to the twentieth century and the postmodern novel or drama or screenplay refers to a genre that is self-consciously opposed to the conventions and expectations characteristic of twentieth-century literature. In literary criticism, of course, *postmodernism* refers to a facile and sophisticated posture toward "texts" disconnected from the intentions of their authors, dissociated from their historical milieux, and promiscuously available for a wide variety of contradictory interpretations, none of which can make a claim to truth, by variously situated readers, none of whom are privileged. The postmodern movement in philosophy, especially in France, has been closely related to and influenced by postmodern literary criticism. However, since by "Modern philosophy" we intellectual historians refer to a period of roughly four hundred years spanning the seventeenth through the twentieth centuries, the natural sense of postModernism in philosophy, as distinct from literary criticism, is the thought that comes after the close of the Modern period in philosophy.

By way of a historical analogy, let me be clear about where I think we stand today. The Ptolemaic-Aristotelian paradigm in Western natural philosophy long reigned during the Middle Ages. Ancillary to that paradigm was Medieval or Scholastic metaphysics, theology, epistemology, ethics, and so on. When the most powerful intellects in the West became convinced that the earth was not the fixed and immobile center of the universe, every other domain of Medieval philosophy was thrown into a state of doubt and confusion. First, the rest of natural philosophy had to be revised to accommodate Copernican astronomy. Gigantic contributions to that effort were made by Galileo and Descartes, to be consolidated by Newton. Then, metaphysics, epistemology, theology, and the rest had to be revised to accommodate and reflect the emerging new integrated natural philosophy. That was Descartes's greatest achievement. We correctly regard Descartes as the father of Modern philosophy, not only because of his immense contribution to the mathematical tools and models of the mechanical worldview and to its metaphysical, theological, and epistemological foundations, but also because his beautiful prose breathes a fiery revolutionary spirit. He speaks forthrightly of doubting everything that he had learnt in the Schools and razing the crumbling edifice of false Scholastic learning so as to rebuild from the ground up.

Intellectually speaking, the twentieth century is analogous to the sixteenth. And I predict that the twenty-first century will be analogous to the seventeenth. Our Nicolaus Copernicus is Albert Einstein. Both Copernicus and Einstein were transitional figures in Western natural philosophy. In some respects, Copernicus was an "ancient" astronomer. He retained three important first principles of ancient astronomy: a center point for the universe, whereat he located the sun; an outermost sphere of fixed stars; and circular orbits for the planets, including the earth. But who can doubt that Copernicus precipitated the Modern scientific revolution? In some respects, Einstein's special and general theories of relativity are "classical"—that is, Modern. But Einstein fundamentally recast our Western concepts of space, time, and matter. Werner Heisenberg,

Niels Bohr, Irwin Schrödinger, Louis de Broglie, Paul Dirac, and the other architects of the quantum revolution in physics completed the postModern revolution in natural philosophy that Einstein began, just as Kepler, Galileo, Descartes, and Newton completed the revolution in natural philosophy begun by Copernicus. By the 1930s, classical mechanics had been swept away and the key conceptual elements of a new integrated postModern natural philosophy had emerged. The development of the theory of evolution and ecology, meanwhile, provided complementary concepts in biology.

Our hopelessly Modern academic philosophers, on both sides of the channel—both the Anglo-American analytic philosophers and those whom we Americans call Continental philosophers, but especially the former—are like the Scholastics whom Descartes summarily dismissed and eventually succeeded. I believe that early in the next century, the twenty-first century, our equivalent of a Descartes and a Newton will reconstruct a convincing and consolidated new postModern paradigm in science, and an associated postModern worldview will emerge.

What will it look like? In this historical moment of doubt and confusion one can only feebly speculate. But before I offer my feeble speculations, let me say something about the more popular version of postModernism in philosophy, deconstructive postModernism.

Though it is not usually understood this way, I think that the deconstructive postModern philosophy—represented most famously by Foucault and Derrida in France and by Richard Rorty in the United States—is, in the final analysis, also a response to the scientific revolution occurring during the twentieth century. In the eighteenth and nineteenth centuries the mechanical model of nature seemed literally true. Science was supposed to picture the real world just the way it actually is. Truth (with a capital "T") was wed to Reality (with a capital "R"). The demise of classical mechanics shakes our faith in the capacity of the human mind to mirror nature, to borrow Rorty's felicitous phrase. If the Newtonian paradigm could be overturned, then can one ever be certain of anything? No—especially not now that Heisenberg's Uncertainty Principle is a cornerstone of the new paradigm in natural philosophy. And if truth be not the criterion of what one might or might not choose to believe and to advocate, what is? Nihilism is one alternative. One might choose to believe and to advocate nothing. Pluralistic relativism is another. One might choose to believe and to advocate whatever one happens to have absorbed from one's cultural ambience—and defend the right of others to do the same. And what might be called hegemonism is a third possibility. One might choose to believe and advocate whatever was self-serving. Those who benefit from the liberal political establishment might cynically admit, as does Rorty, that they believe in it and advocate it simply because they are comfortable members of the currently privileged elite. Those deconstructive postmodern theorists who think of themselves as marginalized or oppressed, such as homosexuals, radical feminists, or persons of color might revise the history of sexuality and race or invent a history of patriarchal oppression to serve their own sexual, ethnic, or gender politics.

TOWARD A RECONSTRUCTIVE POSTMODERN EPISTEMOLOGY

One defining difference between deconstructive and reconstructive postModernism is epistemological. We cannot rid ourselves of all affective bias. More profoundly, we cannot stand outside all tapestries of ideas, all *Weltanshauungen*, and examine each to see if it corresponds to reality as reality actually is. Granted. No cognitive construct is true. But one such construct may be arguably better than others because it is more comprehensive and coherent than others. A pragmatic and evolutionary theory, not of truth, but of tenability, might well replace the Modern paradigm's correspondence theory of truth in the reconstructive postModern paradigm.

Let me elaborate. A worldview that ignores salient and insistent experiential data or that is self-contradictory is not tenable—not because it is false, since no "grand narrative" is true or false, but because it impairs its subscribers' ability to cope with the complexities of contemporary human existence. According to such a pragmatic-evolutionary epistemology, the geocentric worldview died out because it could not comprehend a growing body of astronomical experience. Similarly, creationism is untenable because it cannot account for an overwhelming body of geological and biological experience. State communism collapsed, not because Marxist-Leninist ideology is untrue, but because the central authorities ignored overwhelmingly negative economic, social, and environmental feedback. Capitalist economies may also soon collapse, for exactly the same reasons. Given free reign, Islamic fundamentalism would certainly collapse since that worldview ignores most of human experience accumulated since the seventh century C.E.

To be sure, reconstructive postModernism's pragmatic-evolutionary epistemology is necessarily perspectival, not synoptic. Situated outside the *res extensa*, Modern Cartesian subjects are supposed to have a disinterested and synoptic point of view. But postModern body-subjects are part of the world they try to comprehend and thus can only comprehend it from a finite and engaged point of view.

Situational differences—differences of race, class, gender, culture, nationality—may preclude all people from sharing a single worldview. On the other hand, human difference is not absolute or unleavened with sameness. All human body-subjects are members of one species and live in a common world, a world increasingly unified and homogenized, for better or worse, by contemporary transportation and communication technologies and by transnational economic entities. Further, although each of the various domains of natural science also provide us with a perspectival knowledge of nature, we do not believe that one science can irreconcilably contradict another—as, for example, creationists wrongly argue that the theory of evolution irreconcilably contradicts the more universal second law of thermodynamics. While deconstructive postModernism is content with a patchwork of clashing perspectives, a reconstructive postModern epistemology would strive to integrate diverse human points of view into a coherent and harmonious network—just as diverse sciences form, despite differences of perspective and emphasis, a coherent and harmonious network.

TOWARD A RECONSTRUCTIVE POSTMODERN ONTOLOGY

And now I speculate feebly on the ontology of the emerging reconstructive postModern worldview. If the space-time continuum of general relativity theory is warped or bent, space-time must have substance and body. It cannot be an insubstantial empty theater thinly strewn with externally related substantive bits of matter. We may think that physical entities are not so much *in* space-time as *of* it. We may think, in other words, that the ephemeral quanta are rather less like particles existing in space and time than like knots in the fabric of space-time. When such a particle or knot disappears the underlying continuum shudders and an equivalent wave of energy ripples through it. Thus we might understand Bohr's particle/wave complementarity. In any case, as John Bell's work in quantum physics suggests, the most elementary entities are internally related and mutually defining.

At the other extreme of the hierarchy of sciences, ecology also suggests a nonatomistic ontology of internally related entities. Species are what they are because of their coevolved relationships with one another and with their physical and chemical environments. And species cannot exist apart from a biotic community or ecosystem. Thus, the sciences at the foundation of the hierarchy of sciences, quantum theory and relativity theory, and those at the apex, the theory of evolution and ecology, share a common ontological feature. Both are nonatomistic and nonreductive. In sharp contrast to the reductive, atomistic ontology of classical mechanics, entities in contemporary science, whether at the subatomic level or at the organismic level, cannot be conceived in isolation from their matrices.

If natural philosophy continues to sing the lead part, then the ontological shift in science that is currently underway should be followed shortly by analogous ontological shifts in the satellite domains of philosophy. As noted, the autonomous individual is the analog in Modern moral philosophy of the atom in Modern natural philosophy. What will be the analog in postModern moral philosophy of the internally related entities in postModern natural philosophy?

According to Deep Ecologists Arne Naess and Warwick Fox, it will be a conception of the Self, fully realized; that is, a sense of personal identification with one's social and especially one's environmental milieux. Such a conception of self resonates rather well with a possible ontological interpretation of the New Physics according to which entities are modes of a universal substance, the space-time continuum. Naess was inspired by the monism of classical Indian metaphysics, which the Austrian American physicist-philosopher Fritjof Capra believes to be very similar to the metaphysics of contemporary science.

In contemporary ecology, however, entities retain their distinct identities, although they are more or less systemically integrated. The reconstructed postModern person may, if ecology exerts more influence on social modelling than physics, turn out to be an embedded self, rather than a realized Self. In reconstructed postModern thought one's personal identity, that is, may well derive from one's unique set of relationships to other persons and to place, instead of from one's autonomy, as it does in Modern thought. For example, Who am I? The son of certain loving and constant parents, a loving and constant parent myself, the student of certain charismatic teachers, a professor, a philosopher, and an American, more especially a southern one, at home only in a certain humid climate, in a certain low-lying wooded landscape, and among certain organic odors. If comparison must be made to Asian traditions of thought, such a conception seems more similar to a Confucian than to a Hindu social ontology. But either way, the postModern person will, in any event, be a far cry from the hard-edged, disengaged, dislocated individual of the Modern Western liberal tradition.

And what postModern conception of social order might we expect to be reconstructed? The Modern liberal conception of social order is one of freewheeling citizens of sovereign states whose collisions are minimized by law. The hard edges of the Modern sovereign state are disappearing as I write, blurred by the EC, NAFTA, and GATT. And laws are being supplemented, complemented, and informed by locally shared values and mutual expectations—constantly reformed and fine-tuned by collective discussion and assessment—and collectively enforced by social approbation and disapprobation. Whatever the eventual fate of sovereign states, let us hope that in a mature postModern social order the rule of law—the guarantor of our personal rights and freedoms—remains foundational. In this regard, a comforting fact of history seems to be that new social and political orders retain some of the more humane institutions of their predecessors.

RECONSTRUCTIVE POSTMODERN TECHNOLOGIES

And finally what about technology? After the industrial paradigm, what? Fortunately, here we may leave the unconstrained but perilous realm of speculation and turn instead to characterize what is actually happening.

A writer, such as I, knows rather personally that a profound paradigm shift has occurred in the realm of technique. In the 1950s, when I began to write, the mechanical typewriter was the latest writing technology at a writer's disposal. One pressed a key and the mechanical motion of one's finger moved a series of rods to the last of which a font was affixed that struck an inked ribbon, leaving a letter's imprint on the scrolled paper. (I use the past tense, since today the few writers who cling to typewriters do so as a spiteful form of rebellion against change.) A decade or so later, the electric typewriter came on the scene. It only substituted electrical for muscular energy, a globe (to which the fonts were affixed) for rods, and complicated the mechanical pathway from finger stroke to imprint. The real revolution occurred when the personal computer came on the scene. The writer still mechanically depresses keys on a keyboard, but after that everything happens electronically—from the communication of the keyboard to the central processing unit and from the CPU to the monitor. The computer has few moving parts. One's words appear on a cathode ray screen, as if by magic. The screen itself directly applies quantum physics. And the word processing system is intensely systemic. With one keystroke one can rearrange, insert, or delete a word, sentence, or paragraph, or change the format of a whole document. Even the method of printing letters on paper by means of a laser, in this postModern way of writing, is also an application of quantum physics.

We sometimes call computers "machines." And, indeed, their functions are determinate and algorithmic. Further, they are mass-produced, in the industrial manner, in factories that pollute the environment with toxic chemicals. But, phenomenologically, they are only peripherally and incidentally mechanical. They manifest, quintessentially, the emerging new immaterial and systemic paradigm in contemporary natural philosophy. Let us suppose that the revolution in writing technology epitomizes a gradual and quiet but thoroughgoing revolution in many areas of contemporary technology. If it does, the following process will be repeated. A speedy, quiet, elegant, electronic state system of great power and versatility, which often directly applies domains of the New Physics, replaces a slow, limited, noisy, clumsy, and reductive mechanical apparatus. Another illustrative case is the compact audio disc and CD player, which also employs a laser. It has completely replaced the mechanical long-playing vinyl record and stylus turntable.

In the technological sector, as in the social, we have much to fear as well as much to cheer. A society governed more by mores than by laws is liable to be intolerant of eccentricity and to immoderately impose prevailing popular values. And, as to the ominous side of postModern technology, let us not forget that atomic bombs and smart missiles are as thoroughly informed by the New Physics as are personal computers and compact disc players. Nevertheless, as both Plato and Francis Bacon seem to have understood, philosophers indulge in utopian speculations in order to try to actualize the best and exorcise the worst potentialities of revolutionary moments in history. In the fashion of utopian philosophy, then, let me suggest what the postModern artificial environment could be like. Perhaps we can get an inkling by again employing the method of historical analogy.

Aristotle's own scientific genius lay in biology, and the paradigm of Medieval Aristotelian science represented nature more as a vast organism than as a vast mechanism. Accordingly, preModern technology was decidedly organic. Work was performed by animals. Materials were ingeniously extracted from organic sources: wax for candles from beehives; silken threads for cloth from larval cocoons; other fibers for cloth from various plants and animals; solvents for paints from resins; lubricants from vegetable oils and animal fats; wood for houses from trees; leather for saddles, upholstery, etc. from cattle; and so on and so forth. With the industrial paradigm many of these organic technologies were replaced with mechanical ones. Most obviously, machines have replaced work animals in the transportation and agricultural sectors of industrial economies. But some organic technologies have survived to intermingle with mechanical ones. Most obviously, we still prefer to wear clothes made from silk, wool, and cotton despite the availability of such synthetic fibers as rayon and Dacron. And no one has yet figured out how mechanically to synthesize foodstuffs. Hopefully, no one ever will.

As the reconstructed postModern artificial environment evolves we may, if the present is analogous to the past, expect the new, more elegant, powerful, versatile, and compact electronic state systems to retain, like the computer, mechanical features, and to go on replacing purely mechanical technologies, except when machines proper are irreplaceable. A nonmechanical clothes washing device, for example, is inconceivable—at least I cannot conceive of one. Mechanical technologies will doubtless survive and coexist with the new generation of electronic state systems technologies, just as some of the older organic technologies continue to survive and coexist with those of the Modern industrial era. But the new electronic state systems technologies will, let us hope, recreate the whole artificial environment in their own image. If they do, then, as many predict, we will inhabit a quieter world in which information highways succeed motorways.

And, it seems plausible to suppose that a human economy shifting from industrial production and consumption of material objects to postindustrial production and consumption of information and services will be better adapted to the natural environment. The manufacture of information and provision of services should take less from nature as raw material and be less polluting as well as less noisy. The postModern electronic state systems technological paradigm *is* systemic natural philosophy, just as the Modern industrial paradigm *is* classical mechanics. Hence, we may certainly expect that an artificial environment that embodies it will be better adapted to natural ecological systems than are the mechanical technologies of the industrial era. The emerging new postindustrial paradigm holds out real hope, therefore, that we can achieve a genuine harmony between our artificial environment and the natural environment.

PART VI

TOWARD A NEW PHILOSOPHY
OF CONSERVATION

Whither Conservation Ethics?

Today we face an ever deepening environmental crisis, global in scope. What values and ideals, what vision of biotic health and wholeness should guide our response? American conservation began as an essentially moral movement and has, ever since, orbited around several ethical foci. Here I briefly review the history of American conservation ethics as a context for exploring a moral paradigm for twenty-first-century conservation biology.

Ralph Waldo Emerson and Henry David Thoreau were the first notable American thinkers to insist, a century and a half ago, that other uses might be made of nature than most of their fellow citizens had theretofore supposed (Nash 1989). Nature can be a temple, Emerson (1836) enthused, in which to draw near and to commune with God or the "Oversoul" (Albanese 1990). Too much civilized refinement, Thoreau (1863) argued, can overripen the human spirit; just as too little can coarsen it. In wildness, he thought, lay the preservation of the world.

John Muir (1894, 1901) took the romantic-transcendental nature philosophy of Emerson and Thoreau and made it the basis of a national, morally charged campaign for the appreciation and preservation of wild nature. The natural environment, especially in the New World, was vast enough and rich enough, he believed, to satisfy our deeper spiritual needs as well as our more manifest material needs. Amplifying Thoreau's countercultural theme, Muir strongly condemned prodigal destruction of nature in the service of profligate materialism and greed (Cohen 1984). People going to forest groves, mountain scenery, and meandering streams for religious transcendence, aesthetic contemplation, and healing rest and relaxation put these resources to a "better"—i. e., morally superior—use, in Muir's opinion, than did the lumber barons, mineral kings, and captains of industry hell-bent upon little else than worshipping at the shrine of the Almighty Dollar and seizing the Main Chance (Fox 1981).

Critics today, as formerly, may find an undemocratic and therefore un-American presumption lurking in the romantic-transcendental conservation ethic of Emerson, Thoreau, and Muir. To suggest that some of the human satisfactions that nature affords are morally superior to others may only reflect aristocratic biases and class prejudices (O'Conner 1988). According to utilitarianism—a popular moral and political doctrine introduced by Jeremy Bentham (1823)—human happiness, defined ultimately in terms of pleasure and pain, should be the end of both individual and government action. And one person's pleasure is not necessarily another's. Landscape painters, romantic literati, and transcendental philosophers may find beauty, truth, and goodness in pristine alpine heights, deep forests, and solitary dales, but the vast majority of workaday Americans want affordable building material and building sites, unlimited tap water, cheap food and fiber and good land to raise it on, industrial progress and prosperity generally . . . , and, after all of this, maybe a little easily accessible outdoor recreation.

At the turn of the century, Gifford Pinchot, a younger contemporary of John Muir, formulated a resource conservation ethic reflecting the general tenets of progressivism—an American social and political movement then coming into its own. America's vast biological capital had been notoriously plundered and squandered for the benefit not of all its citizens, but for the profit of a few. Without direct reference to John Stuart Mill (1863)—Bentham's utilitarian protégé, whose summary moral maxim it echoes—Pinchot (1947, 325–26) crystallized the resource conservation ethic in a motto which he credits WJ McGee with formulating: "the greatest good of the greatest number for the longest time." He bluntly reduced the romantic poets' and transcendental philosophers' "Nature" to "natural resources." Indeed, Pinchot insisted that "there are just two things on this material earth—people and natural resources" (1947, 325). He even equated conservation with the systematic exploitation of natural resources. "The first great fact about conservation," Pinchot (1947, xix) enthused, "is that it stands for development." And it was Pinchot (1947, 263) who characterized the Muirian contingent of nature lovers as aiming to "lock up" resources in the national parks and other wilderness reserves.

The first moral principle of the resource conservation ethic is equity—the just or fair distribution of natural resources among present and also future generations of consumers and/or users. Its second moral principle, equal in importance to the first, is efficiency—a natural resource should not be wastefully exploited. Just slightly less obvious, the principle of efficient resource utilization involves the concepts of best or "highest use" and "multiple use."

The "gospel of efficiency," as Samuel Hays (1959) characterized the resource conservation ethic, also implies a sound scientific foundation. The resource conservation ethic thus became wedded to the eighteenth and nineteenth century scientific worldview in which nature is conceived to be a collection of bits of matter, assembled into a hierarchy of externally related chemical and organismic aggregates, which can be understood and successfully manipulated by analytic and reductive methods.

The resource conservation ethic is also wedded to the correlative social science of economics—the science of self-interested rational monads pursuing "preference satisfaction" in a free market. However, because the market, notoriously, does not take account of "externalities"—certain costs of doing business: soil erosion, for example, and environmental pollution—and because standard economic calculations discount the future dollar value of resources in comparison with present dollar value, the free market cannot be relied upon to achieve the most efficient, and certainly not the most prudent, use of natural resources. Pinchot (1947) persuasively argued, therefore, that government ownership and/or regulation of natural resources and resource exploitation is a necessary remedy. Federal and state bureaucracies, accordingly, were created to implement and administer conservation policy as the twentieth century advanced.

Since the resource conservation ethic was based so squarely upon Progressive democratic social philosophy and rhetorically associated with the Modern secular ethic of choice—utilitarianism—it triumphed politically and became institutionalized in the newly created government conservation agencies. The nonconsumptive uses of nature by aesthetes, transcendentalists, and wilderness recreationalists can be accommodated by assigning them a contingent market value or "shadow-price" (Krutilla and Fisher 1985). In some circumstances such uses may turn out to be the highest or most efficient allocation of a given "resource." Thus, an occasional, otherwise worthless wild sop might be thrown to the genteel minority.

The celebrated Schism in the traditional American conservation movement—the schism between the conservationists proper and the preservationists, associated with the legendary names of Pinchot and Muir, respectively— was, thus, in the final analysis a matter of differing moral (and metaphysical) philosophies. Both were essentially human-centered or "anthropocentric," to use the now standard terminology of contemporary environmental ethics. Both, in other words, regarded human beings or human interests as the only legitimate ends and nonhuman natural entities and nature as a whole as means. In the now standard terminology of contemporary environmental ethics, for both conservationists and preservationists only people possess *intrinsic* value; nature possesses merely *instrumental* value. The primary difference is that the preservationists posited a higher transcendental reality above and beyond the physical world and pitted the psychospiritual use of nature against its material use. And they insisted that the one was incomparably superior to the other. The conservationists were more materialistic and insisted, democratically, that all competing uses of resources should be weighed impartially and that the fruits of resource exploitation should be distributed broadly and equitably.

Although Muir's public campaign for the appreciation and preservation of nature was cast largely in terms of the putative superiority of the human spiritual values served by contact with undeveloped, wild nature, Muir also seems to have been the first American conservationist privately to ponder the proposition that nature itself possessed intrinsic value— value in and of itself—quite apart from its human utilities (no matter whether of the more spiritual or more material variety). To articulate this essentially nonanthropocentric intuition, Muir (1916) turned, ironically, to biblical fundamentals for the rhetorical wherewithal (chapter 10). Very directly and plainly stated, God created man and all the other creatures. Each of His creatures—man included, but not man alone—and the creation as a whole are "good" in His eyes (i.e., in philosophical terms they have intrinsic value). Hence, to eradicate a species or to efface nature is to undo God's creative work, and to subtract so much divinely imbued inherent goodness from the world—a most impious and impertinent expression of human arrogance.

More radically than most contemporary exponents of the by-now-familiar Judeo-Christian stewardship environmental ethic, Muir insisted that people are just a part of nature on a par with other creatures and that all creatures (including ourselves) are valued equally by God, for the contribution we and they make to the whole of His creation—whether we can understand that contribution or not. In Muir's own inimitable prose, "Why should man value himself as more than a small part of the one great unit of creation? And what creature of all that the Lord has taken the pains to make is not essential to the completeness of that unit—the cosmos? The universe would be incomplete without man; but it would also be incomplete without the smallest transmicroscopic creature that dwells beyond our conceitful eyes and knowledge" (Muir 1916, 139).

Reading between the lines, we can, I think, easily see that there was another mind set animating Muir's moral vision—an evolutionary and ecological world view. Darwin had unseated from his self-appointed throne the creature Muir sometimes sarcastically called "lord man" and reduced him to but a "small part" of creation, and the likes of H. C. Cowles, S. A. Forbes, and F. E. Clements would soon validate Muir's intuition that there exists a unity and completeness—if not in the cosmos or universe at large, certainly in terrestrial nature—to which each creature, no matter how small, functionally contributes (McIntosh 1985). This worldview held a profound but murky moral import. It fell to Aldo Leopold to bring the ethical implications of the ripening evolutionary-ecological paradigm clearly and fully to light.

Leopold began his career as a professional conservationist trained in the utilitarian Pinchot philosophy of the wise use of natural resources, for the satisfaction of the broadest possible spectrum of human interests, over the longest time (Meine 1988). His ultimately successful struggle for a system of wilderness reserves in the national forests was consciously molded to the doctrine of highest use, and his new technique of game management essentially amounted to the direct transference of the principles of forestry from a standing crop of large plants to a standing crop of large animals (Leopold 1919, 1921). But Leopold gradually came to the conclusion that the Pinchot resource conservation ethic was inadequate, because, in the last analysis, it was untrue.

The resource conservation ethic's close alliance with science proved to be its undoing. Applied science cannot be thoroughly segregated from pure science. Knowledge of ecology is essential to efficient resource management, but during the first half of the twentieth century, ecology began to give shape to a radically different scientific paradigm than that which lay at the very foundations of Pinchot's philosophy. From an ecological perspective, nature is more than a collection of externally related useful, useless, and noxious species furnishing an elemental landscape of soils and waters. It is, rather, a vast, intricately organized and tightly integrated *system* of complex *processes*. As Leopold (1939a, 727) expressed it: "Ecology is a new fusion point for all the sciences. . . . The emergence of ecology has placed the economic biologist in a peculiar dilemma: with one hand he points out the accumulated findings of his search for utility, or lack of utility, in this or that species; with the other he lifts the veil from a biota so complex, so conditioned by interwoven cooperations and competitions, that no man can say where utility begins or ends."

Thus, we cannot remodel our natural *oikos* or household, as we do our artificial ones, without inducing unexpected disruptions. More especially, we cannot get rid of the Early American floral and faunal "furniture" (the prairie flora, bison, elk, wolves, bears) and randomly introduce exotic pieces (wheat, cattle, sheep, English sparrows, Chinese pheasants, German carp, and the like) that suit our fancy without risk of inducing destructive ecological chain reactions.

Conservation, Leopold came to realize, must aim at something larger and more comprehensive than a maximum sustained flow of desirable products (like lumber and game) and experiences (like sport hunting and fishing, wilderness travel, and solitude) garnered from an impassive nature (Flader 1974). It must take care to ensure the continued function of natural processes and the integrity of natural systems. For it is upon these, ultimately, that human resources and human well-being depend.

The Pinchot resource conservation ethic is also untrue on the human side of its people/natural resources bifurcation. Human beings are not specially created and uniquely valuable demigods any more than nature itself is a vast emporium of goods and services, a mere pool of resources. We are, rather, very much a part of nature. Muir (1916) groped to express this bio-egalitarian concept in theological terms. Leopold did so in more honest ecological terms. Human beings are "members of a biotic team," plain members and citizens of one humming biotic community (Leopold 1949, 205). We and the other citizen-members of the biotic community sink or swim together. Leopold's affirmation that plants and animals, soils and waters are entitled to full citizenship as fellow members of the biotic community is tantamount to the recognition that they too have intrinsic, not just instrumental, value. An evolutionary and ecological worldview, in short, implies a land ethic.

In sum, then, examining a core sample of the ethical sediments in the philosophical bedrock of American conservation, one may clearly discern three principal strata of laterally coherent moral ideals. They are the romantic-transcendental preservation ethic, the progressive-utilitarian resource conservation ethic, and the evolutionary-ecological land ethic. American conservation policy and the conservation profession reflect them all—thus giving rise to internal conflict and, from an external point of view, the appearance of confusion. The public agencies are still very much ruled by the turn-of-the-century resource conservation ethic; some of the most powerful and influential private conservation organizations remain firmly rooted in the even older romantic-transcendental philosophy; while contemporary conservation biology is clearly inspired and governed by the evolutionary-ecological land ethic (Soulé, 1985).

As we approach the end of the twentieth century, we face a situation today that is analogous to that faced by our forebears at the end of the nineteenth. Then, the American frontier had closed and what had once appeared to be an effectively boundless and superabundant New World suddenly had palpable limits. At present our generation is pressing hard against the ecological limits not just of the continent, but of the entire planet. We are witnessing the extension of the industrial juggernaut into every corner of the globe. Soils are washing into the sea; toxic chemicals are polluting surface water and groundwater; chain saws and bulldozers are wreaking havoc in tropical forests—and coincidentally exterminating a significant portion of Earth's complement of species—while acid rain is withering the forests and sterilizing the lakes in temperate regions of the Northern Hemisphere; chloroflourocarbons are eroding the planet's protective ozone shield and fossil-fuel consumption is loading Earth's atmosphere with carbon dioxide. Since Leopold's land ethic is fully informed by and firmly grounded in evolutionary and ecological biology, it ought to supplant its nineteenth-century antecedents as our moral anchor in the face of the second wave of the environmental crisis looming threateningly on the horizon—but we need to be very clear about its implications.

The word *preserve* in Leopold's (1949, 224–25) famous summary moral maxim—"A thing is right when it tends to preserve the integrity, stability, and beauty of the biotic community; it is wrong when it tends otherwise"—is unfortunate because it seems to ally Leopold and the land ethic with the preservationists in the century-old preservation versus conservation conflict. We tend to think of Leopold as having begun his career in the latter camp and gradually come over, armed with new arguments, to the former. Leopold's historical association with the wilderness movement cements this impression. But Leopold was from first to last committed as much to active land management as to passive preservation, as a review of Leopold's unpublished papers and published but long-forgotten articles confirms (Flader 1974; Meine 1988). Leopold's vision went beyond the *either* efficiently develop *or* lock up and reserve dilemma of the modern conservation *problematique*. Indeed, Leopold himself was primarily concerned, on the ground as well as in theory, with integrating an optimal mix of wildlife—both floral and faunal—with human habitation and economic exploitation of land.

In a typescript composed shortly after a four-month trip to Germany in 1935—and ironically, but revealingly, entitled "Wilderness"—Leopold wrote,

> To an American conservationist, one of the most insistent impressions received from travel in Germany is the lack of wildness in the German landscape. Forests are there. . . . Game is there. . . . Streams and lakes are there. . . . But yet, to the critical eye there is something lacking . . . . I did not hope to find in Germany anything resembling the great "wilderness areas" which we dream about and talk about, and sometimes briefly set aside, in our National Forests and Parks. . . . I speak rather of a certain quality which should be, but is not found in the ordinary landscape of producing forests and inhabited farms. (Leopold, 1991, 226–27)

In a more fully developed essay entitled "The Farmer as a Conservationist," Leopold (1939b) regales his reader with a rustic idyll in which the wild and domesticated floral and faunal denizens of a Wisconsin farmscape are feathered into one another to create a harmonious whole. In addition to cash and the usual supply of vegetables and meat, lumber and fuelwood, Leopold's envisioned farmstead affords its farm family venison, quail, and other small game, and a variety of fruit and nuts from its woodlot, wetlands, and fallow fields; and its pond and stream yield panfish and trout. It also affords intangibles—songbirds, wildflowers, the hoot of owls, the bugle of cranes, and intellectual adventures aplenty in natural history. To obtain this bounty, the farm family must do more than permanently set aside acreage, fence woodlots, and leave wetlands undrained. They must sow food and cover patches, plant trees, stock the stream and pond, and generally thoughtfully conceive and skillfully execute scores of other modifications, large and small, of the biota that they inhabit.

The pressure of growing human numbers and rapid development, especially in the Third World, implies, I think, that a global conservation strategy focused primarily on "wilderness" preservation and the establishment of nature reserves represents a holding action at best—and a losing proposition at last. I support wilderness and nature reserves—categorically—with my purse as well as my pen. But faced with the sobering realities of the coming century, the only viable philosophy of conservation is, I submit, a generalized version of Leopold's vision of a mutually beneficial and enhancing integration of the human economy with the economy of nature—*in addition to* holding on to as much untrammeled wilderness as we can.

Lack of theoretical justification complements the present sheer impracticability of conserving biodiversity solely by excluding man and his works. Change—not only evolutionary change, but climatic, successional, seasonal, and stochastic change—is natural (Botkin 1990). And "man" is a part of nature. Therefore, it will no longer do to say, simply, that what existed before the agricultural-industrial variety of Homo sapiens evolved or arrived, as the case may be, is the ecological norm in comparison with which all anthropogenic modifications are degradations. To define environmental quality—the integrity, stability, and beauty of the biotic community—dynamically and positively, not statically and negatively, is part of the intellectual challenge that contemporary conservation biology confronts.

Happily, Leopold's conservation ideal of ecosystems that are at once productive and healthy is capable of generalization beyond the well-watered temperate latitudes and pastoral lifestyles characteristic of the upper Midwest. Charles M. Peters, Alwyn H. Gentry, and Robert O. Mendelsohn

(1989) report that the nuts, fruits, oils, latex, fiber, and medicines annually harvested from a representative hectare of standing rain forest in Peru,
for example, is of greater economic value than the sawlogs and pulpwood
stripped from a similar hectare—greater even than if, following clear-cutting and slash-burning, the land is, in addition, converted to a forest
monoculture or to a cattle pasture. They conclude that "without question, the sustainable exploitation of non-wood forest resources represents
the most immediate and profitable method for integrating the use and
conservation of Amazonian forests" (Peters et al. 1989, 656). Arturo
Gomez-Pompa and Andrea Kaus (1988) argue that the greater incidence
of trees bearing edible fruits than would occur naturally in the extant
remnants of Central American rain forest suggests that these "pristine"
habitats may once actually have been part of an extensive Maya
permaculture.

Of course we must remember David Ehrenfeld's (1976) classic warn-
ing that we not put all our conservation eggs in the economic basket. It is
too much to hope that a standard benefit-cost comparison will, in every
case, indicate that the sustainable alternative to destructive development
is more profitable. Certainly I am not here urging an unregenerate return
to the economic determinism of the resource conservation ethic. Rather,
I am simply pointing out that it is often possible for people to make a
good living—and, in some instances, even the best living to be had—
coexisting with rather than converting the indigenous biotic community.
And I am urging that we strive to reconcile and integrate human economic activities with biological conservation. Expressed in the vernacular, I am urging that we think in terms of "win-win" rather than "zero-
sum." Further, I would like explicitly to state—and thereby invite critical
discussion of—Leopold's more heretical, from the preservationist point
of view, implied corollary proposition, viz., that human economic activities may not only coexist with healthy ecosystems, but that they may actually enhance them. Citing Gary Nabhan (1982), in a more recent discussion Ehrenfeld (1989, 9) provides a provocative example:

In the Papago Indian Country of Arizona's and Mexico's Sonoran Desert . . .
there are two oases only thirty miles apart. The northern one . . . is in the U.S.
Organ Pipe Cactus National Monument, fully protected as a bird sanctuary, with
no human activity except bird watching allowed. All Papago farming which has

existed there since prehistory was stopped in 1957. The other oasis, . . . over the border in Mexico, is still being farmed in traditional Papago style. . . . Visiting the oases "on back-to-back days three times during one year," Nabhan, accompanied by ornithologists, found fewer than thirty-two species of birds at the Park Service's bird sanctuary but more than sixty-five species at the farmed oasis.

From this "modern parable of conservation" Ehrenfeld (1986, 9) concludes that "the presence of people may enhance the species richness of an area, rather than exert the effect that is more familiar to us." Is species richness a measure of ecological health? What other standards of ecosystem health can be formulated? How do these norms all fit together to form models of fit environments? Can we succeed, as the Papago seem to have done, in enriching the environment as we enrich ourselves? How does ecosystem health differ from and complement the conservation of biological integrity? These are some of the questions germane to a future conservation philosophy.

Aldo Leopold's Concept
of Ecosystem Health

WHY THE HEALTH METAPHOR

The concept of ecosystem health is metaphorical. "Health" in the literal, nonfigurative sense characterizes only a state or condition of an organism. To employ the concept of ecosystem health metaphorically does not commit one to an implicit endorsement of F. E. Clements's classic, but increasingly unfashionable, organismic paradigm in ecology. To insist that it would would be to suppose that the concept of ecosystem health were intended to have a literal rather than metaphorical sense—the health *sensu stricto* of a superorganism. I do not think that that is what its proponents intend. At least this is not what I intend.

Plato provides a notable historical precedent for using the concept of health metaphorically. In the *Republic*, Socrates says, "Then virtue is the health and beauty and well-being of the soul, and vice the disease and weakness and deformity of the same" (Plato 1937, 709). Plato also provides an instructive historical precedent for why one would want to rhetorically employ the health metaphor. Socrates next asks whether or not a person would prefer to live in accordance with virtue or its opposite—the fundamental question of the whole dialogue. And Glaucon replies, "In my judgment, Socrates, the question now becomes ridiculous. We know that, when the bodily constitution is gone, life is no longer endurable . . . ; and shall we be told that when the very essence of the vital principle is undermined and corrupted, life is still worth having to a man . . . ?" (Plato 1937, 709).

The concept of health, in both its literal and figurative senses, is at once descriptive and prescriptive, objective and normative. Health, literally, is an objective condition of an organism capable of more or less precise empirical description. But it is also an intrinsically valuable state of being. Except under the most unusual circumstances, it is never better to be sick than well. For Plato, health is the good of the body, its appropriate condition of internal order or organization. Similarly, Plato argues, virtue is the good of the soul, *its* appropriate condition of internal order or organization. And, further extending the same metaphor, justice is the intrinsically good, healthy state of the body politic. Today, we could add the ecosystem to Plato's series of analogies. Ecosystem health is a condition of internal order and organization in ecosystems that—no less than analogous conditions of body, soul, and society—is both intrinsically good and objective (and specifiable in principle).

Echoing Plato, Peter Miller (1981, 194) explains why ecosystem health is a good candidate for intrinsic valuation: "[I]t wears the appearance of (a) a value, a basic ingredient in living well or thriving, which (b) characterizes nonhuman and even nonconscious living [systems] (c) independently of human utilities." Thus, as we see, if the health metaphor may be plausibly and persuasively extended to ecosystems, then the fact/value or is/ought dichotomy that has routinely plagued policy debates and applied science can be obviated.

Here, of course, we must be cautious. Assuming the distinction between subject and object common to both Modern philosophy and Modern classical science, all value depends upon a subjective valuer. But as Holmes Rolston III (1981, 114) has eloquently pointed out, what we value is not at all capricious: "We make something a target merely by aiming at it. But our interest in apples is not so arbitrary. It depends in part on something that is found there." Even our purely instrumental valuing depends on fact, or on what Rolston (1981, 114) calls "descriptions." We human beings are also capable of noninstrumental valuing (Callicott 1982, and here in chapter 12). Bodily health is a paradigm case of something that is intrinsically as well as instrumentally valuable; it is good in and of itself, as well as a necessary condition for getting on with our projects. So is virtue and a healthy body politic, Plato would argue; and had the concept of an ecosystem been current in Plato's day, doubtless he would have also argued that ecosystem health too is something valuable for its own sake as well as for its utility. We have a reasonably clear, detailed scientific description of bodily health. The problem for science is to articulate objective norms of ecosystem health. Like the medical norms of bodily health, the norms of ecosystem health would be simultaneously descriptive and prescriptive, objective and nomothetic, instrumentally and intrinsically valuable.

If the concept of ecosystem health turns out to be plausible and persuasive and if the norms and indices of ecosystem health can be specified, the cause of biological conservation may be bolstered. Presently it is being undermined by an insidious skepticism within the scientific community. The erstwhile benchmarks of biological conservation are under withering attack.

THE CRUMBLING CORNERSTONES
OF BIOLOGICAL CONSERVATION

Formerly, one could argue for biodiversity because it was believed to be causally related to ecological stability. The "diversity-stability hypothesis," however, has been severely criticized (May 1973; Goodman 1975)—how decisively, I am not competent to judge. But the mandate for the conservation of biodiversity will be put at risk to the extent that one of its mainstay rationales is suspect.

Wilderness once served as a gross standard of conservation. Wilderness was imagined to be a pristine environment, defined by an Act of the United States Congress as "in contrast to those areas where man and his own works dominate the landscape, an area where the earth and its community of life are untrammeled by man, where man himself is a visitor who does not remain" (Nash 1963, 5). But wilderness preservation, so understood, assumes a pre-Darwinian religious and metaphysical separation of Homo sapiens from the rest of nature. After Darwin, we cannot suppose that "man" is anything but a precocious primate, a denizen of "the earth" and a member of its "community of life." "His own works," therefore, are as natural as those of termites or beavers. Biological conservation via wilderness preservation is also vitiated by ethnocentrism. To suggest that, prior to being "discovered" only half a millennium ago by the European subspecies of Homo sapiens, any landscape in North or South America was "untrammeled by man, where man himself is a visitor," implies either that large portions of North and South America were uninhabited or that the aboriginal inhabitants of the New World had no significant intentional or even unintentional effect upon their lands. Or, worse, it could imply that American Indians were not truly human, were not "man." But, by 1492, all of North and South America were fully if not densely populated (Dobyns 1966). And the effects of more than ten thousand years of human inhabitation of the Western Hemisphere have been profound and, upon the eve of European encroachment, were ongoing (Denevan 1992). After the arrival of Homo sapiens in the Western Hemisphere, some ten thousand or more years ago, the only large land area fitting Congress's description of wilderness was Antarctica (and now a good bit of that continent, and the atmosphere above it, have been thoroughly trammeled). When an area's aboriginal human inhabitants are removed, in order to create a wilderness, the ecologic conditions that existed at the time of their removal, presumably the conditions to be preserved in their "virgin" state, are put at jeopardy (Bonnicksen 1990). Biologic conservation via wilderness preservation thus proves to be based upon an incoherent idea, the wilderness idea (Callicott 1991).

Further, whether a "natural" area has been dominated by Homo sapiens or not, över time it will nevertheless change. The fourth dimension of ecosystems has recently been emphasized by Daniel Botkin (1990). Nature is dynamic. Change at every frequency—diurnal, meteorological, seasonal, successional, climatic, evolutionary, geological, astronomical—is inevitable. According to Botkin, the concept of succession in ecology culminating in a climax community that will perpetuate itself generation after generation until reset by wind, fire, chain saw, plow, or some other disturbance is suspect. While accounting for change, the concept of succession-to-climax, he argues, posits—like Aristotle's physics—rest or a static state as the "natural" condition of ecosystems.

Presenting a more specific and subtle challenge to the rationale for biological conservation, change in the structure of biotic communities has been recently emphasized. According to Michael Soulé (1990, 234), shifts in scientific fashion will facilitate the transition between the traditional view of biogeographic integrity and the postmodern acceptance of cosmopolitanization. . . . The acceptance of the "individualistic paradigm" of community composition, . . . which posits that collections of species that exist in a particular place is a matter of historical accident and species-specific, autecological requirements . . . is reinforced by analyses of Holocene distributions of contemporary species. These studies are undermining typological concepts of community composition, structure, dynamics, and organization by showing that existing species once constituted quite different groupings or "communities."

These recent developments—the impeachment of the diversity-stability hypothesis, the evaporation of the wilderness idea, the diminishing credibility of the Clementsian holistic paradigm and the corresponding ascendency of the Gleasonian individualistic paradigm in theoretical ecology, the impeachment of the community succession-to-climax model and even the typological community, and the emphasis, in general, on change rather than continuity (a kind of neocatastrophism, as it were, supplanting uniformitarianism)—all give aid and comfort to the foes of biological conservation. If change is a fundamental feature of nature; if man is a part of nature and anthropogenic changes are as natural as any other; if, for more than 10,000 years, there have been no large-scale, pristine, untouched terrestrial wilderness environments (outside Antarctica); if species in communities can mix and match as they always have to form novel associations; if diversity is not necessarily necessary to stability; then how can anyone express more than a personal subjective preference in declaring any change whatever that human beings may impose on landscapes to be bad? What's wrong, objectively wrong, with urban sprawl, oil slicks, global warming, or, for that matter, abrupt, massive, anthropogenic species extinction—other than that these things offend the quaint tastes of a few natural antiquarians? Most people prefer shopping malls and dog tracks to wetlands and old growth forests. Why shouldn't their tastes, however vulgar, prevail in a free market and democratic polity? Kristin Shrader-Frechette has explicitly brought us to this omega point:

Ecosystems regularly change and regularly eliminate species. How would one . . . argue that humans should not modify ecosystems or even wipe out species, for example, when nature does this itself through natural disasters, such as volcanic eruptions and climate changes like those that destroyed the dinosaurs? . . . One cannot obviously claim that it is wrong on *ecological grounds* for humans to do what nature does—wipe out species. (Shrader-Frechette 1989, 76, emphasis in original)

The concept of ecosystem health to the rescue. Yes, change is natural, human beings are a part of nature, and anthropogenic changes are no different from other natural changes. But, quite irrespective of the vagaries of taste, we may still argue that some are bad and others good, if we can specify objective norms of ecologic health against which we may evaluate human modifications of the landscape. By the same criteria of course we might evaluate the changes wrought by any other species.

LAND HEALTH

I leave to ecologists the task of determining whether or not the concept of ecosystem health makes scientific sense and, if it does, what the general characteristics and indices of ecosystem health might be. As Plato provides a locus classicus for turning the metaphorical concepts of psychological and political health to moral advantage, Aldo Leopold provides a locus classicus for turning the metaphorical concept of ecosystem health (or "land health," as he more simply denominated it) to conservation advantage. That so distinguished and prescient a conservationist as Leopold thought that the concept had promise, and envisioned its scientific articulation, may be taken as prima facie evidence that the notion is at least worth a close look.

During the last decade of his life, 1938–48, Leopold frequently employed the concept of land health in his sundry writings, including several of the essays in *A Sand County Almanac*. In two of his papers from this period, Leopold provides a sustained discussion of the concept of land health.

Ironically, in view of the foregoing remarks, the first is "Wilderness as a Land Laboratory," in which Leopold offers a novel argument for wilderness preservation. Here he suggests that wilderness may serve as "a base-datum for land-health" and defines "land health" as nature's capacity for "self-renewal," a definition which he reiterates in subsequent usages and a definition that carries, importantly, both dynamic and functional rather than static and structural connotations (Leopold 1941, 3). Though not invoking Clements's organismic ecological paradigm in any strict or specific sense, Leopold here, as he will elsewhere, closely associates the concept of "land health" with an organic image of nature: "There are two organisms in which the unconscious automatic processes of self-renewal have been supplemented by conscious interference and control. One of these is man himself (medicine and public health) and the other is land (agriculture and conservation)" (Leopold 1941, 3).

That Leopold introduces the concept of land health, not as a casual rhetorical device, but as a serious scientific project, is suggested by the way he explores the analogy that he here draws to medicine. In the field of medicine, the symptoms of disease are manifest and doctoring is an ancient art, but medical science is relatively young and still incomplete. Analogously, "the art of land doctoring is being practiced with vigor," he comments, "but the science of land health is a job for the future" (Leopold 1941, 3). In 1941 ecology was not capable of specifying the norms of land health. On the other hand, the "symptoms" of "land-sickness" were all too evident to the discerning conservationist. Among such symptoms, Leopold (1941) mentions soil erosion and loss of fertility, hydrologic abnormalities, and the occasional irruptions of some species and the mysterious local extinctions of others.

While he argues that the most perfect "base-datum of normality" is wilderness, Leopold does not argue that the only way for land to stay healthy is to stay in an untrammeled condition. One may find places "where land physiology remains largely normal despite centuries of human occupation" (Leopold 1941, 3). Such places he believed the well-watered regions of Europe to be. Indeed, the practical raison d'être for a science of land health is precisely to determine the ecologic parameters within which land may be humanly occupied without making it dysfunctional, just as the whole point—or at least the only point that Leopold makes in this paper—of wilderness preservation is to provide a land laboratory in which such a science might be explored.

Leopold's uncritical belief in the existence of wilderness is traceable, I surmise, to the unconscious ethnocentrism that he shared with most of his contemporaries. In a paper written during the same year, he remarks that "the characteristic number of Indians in virgin America was small" (Leopold 1991d, 282). And in a paper published four years earlier he rhetorically reduces one group of American Indians, "the predatory Apache," to a form of less-than-fully-human indigenous wildlife (Leopold 1937, 118). But of course, North America, no less than temperate Europe, had also been subjected to "centuries of human occupation," indeed, more than 100 centuries.

Leopold's other sustained discussion of "land health" is found in an (until now) unpublished 1944 report, "Conservation: In Whole or in Part?" In it, he defines conservation as "a state of health in the land" and land health, once again, "as a state of vigorous self-renewal" (Leopold 1991b, 310). Here Leopold expressly draws out the functional connotation of this definition: "Such collective functioning of interdependent parts for the maintenance of the whole is characteristic of an organism. In this sense land is an organism, and conservation deals with its functional integrity, or health" (Leopold 1991b, 310). The maintenance of land health, therefore, is not necessarily the same thing as maintenance of existing community structures with their historical complement of species. Exotics may immigrate on their own or be deliberately introduced (cautiously) and evaluated, not xenophobically, but on the basis of their impact on the functional integrity of the host community. They may be pathologic, they may be benign, or, conceivably, they may actually enhance ecosystem functions.

In "Conservation: In Whole or in Part?" Leopold affirms the importance of diversity for ecologic function. Referring to the postglacial upper Midwest he writes, "The net trend of the original community was thus toward more and more diversity of native forms, and more and more complex relations between them" (Leopold 1991b, 312). He then draws the classic, but presently impugned, connection between diversity and stability: "Stability or health was associated with, and perhaps caused by this diversity and complexity" (Leopold 1991b, 312). It is a tribute to Leopold's scientific sensibilities that he carefully avoids stating dogmatically that stability was caused by diversity. Indeed, he registers an express caveat: "To assert a causal relation would imply that we understand the mechanism. . . ." But, absent thorough understanding, he argues that "The circumstantial evidence is that stability and diversity in the native community were associated for 20,000 years, and presumably depended on each other. Both now are partly lost, presumably because the original community has been partly lost and greatly altered. Presumably, the greater the losses and alterations, the greater the risks of impairments and disor-ganizations" (Leopold 1991b, 315).

As the science of land health is, for Leopold in the 1940s, only envi-sioned, only programmatic, he suggests that the art of land doctoring can only proceed on such circumstantial evidence and err on the side of cau-tion. The "'rule of thumb'" for "ecological conservation" then should be, he thinks, that "the land should retain as much of its original membership as is compatible with human land-use [and] should be modified as gently and as little as possible" (Leopold 1991b, 315). But, again, it does not take a well-developed science of land health to notice the symptoms of land illness. In addition to those already mentioned in his earlier paper, Leopold here adds the qualitative deterioration in farm and forest prod-ucts, the outbreak of pests and disease epidemics, and boom-and-bust wildlife population cycles.

Further to a governing philosophy of ecological conservation, Leopold suggests something similar to what is known today as holistic and preven-tive, as opposed to reductive and invasive, medicine: "This difference be-tween gentle and restrained, as compared with violent and unrestrained, modification of the land is the difference between organic and mustard-plaster therapeutics in the field of land-health" (Leopold 1991b, 315). Leopold then goes on to outline a unified and holistic conservation strat-egy, as the title of his paper would indicate.

DISCUSSION

The contemporary ecologist looking for substantive norms of ecosystem health—in addition to substantive symptoms of ecosystem illness—which might serve as objective criteria for the evaluation of human modifica-tions of historical ecologic conditions will find a review of Leopold's re-marks about land health unrewarding. Leopold's scientific scruples pre-empted any impulse he may have had speculatively to detail them in the absence of basic ecological research. In general, he closely associates land health with both integrity—which he seems to understand primarily struc-turally—and stability. Leopold equates the integrity of land with the con-tinuity of stable communities over long periods of time. Such integrity and stability, he cautiously suggests, depends upon species diversity and the complexity of relations between native species. In short, we find in Leopold only today's conventional environmental wisdom, which then was new and fresh, but is now a bit tired and tarnished. On the other hand, because Leopold's general definition of land health is more functional than structural, dynamic than static, it is very much in tune with current *fin de (la vingtième) siècle* ecological theory.

In fact there exists a notion in contemporary biology cognate with Leopold's idea of "land health," the concept of "autopoiêsis." Leopold's concept of land health and the concept of autopoiêsis may indeed be mutually reinforcing: The imprimatur of Leopold's enormous reputation could attract greater attention to and exploration of the concept of autopoiêsis and the concept of autopoiêsis could update and more fully and abstractly express what Leopold was groping for with his notion of "land health" characterized as the "capacity of land for self-renewal."

Autopoiêsis is transliterated from two combined Greek words, αυτο and ποιησισ; and, translated from Greek, means self-making. It was coined in 1972 by the Chilean biologists Humberto Maturana and Francisco Varela (1980) to characterize living systems more inclusive than organisms. Thus an organism is autopoiêtic, but so are other biological "entities." Instead of assimilating supraorganic biological systems to organisms, and implausibly attributing to them all sorts of similar characteristics, à la Clements, the concept of autopoiêsis permits a more limited comparison between organisms proper and larger living systems.

Explicitly assimilating Leopold's informal notion of land health with the contemporary formal concept of autopoiêsis could, therefore, rescue the former from guilt by association with the discredited organismic ecological paradigm. Though Leopold, for rhetorical effect, will sometimes say that "land *is* an organism," just as Clements had said that a plant formation *is* an organism, in trying more precisely to articulate what he means by "land health," Leopold focuses on the capacity of land for self-renewal and more carefully says that "*in this sense* land is an organism." Ecosystems and organisms, in other words, are very different and—it here seems that Leopold may have been aware—one would be mistaken to think that the former are just larger and more diffuse versions of the latter. Rather, Leopold thinks, they have one very fundamental, not to say essential, characteristic in common—the capacity for self-organization and self-renewal. More technically expressed, organisms and ecosystems are both autopoiêtic, self-organizing and self-recreating.

The concept of autopoiêsis wears its dynamism on its sleeve, since "poiêsis" is a verb. "Health," on the other hand, is a noun and may therefore suggest a static condition in both organisms and ecosystems. But health, despite the grammar of its name, actually is very much a process, a process of self-maintenance and self-regeneration. In a healthy multicellular organism there is a constant turnover of cells. Further, while there is continuity in the organization of transient cells, over a lifetime there is dramatic ontogeny: from zygote to embryo to fetus to infant; then growth, maturation, reproduction; and finally, decline and senescence. Or, even more dramatically: from egg to larva to pupa to imago. Today, ecologists emphasize that ecosystems also change over time, but, as in healthy organisms, healthy ecosystems maintain a certain continuity and order in the midst of change. Thus radical and discontinuous change is as destructive of autopoiêtic ecosystems as of autopoiêtic organisms.

All the symptoms of land illness that Leopold notes are failures of ecologic function, not merely alterations in composition. While Leopold believed that the compositional integrity of biotic communities guaranteed their continued ecologic function, he acknowledged that functional continuity could be maintained in the midst of gradual and orderly compositional change. According to Maturana and Varela an autopoiêtic system, though by definition a system whose whole and sole business is to regenerate itself, ordinarily undergoes structural changes. But those changes must be orderly and, especially if imposed from outside the system (what they call "deformations"), limited: "Any structural changes that a living system may undergo maintaining its identity must take place in a manner determined by and subordinate to its defining autopoiêsis; hence in a living system loss of autopoiêsis is disintegration as a unity and loss of identity, that is death" (Maturana and Varela, 1980, 112). Hence, human inhabitation and transformation of ecosystems is not, in principle, incompatible with their health—that is, with their autopoiêsis or capacity for self-renewal. Objectively good anthropogenic change is change that benefits people and maintains land health. Objectively bad anthropogenic change is change that results in land sickness or worse in the death of ecosystems. The overgrazed, eroded and unrestorable erstwhile grasslands of the American Southwest are very sick. The barren, laterized soil of an erstwhile tropical rain forest is dead.

Leopold bought into the wilderness myth. Indeed, he was one of the most outspoken advocates of wilderness preservation and one of the architects of the North American wilderness movement. Nevertheless, unlike a Muir or a Murie, he devoted himself primarily to the conservation of humanly occupied and used ecosystems—"a more important and complex task," as he put it (Leopold 1991e, 227). And Leopold certainly acknowledged that long and densely populated and heavily used land could be healthy. In "A Biotic View of Land," he writes, "Western Europe, for example, carries a far different pyramid than Caesar found there. Some large animals are lost; many new plants and animals are introduced, some of which escape as pests; the remaining natives are greatly changed in distribution and abundance. Yet the soil is still fertile, the waters flow normally, the new structure seems to function and persist" (Leopold, 1939, 729).

Susan L. Flader (1974) observes that during the 1930s Leopold underwent a fairly sudden and dramatic shift of attitude toward land management. From the reductive, Cartesian method, set out in *Game Management*, of identifying and manipulating "factors" affecting wildlife populations—such as food, cover, and predation—Leopold shifted to a more holistic, organic approach. Eugene C. Hargrove (1989) compares his new attitude to "therapeutic nihilism" in medicine. This nineteenth-century school of medicine frankly acknowledged that doctors then did not know enough about the physiology of the human organism to be confident that any medical manipulation, invasion, or prescription would do more good than harm. So, they argued, doctors should err on the side of caution, do nothing, and hope their patients would recover on their own. Leopold, similarly, believed that the contemporaneous state of ecological knowledge was so incomplete that any humanly imposed changes on land were altogether unpredictable. Hence, he counseled caution and argued that the functioning of ecosystems could best be assured by preserving, and, where practicable, restoring, their historic structural compositional integrity.

CONCLUSION

I have no idea how much more confident we can be today in the state of ecological knowledge. I can say with assurance, however, that neither manipulative management nor economic development are incompatible, in principle, with Leopold's general concept of land health. Human economic activities and the presence of domestic or exotic species are not inconsistent with land health, as Leopold conceived it, *provided that they do not disrupt ecosystem functions*, as indicated by the incidence or absence of the symptoms (some of which Leopold enumerates) of land-illness.

Of course, Leopold's land ethic may provide other reasons for exercising caution and more stringent constraints on human economic activities. If ecology, for example, could assure us that replacing golden trout with brown in California waters would have no adverse impact on the health of affected aquatic ecosystems, the "biotic right" of species to continuation, advocated by Leopold in "The Land Ethic," might still constitute a compelling reason not to do so. One can imagine all sorts of unnecessary and disfiguring operations that an unscrupulous doctor might perform on an unwitting patient, none of which ultimately compromised the patient's health, to satisfy the doctor's own whims or economic interests. But such operations would certainly compromise the patient's dignity and would violate the patient's rights. Human economic activities should certainly be constrained by considerations of land health. The observance of such constraints is as much a matter of morality as of prudence, since health—personal, social, and ecological—is an intrinsic value. But they should also be constrained by additional ethical and aesthetical considerations—by the "biotic right" of species to continuance and by the beauty of historic biotic communities.

18

The Value of Ecosystem Health

INTRODUCTION

People are familiar with the concept of health, and confidently form opinions about public health issues and health care policy. People are also familiar with metaphorical extensions of the concept of health—"economic health," for example—in the formation and articulation of public policy (Costanza 1995). A new metaphorical extension of the health concept—ecosystem health—has recently made its debut. The beauty of such health metaphors is that they suggest that certain states—of economic systems, of ecological systems—are both objective and normative, actual and valuable (chapter 17). Can the concept of ecosystem health withstand philosophical scrutiny?

I think that it can. Here I review some—but by no means all—of the salient conceptual problems with the concept of ecosystem health. Both elements—*ecosystem* and *health*—of the composite ecosystem health metaphor are problematic. First, I consider—and try to resolve—some of the problems with the ecosystem and health concepts, respectively. Then, I try to clarify the axiological status of health (the status of the *value* associated with health), and, by metaphorical extension, of ecosystem health. Finally, I suggest that we distinguish carefully between biodiversity, biological integrity, and ecosystem health as three different, but not unrelated, conservation desiderata.

THE ECOSYSTEM CONCEPT

According to Worster (1990), after its midcentury heyday, the ecosystem concept is fast fading from ecological theory. He reports surveying recent ecology textbooks and finding "that the concept is not even mentioned in one leading work and has a much diminished place [in comparison with midcentury ecology textbooks] in the others" (Worster 1990, 8). Worster (1990, 17) cites Begon et al. (1986), Putnam and Wratten (1984), Ehrlich and Roughgarden (1987), and Smith (1986).

Perhaps most problematic of all, the very existence of ecosystems has been questioned (Simberloff 1980). Unlike most familiar organisms, ecosystems, especially marine ecosystems, have no obvious spatial boundaries, no delimiting epidermis (Gray 1995). Hence one may wonder whether or not ecosystems are distinct *entities*. One cannot plausibly predicate *health* of ecosystems—even metaphorically—if no such things as ecosystems exist. Some ecologists arbitrarily delimit ecosystems—as, for example, Bormann and Likens (1979), who take them to be coextensive with watersheds. And some ambiguously delimit them—as, for example, O'Neill et al. (1986, 7), who allow an ecosystem to be defined by "the phenomena of interest, the specific measurements taken, and the techniques used to analyze the data," that is, by the "observational set."

While O'Neill et al. (1986) allow ecosystem ontology to be determined by ecological epistemology, they *do* strive for rigor in defining ecosystems. Ecosystems should not be conceived to be "tangible" spatial entities, according to Allen and Hoekstra (1992). Rather, they should be conceived to be "a set of interacting, differently scaled *processes* that may be diffuse in space but easily defined in terms of turnover time . . . . The ecosystem is a much richer concept than just some meteorology, soil, and animals, tacked onto patches of vegetation" (Allen and Hoekstra 1992, 94, 99, emphasis added). Ecosystems, so defined, are hierarchically ordered, both spatially and temporally—sort of like a set of four-dimensional Chinese boxes (O'Neill et al. 1986; Allen and Hoekstra 1992). Hence the prognosis is good that the problematic ontological status of ecosystems can be satisfactorily resolved, albeit at the price of a considerable degree of abstractness.

Potentially just as vitiating, ecosystems, it seems, may not be so highly integrated, so systemic, as they were previously thought to be. Plants may coexist in proximity to one another simply because they are all adapted to similar gradients of soil and climate, not because they are mutually dependent or otherwise closely connected (Gleason 1939; Connell and Slatyer 1977). Over time, moreover, species invade a region—with or without human assistance—and either coexist with or competitively exclude those that preceded them (Elton 1958; OTA 1993). In the past, assemblages of organisms were markedly different from those we find today (Davis 1986; Brubaker 1988). From this we can infer that the assemblages we find today are not units composed of coevolved species strongly connected by tightly linked and delicately orchestrated interactions. There may be no eco-*systems*, in other words; there may only be shifting aggregates of entrepreneurial individuals, composing species populations, which only competitively, not cooperatively, interact.

Here, however, the ecological concept of a community is being confused with the ecological concept of an ecosystem. As Golley (1994) points out, community ecology is a biological science that proceeds, as it were, from the bottom up (beginning with organisms, aggregated into interacting species populations), while ecosystem ecology is a thermodynamical science that proceeds from the top down (beginning with solar energy driving linked processes—everything from movements of air and water to photosynthesis and respiration). It is useful to note, in this regard, that ecosystem processes may remain unaffected by dramatic changes in community composition. "For example," Allen and Hoekstra (1992, 92) point out,

the community structure of forests in the southeastern United States was radically altered by the blight that removed the American chestnut as a critical component of the canopy of the eastern deciduous biome. . . . Meanwhile, the contemporary record at the end of the last century gives no indication that ecosystem function in those same places was altered one jot, even at the height of the epidemic. The chestnut, as indicated by simulation studies, seems to have been merely one workable alternative for primary production and energy capture.

Ecosystems may not be so well integrated that they can be thought to form mature, persistent superorganisms, as Clements (1916) proposed. If not, the concept of ecosystem health is at best a metaphor, since "health" may be predicated literally only of organisms. Ecosystems, furthermore, may be emergent or epiphenomenal. Undeniably, they are dynamic, changing with time (Botkin 1990). But hierarchically linked ecological processes and functions most certainly do occur. Solar energy is captured through photosynthesis and dissipated as it passes up trophic pyramids. Mineral nutrients are extracted from the lithosphere and cycled by organisms working together, though each might be working only for itself. Biomass is produced and accumulated. Detritus is decomposed. Soil is manufactured and retained. The flow of water is modulated. Carbon, oxygen, and nitrogen are exchanged between the atmosphere and the biota. And so on. When such linked processes and functions occur normally (that is, as they have occurred historically) or change normally (that is, at the rates that they have changed historically) then ecosystems may be said to be healthy.

Spatial and temporal scale are crucial in evaluating ecosystem change whether anthropogenic or otherwise. Routine historic change is one possible measure of normality. Some routine historic changes (such as the draining of a pond caused by the breaching of a beaver dam, or the path of devastation wrought by a tornado) are sudden, but local; and some (such as sedimentation and climate change) are ubiquitous but gradual. Hence, sudden, drastic anthropogenic changes *of limited extent and frequency* are consistent with ecosystem health, as are widespread changes that are *sufficiently gradual* to permit the recruitment (or even evolution) of new conduits through which solar energy may flow, nutrients may cycle, and so on.

In sum, then, "health" may be predicated literally and paradigmatically only of organisms. But ecosystems are hardly conceived to be superorganisms, as Clements (1916) proposed. While ecosystems are autopoiêtic (self-organizing and self-renewing), they have no DNA and do not reproduce themselves—at least not in the way that organisms do. And although they may be actual biophysical entities, ecosystems are, therefore, not units of Darwinian selection. But only if we suppose that "health" were *literally* predicated of ecosystems would these dissimilarities between ecosystems and organisms fatally vitiate the concept of ecosystem health. Its leading proponents acknowledge that ecosystem health is, rather, a *metaphorical* concept (Rapport 1995).

The rhetorical purpose of the ecosystem health metaphor is to assimilate ecosystem functions to organismic functions, without claiming that the former are a special case of the latter. While few contemporary ecologists believe that ecosystems are superorganisms, no credible ecologist denies that ecosystems function—that is, that they can recruit, retain, and recycle nutrients; hold soil; modulate the flow of water; etc. And no credible ecologist denies that ecosystems can be made to fail to do such things. One could, I suppose, dispense with the metaphor and describe ecosystem functions and dysfunctions clinically. But then one could also dispense with the literal concepts of health and disease and describe organismic functions and dysfunctions clinically. In both their literal and metaphorical uses, "health" and "disease" are a sort of value-laden shorthand to characterize globally the condition, first and paradigmatically, of organisms, and, by metaphorical extension, of such things as economic systems and ecosystems.

THE CONCEPT OF HEALTH

Perhaps owing to the influence of Foucault (1974), there is some suspicion that health is not an objective state of an organism, as most people naively suppose it to be, but that, rather, health and its opposites are "socially constructed."

Indeed, there are some syndromes that seem to be altogether socially constructed. Many psychological "illnesses" are socially constructed, in the sense that a lot of the idiosyncrasies, eccentricities, and behavioral abnormalities generically labeled "mental illness" may be differently categorized, and thus rendered conceptually discontinuous with physical illnesses—as in fact they usually have been in other social and cultural contexts. Many bad habits and bad traits of character are currently being medicalized—attention deficit syndrome, say, hyperactivity, alcoholism—to relieve those who manifest them of the moral responsibility to correct them and to make weak-willed and undisciplined people appear to be victims, one suspects. And not even all *physical* syndromes are intractable to social construction and reconstruction. Is obesity, for example, a medical condition, requiring therapy, or is it, as in some societies, a sign of wealth? But some diseases won't disappear, unfortunately, if we simply recategorize them. That's too bad; we could save lots and lots of money on health care by replacing doctors and hospitals with a few rhetoricians skilled at persuading people to label their conditions more positively and accept them with pride.

It seems to be an unfortunate tendency of the Western mind to exclude the middle between two nonexclusive alternatives. Some argue, for example, that gender roles are altogether genetically programmed, while others insist that gender roles are completely socially constructed. But surely both nature and nurture play a substantial part in men's and women's different preferences and proclivities. Similarly, health seems to be a concept that designates an objective organic condition, but a concept that also seems to have sufficient indeterminacy or imprecision to allow for some personal and social determination or refinement. People in the final stages of cancer or AIDS are objectively and unequivocally ill. Socially and psychologically well-adjusted athletes in top physical condition are objectively and unequivocally healthy. What about people who have smoked cigarettes for twenty years but who, so far, have no detectable emphysema, lung cancer, or heart disease? Or people whose bodies are 30 percent fat, eat junk food, and get no vigorous exercise? Are such people healthy or unhealthy? Deciding that is what's known as a "judgment call."

If "health," when literally predicated of human beings, appears to leave considerable room for personal and social construction, then we should expect that it would allow much more room for personal and social construction when predicated metaphorically of ecosystems. Thus, Rapport (1992a, 145) somewhat recklessly declares that "a healthy ecosystem is whatever ecologists, environmentalists, and the public at large deem it to be." This ambiguous statement might be taken to mean that while ecologists and environmentalists, on the one hand, may deem an eroding clear-cut watershed drained by a silted-out (former) salmon stream to be unhealthy, the timber industry, on the other hand, may deem it to be healthy, and, through an expensive advertising campaign, convince the public at large to think so as well. So which is it: healthy, or not? One interpretation of Rapport's dictum is that objectively a forest ecosystem in such a condition is neither: Health is in the eye of the beholder. A close scrutiny of the context, however, indicates that Rapport (1992a) is not offering a radical Foucaultian account of ecosystem health. He seems to mean rather that the metaphorical concept of ecosystem health, no less than the concept of organic health proper, is partially, but not wholly, open to personal and social determination. In a subsequent essay, Rapport (1995, 13) has more carefully stated his position: "Ecosystem health is partly a matter of social values and partly a matter of the requirements for persistence or resilience of ecosystems. The fact that social values play a role has lead some to claim that any condition of the ecosystem might be found, at least by some, to be healthy. This argument ought to be rejected."

In the policy model that Rapport (1995) seems to be suggesting, ecologists and environmentalists try to determine the objective *parameters* of healthy ecosystems; and within those parameters the public at large, either through the market or through democratic political processes, can determine how ecosystems should be altered to achieve a variety of social ends. Denuded and eroding watersheds are not "healthy" simply because loggers and timber executives deem them to be, anymore than HIV hosts in the terminal stages of AIDS are healthy simply because members of ACT UP deem *them* to be. On the other hand, forest ecosystems can be managed in a variety of ways, with different outcomes, and remain within the general constraints of ecosystem health. Allen and Hoekstra's comment about the absence of ecological consequences upon the disappearance of the American chestnut from the forests of the southeastern United States suggests that silviculture in similar forests could be practiced without a reduction in primary productivity; species diversity; nutrient recruitment, retention, and cycling; pollination; decomposition; etc.—in general, without appreciably disrupting the *processes* that constitute a *functioning* forest ecosystem.

Schrecker (1994) worries that the concept of ecosystem health will abet a conspiracy to transfer the power of making land-use decisions from laypersons (where it belongs?) to environmentalists who are insidiously attempting to realize their actually subjective land-use preferences by appeal to the culturally bestowed authority of science and its pretence of objectivity. The etiology of Schrecker's phobia seems to be the aforementioned habit of either/or thinking. *Either* ecosystem health is an objective condition *or* it is socially constructed. If totally objective, then land-use decisions should be made by ecosystem ecologists and by no one else; if totally socially constructed, then such decisions should remain with the "people" and the "experts" should be dismissed as a cadre of power-hungry charlatans. But the middle path is both open and inviting: Health is an objective condition of organisms and, by metaphorical extension, of ecosystems. There remains, nonetheless, a lot of room for personal and social determination or "construction" of what constitutes both organic and ecosystemic health. Therefore, in making rational, democratic land-use decisions the roles of experts and laypersons can be regarded as cooperative and complementary rather than as competitive and mutually exclusive. The experts do their best to set out the parameters of ecosystem health and within those parameters we the people decide how we want to use and manage the ecosystems that we inhabit.

THE AXIOLOGY OF ECOSYSTEM HEALTH

"Health" is, to some degree, an objective condition of ecosystems. Is the *value*—the goodness, so to speak—of ecosystem health also objective?

Elsewhere, I argued that the concept of health was at once descriptive and prescriptive, that the condition of health was at once factual and valuable, basing my argument, in part, on historical precedent (chapter 17). Plato (1937), for example, argues that if justice is the health of the body politic and virtue is the health of the soul, then justice and virtue are unquestionably valuable. And Leopold (1949, 1991a, 1991b) extends the concept of health to "land" on the assumption that "land health" is intrinsically good and "land pathology" inherently bad. Though ecosystem health is valu*able*, in a variety of ways (including intrinsically valuable), I was careful to avoid committing myself to the *objectivity* of the value of ecosystem health—or of anything else, for that matter.

If the *value* of ecosystem health is not objective, we had damn well better take the *condition* of ecosystem health —which is, as just noted, to some considerable extent objective—into consideration, anyway, when our actions threaten it. Human economic systems are embedded in and depend upon ecosystems. If ecosystem dysfunctions become epidemic, human economic systems will therefore be imperilled. Rapport (1995) argues that healthy ecosystems supply us human beings with valuable services—such as flood control, water purification, pollination, and so on—free of charge, while such services are not rendered, or are rendered only in diminished degree, by dysfunctional ecosystems. Unhealthy ecosystems, in short, will soon engender unhealthy economic systems. In some regions of the world, advanced ecosystem morbidity has already produced massive social dislocations (Homer-Dixon 1991). Not instrumentally to value (verb transitive) ecosystem health is very imprudent.

Most—if not all—of us human beings value our own health. We do so, moreover, intrinsically as well as instrumentally. That is, although being healthy enables us to get on with our projects, we had rather be well than ill, even when we are completely idle. And the value we place on our own health transcends preferring to *feel* great rather than lousy. Hypertension, for example, is attended by no pain or discomfort. Yet many of those afflicted by it treat their hypertension with behavior modification and medicine. One may well argue that the hypertensives who do so do so from a prudential fear of a stroke—which could very well be attended by pain, disability, and death. Granted. But I still think that, over and above such prudential considerations, people value being in the pink for its own sake. Moral people, moreover, are well meaning; they intrinsically value the health of other persons as well as their own. And, notice, it is harder plausibly to reduce the way we value the health of others to instrumental or prudential concerns—such as lowering our own health insurance premiums—than it is to reduce to instrumental or prudential concerns the way we value our own health. If we can intrinsically value our own health and the health of other people, then we can also intrinsically value the "health" of ecosystems. That is, we may value (verb transitive) ecosystem health *for its own sake*—no less than we may value for its own sake our own health and the health of other people.

Nelson (1995), however, provides a new and interesting argument for the objectivity of the value of ecosystem health. Some of our most important moral concepts, Nelson points out, are "thick" descriptors with ineluctable axiological overtones. Betrayal, treachery, brutality, and wisdom, for example, all have prescriptive as well as descriptive connotations. Unfortunately, cases of betrayal, treachery, and brutality do exist, objectively, though with them too there is room for some personal and social construction. (It's currently called "spin control.") Moreover, acts of betrayal, treachery, and brutality, when they take place, are, without exception, bad (deontologically, at any rate, if not always consequentially). Wise decisions also take place in reality as well as in imagination. And wisdom per se is always a good thing. Health is also such a thick descriptor, according to Nelson. Health is a more or less objective condition of organisms; and health is, without exception, also a good thing. Thick descriptors are indivisible gestalts: description is always accompanied by prescription; fact by value. Therefore, Nelson concludes, if the health of organisms is (more or less) objective so the attendant goodness of health must also be objective. To say that health is always, without exception a good, that is, a valued thing may be to go too far. Sometimes illness is valued by some people under some circumstances (Brody 1991). But it is hard to imagine a society in which illness was the valued *norm,* in which people rejected potential spouses because they were not diseased; in which parents regularly induced diseases in their children; in which people paid premiums for disease insurance, so that they could pay physicians to make and keep them sick; and so on.

But is "health" a thick descriptor? One can no more think of an evil saint, a good act of betrayal (or treachery or brutality), or a bad wise decision than of a spherical cube. Can we think that the healthy condition of an organism is bad and its diseased condition good? Yes, we often think so. For example, when the scheme to control rabbits in Australia, by deliberately introducing myxomatosis, worked, and rabbits were succumbing to the disease in droves, doubtless most Australians and ecologists everywhere thought that that was very good. And one might well think that it were good if some brutal dictator, who was responsible for the misery of millions of people, had been found to have a cancerous brain tumor and thus that his treachery would perforce soon cease to plague the world.

However, when we examine these kinds of cases more closely, we find that health is what Nelson (1995) calls a defeasible, not an absolute, good. Only a cruel and barbarous person would think that sickness in a rabbit or in any other organism was good per se. Rabbits in Australia were deliberately, but (I hope everyone would agree) regrettably, infected with myxomatosis to achieve a *greater* good. (And that greater good was, as a matter of fact, the health of Australian ecosystems.) "Health" is a thick descriptor. That is, it is a value-laden concept. It designates a good condition of organisms and by metaphorical extension of ecosystems, but a good condition that is defeasible, that may be eclipsed by some greater good.

But is the value—the goodness and badness—indicated by thick descriptors really objective? Objectively existing values have an air of mystery about them. While I quite agree that such concepts as betrayal, treachery, brutality, wisdom, *and health* are all thick descriptors, I am not convinced that they cannot be sliced into their separate descriptive and prescriptive, ontological, and axiological components. One might say that at the level of *normative* ethical analysis they designate objective conditions or circumstances that are by their natures good or bad, respectively—and therefore they designate, a fortiori, "objective" values. One never hears a sound without both pitch and timbre or sees a color without both intensity and hue, but pitch may nevertheless be distinguished from timbre and intensity from hue. Similarly, one might also insist, at the level of *metaethical* analysis, that the descriptive and prescriptive, factual and valuational, objective and normative components of thick descriptors may be sorted out.

In what sense do thick descriptors designate "objective" values at the level of normative ethical analysis? In this sense: One feature of objective things is that they exist independently of any subject's belief, will, or feeling. Whether I believe it or not, like it or not, the Mississippi River exists. The value dimension of a thick descriptor functions like a designator of something objective, because a moral person has no choice in the matter. A moral person can like ice cream or not like it, but a moral person cannot like cruelty. A moral person can approve or disapprove of retributive punishment, but not of injustice; of fornication, but not of rape; of killing, but not of murder. A metaethical axiology that renders their value penumbra dependent on consciousness is perfectly consistent with normatively implacable thick descriptors.

Nelson (1995) frets that if we cannot make a convincing case for the proposition that the goodness of ecosystem health is literally objective, then ecosystem management and use will be held hostage to the vagaries of human whims. His example is the Chesapeake Bay. If its health is not an objective good, then how can environmentalists command the moral high ground in their campaign to get people not thoughtlessly to treat the Chesapeake as merely a sewer and a liquid highway. If my analysis is correct, ecosystem health, as a thick descriptor, is functionally equivalent to an objective value (whatever the metaethical oxymoron "objective value" may mean). Like the health of people or of rabbits, ecosystem health directly appeals to the moral sentiments of moral people (chapter 12). Ecosystem health, like the health of people or of rabbits, is intrinsically valuable— that is, valuable for its own sake.

Also like the health of people or of rabbits, ecosystem health is, however, a defeasible good. It may be compromised or sacrificed in order to achieve ends that we value more highly. But—and this is the policy difference made by the concept of ecosystem health—compromising or sacrificing ecosystem health requires sufficient justification (Fox 1993). The burden of proof shifts from those who would preserve ecosystem health to those who would, at the drop of a hat, compromise or sacrifice it (Fox 1993). No responsible person, for example, could approve visiting a myxomatosis epidemic on the well-behaved rabbit population of Canada, just for the hell of it. To assault the health of so many organisms requires considerable justification. By parity of reasoning, to assault the health of an ecosystem, such as the Chesapeake Bay, ought also to require considerable justification.

Jamieson (1995) characterizes as "quite crude" the supposition that some values are objective while others are merely subjective. Nevertheless, he seems quite content to pander to this crude supposition and, while tacitly acknowledging that all values are irredeemably subjective, considers which are and which are not, "good candidates for objectification." According to Jamieson, we are right to objectify the value of human health, but not of ecosystem health.

In standard English, something is objective if it exists independently of consciousness; something is subjective if it is dependent upon consciousness for its existence. For example, trees are objective, unless you accept George Berkeley's philosophy; and hope is subjective. (Because values so obviously depend upon consciousness for their existence is precisely why the phrase *objective values* seems mysterious, upon first hearing, and oxymoronic after philosophical reflection.) In the view that Jamieson characterizes as "quite crude," reasons, desires, dispositions, and values are subjective if they are "an individual's idiosyncratic states or preferences"; they are objective "when they are widely shared."

Should we pander to the crude and philosophically unjustifiable claim that some values—the widely shared ones—are objective, while new or unconventional values are merely subjective? I think not. All the usual arguments against cultural relativism spring to mind, especially as Jamieson declares—tacitly endorsing the vulgar view—that "objectivity is . . . the creation of a common culture and way of life." Among the ancient Greeks, slavery was a way of life, a foundational aspect of a common culture.

Hence, by Jamieson's creation-of-a-common-culture account of the objectification of values, in that time and place, the value of slavery was appropriately objectified, while on the crude view it was *objectively* good without qualification. Need I go on to mention the caste system in India, the subordination of women in Islamic societies, the suppression of human rights in China, etc., etc., etc.? And all the usual arguments against conventionalism also spring to mind. By being accorded "objectivity," values that happen to prevail at a given place and time are alleged to be part of the recalcitrant nature of things—the way the world is—while new or unconventional values are marginalized as merely "subjective," "person-specific," and "idiosyncratic." Thus does the reigning interest group in a culture silence any challenge to its preferred way of life, to business as usual. Jamieson (1995) expressly rejects "the false dichotomy that values are either a part of the fabric of the world or mere subjective states." But the dichotomy is not a false one. Values—all of them—are subjective states. To believe that some are objective is to believe falsely. To objectify values is not only deceptive, it is pernicious. Insisting upon the wholesale subjectivity of values is liberating because it allows all values—both those that are conventional and those that are not—to compete on a level playing field. *All* values are subjective, and, in this respect, all are, therefore, equal.

But how do values compete? Jamieson (1995) is quite right to think that values—though they all may be entirely subjective, as I insist—are not "arbitrary," and that "reasons can be given as to why others should value [things] in the way in which we do." Debates about values are not, that is, like disputes among children about which color is prettiest; they may be rationally resolved (chapters 5 and 6). Jamieson goes on to give some good reasons why we should value human health and the health of sentient animals. Nelson (1995) gives some good reasons why ecosystem health is valuable. What additional reasons can I give for valuing ecosystem health? Prudential reasons: Ecosystem illness threatens the human socioeconomic systems that are embedded in them and dependent upon them. Consider, for example, what is happening to the socioeconomic systems in the sick ecosystems of the Sahel in Africa (Homer-Dixon 1991). Aesthetic reasons: Healthy ecosystems, like healthy people, are more attractive than sick ones, better to look at and to be in (Francis et al. 1979; Leopold 1949). And ethical reasons: Ecosystem health is intrinsically valuable (though it may not be an objective value). Thoughtlessly mutilating ecosystems is not only imprudent, nor only offensive to a refined taste in natural objects, it is immoral. We should have the same prima facie respect for ecosystem health as we have for organismal health and compromise or sacrifice it only with sufficient justification.

BIODIVERSITY, ECOSYSTEM HEALTH, AND BIOLOGICAL INTEGRITY

"Integrity" is also a thick descriptor in conservation discourse going back at least to the United States Clean Water Act of 1972 (Karr 1981). "Biodiversity" has not been in wide use quite that long in conservation discourse, becoming common with the emergence of conservation biology in the mid-1980s (Wilson 1988). Rapport (1995) has traced the use history of "ecosystem health" in conservation discourse. When they are first iterated such concepts as biodiversity, biological integrity, and ecosystem health often only have vague respective meanings—unless those who coin such terms give them precise meanings, and everyone else who uses them conforms to the founders' definitions. "Health," as already noted, is imprecise in common parlance. "Ecosystem health" (like "biodiversity" and "biological integrity") when first iterated in conservation discourse only had a vague meaning, and is now in the process of acquiring a more precise, technical definition. Words are tools, artifacts without a predestined form, and we are free to shape them, within the loose constraints of ordinary language, to suit our purposes. I suggest that, since three distinct terms—"biodiversity," "biological integrity," and "ecosystem health," with three distinct histories of use—are presently at hand, we carefully shape each to serve a distinct and different purpose in conservation discourse.

In comparing the concepts of biodiversity and biological integrity, Angermeir and Karr (1994, 691) note that "biodiversity" when first iterated was understood to refer to numbers of species in biotic communities, but that it is now commonly used in reference to "multiple organizational levels" including genetic diversity within populations, diversity among communities of interacting populations in a landscape, diversity of landscapes within biomes, and diversity of biomes within the biosphere. Noss (1990) explicitly includes ecosystems and ecological processes in a definition of biodiversity at multiple organizational levels, but Angermeir and

Karr (1994) argue that ecological processes cannot be (or should not be) embraced by the concept of biodiversity (for reasons too technical to rehearse here): Biological "diversity [properly] describes only the elements," while biological "integrity is reflected in both the biotic elements and the processes that generate and maintain those elements," proclaim Angermeir and Karr (1994, 692).

Angermeir and Karr (1994, 692) also argue that biological integrity should replace biodiversity as the conservation concept of choice—at least among purists—because "naturally evolved assemblages possess integrity, but random assemblages do not; adding exotic species or genes from distant populations may increase local diversity, but it reduces integrity." Angermeir and Karr (1994) do not explain what they mean to indicate by "random assemblages," though "adding exotic species or genes from distant populations" is clear enough.

However biological integrity and biodiversity may differ from one another, it seems clear that both also differ from ecosystem health, as that concept is taking more definite shape. Biodiversity is clearly a concept more in keeping with the conservation desiderata suggested and supported by community or evolutionary ecology than the conservation desiderata suggested and supported by ecosystem ecology, if Angermeir and Karr (1994) are right to limit the concept of biodiversity to "elements"—that is, components: genes within populations of organisms, populations of organisms within biotic communities, biotic communities within landscapes, landscapes within biomes, and biomes within the biosphere. While Angermeir and Karr (1994) include the ecological processes that constitute ecosystems in their definition of it, two features of "biological integrity," so defined, sharply distinguish the meaning of that term from the meaning of "ecosystem health" that is taking shape in this and similar discussions.

First, "most uses of the integrity concept focus on the 'community' level of organization," while, as already noted here, most uses of the health concept relate to the ecosystem approach to comprehending nature's organization (Angermeir and Karr 1994, 692). And Angermeir and Karr (1994, 691) understand the difference exactly as reported here: "community perspectives are grounded in evolutionary biology and focus on dynamics of organism distribution and abundance; ecosystem perspectives are grounded in thermodynamics and focus on the dynamics of energy and materials through and around organisms."

Second, according to Angermeir and Karr (1994, 692), "integrity refers to conditions under little or no influence from human actions," while, as already noted here, ecosystems that have been radically altered—or even created de novo (agro-ecosystems, for example)—by human action may be healthy. The fact that nearly all biotic communities have been substantially influenced by human actions for millennia creates a dilemma for Angermeir and Karr: Either they must ignore the considerable influence of indigenous peoples in deciding which communities manifest biological integrity or they must regard such peoples as wildlife and their influence as no different from that of any other indigenous omnivore. Ignoring a significant influence on nature is bad natural science and regarding any group of people as wildlife is bad social science (as well as questionable ethics).

How to incorporate indigenous human influence into a definition of biological integrity is a problem for future philosophical research. Meanwhile, I suggest the following working definitions. Let "ecosystem health" mean a condition of normality in the linked processes and functions that compose *ecosystems*. Let "biological integrity" mean "the capability of supporting and maintaining a balanced, integrated, adaptive *community* of organisms having a species composition, diversity, and functional organization comparable to that of *natural* habitat in the region" (Angermeir and Karr 1994, 692, emphasis added). And let "biodiversity" mean the variety of *components* (or elements) at every level of biotic *community* organization.

Allen and Hoekstra's aforementioned example of the loss of the American chestnut from the forest communities of the southeastern United States, with no discernible effect on the forest ecosystems of the same region, offers a good case for exercising these terms. The integrity of the affected forest communities was certainly compromised, but the health of the forest ecosystems was not impaired (if Allen and Hoekstra are right that there were in fact no discernible ecosystemic effects). The net biodiversity of the forest community may have been reduced, with the loss of the American chestnut; or come out a wash, if we count the ascomycete that did it in as an addition; or even increased if we focus not just on the American chestnut and its nemesis but expand our inventory and count the other exotic species of flora and fauna that also invaded the community along with *Homo sapiens europi;* while the biodiversity of the planet was clearly reduced with the virtual loss of a species (the American chestnut) and with the actual loss of a distinctive community type (the pre-Columbian forest communities of southeastern North America).

So defined, biological integrity and ecosystem health are not, however, totally unrelated. The loss or significant reduction of keystone species in biotic communities (such as the alligator in the swamps of the southeastern United States); sudden, massive species extirpation in biotic communities (such as that attending the deforestation of the moist tropics); and the invasion of biotic communities by exotic species (such as the sea lamprey invasion of the Great Lakes) can have catastrophic consequences on ecosystem health. One *sure* way to maintain ecosystem health is to maintain biological integrity, a point Karr (1995) makes emphatically.

Preserving the integrity of biotic communities—more reductively, that is, preserving *native* species populations, in their characteristic numbers, with their evolved or historic interactions—is an instrumentally, aesthetically, and intrinsically valuable conservation goal parallel to the maintenance of ecosystem health (Callicott 1994; Meffe et al. 1994). The integrity of biotic communities is best secured by large reserves, from which human habitation and economic activity are excluded. But we human beings have to live somewhere and we have to make a living somehow. Ecosystem health is the appropriate conservation norm for those parts of the planet in which we human beings live and work (Costanza 1995).

Biological integrity and ecosystem health are, therefore, complementary conservation norms and together represent a coherent ideal for which we might strive in the future: To foster global biodiversity at every level of organization from gene to biome, let us set aside as many representative biotic communities as we can, and manage these nature reserves in such a way as to maintain their biological integrity. And to foster a sustainable livelihood for ourselves and for future generations of Homo sapiens, let us inhabit and exploit those ecosystems lying outside nature reserves in ways that do not compromise their health.

SUMMARY AND CONCLUSION

Ecosystems exist, although they are turning out to be nested sets of linked process-functions with temporal boundaries, not tangible superorganisms with spatial boundaries. Ecosystem health—or normal occurrence of ecological processes and functions—is an objective condition of ecosystems, although the concept of ecosystem health allows some room for personal and social determination or construction. Ecosystem health is prudentially, aesthetically, and intrinsically valuable, although the value of ecosystem health, like the value of anything else under the sun, is subjectively conferred. Biodiversity, biological integrity, and ecosystem health, while related, are not identical or interchangeable concepts. Together they represent complementary conservation norms.

19

Ecological Sustainability as a
Conservation Concept

INTRODUCTION

Like "biodiversity," "sustainability" is a buzzword in current conservation discourse. And like "biodiversity," "sustainability" evokes positive associations. According to Allen and Hoekstra (1993: 98), "everyone agrees that sustainability is a good thing." Both "sustainability" and "biodiversity," however, are at grave risk of being coopted by people primarily concerned about things other than biological conservation. As Noss (1995, 26) notes, "virtually everyone who has used the term ['sustainability'] seems to have had 'human needs and aspirations' as their primary concern." Angermeier (1994) and Angermeier and Karr (1994) point out that local biodiversity can be artificially increased (at least temporarily) by introducing nonindigenous species into a biotic community; and, indeed, sports fisherpersons more concerned about angling opportunities than about biological conservation have cloaked their argument for introducing nonindigenous game fish to the Great Lakes in the mantle of enhanced biodiversity (Thomas 1995).

One response would be for conservation biologists to write both "biodiversity" and "sustainability" off as hopelessly tainted terms. We believe that a better response would be to try to define them in ways that facilitate biological conservation and expand conservation options. Concepts (and the terms that label them) are tools. Within the limits of their etymologies and lexical definitions, terms can be defined to suit the needs and purposes of a particular discipline—conservation biology, in this case. Noss (1995) has sharpened the concept of biodiversity for purposes of biological conservation, arguing that while local biodiversity may be artificially increased, sensitive endemic species may go extinct, as a result, through competitive exclusion by weedy cosmopolitan exotics—thus diminishing landscape diversity regionally and species diversity globally. In accordance with a suggestion by Lélé and Norgaard (1996)—that scientists reflect upon and make their own values and biases clear—here we try to reshape the concept of sustainability for purposes of biological conservation. And the "discourse" of the "like-minded community" that our discussion "privileges" (Lélé and Norgaard 1996) is the international, ethnically diverse community of conservation biologists. Our discussion of the concept of sustainability is stipulative rather than descriptive. Lélé and Norgaard (1996) point out that sustainability means many different things to many different people. We are concerned less, however, with how the concept of sustainability is variously interpreted—explicitly or implicitly—and more with how it might best be crafted to serve conservation desiderata.

Two familiar conservation-related concepts sprouting from the *sustain* radical can be immediately identified: (maximum/optimum) sustained yield and sustainable development. Here we give shape to a third *sustain*-rooted conservation concept: ecological sustainability. For purposes of biological conservation, we suggest that the concept of ecological sustainability be sharply distinguished from both sustained yield and sustainable development. Both sustained yield and sustainable development, on the other hand, are associated with the human use and/or inhabitation of nature. As a member of the *sustain* family of conservation-related concepts and in deference to common usage, ecological sustainability should, therefore, also be crafted for conserving the biota of ecosystems that are humanly inhabited and economically exploited. Other concepts, such as ecological integrity, might more appropriately guide the conservation of biodiversity reserves (Woodley et al. 1993; Angermeier and Karr 1994; Westra 1994; Noss 1995).

Salwasser (1990) initiated a debate about the extent to which the concept of sustainability should guide conservation biology. He argues that achieving sustainability should be the principal goal of conservation biology (Salwasser 1990). Though Salwasser (1990, 214) proposes "to put some flesh on the skeleton of the concept of sustainability," his discussion is more programmatic than substantive. He provides, that is, no clear definition of sustainability; instead, he mostly criticizes the not-in-my-backyard (or NIMBY) attitude and the lack of effective policies to curb resource demand and encourage recycling, while insinuating that wildlands preservation may be a quixotic conservation strategy in a world that is already way overpopulated (with no end to exponential human population growth yet in sight).

Salwasser's proposal was not warmly welcomed by orthodox conservation biologists. For example, Noss (1991, 120) inveighs against "the paradigm shift" from "wilderness preservation to sustainable management" that he understands Salwasser (1990) and others (Brown 1988; USDA Forest Service 1989; Callicott 1990a) to be advocating. Noss's hostility is not unwarranted. Salwasser (1990) proffers the sustainability philosophy of conservation (however it might eventually be specified) as a successor not only to the traditional "crop-oriented" but also to the traditional "preservation-oriented" conservation philosophy. While, in respect to conservation desiderata, the concept of wilderness is problematic (Guha 1989; Callicott 1992; Denevan 1992; Gomez-Pompa and Kaus 1992; Cronon 1995), we certainly do not propose that every nook and cranny of the biosphere be humanly inhabited and exploited, provided such inhabitation and exploitation be ecologically sustainable. On the contrary, in sharp contrast to Lélé and Norgaard (1996), who demean this conservation stratagem as "police and prohibit," we emphatically endorse the establishment of biodiversity reserves (the bigger and more numerous the better), understood as areas from which human habitation and economic activities are largely if not completely excluded in order to provide habitat for viable populations of other species. Sustainably inhabiting and using some areas and establishing biodiversity reserves in others should be regarded as complementary, not as either competing or mutually exclusive, approaches to conservation. Particularly sensitive species, interior species, and species that may come into conflict with Homo sapiens need habitat that is not rendered unfit for them by human residency and/or human economic activities. We propose that ecological sustainability be the guiding conservation concept for those areas that remain humanly inhabited and economically exploited.

We develop the concept of ecological sustainability in contradistinction to the two more familiar conservation-related concepts derived from the *sustain* radical—sustained yield and sustainable development—with which it is liable to be confused. We then link ecological sustainability to another emerging conservation concept, ecosystem health. And we argue that while biological integrity may well serve as a conservation norm for areas that are preserved or protected, ecosystem health may serve as a complementary conservation norm for those humanly inhabited and used areas that we can deem to be ecologically sustainable. Finally, for purposes of illustration, we review some examples of ecologically sustainable humanly inhabited and economically exploited ecosystems.

Ecosystem health, as we explain, provides an ecological norm in reference to which the sustainability of a variety of human economic goals, determined by different groups with different cultural values and attitudes, can be measured. As Lélé and Norgaard (1996) note, lexically "sustainability is simply the ability to maintain something undiminished over some time period." Constraints that limit the ability to maintain something undiminished over some time period come in all shapes and sizes—some are economic, some political, some social, some physical, chemical, and biological. Here we restrict our discussion to the ecological constraints on the ability to maintain various culturally selected economic activities. We propose that ecological sustainability, as a conservation concept, therefore, be understood to be the maintenance, in the same place at the same time, of two interactive "things": culturally selected human economic activities and ecosystem health. The spatial scale of ecological sustainability can vary from the watershed to the biosphere. The temporal scale of ecological sustainability can also vary from the proverbial seven generations out to the indefinite future.

SUSTAINED YIELD AND SUSTAINABLE DEVELOPMENT

As Salwasser (1990) and Callicott (1990b) indicate, two conservation philosophies dominated the first three quarters of the twentieth century: resource conservation (resourcism) and wilderness preservation (preservationism). Resourcism is thoroughly anthropocentric: nature is valued only to the extent that it is humanly useful. In the resourcist view, some "natural resources" (such as fossil fuels) are assumed to be finite and nonrenewable; others (such as metals) are assumed to be finite, but recyclable; and still others (such as usable trees, huntable wildlife, and edible fishes) are regarded as indefinitely renewable, either through natural or artificial propagation. One primary desideratum of resource conservation is to achieve sustained yield of these renewable natural resources—be they Douglas firs, white-tailed deer, or sockeye salmon. Biotic communities and ecosystems are valued only incidentally. If their existence is acknowledged at all, they are treated as the machinery that produces the goods.

Larkin (1977, 1) characterizes the concept of sustained yield thus: "any species each year produces a harvestable surplus, and if you take that much and no more, you can go on getting it forever and ever." In addition to the recruitment rates of the targeted species populations, the theoretical models of sustained yield are complicated by such biological variables as the growth rates and optimum harvest sizes and ages of the targeted organisms (Larkin 1977). Without criticizing resourcism per se, Larkin (1977) reviews the biological, ecological, and socioeconomic factors that render the concepts of maximum and optimum sustained yield problematic. But even if the concept of sustained yield were to be successfully operationalized, it would hardly be adequate for biological—as opposed to resource—conservation. Most species are not harvestable resources. And most of the species in danger of genetic impoverishment, local extirpation, and global extinction are not at risk because they are being overharvested, but because their habitats are being polluted and destroyed (Ehrlich 1988).

As sustained yield is historically wedded to resourcism, the more recently fashioned concept of sustainable development is betrothed to neoclassical economics—though environmental and ecological economists are rising to speak out against the marriage (Costanza and Daly 1992).

In the vernacular, "development" often means the wholesale replacement of wild biotic communities with tract houses, shopping malls, office buildings, industrial "parks," and pavement. The term is also often used to refer to a shift from subsistence-oriented foraging or agrarian economies (many of which are ecologically sustainable) to money-oriented market economies—as when "Third World" nations are said to undergo "development." "Development" thus commonly denotes urbanization, the industrialization of agriculture, and, more abstractly, an expanding market economy. Hence it is not surprising that "sustainable development" has been interpreted to mean sustaining (at least until the next election) economic growth (Clinton and Gore 1992). So interpreted, the concept is antithetical to the concerns of conservation (Willers 1994): It implies an indefinite expansion of areas covered by lifeless manufactured materials (such as concrete, glass, asphalt, and lumber) or by living monocultures of domesticated plants (such as eucalyptus trees, soybeans, and maize), and a corresponding indefinite shrinkage of diverse forests, grasslands, and other "undeveloped" landscapes, many of them humanly inhabited by foragers and subsistence agriculturists (O'Neal et al. 1995).

Hoping to rescue the concept of sustainable development from conflation with indefinitely sustained economic growth, Costanza and Daly (1992) carefully distinguish between economic growth and economic development. In their account, growth consists of "pushing more matter-energy through the economy," while development consists of "squeezing more human want satisfaction out of each unit of matter-energy that passes through" (Costanza and Daly 1992, 43). Unsustainable economic growth is tantamount to increased throughput; sustainable economic development is tantamount to increased efficiency.

We might add that a no-growth conception of sustainable development should also involve a reassessment of human wants. Suppose people started wanting fewer material goods (such as superfluous gadgets and appliances) and more amenities (such as clean air and water) and services (such as education and information). Jobs would be created (in fields such as ecological restoration and computer programming). Profits would be made. That would be economic development. But it would be achieved less through efficiency than through a demand-driven shift from an environmentally destructive manufacturing/consuming economy to an environmentally benign amenity/service economy.

Another aspect of steady-state sustainable development might involve the concentration and miniaturization of the human sphere. Suppose people started wanting to more densely inhabit cozier spaces proximate to pedestrian-scaled shops, restaurants, saloons, theaters, and other urban attractions. Suburban and exurban sprawl would be reversed; and the living space available for nonhuman species might increase proportionately.

Further, the need for transportation would be reduced, also reducing all the untoward environmental consequences of manufacturing and powering automobiles.

Beginning with the Brundtland Report (World Commission on Environment and Development 1987) and culminating in the 1992 United Nations Conference on Environment and Development in Rio de Janeiro, economic development and environmental quality have been positively linked. "Sustainable development" has thus been commonly understood to mean economic development that does not appreciably harm the natural environment (World Resources Institute 1992). The definition of 'sustainable development' in *Our Common Future*—"development that meets the needs of the present without compromising the ability of future generations to meet their own needs"—has been widely accepted as authoritative (Willers 1994). Note, however, that this definition includes no reference to environmental quality, biological integrity, ecosystem health, or biodiversity.

Further, the axiom of substitutability, fundamental to neoclassical economics, makes the definition of "sustainable development" in the Brundtland Report—a definition that is rapidly becoming standard—particularly ominous, from a conservation point of view. In the world according to neoclassical economics, as a heavily exploited natural resource becomes scarce its price increases, making investment in finding or inventing a substitute increasingly attractive (Barnett and Morse 1963). From this point of view, there is no reason to conserve any particular natural resource. When we begin to run short of copper for making telephone wires, someone will (as indeed someone did) invent fiber optics. Such accumulated anecdotal evidence suggests that market forces will always stimulate the discovery or invention of substitutes for any natural resource—from petroleum to Madagascar periwinkles. According to this way of thinking, we can, therefore, meet the needs of the present by rapidly exploiting current organic natural resources to commercial if not to biological extinction and bequeath a legacy of wealth and technology and a culture of business and inventiveness to future generations—by means of which they can meet their own needs. As Willers (1994) suggests, in the Brundtland Report, 'sustainable development' means pretty much business as usual.

ECOLOGICAL SUSTAINABILITY

While technological optimists may suppose that substitutes for the current inventory of natural resources can be discovered or invented, no one, to our knowledge, has suggested that substitutes for ecological services—such as pollination, nitrogen fixation, water purification, and so on—can be invented. Indeed, some ecologists and conservationists have pointed out that it is preposterous to suppose that engineers can devise artificial substitutes for the ecological processes and functions in the economy of nature that provide free services to the human economy (Ehrlich 1989; Kaufmann 1995). Though it too has been the subject of strident criticism by conservationists (Robinson 1993a; Willers 1994), another influential international document, *Caring for the Earth*, (International Union for the Conservation of Nature and Natural Resources/United Nations Environmental Program/The World Wide Fund for Nature 1991) provides a more conservation-friendly account of sustainability than does *Our Common Future*. Its subtitle is "A Strategy for Sustainable Living," not "A Strategy for Sustainable Development." Sustainable living, as opposed to sustainable development, might be understood as human economic activity that does not seriously disrupt ecological processes and functions; or, alternatively, as devising artificial ecosystems (human economies) that are symbiotically adapted to proximate natural ecosystems as sketched by Jackson (1980; 1987).

Following a suggestion by Robinson (1993b), we propose that the goal of biological conservation be pursued on two fronts simultaneously. The first approach is consonant with the century-old American preservationist tradition and depends principally on biodiversity reserves. Classic preservationism was, with few exceptions (Muir 1916), valuatively anthropocentric. Areas were set aside primarily for human recreation, esthetic enjoyment, and spiritual elevation (Foreman 1995a). Biological conservation was a side effect (Foreman 1995b). The contemporary preservationist approach differs from its early-twentieth-century antecedent in being biocentric (Noss 1995). The biota is valued for its own sake. Accordingly, priority is assigned to biological conservation over recreation and other nonconsumptive human uses of protected areas, and reserves are selected, delimited, connected, and managed in accordance with the best available science, irrespective of their conventional recreational, esthetic, or spiritual appeal (Foreman et al. 1992). Though use-oriented, the second approach is not an extension of the century-old resourcist tradition. Rather, it emerges from a more recently evolved conception of nature as a hierarchically integrated set of ecosystems (Allen and Starr 1982; O'Neill et al. 1986; Allen and Hoekstra 1992) in which human economies are inescapably embedded (Costanza and Daly 1992; Allen and Hoekstra 1993).

We propose that ecological sustainability be the paradigm for this second approach to biological conservation. This approach is complementary to—not a substitute for—the contemporary preservation-oriented approach. Human economic activities have traditionally—in theory, at least—been limited by an economic constraint: the bottom line. A proposed development—be it a hydroelectric impoundment in the Amazon or a shopping mall in Arizona—is deemed unworthy of undertaking if its costs will exceed its returns on investment. Following Charles (1994), we suggest that, in addition to this familiar economic constraint, human activities also be judged by an ecologic constraint: ecological sustainability. A proposed economic venture—be it the reestablishment of harvestable herds of native ungulates on the North American great plains or the creation of an agroforest in Thailand—should be deemed unworthy of undertaking not only if its costs exceed its benefits, but if it will compromise the health of the (relatively) macroscale ecosystems in which it is embedded and the (relatively) microscale ecosystems on which it is imposed.

This ecological interpretation of sustainability thus interfaces with another inchoate conservation concept—ecosystem health. The concept of ecosystem health, however, is also in process of refinement and elaboration (Costanza et al. 1992; Callicott 1995; Rapport et al. 1995). The coupling of ecological sustainability and ecosystem health is parallel to the coupling of biological preservation and ecological integrity by Angermeier and Karr (1994) and Noss (1995). Following Angermeier and Karr (1994), let ecological integrity denote the historic species composition and structure of biotic communities. Humanly inhabiting and economically exploiting an area will necessarily compromise its ecological integrity, except if such inhabitation and exploitation be extremely diffuse, surgical, or primitive (Robinson 1993a). A mesoscale ecosystem may remain healthy, however, even when the mesoscale complement of species it comprises have been altered to suit human specifications (Rapport 1995a; Rapport 1995b). That is, ecological processes such as primary production, nutrient retention and cycling, nitrogen fixing, soil stabilizing, water purification, etc., can occur normally when less desirable species are carefully replaced by more desirable ones—desirability to be determined politically and economically (Rapport 1995a; Rapport 1995b). We therefore suggest that sustainable human inhabitation and economic land use (and water use) be understood as inhabitation and use that may to some degree compromise ecological integrity—the less so the better—but that may not appreciably compromise ecosystem health.

Ecological sustainability and its associated norm, ecosystem health, have both anthropocentric and ecocentric value dimensions. Humanly inhabited and economically exploited ecosystems produce not only instrumentally valuable goods (food, fodder, thatch, fuelwood, etc.), but, if healthy, they may also afford instrumentally valuable services (clean air, potable water, flood control, crop pollination, various amenities). In sharp contrast to Lélé and Norgaard (1996), who dismiss the idea that "Earth's natural processes and biodiversity [are] inherently good, even if there were no human beings on the planet to benefit from these phenomena" as being "absurd when presented so baldly," we assert that ecosystems and their component processes are intrinsically as well as instrumentally valuable. As Noss (1995, 26) notes "Sustainability need not be interpreted anthropocentrically.... A biocentric or holistic concept of sustainability focuses on sustaining natural ecosystems and all their components for their own sake, with human uses included only when they are entirely compatible with conservation of the native biota and natural processes." We agree with this statement, with one proviso—that the "components" of ecosystems are understood to be ecological processes, not the several sets of species that compose various biotic communities. In our account of ecological sustainability, the components of biotic communities and the native biota may be intrinsically valued, but only subordinately or secondarily—to the extent that they are functional moments in ecosystems—while in our account of ecological integrity, as in that of Angermeier and Karr (1994), Westra (1994), and Noss (1995), the components of biotic communities and the native biota have primary, unqualified intrinsic value. This ecocentric valuation—from the perspective of the ecological sustainability/ ecosystem health conceptual complex—principally of ecosystems and ecological processes is not arbitrary. It devolves from a hierarchical ecosystem worldview, in which ecological entities are defined and delimited in terms of trophic-dynamic processes and functions, such as nutrient cycling, not in terms of interacting populations of organisms (Allen and Starr 1982; O'Neill et al. 1986; Allen and Hoekstra 1992). Allen and Hoekstra (1992, 92) provide a dramatic illustration of the difference between the population-community and ecosystem perspectives in ecology:

The community structure of forests in the southeastern United States was radically altered by the blight that removed the American chestnut as a critical component of the canopy of the eastern deciduous biome. . . . Meanwhile, the contemporary record at the end of the last century gives no indication that ecosystem function in those same places was altered one jot, even at the height of the epidemic. The chestnut, as indicated by simulation studies, seems to have been merely one workable alternative for primary production and energy capture.

If Allen and Hoekstra here have their facts straight, from the point of view of community ecology the chestnut blight was an ecological disaster, while from the point of view of ecosystem ecology, far from a disaster, it was virtually a nonevent. Other canopy dominants stepped forward to take over the erstwhile role of the chestnut in primary production, nutrient recruitment, soil stabilization, etc.

Noss (1995, 21) explains the distinction between the health of ecosystems and the integrity of biotic communities in logical terms: "health is necessary for integrity, [but] it is not sufficient," while ecological integrity is sufficient for ecosystem health, but not necessary (Westra 1994). And Noss's hypothetical illustration of the difference is more extreme than Allen and Hoekstra's (1992) historical illustration: "One can imagine many ecosystems that are quite healthy yet lack integrity. A tree farm, for example, might be considered healthy if it vigorously adds biomass, but it surely lacks integrity. Many species could be lost from an ecosystem before any overt signs of ill-health are evident; but with each loss of a native species the integrity of the ecosystem declines" (Noss 1995, 21).

The real world is one. Historically, however, ecologists have modelled it in two fundamentally different ways—biologically and thermodynamically (Elton 1927; Lindeman 1942). According to the "bottom up" biological approach, the fundamental entities treated by ecology are organisms, aggregated into gene-exchanging species populations, interacting in biotic communities (Begon et al. 1986). The extirpation of a species population or extinction of a species globally, from the point of view of community ecology, is a signal event; it represents the erasure of a fundamental bio-ecological unit (Wilson 1992). According to the second, "top down" thermodynamical approach, the fundamental entities treated by ecology are ecosystems, the components of which are not organisms, species populations, and biotic communities, but multiscaled interacting processes, such as photosynthesis, energy transfer from one trophic level to the next, and nutrient cycling (Allen and Starr 1982; O'Neill et al. 1986; Allen and Hoekstra 1992). The specific identity of the organisms that are moments in these processes is incidental and the loss or replacement of one by another is often of little consequence (except when function is interrupted and impaired) and therefore of little ecological interest—or concern (Allen and Hoekstra 1993). These two approaches to ecology—the biologic and thermodynamic—are not competing, but complementary. They are two equally valid ways of modelling the same reality.

We propose a corresponding doctrine of complementarity in conservation biology. The norm for biodiversity reserves, in which human inhabitation and use are severely restricted, should be ecological integrity. The norm for sustainably inhabited and used ecosystems should be ecosystem health.

APPLICATIONS

How can these conservation concepts be applied in the real world? Like the neopreservationist program (Foreman et al. 1992), ecological sustainability in humanly inhabited and economically exploited ecosystems is a long-range conservation goal that can only be achieved, given where we have to start, gradually and incrementally. The global biosphere reserve initiative embodies, in a microcosm, the complementary, two-front approach to conservation that we are recommending here. The biosphere reserve model differs from the classic national park, wildlife sanctuary, or designated wilderness area model by including, in addition to a strictly protected core area, humanly inhabited and economically exploited buffer and transition zones (von Droste 1988). The core zones of a global system of biosphere reserves are intended to slow the loss of biological diversity and integrity. The buffer and transition zones of biosphere reserves can complement the core zones in two ways: first, by insulating the cores from various outside threats, and second, by serving as laboratories for exploring ecologically sustainable forms of human livelihood. We hope that, eventually, protected areas will be enlarged as envisioned in the Wildlands Project (Foreman et al. 1992). We also hope that all the remaining humanly inhabited and economically exploited regions of the earth will, eventually, be humanly inhabited and economically exploited sustainably. In the meantime, we suggest that, by way of a start, the conservation norm for the humanly inhabited and economically exploited buffer and transition zones of biosphere reserves be ecological sustainability, as defined here in terms of ecosystem health.

Establishing biosphere reserve cores, while politically the most difficult, is technically the least difficult part of setting up a biosphere reserve program. You identify areas that are unusually diverse or that contain endemic, rare, or endangered species and exclude as much area as you can from human habitation and use (Noss 1995). We do not mean to minimize the challenge of effectively managing core zones of biosphere reserves, especially if they remain small and subject to the effects of illegal human encroachment, air and water borne industrial pollutants, and invasive nonindigenous species. But the challenge of figuring out ecologically sustainable economic activities for the matrices surrounding biosphere reserve cores—the buffer and transition zones—has been daunting (Batisse 1993). Nevertheless, there are some examples of ecologically sustainable ways of humanly inhabiting and economically exploiting ecosystems and we mention a few of them here to illustrate the ecological sustainability/ecosystem health conceptual complex in action.

An example of sustainable forestry may be found on the Menominee Indian reservation in northeastern Wisconsin. The 100,000-hectare Menominee forest, managed by Menominee Tribal Enterprises, produces more sawlogs than the contiguous 265,000-hectare Nicolet National Forest, managed by the USDA Forest Service (Davis 1998). Yet the selectively harvested old-growth Menominee forest has more large, late-successional trees (characteristic of the Northern Hardwoods-Hemlock-White Pine association), is more dense, and has a more diverse mix of species, than the adjoining national forest (Alverson et al. 1994; Davis 1998). The presence of large organisms and species diversity is indicative of ecosystem health (Rapport 1995a, 1995b). Preservation of the historic biotic community structure and harvest of forest products in perpetuity are the express priorities of Menominee forest management, to which turning a profit for Menominee Tribal Enterprises is subordinate (Davis 1998).

In the humid northeastern hill region of India, forest dwellers have employed a traditional method of shifting agriculture called *jhum* for centuries (Ramakrishnan 1992). Traditional *jhum* agriculture employs mixed cropping practices, which are both economically and ecologically sustainable. As the system has evolved, a wide variety of cultivars form multiple layers of leaves, with a high leaf area index, topped by a canopy; underground, a similarly tiered root mass optimizes water and nutrient uptake (Ramakrishnan 1992). These artificial ecosystems are punctuated by fallows colonized by uncultivated species on a ten-year cycle. *Jhum* agroecosystems are characterized by indicators of ecosystem health as identified by Rapport (1995a; 1995b)—species diversity, complex community structure, high rates of primary productivity, and accumulation of biomass—that are comparable to those in old-field uncultivated plant formations (Ramakrishnan 1992).

Agroforestry combines cultivation of tree species with annual and perennial crops. Deep-rooted trees make subsurface nutrients available to annuals, while legumes supply their neighbors with nitrogen (National Research Council 1993). In addition to the ecological services they provide, the woody species composing these artificial ecosystems may be chosen to provide fodder for livestock. A particular type of agroforestry, practiced on several farms in Nigeria, is called alley cropping, in which annual crops, such as maize, are grown between rows of trees or shrubs that build and hold topsoil and recruit and retain nutrients (Plucknett 1990). Soil stability and nutrient recruitment and cycling are, again, indicators of ecosystem health (Rapport 1995a; Rapport 1995b).

In the U.S. Midwest, "conventional" dairy and beef operations—characterized by high inputs of fossil fuels, fertilizers, and pesticides for growing row crops, and large enclosed pastures for continuous grazing—lead to soil compaction and losses from the soil of organic matter, nutrients, and microorganisms (National Research Council 1989). Increased compaction and reduced organic matter in the soil reduce water infiltration and retention and increase runoff, disrupting the normal hydrology at the landscape scale in which the cultivated and continuously grazed patches are embedded (National Research Council 1989). Loss of soil microorganisms impedes the breakdown of crop residues and animal waste, and, therefore, disrupts nutrient cycling (National Research Council 1989). These are all indications of ecosystem dysfunction or ill-health (Rapport 1995a, 1995b).

Several farmers in southern Minnesota have converted from such conventional methods to a regime called the "management intensive grazing system," in which land is relieved of row crops and continuous grazing and converted to pasture divided into paddocks (Land Stewardship Project 1995). Animals are rotated between paddocks, based on farmers' observations of stand quality. Preliminary studies indicate that timely movement of animals prevents overgrazing. Prevention of overgrazing reduces soil compaction and erosion. Elimination of chemical fertilizers, pesticides, and herbicides and reduced soil compaction allows microorganisms to flourish, thereby restoring normal decomposition of animal waste and plant detritus—and thus restoring normal nutrient cycling. Reduced soil compaction improves water infiltration and retention—thus restoring normal hydrologic processes. Farmers practicing management intensive grazing note an increase in the diversity of plant species in their pastures and observations of increased numbers of grassland birds suggest that these pastures are being used as nesting sites. Soil stability and flocculation, hydrologic modulation, nutrient retention and cycling, complex community structure, and biological diversity at every scale—from microorganisms to migratory avifauna—are all, once more, indications of ecosystem health (Rapport 1995a, 1995b).

CONCLUSION

For nearly a century, conservation philosophy has been divided into two schools of thought—resourcism and preservationism. These two philosophies of conservation are mutually incompatible. The former understood conservation to mean maximum sustained yield of renewable resources (along with equitable distribution of the spoils), the latter understood conservation to mean excluding human inhabitation and economic exploitation from remaining areas of undeveloped nature. From the point

of view of contemporary conservation biology, classic resourcism is hopelessly reductive and ignores nonresources (Ehrenfeld 1976), while classic
preservationism was driven by nonbiological concerns—for such things
as scenery, solitude, and recreation (Foreman 1995a). More recently,
preservationism has been retooled and adapted to conservation biology
(Foreman et al. 1992; Foreman 1995b). Though they may still be scenic
and inspiring, national parks, designated wilderness areas, and the other
legacies of the historic nature preservation movement now have another,
more vital conservation role to play—as reservoirs of biodiversity and ecological integrity (Foreman et al. 1992; Foreman 1995a; Foreman 1995b).
We endorse the goal of the Wildlands Project, which is to expand the
areas from which human habitation and economic exploitation are largely
excluded. But we think that conservation efforts should also target the
extensive areas that are humanly inhabited and economically exploited.

Resourcism is beyond rehabilitation as a contemporary philosophy of
biological conservation. Instead, we suggest a new approach to conserving humanly inhabited and economically exploited ecosystems under the
rubric of 'ecological sustainability.' The neopreservationist approach to
conservation is informed principally by population biology and evolutionary and community ecology. And it aims at preserving ecological integrity (Angermeier and Karr 1994; Noss 1995) and biodiversity at every
organizational level (Noss 1990). The sustainability approach is informed
principally by hierarchy theory and more generally ecosystem ecology and
aims at preserving ecosystem health—that is, normal ecological processes
and functions, irrespective of which species perform them. But just as a
whole and complete science of ecology must integrate the community
and ecosystem perspectives (Allen and Hoekstra 1992), so must a whole
and complete conservation biology embrace both preserving biodiversity
and ecological integrity, on the one hand, and sustaining ecosystem health,
on the other. For the sake of clarity, we have illustrated these complementary approaches to biological conservation in reference to reserve cores
and their humanly inhabited and exploited matrices, respectively, but
biodiversity and sustainability, ecological integrity and ecosystem health
are not unrelated. Areas that retain their biological diversity and ecological integrity are quite likely to comprise healthy ecosystems (Noss 1995),
and one indicator of ecosystem health is biological diversity (Rapport
1995a, 1995b).

BIBLIOGRAPHY

Aiken, W. 1984. "Ethical Issues in Agriculture." In *Earthbound: New Introductory Essays in Environmental Ethics,* edited by T. Regan, 74–288. New York: Random House.

Albanese, C. L. 1990. *Nature Religion in America: From the Algonkian Indians to the New Age.* Chicago: University of Chicago Press.

Allen, T. F. H., and T. B. Starr. 1982. *Hierarchy: Perspectives for Ecological Complexity.* Chicago: University of Chicago Press.

Allen, T. F. H., and T. W. Hoekstra, 1992. *Toward a Unified Ecology.* New York: Columbia University Press.

———. 1993. "Toward a Definition of Sustainability." In *Sustainable Ecological Systems: Implementing an Ecological Approach to Land Management,* edited by W. W. Covington, and L. F. Debano, 98–107. Fort Collins, Colo.: Rocky Mountain Forest and Range Experiment Station, USDA.

Alexander, S. 1968. *Beauty and Other Forms of Value.* New York: Thomas Y. Crowell.

Alverson, W. S., W. Kuhlman, and D. M. Waller. 1994. *Wild Forests: Conservation Biology and Public Policy.* Washington, D.C.: Island Press.

Angermeier, P. L. 1994. "Does Biodiversity Include Artificial Diversity?" *Conservation Biology* 8:600–602.

Angermeir, P. L., and J. R. Karr. 1994. "Biological Integrity Versus Biological Diversity as Policy Directives: Protecting Biotic Resources." *Bioscience* 44:690–97.

Attfield, R. 1981. "The Good of Trees." *The Journal of Value Inquiry* 15:35–54.

———. 1983. *The Ethics of Environmental Concern*. New York: Columbia University Press.

Bakr, A., A. B. Kader, A. L. T. E. S. A. Sabbagh, M. A. S. A. Glenid, and M. Y. S. Izzidien, eds. 1983. *Islamic Principles for the Conservation of the Natural Environment*. Gland, Switzerland: IUCN.

Badè, W. F. 1916. Foreword to *A Thousand-Mile Walk to the Gulf*, by J. Muir. Edited by W. F. Badè. Boston: Houghton Mifflin.

Barnett, J., and C. Morse. 1963. *Scarcity and Growth: The Economics of Natural Resource Availability*. Baltimore: Johns Hopkins University Press.

Barr, J. 1972. "Man and Nature: The Ecological Controversy and the Old Testament." *Bulletin of the John Rylands Library* 55:9–32.

Batisse, M. 1993. "Biosphere Reserves: An Overview." *Nature and Resources* 29:3–5.

Baxter, W. F. 1974. *People or Penguins: The Case for Optimal Pollution*. New York: Columbia University Press.

Begon, M., J. L. Harper, and C. R. Townsend. 1986. *Ecology: Individuals, Populations, and Communities*. Sunderland, Mass: Sinauer Associates.

Bentham, J. 1823. *An Introduction to the Principles of Morals and Legislation*. Oxford: Clarendon Press.

Berry, W. 1981. *The Gift of Good Land*. San Francisco: North Point Press.

Black, J. 1970. *The Dominion of Man: The Search for Ecological Responsibility*. Edinburgh: Edinburgh University Press.

Bohm, D. 1977. "Science as Perception-Communication." In *The Structure of Scientific Theories*, edited by F. Suppe, 2d ed., 376–91. Urbana: University of Illinois Press.

———. 1983. *Wholeness and the Implicate Order*. London: Routledge and Kegan Paul.

Bonnicksen, T. M. 1990. "Restoring Biodiversity in Park and Wilderness Areas: An Assessment of the Yellowstone Wildfires." In *Wilderness Areas: their Impacts*, edited by A. Rassmusen, 25–32. Logan: Utah State University Cooperative Extension Service.

Bormann, F. H., and G. E. Likens. 1967. "Nutrient Cycling." *Science* 155:424–29.

———. 1979. *Pattern and Process in a Forested Ecosystem*. New York: Springer-Verlag.

Botkin, D. 1990. *Discordant Harmonies: A New Ecology for the Twenty-first Century*. New York: Oxford University Press.

Brennan, A. 1988. *Thinking About Nature: An Investigation of Nature, Value, and Ecology*. Athens: University of Georgia Press.

———. 1992. "Moral Pluralism and the Environment." *Environmental Values* 1:15–33.

Brody, H. 1987. *Stories of Sickness*. New Haven: Yale University Press.

Brown, J. H. 1988. "Alternative Conservation Priorities and Practices." Paper presented at 73rd Annual Meeting, Ecological Society of America, Davis, California, August 1988.

Brubaker, L. B. 1988. "Vegetation History and Anticipating Future Vegetation Change." In *Ecosystem Management for Parks and Wilderness*, edited by J. K. Agee, 42–58. Seattle: University of Washington Press.

Burtt, E. A. 1954. *The Metaphysical Foundations of Modern Science*. Garden City, N.Y.: Anchor Books.

Cahen, H. 1988. "Against the Moral Considerability of Ecosystems." *Environmental Ethics* 10:195–216.

Callicott, J. B. 1979. "Elements of an Environmental Ethic: Moral Considerability and the Biotic Community." *Environmental Ethics* 1:71–81

———. 1980. "Animal Liberation: A Triangular Affair." *Environmental Ethics* 2:311–38.

———. 1982. "Hume's Is/Ought Dichotomy and the Relation of Ecology to Leopold's Land Ethic." *Environmental Ethics* 4:163–74.

———. 1984. "Non-anthropocentric Value Theory and Environmental Ethics." *American Philosophical Quarterly* 21:299–309.

———. 1985. "Intrinsic Value, Quantum Theory, and Environmental Ethics." *Environmental Ethics* 7:275–85.

———. 1986. "The Search for an Environmental Ethic." In *Matters of Life and Death*, edited by T. Regan, 2d ed., 381–424. New York: Random House.

———. 1987. "The Conceptual Foundations of the Land Ethic." In *Companion to "A Sand County Almanac": Interpretive and Critical Essays*, edited by J. B. Callicott, 186–217. Madison: University of Wisconsin Press.

———. 1988. "Animal Liberation and Environmental Ethics: Back Together Again." *Between the Species* 4:163–69.

———. 1989. *In Defense of the Land Ethic: Essays in Environmental Philosophy*. Albany: State University of New York Press.

———. 1990a. "Standards of Conservation: Then and Now." *Conservation Biology* 4:229–32.

———. 1990b. "Whither Conservation Ethics?" *Conservation Biology* 4:15–20.

———. 1991. "The Wilderness Idea Revisited: The Sustainable Development Alternative." *Environmental Professional* 13:235–47.

———. 1994. "Conservation Values and Ethics." In *Principles of Conservation Biology*, edited by G. K. Meffe and C. R. Carroll, 24–49. Sunderland, Mass.: Sinauer Associates.

———. 1995. "Some Problems with the Concept of Ecosystem Health." *Ecosystem Health* 1:101–12.

Callicott, J. B., and R. T. Ames. 1989. "Epilogue: On the Relations of Idea and Action." In *Nature in Asian Traditions of Thought: Essays in Environmental Philosophy*, edited by J. B. Callicott and R. T. Ames, 279–89. Albany: State University of New York Press.

Callicott, J. B., and T. W. Overholt. 1993. "American Indian Attitudes toward Nature." In *Philosophy from Africa to Zen: An Invitation to World Philosophy*, edited by R. C. Solomon and K. M. Higgins, 55–80. Lanham, Md.: Rowman and Littlefield.

Capra, F. 1982. *The Turning Point: Science, Society and the Rising Culture.* New York: Simon and Schuster.

Chandler, J. 1991. "Ethical Philosophy." In *The Sociobiological Imagination*, edited by M. Maxwell. Albany: State University of New York Press.

Charles, A. T. 1994. "Towards Sustainability: The Fishery Experience." *Ecological Economics* 11:201–11.

Cheney, J. 1989a. "Postmodern Environmental Ethics: Ethics as Bioregional Narrative." *Environmental Ethics* 11:117–34.

———. 1989b. "The Neo-Stoicism of Radical Environmentalism." *Environmental Ethics* 11:293–325.

Clements, F. E. 1916. *Plant Succession: An Analysis of the Development of Vegetation.* Washington, D.C.: Carnegie Institution.

Clinton, B., and A. Gore. 1992. *Putting People First: How We Can All Change America.* New York: Time Books.

Cohen, M. P. 1984. *The Pathless Way: John Muir and the American Wilderness.* Madison: University of Wisconsin Press.

Comstock, G. L. 1995. "Do Agriculturalists Need a New, an Ecocentric Ethic?" *Agriculture and Human Values* 12:2–15.

Connell, J. H., and R. O. Slatyer. 1977. "Mechanisms of Succession in Natural Communities and their Role in Community Stability and Organization." *American Naturalist* 111:1119–44.

Cornford, F. M. 1952. *Principia Sapientia: The Origins of Greek Philosophical Thought.* Cambridge: Cambridge University Press.

Costanza, R. 1995. "Ecological and Economic System Health and Social De-
cision Making." In *Evaluating and Monitoring the Health of Large-Scale
Ecosystems,* edited by D. J. Rapport, C. Gaudet, and P. Calow, 103–26.
Heidelberg: Springer-Verlag.

Costanza, R., and H. E. Daly. 1992. "Natural Capital and Sustainable Development." *Conservation Biology* 6:37–46.

Costanza, R., B. G. Norton, and B. D. Haskell. 1992. *Ecosystem Health: New
Goals for Environmental Management.* Washington, D.C.: Island Press.

Cronon, W. 1995. "The Trouble with Wilderness: Or Getting Back to the
Wrong Nature." In *Uncommon Ground: Toward Reinventing Nature,* edited by W. Cronon, 23–90. New York: W. W. Norton.

Degan, H., A. V. Holden, and L. F. Olsen. 1987. *Chaos in Biological Systems.*
New York: Plenum Press.

Darwin, C. R. 1871. *The Descent of Man and Selection in Relation to Sex.*
London: J. Murray.

Davis, M. B. 1984. "Climatic Instability, Time Lags, and Community
Disequilibrium." In *Community Ecology,* edited by J. Diamond and T. J.
Case,269–84. New York: Harper and Row.

Davis, T. 1998. *Sustaining the Forest, the People, and the Spirit.* Albany: State
University of New York Press.

Dawkins, R. 1976. *The Selfish Gene.* New York: Oxford University Press.

Denevan, W. 1992. "The Pristine Myth: The Landscape of the Americas in
1492." *Annals of the Association of American Geographers* 82:369–85.

Derrida, J. 1981. *Positions.* Translated by A. Bass. Chicago: University of Chicago Press.

Descartes, R. 1641. *Meditations de Prima Philosophia.* Paris: Michaelem Soly.

Devall, B., and G. Sessions, 1985. *Deep Ecology: Living as if Nature Mattered.*
Salt Lake City: Peregrine Smith Books.

Dobel, P. 1994. "The Judeo-Christian Stewardship Attitude Toward Nature."
In *Environmental Ethics: Readings in Theory and Application,* edited by
Louis P. Pojman, 20–24. Boston: Jones and Bartlett.

Dobyns, H. F. 1966. "Estimating Aboriginal American Population: An Appraisal of Techniques with a New Hemispheric Estimate." *Current Anthropology* 7:395–412.

Ehrenfeld, D. W. 1976. "The Conservation of Non-resources." *American Scientist* 64:647–55

———. 1988. "Why Put a Value on Biodiversity?" In *Biodiversity,* edited by
E. O. Wilson, 212–16. Washington, D.C.: National Academy Press.

————. 1989. "Life in the Next Millennium: Who Will Be Left in the Earth's Community?" *Orion Nature Quarterly* 8, no. 2:4–13.

Ehrenfeld, D. W., and P. J. Bently. 1985. "Judaism and the Practice of Stewardship." *Judaism: A Quarterly Journal of Jewish Life and Thought* 34:301–11.

Ehrlich, P. R. 1988. "The Loss of Diversity: Causes and Consequences." *Biodiversity,* edited by E. O. Wilson, 21–27. Washington, D.C.: National Academy Press.

————. 1989. "The Limits to Substitution: Meta-resource Deletion and a New Economic-ecological Paradigm." *Ecological Economics* 1:9–16.

Ehrlich, P. R., and A. H. Ehrlich. 1981. *Extinction: The Causes and Consequences of the Disappearance of Species* New York: Random House.

Ehrlich, P. R., and J. Roughgarden. 1987. *The Science of Ecology*. New York: Macmillan.

Elliot, R. 1992. "Intrinsic Value, Environmental Obligation, and Naturalness." *Monist* 75:138–60.

Elton, C. 1927. *Animal Ecology*. London: Sidgwick and Jackson.

————. 1958. *The Ecology of Invasions by Animals and Plants*. London: Methuen.

Emerson, R. W. 1836. *Nature*. Boston: James Monroe.

Feinberg, J. 1974. "The Rights of Animals and Unborn Generations." In *Philosophy and Environmental Crisis,* edited by W. Blackstone, 43–68. Athens: University of Georgia Press.

Ferré, F. 1996a. "Persons in Nature: Toward an Applicable and Unified Environmental Ethics." *Ethics and the Environment* 1:15–25.

————. 1996b. *Being and Value: Toward a Constructive Postmodern Metaphysics*. Albany: State University of New York Press.

Flader, S. 1974. *Thinking Like a Mountain: Aldo Leopold and the Evolution of an Ecological Attitude toward Deer, Wolves, and Forests*. Columbia: University of Missouri Press.

Foreman, D. 1983. "More on *Earth First!* and *The Monkey Wrench Gang.*" *Environmental Ethics* 5:95–96.

————. 1991. "The New Conservation Movement." *Wild Earth* 1, no. 2:6–12.

————. 1995a. "Wilderness: From Scenery to Nature." *Wild Earth* 5, no. 4:8–16.

————. 1995b. "Wilderness Areas and National Parks." *Wild Earth* 5, no. 4:60–63.

Foreman, D., J. Davis, D. Johns, R. Noss, and M. Soulé. 1992. "The Wildlands Project Mission Statement." *Wild Earth,* 3–4. The Wildlands Project special issue.

Foucault, M. 1974. *Birth of the Clinic: An Archeology of Medical Perception.* New York: Random House.

Fox, S. 1981. *John Muir and His Legacy: The American Conservation Movement.* Boston: Little, Brown.

Fox, W. 1985. "A Postscript on Deep Ecology and Intrinsic Value." *Trumpeter* 2, no. 4:20–23.

———. 1990. *Toward a Transpersonal Ecology.* Boston: Shambhala Publications.

———. 1993. "What Does the Recognition of Intrinsic Value Entail?" *Trumpeter* 10:101.

Francis, G. R., J. J. Magnuson, H. A. Regier, and D. R. Talhelm. 1979. *Rehabilitating Great Lakes Ecosystems, Technical Report No. 37.* Ann Arbor, Mich.: Great Lakes Fishery Commission.

Frey, R. G. 1980. *Interests and Rights: The Case Against Animals.* Oxford: Clarendon Press.

Friedman, R. E. 1987. *Who Wrote the Bible?* New York: Summit Books.

Fritsch, A. J. 1980. *Environmental Ethics: Choices for Concerned Citizens.* Garden City, N.Y.: Anchor Press.

Galileo Galilei. 1623. *Il Saggiatore.* Rome: Appresso Giacomo Mascardi.

Geertz, C. 1973. *The Interpretation of Cultures.* New York: Basic Books.

Gilligan, C. 1982. *In a Different Voice: Psychological Theory and Women's Development.* Cambridge: Harvard University Press.

Gleason, H. A. 1939. "The Individualistic Concept of the Plant Association." *American Midland Naturalist* 21:92–10.

Gleik, J. 1987. *Chaos: The Making of a New Science.* New York: Viking.

Godfrey-Smith, W. 1980. "The Rights of Non-humans and Intrinsic Values." In *Environmental Philosophy,* edited by D. Mannison, M. McRobbie, and R. Routley, Monograph Series no. 2, 30–47. Canberra: Department of Philosophy, RSSS, Australian National University.

Golley, F. B. 1994. *A History of the Ecosystem Concept in Ecology.* New Haven: Yale University Press.

Gomez-Pompa, A., and A. Kaus. 1988. "Conservation by Traditional Cultures in the Tropics." In *For the Conservation of the Earth,* edited by Vance Martin, 183–89. Golden, Colo.: Fulcrum.

———. 1992. "Taming the Wilderness Myth." *Bioscience* 42:271–79.

Goodman, D. 1975. "The Theory of Diversity-Stability Relationships in Ecology." *Quarterly Review of Biology* 30:237–66.

Goodpaster, K. E. 1978. "On Being Morally Considerable." *Journal of Philosophy* 75:308–25.

———. 1979. "From Egoism to Environmentalism." In *Ethics and Problems of the Twenty-first Century,* edited by K. E. Goodpaster and K. E. Sayre, 21–35. Notre Dame, Ind.: University of Notre Dame Press.

Gough, J. W. 1957. *The Social Contract.* Rev. ed. Oxford: Clarendon Press.

Gray, J. S. 1995. "New Approaches to the Assessment of Marine Ecosystem Health." In *Evaluating and Monitoring the Health of Large-Scale Ecosystems,* edited by D. J. Rapport, C. Gaudet, and P. Calow, 127–36. Heidelberg: Springer-Verlag.

Guha, R. 1989a. *The Unquiet Woods: Ecological Change and Peasant Resistance in the Himalaya.* Berkeley: University of California Press.

———. 1989b. "Radical American Environmentalism and Wilderness Preservation: A Third World Critique." *Environmental Ethics* 11:71–83.

Hallowell, A. I. 1960. "Ojibwa Behavior, Ontology, and World View." In *Culture in History,* edited by S. Diamond, 19–52. New York: Columbia University Press.

Hamilton, W. D. 1964. "The Genetical Theory of Social Behaviour." *Journal of Theoretical Biology* 7:1–52.

Hardin, G. 1982. "Discriminating Altruisms." *Zygon* 17:163–86.

Hargrove, E. C. 1985. "The Role of Rules in Ethical Decision Making." *Enquiry* 28:30–39.

———. 1986. "Religion and Environmental Ethics: Beyond the Lynn White Debate." In *Religion and Environmental Crisis,* edited by E. C. Hargrove, ix–xix. Athens: University of Georgia Press.

———. 1989. *Foundations of Environmental Ethics.* Englewood Cliffs, N.J.: Prentice-Hall.

———. 1992. "Weak Anthropocentric Intrinsic Value." *Monist* 75:183–207

———. 1993. "Callicott and Moral Pluralism." Paper presented to the ninety-first annual meeting of the American Philosophical Association-Central Division, Chicago, 24 April 1993.

Hays, S. P. 1959. *Conservation and the Gospel of Efficiency: The Progressive Conservation Movement.* Cambridge: Harvard University Press.

Heisenberg, W. 1962. *Physics and Philosophy: The Revolution in Modern Science.* New York: Harper and Row.

Helfand, J. 1971. "Ecology and the Jewish Tradition." *Judaism* 20:330–35.

Homer-Dixon, T. F. 1991. "On the Threshold: Environmental Changes as Causes of Acute Conflict." *International Security* 16, no. 2:76–116.

Hume, D. [1739] 1960. *A Treatise of Human Nature.* Reprint, Oxford: Clarendon Press.

———. [1751] 1957. *An Enquiry Concerning the Principles of Morals.* Reprint, New York: Library of Liberal Arts.

International Union for the Conservation of Nature and Natural Resources/ United Nations Environmental Program/The World Wide Fund for Nature. 1991. *Caring for the Earth: A Strategy for Sustainable Living.* Gland, Switzerland: IUCN.

Jackson, W. 1980. *New Roots for Agriculture.* Lincoln: University of Nebraska Press.

———. 1987. *Altars of Unhewn Stone.* San Francisco: North Point Press.

Jamieson, D. 1995. "Ecosystem Health: Some Preventive Medicine." *Environmental Values* 4:331–34.

Johnson, L. E. 1991. *A Morally Deep World: An Essay on Moral Significance and Environmental Ethics.* Cambridge: Cambridge University Press.

Jones, R. S. 1972. *Physics as Metaphor.* New York: New American Library.

Kant, I. 1785. *Grundlegung zur Metaphysik der Sitten.* Riga: Johann Friedrich Hartknoch.

———. 1787. *Kritik der Reinen Vernunft.* Riga: Johann Friedrich Hartknoch.

———. 1959. *Foundations of the Metaphysics of Morals.* Translated by L. W. Beck. New York: Bobbs-Merrill.

Karr, J. R. 1981. "Assessment of Biotic Integrity Using Fish Communities." *Fisheries* 6, no. 6:21–27

———. 1995. "Using Biological Criteria to Protect Ecological Health." In *Evaluating and Monitoring the Health of Large-Scale Ecosystems,* edited by D. J. Rapport, C. Gaudet, and P. Calow, 137–52. Heidelberg: Springer-Verlag.

Karr, J. R., and D. R. Dudley. 1981. "Ecological Perspective on Water Quality Goals." *Environmental Management* 5:55–68.

Kaufmann, R. K. 1995. "The Economic Multiplier of Environmental Life Support: Can Capital Substitute for a Degraded Environment?" *Ecological Economics* 12:67–79.

Kay, J. 1988. "Concepts of Nature in the Human Bible." *Environmental Ethics* 109:309–27.

———. 1989. "Human Dominion Over Nature in the Hebrew Bible." *Annals of the Association of American Geographers* 79:214–32.

Krutilla, J., and A. Fisher. 1985. *The Economics of Natural Environments: Studies in the Valuation of Commodity and Amenity Resources*. Rev. ed. Washington, D.C.: Resources for the Future.

Kselman, J. S. 1985. "Adamah." In *Harper's Bible Dictionary*, edited by Paul J. Achtyemeier, 12. San Francisco: Harper and Row.

Kuhn, T. 1961 *The Structure of Scientific Revolutions*. Chicago: The University of Chicago Press.

The Land: God's Giving, Our Caring. 1982. Minneapolis: Augsburg Publishing House.

Land Stewardship Project. 1995. *Biological, Financial, and Social Monitoring to Develop Highly Sustainable Farming Systems: Progress Report for 1995*. White Bear Lake, Minn.: Land Stewardship Project.

Larkin, P. A. 1977. "An Epitaph for the Concept of Maximum Sustained Yield." *Transactions of the American Fisheries Society* 106:1–11.

Lélé, S., and R. B. Norgaard. 1996. "Sustainability and the Scientist's Burden." *Conservation Biology* 10:354–65.

Leopold, A. 1918. "Forestry and Game Conservation." *Journal of Forestry* 16:404–11.

———. 1921. "The Wilderness and Its Place in Forest Recreation Policy." *Journal of Forestry* 19:718–21.

———. 1931. "Game Methods: The American Way." *American Game* 20 (March–April): 29–31.

———. 1933a. *Game Management*. New York: Charles Scribner's Sons.

———. 1933b. "The Conservation Ethic." *Journal of Forestry* 31:634–43.

———. 1937. "Conservationist in Mexico." *American Forests* 43:118–20.

———. 1939a. "A Biotic View of Land." *Journal of Forestry* 37:727–30.

———. 1939b. "The Farmer as a Conservationist." *American Forests* 45:294–99, 316, 323.

———. 1941. "Wilderness as a Land Laboratory." *The Living Wilderness* 6 (July): 3.

———. 1942. "The Role of Wildlife in a Liberal Education." *Transactions of the Seventh North American Wildlife Conference*, 485–89.

———. 1945. "The Outlook for Farm Wildlife." *Transactions of the Tenth North American Wildlife Conference*, 165–68.

———. 1949. *"A Sand County Almanac" and "Sketches Here and There."* New York: Oxford University Press.

———. 1953. *Round River: From the Journals of Aldo Leopold*. New York: Oxford University Press.

―――. 1979. "Some Fundamentals of Conservation in the Southwest." *Environmental Ethics* 1:131–41.

―――. 1991a. "Land Pathology." In *The River of the Mother of God and Other Essays by Aldo Leopold,* edited by S. L. Flader and J. B. Callicott, 212–17. Madison: University of Wisconsin Press.

―――. 1991b. "Conservation in Whole or in Part?" In *The River of the Mother of God and Other Essays by Aldo Leopold,* edited by S. L. Flader and J. B. Callicott, 310–19. Madison: University of Wisconsin Press.

―――. 1991c. "Engineering and Conservation." In *The River of the Mother of God and Other Essays by Aldo Leopold,* edited by S. L. Flader and J. B. Callicott, 249–54. Madison: University of Wisconsin Press.

―――. 1991d. "Means and Ends in Wildlife Management." In *The River of the Mother of God and Other Essays by Aldo Leopold,* edited by S. L. Flader and J. B. Callicott, 235–38. Madison: University of Wisconsin Press.

―――. 1991e. "Ecology and Politics." In *The River of the Mother of God and Other Essays by Aldo Leopold,* edited by S. L. Flader and J. B. Callicott, 281–86. Madison: University of Wisconsin Press.

―――. 1991f. "Wilderness." In *The River of the Mother of God and Other Essays by Aldo Leopold,* edited by S. L. Flader and J. B. Callicott, 226–29. Madison: University of Wisconsin Press.

Lindeman, R. L. 1942. "The Trophic-Dynamic Aspect of Ecology." *Ecology* 23:399–418.

Locke, J. 1690. *An Essay Concerning Human Understanding.* London: Awnsham and John Churchill.

Lovelock, J. 1988. *The Ages of Gaia: A Biography of Our Living Earth.* New York: W. W. Norton.

Macpherson, C. B. 1962. *Political Theory of Possessive Individualism: Hobbes to Locke.* New York: Random House.

Margulis, L., and D. Sagan. 1991. *Microcosmos.* New York: Simon and Schuster.

Mathews, F. 1988. "Conservation and Self-Realization: A Deep Ecology Perspective." *Environmental Ethics* 10:347–55.

Maturana, H. R., and F. J. Varel, 1980. "Autopoiesis: The Organization of the Living." In *Autopoiesis and Cognition,* 59–140. Boston: D. Reidel.

May, R. M. 1973. *Stability and Complexity in Model Ecosystems.* Princeton: Princeton University Press.

―――. 1974. "Biological Populations with Nonoverlapping Generations: Stable Points, Stable Cycles, and Chaos." *Science* 186:645–47.

McIntosh, R. P. 1985. *The Background of Ecology: Concept and Theory.* Cambridge: Cambridge University Press.

Meffe, G. K., C. R. Carroll, and S. L. Pimm. 1994. "Community-level Conservation: Species Interactions, Disturbance Regimes, and Invading Species." In *Principles of Conservation Biology,* edited by G. K. Meffe and C. R. Carroll, 209–36. Sunderland, Mass.: Sinauer Associates.

Meine, C. 1988. *Aldo Leopold: His Life and Work.* Madison: University of Wisconsin Press.

Meyer, M. J. 1992. "Rights between Friends." *Journal of Philosophy* 89:467–83.

Midgley, M. 1983. *Animals and Why They Matter.* Athens: The University of Georgia Press.

Mill, J. S. 1863. *Utilitarianism.* London: Parker, Son and Brown.

———. [1874] 1969. "Three Essays on Religion." Reprinted in vol. 10 of *Collected Works of John Stuart Mill,* edited by J. M. Robson. Toronto: University of Toronto Press.

Miller, P. 1981. Is Health an Anthropocentric Value? *Nature and System* 3:193–207.

———. 1982. "Value as Richness: Toward a Value Theory for the Expanded Naturalism in Environmental Ethics." *Environmental Ethics* 4:101–14.

———. 1989. "Descartes' Legacy and Deep Ecology." *Dialogue* 28:183–202.

Morowitz, H. 1972. "Biology as a Cosmological Science." *Main Currents in Modern Thought* 28:151–57.

Muir, J. 1894. *The Mountains of California.* New York: Century.

———. 1901. *Our National Parks.* Boston: Houghton Mifflin.

———. 1913. *The Story of My Boyhood and Youth.* Boston: Houghton Mifflin.

———. 1916. *A Thousand-Mile Walk to the Gulf.* Edited by W. F. Badè. Boston: Houghton Mifflin.

Nabhan, G. P. 1982. *The Desert Smells Like Rain: A Naturalist in Papago Country.* San Francisco: North Point Press.

Naess, A. 1973. "The Shallow and the Deep, Long-Range Ecology Movement: A Summary." *Inquiry* 16:95–100.

———. 1987. "Self-Realization: An Ecological Approach to Being in the World." *Trumpeter* 4, no. 3:35–42.

Nash, R. F. 1967. *Wilderness and the American Mind.* New Haven: Yale University Press.

———. 1988. *The Rights of Nature: A History of Environmental Ethics.* Madison: University of Wisconsin Press.

National Research Council. 1989. *Alternative Agriculture*. Washington, D.C.: National Academy Press.

———. 1993. *Sustainable Agriculture and the Environment in the Humid Tropics*. Washington, D.C.: National Academy Press.

Nelson, J. L. 1995. "Health and Disease as 'Thick' Concepts in Ecosystemic Contexts." *Environmental Values* 4:311–22.

Nelson, M. 1996. "Holists and Fascists and Paper Tigers . . . Oh My!" *Ethics and the Environment* 2:103–17.

Norton, B. G. 1986. "Conservation and Preservation: A Conceptual Rehabilitation." *Environmental Ethics* 8:195–220.

———. 1987. Review of *Respect for Nature*, by Paul Taylor. *Environmental Ethics* 9:261–67.

———. 1988 "Commodity, Amenity, and Morality: The Limits of Quantification in Valuing Biodiversity." In *Biodiversity*, edited by E. O. Wilson, 200–205. Washington, D.C.: National Academy Press.

———. 1991. *Toward Unity Among Environmentalists*. New York: Oxford University Press.

———. 1992. "Epistemology and Environmental Value." *Monist* 75:208–26.

Noss, R. F. 1990. "Indicators for Monitoring Biodiversity: A Hierarchical Approach." *Conservation Biology* 4:335–64.

———. 1991. "Sustainability and Wilderness." *Conservation Biology* 5:120–22.

———. 1995. *Maintaining Ecological Integrity in Representative Reserve Networks*. Toronto and Washington: World Wildlife Fund Canada/World Wildlife Fund-United States.

O'Conner, J. 1988. "Capitalism, Nature, Socialism: A Theoretical Introduction." *Capitalism, Nature, Socialism* 1:3–38.

Odum, E. P. 1953. *Fundamentals of Ecology*. 1st ed. Philadelphia: Saunders.

———. 1959. *Fundamentals of Ecology*. 2d ed. Philadelphia: Saunders.

———. 1971. *Fundamentals of Ecology*. 3d ed. Philadelphia: Saunders.

O'Neal, A. E., A. S. Pandian, S. V. Rhodes-Conway, and A. H. Bornbush. 1995. "Human Economies, the Land Ethic, and Sustainable Conservation." *Conservation Biology* 9:217–20.

O'Neill, J. 1992. "The Varieties of Intrinsic Value." *Monist* 75:119–37.

O'Neill, R. V., D. L. DeAngelis, J. B. Waide, and T. F. H. Allen. 1986. *A Hierarchical Concept of Ecosystems*. Princeton: Princeton University Press.

OTA. 1993. *Harmful Non-indigenous Species in the United States*. OTA-F-565. Washington, D.C.: U.S. Government Printing Office.

Passmore, J. 1974. *Man's Responsibility for Nature: Ecological Problems and Western Traditions*. New York: Scribner's.

Peters, C. M., A. H. Gentry, and R. O. Mendelsohn. 1989. "Valuation of an Amazonian Rainforest." *Nature* 339:656–57.

Pickett, S. T. A., and P. S. White. 1985. *The Ecology of Natural Disturbance and Patch Dynamics*. Orlando, Fla.: Academic Press.

Pickett, S. T. A., and R. S. Ostfeld, 1995. "The Shifting Paradigm in Ecology." In *A New Century for Natural Resources Management*, edited by R. L. Knight and S. F. Bates. Washington, D.C.: Island Press.

Pimm, S. 1991. *The Balance of Nature?* Chicago: University of Chicago Press.

Pinchot, G. 1947. *Breaking New Ground*. New York: Harcourt, Brace.

Pister, E. P. 1985. "Desert Pupfishes: Reflections on Reality, Desirability, and Conscience." *Fisheries* 10, no. 6:10–15.

———. 1987. "A Pilgrim's Progress from Group A to Group B." In *Companion to "A Sand County Almanac": Interpretive and Critical Essays*, edited by J. B. Callicott, 221–32. Madison: University of Wisconsin Press.

Plato. 1937. *Republic*. In vol. 1B of *The Dialogues of Plato*, translated by B. Jowett, 591–879. New York: Random House.

Plucknett, D. 1990. "International Goals and the Roleg International Agricultural Research Centers." In *Sustainable Agricultural Systems*, edited by R. Lal, P. Madden, R. H. Miller, and G. House, 33–49. Ankeny, Iowa: Soil and Water Conservation Society.

Putnam, R. J., and S. D. Wratten. 1984. *Principles of Ecology*. Berkeley: University of California Press.

Rachels, J. 1990. *Created From Animals*. New York: Oxford University Press.

Ramakrishnan, P. S. 1992. *Shifting Agriculture and Sustainable Development*. Man and the Biosphere, vol. 10. Park Ridge, N.J.: The Parthenon Publishing Group.

Rapport, D. J. 1992a. "What is Clinical Ecology?" In *Ecosystem Health: New Goals for Environmental Management*, edited by R. Costanza, B. G. Norton, and B. D. Haskell, 144–56. Washington, D.C.: Island Press.

———. 1992b. "Evaluating Ecosystem Health." *Journal of Aquatic Ecosystem Health* 1:15–24.

———. 1995a. "Ecosystem Health: An Emerging Integrative Science." In *Evaluating and Monitoring the Health of Large-Scale Ecosystems*, edited by D. J. Rapport, C. Gaudet, and P. Calow, 5–32. Heidelberg: Springer-Verlag.

———. 1995b. "Ecosystem Health: More than a Metaphor?" *Environmental Values* 4:287–309.

Raup, D. M. 1988. "Diversity Crises in the Geologic Past." In *Biodiversity*, edited by E. O. Wilson, 51–77. Washington, D.C.: National Academy Press.

———. 1991. *Extinction: Bad Genes or Bad Luck?* New York: W. W. Norton.

Raup, D. M., and J. J. Sepkoski. 1984. "Periodicity of Extinctions in the Geologic Past." *Proceedings of the National Academy of Sciences USA* 81:801–5.

Rawles, K. E. 1990. "Animal Welfare and Environmental Ethics." Master's thesis, Colorado State University.

Regan, T. 1976. "Feinberg on What Sorts of Beings Can Have Rights." *Southern Journal of Philosophy* 14:485–98.

———. 1979. "An Examination and Defense of One Argument Concerning Animal Rights." *Inquiry* 22:189–219.

———. 1981. "The Nature and Possibility of an Environmental Ethic." *Environmental Ethics* 3:19–34.

———. 1983. *The Case for Animal Rights*. Berkeley: University of California Press.

Robinson, J. G. 1993a. "The Limits to Caring: Sustainable Living and the Loss of Biodiversity." *Conservation Biology* 7:20–28.

———. 1993b. "Believing What You Know Ain't So: Response to Holgate and Munro." *Conservation Biology* 7:941–42.

Rolston III, H. 1975. "Is There an Ecological Ethic?" *Ethics* 85:93–109

———. 1981. "Values in Nature." *Environmental Ethics* 3:113–28.

———. 1986. *Philosophy Gone Wild: Essays in Environmental Ethics*. Buffalo, N.Y.: Prometheus Books.

———. 1988. *Environmental Ethics: Duties to and Values in the Natural World*. Philadelphia: Temple University Press.

———.1989. Review of *Thinking About Nature: An Investigation of Nature, Value, and Ecology*, by Andrew Brennan. *Environmental Ethics* 11:259–67.

———. 1994. *Conserving Natural Value*. New York: Columbia University Press.

Rorty, R. 1979. *Philosophy and the Mirror of Nature*. Princeton: Princeton University Press.

Routley, R. 1973. "Is There a Need for a New, an Environmental Ethic?" In *Proceedings of the Fifteenth World Congress of Philosophy*, edited by the Bulgarian Organizing Committee, 205–10. Sophia, Bulgaria: Sophia Press.

Routley, R., and V Routley. 1980. "Human Chauvinism and Environmental Ethics." In *Environmental Philosophy*, edited by D. Mannison, M. McRobbie,

and R. Routley, monograph series no. 2, 96–189. Canberra: Department of Philosophy, RSSS, Australian National University.

Sagoff, M. 1985. "Fact and Value in Ecological Science." *Environmental Ethics* 7:99–116.

————. 1988. *The Economy of the Earth.* Cambridge: Cambridge University
Press.

Salwasser, H. 1990. "Sustainability as a Conservation Paradigm." *Conservation Biology* 4:213–16.

Sayre, K.M. 1991 "An Alternative View of Environmental Ethics." *Environmental Ethics* 13:195–213.

Schaeffer, F. 1970. *Pollution and the Death of Man: The Christian View of
Ecology* New York: Hodder and Stoughton.

Schneider, S. H. 1989. *Global Warming: Are We Entering the Greenhouse Century?* San Francisco: Sierra Club Books.

Schopenhauer, A. 1961. *The World as Will and Idea.* Translated by R. B.
Haldane and J. Kemp. Garden City, N.Y.: Doubleday.

Schrecker, T. 1994. "Constructing Ecosystem Health: The Perils of Organic
and Medical Metaphors." Paper for the First International Symposium
on Ecosystem Health and Medicine, 19–23 June, Ottawa, Ont.

Schweitzer, A. [1923] 1994. *Philosophy and Civilization.* Translated by J. Naish.
Reprinted (excerpts) in *Environmental Ethics: Readings in Theory and Application,* edited by L. P. Pojman, 65–71. Boston: Jones and Bartlett.

Seed, J. 1985. "Anthropocentrism." Appendix E in *Deep Ecology: Living as if
Nature Mattered,* by B. Devall and G. Sessions, 243–46. Salt Lake City:
Peregrine Smith.

Shrader-Frechette, K. S. 1989. "Ecological Theories and Ethical Imperatives:
Can Ecology Provide a Scientific Justification for the Ethics of Environmental Protection?." In *Scientists and their Responsibility,* edited by W. R.
Shea and B. Sitter, 73–104. Canton, Mass.: Watson Publishing International.

————. 1990. "Biological Holism and the Evolution of Ethics." *Between the
Species* 6:185–92.

————. 1996. "Individualism, Holism, and Environmental Ethics." *Ethics
and the Environment* 1:55–69.

Shrader-Frechette, K. S., and E. D. McCoy. 1993. *Method in Ecology: Strategies for Conservation.* Cambridge: Cambridge University Press.

Shepard, P. 1969. "Introduction: Ecology and Man—A Viewpoint." In *The
Subversive Science: Essays Toward and Ecology of Man,* edited by P. Shepard

and D. McKinley, 1–10. Boston: Houghton Mifflin.

————. 1978. *Thinking Animals: Animals and the Development of Human Intelligence.* New York: Viking.

Shiva, V. 1991. *The Violence of the Green Revolution: Third World Agriculture, Ecology, and Politics.* London: Zed Books.

Simberloff, D. 1980. "A Succession of Paradigms in Ecology: Essentialism to Materialism and Probabilism." *Synthese* 43:3–39.

Singer, P. 1977. *Animal Liberation: A New Ethics for Our Treatment of Animals.* New York: Avon.

————. 1982. *The Expanding Circle: Ethics and Sociobiology.* New York: Farrar, Straus, and Giroux.

Smith, A. 1759. *Theory of the Moral Sentiments.* Edinburgh: A. Millar, A. Kinkaid, and J. Bell.

Smith, R. L. 1986. *Elements of Ecology.* 2d ed. New York: Harper and Row.

Soulé, M. E. 1985. "What is Conservation Biology?" *BioScience* 35:727–33.

————. 1990. "The Onslaught of Alien Species, and Other Challenges in the Coming Decades." *Conservation Biology* 4:233–43.

————. 1995. "The Social Siege of Nature." In *Reinventing Nature?: Responses to Postmodern Deconstruction,* edited by M. E. Soulé and G. Lease, 137–70. Washington, D.C.: Island Press.

Speck, F. 1938. "Aboriginal Conservatores." *Bird Lore* 40:258–61.

Speiser, E. A. 1964. *Genesis: Introduction, Translation, and Notes.* Garden City, N.Y.: Doubleday.

Stegner. W. 1987. "The Legacy of Aldo Leopold." In *Companion to "A Sand County Almanac": Interpretive and Critical Essays,* edited by J. B. Callicott. Madison: University of Wisconsin Press.

Steverson, B. K. 1994. "Ecocentrism and Ecological Modeling." *Environmental Ethics* 16:71–88.

Stone, C. D. 1972. "Should Trees Have Standing?—Towards Legal Rights for Natural Objects." *Southern California Law Review* 45:450–501.

————. 1974. *Should Trees Have Standing?: Toward Legal Rights for Natural Objects.* Los Altos, Calif.: William Kaufmann.

————. 1987. *Earth and Other Ethics: The Case for Moral Pluralism.* New York: Harper and Row.

————. 1988. "Moral Pluralism and the Course of Environmental Ethics." *Environmental Ethics* 10:139–54.

Strangers and Guests: Toward Community in the Heartland. 1980. Des Moines, Iowa: Heartland Project.

Suppe, F. 1977. "The Search for Philosophic Understanding of Scientific Theories." In *The Structure of Scientific Theories*, ed. F. Suppe, 2d ed., 1–32. Urbana: University of Illinois Press.

Tansley, A. G. 1935. "The Use and Abuse of Vegetational Concepts and Terms." *Ecology* 16:192–203.

Taylor, P. W. 1981. "The Ethics of Respect for Nature." *Environmental Ethics* 3:197–218.

———. 1983. "In Defense of Biocentrism." *Environmental Ethics* 5:237–43.

———. 1986. *Respect for Nature: A Theory of Environmental Ethics*. Princeton: Princeton University Press.

Tilman, D., and J. A. Downing. 1994. "Biodiversity and Stability in Grasslands." *Nature* 367:363–65.

Thoreau, H. D. 1863. *Excursions*. Boston: Ticknor and Fields.

Thomas, D. 1995. *Lake Trout Restoration Program: Who Profits, Who Pays?* Ann Arbor, Mich.: Special Publication of the Great Lakes Sport Fishing Council.

Trible, P. 1978. *God and the Rhetoric of Sexuality*. Philadelphia: Fortress Press.

Tuan, Y.-F. 1968. "Discrepancies Between Environmental Attitude and Behaviour: Examples from Europe and China." *The Canadian Geographer* 12:176–91.

———. 1970. "Treatment of the Environment in Ideal and Actuality." *American Scientist* 58:244–49.

USDA Forest Service. 1989. *New Perspectives: An Ecological Path for Managing Forests*. Redding, Calif.: Pacific Northwest Research Station, Portland, Oregon, and Pacific Northwest Research Station.

Varner, G. E. 1988. Review of *Earth and Other Ethics: The Case for Moral Pluralism*, by C. D. Stone. *Environmental Ethics* 10:259–65.

———. 1991. "No Holism without Pluralism." *Environmental Ethics* 19:175–79.

von Bertalanffy, L. 1967. *Robots, Men, and Minds*. New York: Braziller.

von Droste, B. 1988. "The Role of Biosphere Reserves at a Time of Increasing Globalization." In *For the Conservation of Earth*, edited by V. Martin, 89–93. Golden, Colo.: Fulcrum.

Warren, M. A. 1983. "The Rights of the Non-human World." In *Environmental Philosophy: A Collection of Readings*, edited by R. Elliot and A. Gare, 130–31. University Park: The Pennsylvania State University Press.

Weiser, A. 1961. *The Old Testament: Its Formation and Development.* New York: Association Press.

Wenz, P. S. 1988. *Environmental Justice.* Albany: State University of New York Press.

———. 1992. "Minimal, Moderate, and Extreme Moral Pluralism." *Environmental Ethics* 15:61–74.

Weston, A. 1991. "On Callicott's Case Against Moral Pluralism." *Environmental Ethics* 13:283–86.

———. 1992. "Before Environmental Ethics." *Environmental Ethics* 14:321–38.

Westra, L. 1994. *An Environmental Proposal for Ethics: The Principle of Integrity.* Lanham, Md.: Rowman and Littlefield.

White, L. W. 1967. "The Historical Roots of Our Ecologic Crisis." *Science* 155:1203–7.

———. 1973. "Continuing the Conversation." In *Western Man and Environmental Ethics,* edited by I. Barbour, 55–64. Reading Mass.: Addison Wesley.

Willers, B. 1994. "Sustainable Development: A New World Deception." *Conservation Biology* 8:1146–48.

Wilson, E. O. 1975. *Sociobiology: The New Synthesis.* Cambridge: The Belknap Press of Harvard University Press.

———. 1984. *Biophilia.* Cambridge: Harvard University Press.

———. 1988. "The Current State of Biological Diversity." In *Biodiversity,* edited by E. O. Wilson, 3–18. Washington, D.C.: National Academy Press.

———. 1992. *The Diversity of Life.* Cambridge: The Belknap Press of Harvard University Press.

Wittbecker, A. E. 1990. "Metaphysical Implications from Physics and Ecology." *Environmental Ethics* 12:275–82.

Woodley, S., J. Kay, G. Francis. 1993. *Ecological Integrity and the Management of Ecosystems.* Delray Beach, Fla.: St. Lucie Press.

World Commission on Environment and Development. 1987. *Our Common Future.* Oxford: Oxford University Press.

World Resources Institute. 1992. *World Resources, 1992–93.* Oxford: Oxford University Press.

Worster, D. 1979. *Nature's Economy: The Roots of Ecology.* 1st ed. Garden City, N.Y.: Anchor Books.

———. 1988. Review of *The Pathless Way,* by Michael P. Cohen. *Environmental Ethics* 10:267–70.

————. 1990. "The Ecology of Order and Chaos." *Environmental History Review* 14:1–18.

————. 1994. *Nature's Economy: The Roots of Ecology.* 2d ed. Garden City, N.Y.: Anchor Books.

Zimmerman, M. E. 1995. "The Threat of Ecofascism." *Social Theory and Practice* 21:207–38.

INDEX